The Official History of Colonial Development

VOLUME 2

DEVELOPING BRITISH COLONIAL RESOURCES,
1945–1951

The author has been given full access to
official documents. He alone is
responsible for the statements made
and the views expressed.

The Official History of Colonial Development

VOLUME 2

DEVELOPING BRITISH COLONIAL RESOURCES, 1945–1951

D. J. Morgan

First published 1980 by
THE MACMILLAN PRESS LTD
London and Basingstoke
Associated companies in Delhi
Dublin Hong Kong Johannesburg Lagos
Melbourne New York Singapore Tokyo

Printed in Great Britain by
Unwin Brothers Ltd,
The Gresham Press, Woking, Surrey

British Library Cataloguing in Publication Data

Morgan, David John
    The official history of colonial development
    Vol. 2: Developing British colonial resources,
    1945–1951
    1. Great Britain – Colonies – Economic policy
    2. Economic assistance, British
    I. Title   II. Developing British colonial
    resources, 1945–1951
    338.91′171′241041   HC259
    ISBN 0-333-26230-1 |ε|0|
    ISBN 0-333-28800-9 (5 volume set)

338·9142DR

Contents

List of Tables

Preface

My interest in the field of Colonial and Commonwealth economic policy was aroused in 1941 when, on joining the staff of Dr Arnold J. Toynbee's Foreign Research and Press Service in Oxford, I was required to prepare a study of the economic background and implications of the Ottawa Trade Agreements, 1932. Over the following years – at the University of Liverpool, the London School of Economics, the University of the West Indies, the University of Manchester, the Overseas Development Institute, and the Institute of Commonwealth Studies of the University of London – I extended my interest beyond trade policy to the problems of development and aid. This was enormously assisted in the first place by my residence in Jamaica over the years 1955–59 whilst I was Head of the Department of Economics at the University College. During those years I was able to gain first-hand knowledge of the economies and economic problems of the Caribbean area: Mexico and Central America, Venezuela and Guyana, the British, French and Dutch islands, Cuba, Haiti and Puerto Rico. It was assisted in the second place by the privileged access to the files of the Colonial Office in order to prepare a short history of the origins and nature of British aid to developing countries, which was published by the Overseas Development Institute in 1964 under the title of *Colonial Development*. In the third place, there were study-visits to the New Commonwealth. In 1964 a Houblon-Norman award enabled me to renew my acquaintance with the West Indies, beginning with Bermuda and the Bahamas, in order to study banking developments and aid problems. A Hayter grant in 1966 and a Leverhulme award in 1969 enabled me to become acquainted with the economies and economic problems of East and Central Africa, Ethiopia and Egypt. In particular, I studied the working of joint ventures between local and expatriate interests, including among the former the local development corporations and among the latter both the Commonwealth Development Corporation and the Commonwealth Development Finance Company. I was fortunate to meet Governors, Ministers and officials, Governors of Central Banks, staffs of local development corporations, banks and businesses of many kinds, economists in the

Universities and Research Institutes, and the Regional Controllers and staffs of the CDC, who gave me the benefit of their experience.

The invitation to prepare a full-scale study of Colonial Development in the new Peacetime Series of Official Histories was exciting and challenging. Because of the sheer mass of official documentation made available, it was also daunting. Thus, for one fairly self-contained episode, namely the East African Groundnuts Project over the years 1946–51, when it was the responsibility of the Ministry of Food, between 600 and 700 files were 'put by' by that Ministry, while the Lord President's Office, the Cabinet Office, the Treasury, the Foreign Office, the Commonwealth Relations Office and the Colonial Office added an assortment of complementary files. In order to decide on a firm outline for the whole History, I began by reading through the Cabinet Conclusions for the years 1935–65, so that the topics which engaged the attention of Ministers in the broad field of Colonial Development were known in the context of the concerns and decisions of the time. Topics were then followed, in turn, through Cabinet Committees to departmental files, where internal and inter-departmental discussions led up to Briefs for Ministers. In the Treasury, the Chancellor of the Exchequer customarily awaited on an agreed draft from his senior officials before he was prepared to discuss even with his Cabinet colleagues. Once Ministers have come to their decisions, matters are returned to officials for implementation. The more general the decision – and Cabinet decisions are necessarily often in somewhat general terms – the more discretion there is in implementation. Officials might even feel justified in providing favoured treatment in cases where Ministers deny any preference, as happened over the allocations to the Overseas Food Corporation discussed in Volume 2, Chapter 5, Section xii. Without the ready assistance of experienced records officers, the whole operation would have been imperilled. It is a pleasure to thank those in the Departments concerned, namely the Foreign and Commonwealth Office, the Cabinet Office, the Treasury, the Ministry of Agriculture, Fisheries and Food, and the Ministry of Overseas Development. Many others, particularly in the Historical Section of the Cabinet Office, did much over the years to facilitate the study and deserve my gratitude. I have acknowledged at the appropriate places in the text my indebtedness to those with whom I discussed while the study was being prepared.

In the course of his announcement of the Peacetime Series (H. of C. Deb., Vol. 793, cols 411–12, 18 December 1969), the Prime Minister, Mr Harold Wilson, stated that the Series 'would enable important periods in our history to be recorded in comprehensive and authoritative narratives, written while the official records could still be supplemented by reference to the personal recollections of the public men who were involved'. In accordance with this intention, the following persons have kindly commented on the part of the draft where they had first-hand knowledge: Sir William Gorell Barnes, the Viscount Boyd of Merton, Sir Sydney Caine, Mrs E. M. Chilver, the Lord Greenwood of Rossendale, Sir Stephen Luke, the Rt Hon. Malcolm MacDonald, Sir Leslie Monson, the Lord Ogmore, the Earl of Perth, Sir David Pitblado, Sir Hilton Poynton, Sir Philip Rogers, Sir David Serpell, Sir John Winnifrith.

I am grateful to them for their kindness in reading the draft and discussing it with me; additions to and other improvements of the text resulted. I should like also gratefully to acknowledge the interest in the History shown by Mr Harold Macmillan at a critical time.

Finally, my wife Eleanor took a keen interest in the whole project from beginning to end and many improvements in the text were suggested by her: I am happy to acknowledge her assistance. As always, the remaining shortcomings and blemishes, great and small, are entirely the responsibility of the author.

D. J. MORGAN

21 April 1978

List of Abbreviations

AACC	Anglo-American Caribbean Commission
CAO	Central African Office
CCD	Committee on Colonial Development
CCED	Committee on Commonwealth Economic Development
CDAC	Colonial Development Advisory Committee
CDC	Colonial Development Corporation (1948–1963) then Commonwealth Development Corporation
CDF	Colonial Development Fund
CD & W	Colonial Development and Welfare
CDWAC	Colonial Development and Welfare Advisory Committee
CDWP	Colonial Development Working Party
CEAC	Colonial Economic Advisory Committee
CEDC	Colonial Economic and Development Council
CEPS	Central Economic Planning Staff (Treasury)
CPC	Colonial Policy Committee (Cabinet)
CRO	Commonwealth Relations Office
DTC	Department of Technical Co-operation
D & W Organisation	Development and Welfare Organisation (Barbados)
ECA	Economic Co-operation Administration (United States)
EEC	European Economic Community
EFTA	European Free Trade Association
EPC	Economic Policy Committee (Cabinet)
ERP	Economic Recovery Programme (United States)
GATT	General Agreement on Tariffs & Trade
HMOCS	Her Majesty's Oversea Civil Service
IBRD	International Bank for Reconstruction and Development

ODM	Ministry of Overseas Development
OFC	Overseas Food Corporation
ORD Acts	Overseas Resources Development Acts
REC	Regional Economic Committee (West Indies)
SCAC	Standing Closer Association Committee
SEAF	Committee on Food Supplies from South-East Asia
UAC	United Africa Company
WFS	Ministerial Committee on World Food Supplies

1 Economic Policy and Supplies to the Colonies

1. PROBLEMS AND ISSUES

The ending of the wars in Europe and the Far East was expected to usher in a period of faster growth in the Colonial Empire. Achievements were in fact quite striking in several fields.[1] A major success was gained in the Colonial export drive: in the first half of 1948, the index of volume of Colonial exports was 148 compared with 100 in 1946, 132 in 1947 and 117 in 1936. Gross dollar earnings in the first six months of 1948 were at an annual rate of $600–700 million. The Colonial Empire, which was in deficit for dollars in 1945, was by July–September 1948 a net dollar earner at the rate of $200 million per annum. The contribution of the Colonies to United Kingdom imports rose from 5.4 per cent by value in 1938 to 10.2 per cent in the first half of 1948, and thus saved foreign exchange which would otherwise have had to be spent. The total public revenue of Colonial Governments, apart from CD & W assistance, was approximately £58 million in 1938, some £115 million in 1946 and approximately £140 million in 1947. In addition, substantial sums had been accumulated in special funds on behalf of Colonial producers for future price stabilisation and development instead of being absorbed in general revenue. At the end of September 1948 these funds totalled £81 million, the three biggest being West African Cocoa Funds (£52 million), West African Oilseeds Funds (£15 million), and Uganda Cotton Funds (£9.5 million).

Perhaps the most striking achievement was the restoration of civil Government in the territories in the Far East which had been overrun by the Japanese. A record output of rubber and a rapid rise of tin production followed. Hong Kong provided an example of prosperity and financial stability in the midst of surrounding chaos. The civil Government of Sarawak and North Borneo had to be built from virtually nothing, and the latter had produced a ten-year plan for reconstruction and development. The rehabilitation of the

Governments in the Far East, and the absence of recruiting during the war, necessitated a large-scale effort to recruit staff for all Colonial governments. Between June 1945 and the end of September 1948 approximately 4100 vacancies had been filled in the Colonial Service as a whole, equivalent to seven or eight times the pre-war average recruitment rate.

It is true that, in the first few years of peace, the major part of the practical achievements realised on the economic side resulted from the rehabilitation and expansion of existing industries, in particular those destroyed by the war, of which Malayan tin mining was a notable example. Rice acreage in the Federation of Malaya had increased by 7 per cent in the 1947–48 season compared with the previous year. Colonial development proper, partly because of its inevitably long-term nature, had not shown such striking achievements, although many projects were in hand. A considerable mileage of new first and second-class roads and some extensions of railways, such as an extension of 125 miles to the Mpanda lead mines in Tanganyika, were under construction, or completed. Construction had begun on the Freetown deep-water quay and on the groundnut port of Mikindani, Tanganyika; the construction of the Changi Airport at Singapore was well on the way, while some 378,000 square miles – over four times the area of Britain – had been air-photographed by the Colonial Geodetic and Topographical Survey, and maps had been prepared for 50,000 square miles of the area. New plant for copper, cobalt and lead was in course of erection in Northern Rhodesia, and preliminary site work had started on the £10.5 million Owen Falls Hydro-Electric Scheme in Uganda. Much work had been done, particularly in East Africa, on soil conservation. Thus, in 1947, over 700 miles of contour banking was constructed in the central provinces of Tanganyika, and every farm in a complete District of its Southern Highlands Province had been laid out to control erosion.

In the field of social achievements, the anti-malarial campaign in Cyprus and on the coastal belt of British Guiana had made rapid progress. The Anchau Scheme in Northern Nigeria provided valuable experience in tsetse clearance and resettlement of African populations; a corridor 70 miles long and 10 miles wide was cleared of tsetse, 5000 people resettled in new villages and in one new town, and 60,000 people freed from the menace of sleeping sickness. A start had been made with the building of new schools and some, such as the Central Medical School in Fiji, were operational. The Colonial Universities in Jamaica, Ibadan and Achimota had opened in temporary accommodation.

All this was gratifying but the general position had changed since the CD & W Acts of 1940 and 1945 had been passed. When these Acts were conceived it was thought, firstly, that if provision was thus made for the necessary expansion of the basic economic and social services, the launching of more productive undertakings could sometimes be undertaken by public enterprise but usually be left to private enterprise; and, secondly, that finance would once again, as between the two wars, be the main limiting factor and that, if the finance were made available, there would be little or no difficulty in obtaining the necessary materials, equipment and manpower.

The first of these two assumptions was always questionable. In fact, the Colonial Office took the initiative in exploring the idea of setting up a public corporation, not necessarily to take the place of private enterprise, but to undertake productive work of all kinds and especially of a kind which private enterprise might not be able or willing to undertake; and, where necessary and suitable, to give support and encouragement to private enterprise whether by entering into partnership with it or by standing behind it with finance. Further consideration of this idea led in due course to the Overseas Resources Development Act, which received the Royal Assent in 1948, and to the establishment by that Act of the Colonial Development Corporation and the Overseas Food Corporation.

In 1946 the second assumption – namely, that finance would be the main limiting factor – seemed less unreasonable. On the home front the reconversion of industry from war to peace production was proceeding smoothly and the volume of United Kingdom production for peaceful purposes was rapidly mounting. There seemed little reason to expect the degree of deterioration in the international situation which subsequently took place and falsified our hopes of early recovery. It was not only in the field of Colonial policy that this overoptimism prevailed.

In these circumstances it was not unreasonable to expect that within a relatively short time it would be possible for the necessary material goods to be made available without too much difficulty to carry out the programmes of Colonial development for which finance had been provided. This was, in fact, the expectation at that time; and so far from planning in the Colonial Office an organisation which would be capable of more extended programming and screening of Colonial requirements and of working with a United Kingdom planning organisation to secure the integration of Colonial and United Kingdom plans, it was expected that the wartime organisation would be adjusted to meet the expected peacetime situation. Then came two serious blows. First, there was the fuel crisis of February 1947, and the overriding priorities in favour of certain British industries to which that crisis led; and, secondly, the balance of payments crisis of August 1947, and the policy of bilateral agreements and dollar conservation to which that crisis led. All these things suddenly caused heavy pressure on the margin of United Kingdom supplies of various kinds on which the Colonies were relying, at a time when, as the Secretary of State, Mr Creech Jones, 'confessed' in a paper that he addressed on 10 February 1949 to the Economic Policy Committee on Colonial Office organisation,[2] the Office 'was not adequately organised to resist such pressure, or indeed, to realise at once that it was taking place, and with what effect'.

11. IMPACT OF THE ECONOMIC CRISIS OF 1947

It had been assumed that finance would be the main limiting factor once the war was over. But this was not to be, as the Secretary of State explained in the first paragraph of his report to Parliament, *The Colonial Empire (1947–48)*,[3]

the economic disruption in Europe could well throw back development in the overseas territories . . . it became necessary to ask what more was possible to strengthen the economies of the territories, to meet their needs and to increase the production of foodstuffs and materials in short supply in the world; moreover, what could be done to fortify, not only their own, but Britain's and Europe's long-term economy?

On 20 August 1947 a personal message had been sent by the Secretary of State to all Colonies. It began:

The United Kingdom is facing an economic crisis as serious as any in her long history. Our ability to surmount it is a great test and requires in the economic field efforts as strenuous as we made in the major crises of the war. I am sure the Colonial peoples will want to understand the nature of these economic difficulties, how they affect Colonial territories and what Colonial peoples can do in collaboration with us to win through to conditions of greater stability and prosperity.[4]

The message described the causes of the United Kingdom's weakness, especially wartime sacrifices and the rise of import prices, and the United Kingdom's response by reducing imports and raising production. The Colonies were asked to limit imports to what could be paid for from current earnings or, where possible, below that level, and to increase supplies of goods which the United Kingdom had otherwise to import from dollar sources, or which could be sold for dollars. The increase of Colonial production was seen to be 'the major long-term contribution' which Colonial territories could make, the world shortage of food and raw material offering 'unprecedented opportunity for the Colonies to develop their production and their trade on lines which, as with all soundly organised trade, will bring mutual advantage to both parties to it.' His Majesty's Government would assist with technical assistance and capital but the whole-hearted co-operation of the Governments and peoples of the Colonies was also necessary. His Majesty's Government was confident of receiving that co-operation.

Two Colonies reacted quickly and rather unexpectedly. The Governor of the Seychelles immediately offered to forgo the CD & W allocation for 1947–51, amounting to £25,000 a year, or else to make a voluntary gift of £10,000 to the United Kingdom.[5] This was declined as unnecessary; cuts in consumption and increases in taxation were suggested instead.[6] However, the Members of the Executive Council and the Members of the Legislative Council unanimously voted an interest-free loan of £10,000 to His Majesty's Government, which the latter accepted as not an unduly expensive gesture on condition that it would be returned if needed locally. The Governor of Northern Rhodesia, besides being worried about drawing on sterling balances and about raising a loan for development purposes in 1949–50, asked for guidance as the Unofficial Members of the Legislative Council wished to decline CD & W assistance of £2.5 million as a gesture of support.[7] It was believed in the Colonial Office that the Northern Rhodesian Legislature regarded the administration and financial control of CD & W schemes as unduly restrictive and, if curtailment of development plans was in any case necessary, would gladly jettison their CD & W allocation in return for freedom from Whitehall interference.[8] Just as a sacrifice by the Seychelles was regarded as unnecessary so also was a renunciation of the rights of the Northern Rhodesian native to the benefits of CD & W assistance regarded as unfortunate.[9] Instead, it was suggested that calls on United Kingdom production of plant should be limited to items permitting an increase in productive efficiency.[10]

This last point was echoed by the Conference of East African

Governors in October 1947. Their Economic Adviser pointed out that increased exports would be possible only if the railways received more rolling stock, and the necessary machinery, materials and containers, including jute bags, were made available, and – more important than capital goods – agricultural labour was made attractive, possibly by the supply of incentive goods.[11] The Conference, while awaiting the results of separate discussions in each of the Territories concerning import policy, agreed that priority should be given to housing improvements and welfare amenities designed to attract labour.[12] It was considered that a substantial increase in the direct taxation of Africans would not be politically feasible.

The attitude of Governors was further shown by their responses to a memorandum, 'The Colonial Empire and the Economic Crisis', which was circulated with a covering letter from the Permanent Under-Secretary on 26 July 1948.[13] These arose from a suggestion that the Finance Department should consider whether anything new could be added to the familiar exhortations to Colonial Governments to raise taxation in order to reduce general purchasing power.[14] A draft was submitted which, in view of action in Kenya involving an income tax refund of £10 to those with incomes in excess of £7000 per annum, was thought salutary in 'impressing on Governors their economic responsibility and that they should be guided in this by the Secretary of State, and not by their European unofficials to whose point of view some of them are too prone to bow.'[15] The draft was circulated in the Colonial Office and sent to the Treasury for approval, but owing to the delay in receiving comments it was redrafted as a memorandum. Sir Charles Jeffries suggested that 'the very shortage of "consumer goods" which we are apt to deplore gives us, in fact, a golden opportunity to correct the materialist tendency of the past, to play down the old theme of offering rewards in the shape of Western manufactures, and to play up the idea of self-help, self-improvement and self-reliance.'[16] However commendable in itself, this was seen to be contrary to the general thesis underlying the memorandum, which was founded on the mutual benefit of trading activities between the United Kingdom and the Colonies, and also to require a considerable psychological revolution in order to obtain the willing acquiescence of Colonial peoples.[17] Later, Sir Charles Jeffries returned to the attack. While agreeing with the draft within the context of the current attitude towards Colonial development, he said he thought that attitude was wrong. Nor did he believe that the memorandum would be good propaganda, because it did 'not explain (because it can't) how the Colonial people can be convinced that the United Kingdom is in a serious plight when the standard of living of the mass of the people here is so immensely superior to that of the Colonial populations'.[18] Others also pointed the difference between the United Kingdom's problems and requirements and those of the Colonies, one official minuting: 'I think the danger – or at least the temptation – of our exploiting the Colonies at this particular and most difficult time is real.'[19] Another agreed, believing that the Ministry of Food was one-sided and suggesting that the term 'Mother Country' was out-dated.[20] The Treasury would have preferred 'something with more punch about the need to increase taxation' and suggested that the Colonies should be given further technical advice on possible taxation developments.[21] Following a further recasting, the memorandum and covering letter were sent to 34 Colonies on 26 July 1948. The tone of the letter was markedly defensive: 'It hardly needs to be said that there is no intention on the part of His Majesty's Government to exploit the Colonial Empire for the sake of selfish United Kingdom interests, or to impede in any way the political progress of the Colonial people, even if some individual statements made, or action taken under pressure of present circumstances, may perhaps expose us to doubt from certain types of critic.'[22] It was intended to use the exigencies of the situation to demonstrate 'that the inter-dependence of the Colonial territories and Britain is a real and powerful thing'[23] and the memorandum had been prepared as a first essay in this task of 'telling the facts'.[24] It was not intended to be published, though the substance of it might be used in public statements. The memorandum explained the United Kingdom's balance of payments position and the measures adopted, including the European Recovery Programme, to relieve it. Despite such an unfavourable situation, it was stated that the United Kingdom was determined 'to play its full part in the development of the Colonies' – the 1945 CD & W Act, the 1948 ORD Act, double taxation arrangements which transferred revenue from the United Kingdom Exchequer to the Colonies in which United Kingdom companies operated, and efforts to provide a fair share of iron and steel and other capital goods to Colonies, were mentioned as proof of this resolve. The reasons for the resolve were, first, the demand of Colonial peoples for higher standards of living and, secondly, the long-term advantage to the sterling area balance of payments from the development of Colonial economic resources. In the short term, this policy carried obvious dangers, because it could raise the demand for both capital and consumer goods above what could be met. Therefore, Colonial Governments were asked (a) to control, or supervise, the use of scarce capital goods; (b) to control imports, particularly from dollar sources, though it was acknowledged that, in the dollar-earning territories of the Gold Coast and Malaya, it would be 'much more difficult to convince public opinion of the need to restrict dollar expenditure'; and (c) to raise savings and taxation in order to cope with the inflationary problem resulting from the high prices of Colonial exports, apart from rubber, and of the expenditure of development finance. 'In the Colonies, where the physical controls exercised in the United Kingdom are absent or less efficacious, it is all the more essential to employ the fiscal measures of surplus and increased revenue.'

The memorandum was appreciated by Governors, some of whom regarded it as 'rather strong meat', which convinced the Colonial Office that it had been justified in resisting pressure from the Treasury in favour of stiffening up the memorandum still further.[25] Four Governors in the West Indies wished to publish any future such memoranda as it was so difficult 'to disseminate background information in a prompt, effective and "popular" manner'.[26] But there were rejoinders also. The Governor of the Bahamas, Sir William Murphy, wrote of the difficulty of obtaining sufficient goods from the United Kingdom, and of excessive wholesale prices. He regarded the lack of statistics and the attitude of the Legislature as severe handicaps in dealing with the local problem of inflation.[27] The Governor of Kenya, Sir Philip Mitchell, wrote at greatest length and most critically, arguing that

a large part of the Colonial public of British origin and also the majority of English-speaking Indians out here, while readily admitting that the United Kingdom is in a mess, think it is a mess of her own Government's making; that British workmen no longer work hard, and that British business has little enterprise left because it has no incentive, and that what is really needed is a change of Government in the United Kingdom and, of course, of policy. The African, on the other hand, is, generally speaking, now enjoying better wages, food and – in towns anyhow – a prospect at least and, in increasing numbers, the reality of better housing than he has ever dreamt of; he is continuously bombarded in speeches and his own newspapers with subversive, anti-British, and anti-Government matters, and if, as a small proportion do, he is able to understand it at all, he comes to the conclusion that there may be a chance of considerable loot because the British Government has become so weak that it can be abused and flouted with impurity. The majority do not understand anything about it at all, but, although they are demonstrably better off than ever before, they are constantly told that the Europeans and Indians are oppressing them, and so they readily become susceptible to gang leadership. To the outside observer, it seems difficult to say that a rise in wages from near-starvation to current subsistence level can be called inflation – especially when the latter figure is about 12/– a week in the towns and 2/– to 6/– in the country.[28]

He criticised the lowness of the fixed price of gold, the irrelevance of the nationalisation of steel, food subsidies in the United Kingdom as an anti-inflationary measure, the bias in CD & W towards welfare instead of development, the irrelevance of OFC and CDC to the immediate problem of shortage of capital equipment, and so forth. As he stated in a further letter, it was all summed up in a cartoon in *Punch* showing a small box labelled 'Fresh Constitutions' being loaded on a ship for the Colonies while large boxes of exports were stacked on the quayside for 'Hard Currency Areas Only'.[29]

It was felt necessary to tell the Governor as much as possible of the efforts being made and success achieved in improving supplies to the Colonies.[30] The Parliamentary Under-Secretary, Mr D. Rees-Williams, later Lord Ogmore, was surprised 'how even an intelligent, sympathetic man can get out of touch and how many misunderstandings can arise' and thought everything possible should be done to explain HMG's policy and the United Kingdom's difficulties and achievements to the Colonial public.[31] After discussion in the Office, a reply was sent to the Governor which, while it contested some of his detailed criticisms such as those concerning food subsidies, the price of gold, and nationalisation, admitted that the memorandum had (*a*) insufficiently stressed that, under conditions of full employment, increased production depended on increasing productivity; and (*b*) overemphasised taxation as a cure for inflation and understated the possible and largely preferable use of stabilisation funds and promotion of savings.[32] The Governor was not convinced and, in respect of education, expressed concern as technical education was not being adequately developed, with the result that 'practically all the technical services required by the local population are provided by immigrant Europeans and Indians', though the situation was being tackled.[33] Sir T. Lloyd spoke to Sir P. Mitchell about this on 4 January 1949.[34]

The need for a revision of Colonial Office procedure was expressed in much the same terms from other quarters. Thus the Economic Adviser to the Comptroller for Development and Welfare in the West Indies, in a confidential memorandum following the completion of the

POOR POLICY

'And is *this* all you've got for the Colonies?'

Punch, 11 August 1948

1945–46 Report, stated that, while there was no real difficulty in putting forward a convincing case that Colonial Office policy had made a substantial contribution to the restoration of well-being in that area over the years since 1940, it was unlikely to be true of the next few years 'unless there are major changes in the administrative set-up, which is most inadequate to the needs of the area, and unless there is considerable revision in the relation of the Colonial Office to these Governments'. Revenue collection, customs administration, and price control were alike in urgent need of overhaul in the light of the shortage and lack of skill of the staff. While the primary need was to modernise the administration, the clamant need at the time was to bring down the inflated cost of living. The prescription for this was to terminate unrealistic mark-ups on readily-saleable goods, and open marketing to competition, thus bringing a halt to the accumulation of wealth – and, therefore, of power – of the largely expatriate groups of retailers and wholesalers. The lack of realism of the Colonial Office was seen to be in not realising that these were the weaknesses, while the provision of haphazard subventions merely worsened the position. [Memorandum by Professor C. G. Beasley entered on file 71409, West Indies 1947, on 1 July 1947. The file has been Destroyed Under Statute but a copy of the memorandum survives. Professor Beasley, after pointing to 'the poor type of Colonial administration with which the area is saddled, ranging from mediocre at best to culpably negligent at worst', felt that the Secretary of State could in any Parliamentary discussion arising from the 1945–46 Report of the Development and Welfare Organisation reasonably 'point to the continuous political development and the movement towards federal organisation as the most promising method of improving the administration of the region especially by making possible the employment of technical officers for customs administration and for financial control'.]

The Economic Adviser's strictures received confirmation in a report by an official who visited the West Indies in 1949.[35] The staff position was said to be critical, particularly in Trinidad and British Guiana, mainly because of the comparatively low salaries and insufficiently attractive conditions of service. It was thought that wasteful expenditure occurred in various projects through the errors in estimates and planning made by staff of insufficient calibre. In the short term, it was recommended that greater control and inspection over the expenditure of CD & W money should be instituted, but the longer-term solution was the constitution of a 'proper system of recruitment to the Civil Service in the West Indies'. Meantime, steps were being taken to

improve estimates by the appointment of Financial Secretaries and
Economic Advisers, and by the training provided by the O and M
Division of the Treasury. Any case where a Governor appeared to pay
too little attention to financial advice should be dealt with in-
dividually. On supplies, it was agreed that Colonial Governments
should make 'every effort to educate the peoples of the West Indies as
to the true position of the Sterling Area, and the necessity for
economising in dollars'. In this the West Indies were unique, because
during the war West Indian purchases had been switched to the
United States owing to the shortage of shipping and, as a result, had
not experienced the same austerity as the United Kingdom and other
Colonies. While dollar purchases were being reduced through an
examination of import programmes this, because of past policy and the
fact that American goods were often cheaper, could not result in
substantial dollar savings in the near future.

In many ways, the circumstances in the Gold Coast were the reverse
of those in the West Indies. At Accra on 28 February 1948 the police
had resorted to the use of firearms when disorders and looting took
place. An independent Commission of Enquiry was set up. The
Chairman was Mr Aiken Watson, KC. The Report was signed on 8
June 1948. Its recommendations were radical and quickened the pace
of change not only in the Gold Coast but in Nigeria and elsewhere.[36]
Suspicion in the Gold Coast surrounding all Government activity was
reported.[37] The underlying causes of the disturbances were said to be
political, economic and social and, in the opinion of the Commission,
'The remedy for the distrust and suspicion with which the African
views the European, and which is today poisoning life in the Gold
Coast, demands an attack on all three causes. None of them may be
said to take precedence.'[38] For present purposes, attention will be
concentrated on the economic causes, which the Commission summarised thus:

(i) The announcement of the Government that it would remain
neutral in the dispute which had arisen between the traders and the
people of the Gold Coast over high prices of imported goods and
which led to the organised boycott of January–February, 1948.
(ii) The continuance of war-time control of imports, and the
shortage and high prices of consumer goods which were widely
attributed to the machinations of European importers.
(iii) The alleged unfair allocations and distribution of goods in
short supply by the importing firms.
(iv) The Government's acceptance of the scientists' finding that the

only cure for Swollen Shoot disease of cocoa was to cut out diseased trees, and their adoption of that policy combined with allegations of improper methods of carrying it out.

(v) The degree of control in the Cocoa Marketing Board which limited the powers of the farmers' representatives to control the vast reserves which are accumulating under the Board's policy.

(vi) The feeling that the Government had not formulated any plans for the future of industry and agriculture and that, indeed, it was lukewarm about any development apart from production for export.[39]

The Economist (7 August 1948) ended a comment on the Report with this question: 'Can anything fundamental be done to a Colony whose inhabitants allow their biggest asset, the cocoa trees, to be ruined by swollen shoot disease and then refuse to co-operate with their government in stamping it out?' According to the Governor, the United Gold Coast Convention was 'certainly behind, and almost wholly responsible for, the bitterness and violence connected with the opposition to the swollen shoot cutting-out campaign'.[40]

However, for the present purpose, points (iv), (v) and (vi) do not require further consideration. It is sufficient to concentrate attention on supplies, prices and distribution. Total supplies of consumer goods were said to be below the level of pre-war years, while population and incomes had sharply increased. Inevitably prices had risen considerably, particularly in 1946 and 1947. Most of the complaints about unfair distribution were concerned with imported goods and related to:

(*a*) The continuation of licensing and other import controls.

(*b*) The monopolistic position of the importing firms and restriction of African enterprise.

(*c*) The basing of import quotas on past performance.

(*d*) The methods of sale employed by importing firms.

(*e*) Conditional sales.

(*f*) Excessive margins and distributive costs.

(*g*) The wide gap between the prices paid in the retail stores of the importing firms and the price paid by the African buying from a petty trader.[41]

These points were separately discussed by the Commission and, like the rest of the Report, were commented on publicly by the Secretary of State in the *Statement by His Majesty's Government on the Report of the*

Commission of Enquiry into Disturbances in the Gold Coast.[42] This closely reflected 'the views of the Office on the Report'.[43]

With regard to supplies, the Secretary of State claimed that statistics for 1946 and 1947 'show that, although a number of shortages persisted, the total imports into the Gold Coast in 1947 were in value approximately 70 per cent greater than in the previous year'.[44] Both foodstuffs and other essential goods, such as textiles, shared in that increase, and the Secretary of State concluded that 'the improvement which has already taken place will undoubtedly reduce some of the pressure towards inflated prices to which the Commission drew attention. This will however, be offset to some extent if there is any increase in the price paid to the producer for cocoa.'[45]

The last point turned out to be highly relevant. On 20 July 1948, Mr, later Sir William, Gorrell Barnes, a visiting Colonial Office official attending in Import Control Conference, sent a telegram to the Secretary of State warning that, in view of larger cash payments to cocoa growers and the limited contribution to be expected from tax policy, 'it seems clear that there is possibility of trouble unless there is a rapid increase in imports of goods in short supply, including allocated commodities and those lines of other goods which Africans will buy.'[46] Owing to the lack of data, lack of ability in some cases and willingness in others of Departments to intervene, and insufficient attention to the needs of particular Colonies, he felt the matter needed special and urgent attention, arguing that, unless appropriate action could be taken quickly, restrictions on hard currency imports should be relaxed, or even lifted altogether. It was realised that such a policy could not be limited to the Gold Coast, but would have to be extended to other Colonies with similar problems, and this would include Nigeria. Also, although the seriousness of the position of sterling was acknowledged, it was urged that the stability of a dollar-earning Colony – or Colonies – was at issue.

Mr Gorell Barnes believed that action along these lines would require a new type of organisation in the Colonial Office, which he broadly sketched in a further telegram.[47] It was proposed that there should be a Colonial Economic Policy Committee reporting to the Economic Policy Committee of the Cabinet, with two full-time alternate chairmen and a considerable full-time Secretariat, one of the chairmen and a proportion of the Secretariat being, in turns, always in the Colonies. While the provision of supplies was put first among the duties, other aspects, such as finance, production and marketing, would also be taken in hand in what was termed 'planning with a vengeance' in an organisation that would require a smaller staff than the 'present rather frustrated organisation in the Colonial Office'.[48] The reaction in the Colonial Office was one of caution, as it was felt that the Treasury would not be easy to convince over loosening controls on dollar imports.[49] The Board of Trade was first to react, stating that there was doubt whether there was much, 'if anything, we, as a Department, can do to implement your thesis that supplies needed to beat the danger of inflation should be classed as essential', adding that 'in general, this is out of the question', in reference to the proposal that administrative priority should be given to supplies to the Gold Coast that would mop up purchasing power.[50] Meantime, the Governor had warmly endorsed the views put forward, providing both a list of priority commodities and a request for any others that could be sold in the Colony.[51]

An inter departmental meeting was held at the Colonial Office on 30 July 1948, to discuss the supply of consumer goods to the Gold Coast and Nigeria.[52] Besides a contingent of six from the Colonial Office, the Treasury, Board of Trade, Ministry of Food and Ministry of Fuel and Power were represented. The chairman, Mr Gorell Barnes, said that the increased payment of at least an additional £7 million to cocoa producers in the Gold Coast and about a similar amount in Nigeria would sharply raise purchasing power. The effect was likely to be particularly serious in the Gold Coast. Consequently, there was need for both (a) sufficient goods to meet the inflationary danger and (b) the supply of increased quantities of commodities in which shortages had led to black market and conditional sales. With reference to (a), a meeting with firms trading with West Africa was suggested to examine the problem, while, as regards (b), the Gold Coast Government was to be asked for further details. In the meantime, the relevant Departments agreed to consider possible action.

When this upshot was reported to the Governors of the Gold Coast and Nigeria,[53] the former feared that the suggested meeting in London of firms with headquarters in the United Kingdom which traded in West Africa could give credence to allegations that the Colonial Government was in league with big European firms. Instead, he proposed to meet businessmen and traders in Accra in order to get a list of goods that would find a ready market.[54] The meeting in London was not called,[55] and the Governors sent a stream of telegrams asking for additional flour, sugar, soap, butter and cheese, Ovaltine, salt, textiles, sewing thread, Swiss watches and Czechoslovak clocks, petroleum products, sewing machines, kerosene, unmanufactured tobacco, corned beef, dressed leather, canned fish, bicycles, shotguns, whisky and gin. An unprecedented search for supplies followed and was highly successful. By October 1948 the only goods not subject to allocation or control which were still in short supply were the shotguns and Singer sewing machines, whose supply was allocated by the American parent firm and supplied by the sole agent, the United Africa Company, to whom it was suggested representations should be made by the Colonial Government. The problem can be appreciated once it is realised that, compared with imports into Nigeria of 6640 sewing machines in 1947, the requirements for 1949 were said to be 24,000.[56] Other interesting points about particular items emerge from File 17265. It was explained that hitherto the bulk of supplies of butter and cheese had been consumed by Europeans but now Africans, particularly returning soldiers, had developed a taste for them. This provided an opening for political agitation if the demand was not satisfied, it was said in Telegram No. 677 of 18 August 1948 from the Governor, Sir G. Creasy, to the Secretary of State – item 77 in the file. The Parliamentary Under-Secretary, Mr Rees-Williams, strongly supported the Governor's requests in a secret telegram from Accra on 24 August 1948 (no. 699–ibid., item 99) in which he asked for the Minister of Food and President of the Board of Trade to be told of the inflationary pressure in the Gold Coast. This telegram was prompted by one from W. L. Gorell Barnes – item 85. The Ministry of Food responded handsomely – item 118. As for bicycles, although supplies of other makes were available in the shops, the demand was for 'Raleigh' machines – see memorandum by Mr Gorell Barnes with item 135. There was a strong African demand for shotguns with 34-inch and 36-inch barrels, which were made only in Belgium. The 1500 required had to be obtained from Belgium – ibid. and items 163, 174 and 179 in Part II of the file (CO 852/801).

These tremendous efforts were necessary because, at a time when virtually everything was subject to allocation of one kind or another, there was no machinery for ascertaining the essential requirements of the Colonies, or even of knowing what they were obtaining. In fact, in the absence of requirements programmes, Colonial needs from this country were largely going by default, with the twofold result that their development suffered and more dollars had to be allowed than would otherwise have been necessary. The strategy, therefore, was, on the one hand, to ascertain requirements and persuade – or cajole – home Departments that reasonable allocation should be made to meet them, and, on the other hand, to persuade the Colonies that, provided their essential requirements were met from one source or another, it was sensible for them, as members of the sterling area with their reserves in sterling, to restrict their purchases from the dollar area. All this involved not only securing allocations from the United Kingdom suppliers, but also ensuring that licensing, which was necessary to safeguard sterling, was not used unnecessarily merely to protect United Kingdom industry, as when better or cheaper supplies were available from the soft-currency European suppliers or, within the limits of the bilateral payments agreement, from Japan. In all this the *ad hoc* arrangements beginning in July 1948, achieved notable success, and it seems likely that had they begun twelve months earlier the atmosphere which enabled the disturbances of February 1948 to be sparked off would not have formed. Be that as it may, no further threatening situations were allowed to arise again because of lack of supplies.

III. THE COLONIAL DEVELOPMENT WORKING PARTY

The disturbances in the Gold Coast highlighted the supplies problem. However, the need for a review of the general economic problems facing the Colonies had been recognised at roughly the time when the Acting Governor first wrote from the Gold Coast. In a minute of 10 November 1947 it was suggested that the Secretary of State might propose to other interested Ministers the formation of an inter-departmental working party to consider certain general problems concerning Colonial economic development.[57] It was felt that the character of the problems involved in such development needed exploration, and there was need also to ensure that all possible assistance was being given by HMG as a whole. The various immediate practical problems of a general character requiring such attention included:

(*a*) the general problem of the order of priority to be given to the supplies required for Colonial development, and the place of such projects in HMG's general programme of capital investment, with consideration of the ways in which such priorities could be implemented;

(*b*) whether and, if so, how foreign borrowing, in particular in the United States, through the International Bank or otherwise, should be sought;

(*c*) possible collaboration, including co-ordination of plans, with other Colonial powers, especially in Africa; and

(*d*) possible utilisation of the resources of other Departments,

including the Service Departments, in surmounting difficulties due
to shortages of skilled and technical personnel. The desirability of
such a means of focusing inter-departmental interest on the subject
had been felt by the Central Planning Staff, and elsewhere in the
Treasury, where Sir Wilfred Eady felt concern.[58]

The Secretary of State wrote accordingly to the Chancellor of the
Exchequer, Sir Stafford Cripps.[59] The Working Party on Colonial
Development met on 27 November 1947, under the chairmanship of
Sir Edwin, later Lord, Plowden, who was Chief Planning Officer and
Chairman of the Economic Planning Board, 1947–53. It was agreed
that the Working Party (CDWP) should (a) review Colonial requirements for capital equipment in relation to competing needs for home
investment and export; (b) assess the resources likely to be available for
implementing Colonial investment programmes, and make recommendations on the extent to which the programmes required modification in order to make the most effective use of these resources;
(c) make proposals on the relative priorities which should be observed
in dealing with existing and new projects; and (d) examine the
arrangements for determining the allocation of capital goods needed
for the maintenance and development of the Colonial economies, and
make recommendations on the extent to which these arrangements
required modification. Apart from the Central Economic Planning
Staff and the Colonial Office, the Board of Trade, Ministry of Food
and Ministry of Supply were represented.

   In an economy of scarcity and planning, the Working Party and its
particular terms of reference were inevitabilities. Yet the early work of
the CDWP lacked relevance to the pressing problems, and, after a
frank discussion on 12 January 1948, it was agreed that the CDWP
should (i) establish as soon as possible what supplies of materials and
equipment were required (a) to maintain Colonial economies at
current levels, (b) to increase Colonial output quickly, e.g. by
providing rolling-stock, and (c) to carry out capital works likely to
produce substantial returns in the period 1952–57; (ii) identify and, as
far as possible, quantify projects in categories (a), (b) and (c) which
were likely to save dollars. As a result, the CDWP produced in April
1948 an interim report on the main obstacles to the increase of
Colonial production, and made various general recommendations to
relieve them. Perhaps, at a time of obvious shortage, it was useful to
conclude that materials, equipment and skilled manpower limited
expansion rather than finance. The real question was: what shortages
and where? A pioneer pilot enquiry was made into Nigeria's needs for

capital goods over the years 1948–50. It showed that shortage of iron and steel limited production, trained manpower was a problem, and supplies of railway materials and consumer goods needed attention. Consequently, the CDWP recommended that: existing resources should be repaired and improved before new resources were developed, and special attention should be given to transport and communications; further efforts should be made to recruit skilled personnel; investment in the Colonies of loan and equity capital from foreign and Dominion sources should be encouraged. The interim report was a brave first essay, which tended to generalise because it had little precise to contribute. Its recommendations were approved by the Cabinet Economic Policy Committee,[60] and the detailed working out of its recommendations was divided between Departments, mainly the Central Economic Planning Staff and the Colonial Office.

Agreement in principle was one thing, even though fundamental, while implementation was another. This latter depended in the first place on the availability and collation of data, which was no easy matter. In the first paper submitted to CDWP the Colonial Office had attempted to summarise the known capital investment projects. These totalled £61 million for 1948–49 and £444 million for the four subsequent years.[61] This was thought to be a useful exercise, although it could well be wrong by £100–125 million in either direction.[62] The details of private investment were thought to be least complete and the figures most liable to error.[63] The estimate of public investment was compiled from the development plans of 17 Colonies, which did not include either the Gold Coast, which had funds but few projects, or the Malayan Union, which was considering ambitious programmes of capital works with, as yet, limited funds. It was clear that information in London needed supplementing and Colonial Governments were asked for estimates of requirements for 1948 and 1949 of iron and steel,[64] cement and various types of machinery. The circular made known the establishment of CDWP and listed its purposes. Colonies were urged to provide information so that 'Colonial development is not impeded by failure to get due share of capital equipment.'[65] The replies, with rare exception, gave little indication of expected aggregate expenditure, the interpretation given to 'capital investment' varied, while estimates for the private sector were hardly more than guesswork. The Governor of Trinidad, Sir John Shaw, complained that, as there was no department or body in the Colony co-ordinating all plans for development, much unproductive labour had been used to collect unreliable figures that could not be of genuine use for planning purposes.[66] Taking from the replies the estimates that could be regarded as realistic and otherwise using data available in London, the Central Economic Planning Staff (CEPS) produced a paper,[67] which showed that the total of capital expenditure required in all the Colonies could be estimated at the rate of approximately £185 million a year, of which £161,500,000 was accounted for by the 18 major Colonies which had been studied in detail. Local costs accounted for two-fifths of the total, most of it on labour. Imports were put at £110 million. Such were the figures on which most reliance could be placed, and it was asked whether the exercise was of any practical use because the Colonial Empire could not be treated as a homogeneous whole. Although it was felt that regular surveys in each of the major Colonies might produce results valuable to the United Kingdom as well as to the Colonies themselves, the advantage was not considered sufficient to make the exercise worth repeating.[68]

The paper arising was submitted by CEPS to the CDWP and discussed at the eleventh meeting on 15 September 1948,[69] when it was thought to be useful in giving the order of magnitude of investment in the Colonies and also the general pattern of investment. It was agreed that it was inadvisable to attempt a similar exercise again until individual Colonies had built up their own economic studies. Meanwhile, CEPS was invited, in conjunction with other Departments, to produce a paper for the assistance of Colonies on the techniques of undertaking an enquiry of this kind. Notes were circulated and a meeting held.[70] As it was likely that overall capital investment figures for the Colonies would be required again in 1949, it was suggested that Colonies should be assisted by a visiting expert.[71] The day of the fruitful comprehensive review had not come. Improvisation was successful in the Gold Coast and Nigeria and could be so elsewhere. The Colonial Office rather than the CEPS was the right place for working estimates to be made.

IV. BROADENING THE PERSPECTIVE

Early in January 1948 Ministers discussed a report by the Chief of the Imperial General Staff, Field-Marshal Montgomery, on his visit to Africa.[72] The Secretary of the Cabinet, Sir Norman Brook, later Lord Normanbrook, assured the Permanent Under-Secretary at the Colonial Office on the following day that Ministers had not concentrated so much attention on the development of Africa's economic resources wholly, or mainly, because of the views of the CIGS, which, in fact, they regarded as over-simplified. Rather it was

> their study of the future course of the United Kingdom economy which had led them to the view that, when the period of Marshall Aid was over, this country would have to rely far more than ever before on the dollar-earning capacity of the Commonwealth and Empire. Another strand in this thought was the idea of a political union of Western Europe – for Ministers believed that a Western European bloc could not stand on terms of equality with the Soviet and the American blocs unless it included the African Colonial possessions of the Western European powers.[73]

Ministers felt that more should have been done to develop African economic resources, and it was suggested that the Colonial Office should (i) press forward with promising schemes of economic development and improve its own organisation to facilitate this, and (ii) ensure that the Colonial Empire received its fair share of the resources for capital development which were at the disposal of His Majesty's Government.

While the first of these was a matter primarily for the Colonial Office, the second involved inter-departmental organisation. In December 1948 the Economic Policy Committee (EPC) approved a recommendation of the Colonial Development Working Party (CDWP) that a permanent inter-departmental Committee of officials should be set up to keep the broad aspects of Colonial Development under continuous review.[74] The Committee on Colonial Development (CCD) was accordingly appointed to do so, with the tasks of co-ordinating United Kingdom and Colonial economic policy, assessing progress in Colonial export targets and development schemes, advising on major deficiencies, and generally following up the recommendations of CDWP. The Committee met once in 1948, 16 times in 1949, eight times in 1950 and twice in 1951, circulating respectively three, 50, 33 and 18 papers. After the review of Committees by the new Government, it was announced at the meeting of 20 November 1951 that the Prime Minister had decided to dissolve the CCD. At the first meeting, which took place on 21 December 1948,[75] the CCD accepted as one of its first tasks the determination of what should be published in the field of Colonial development, as it had been decided not to publish the report of the CDWP. The Committee examined the recommendations of that report in order to ensure that any necessary action by other Departments was in hand. It approved the proposal by the Colonial Office to set up a Sub-Committee to consider Colonial import programmes. The Colonial Office, in turn, was invited (i) to ascertain the import requirements of the Colonial Development Corporation, and (ii) to draft instructions to the Colonies for interim dollar expenditure. At its second meeting, the Colonial Office representative reported instances where manufacturers in the United Kingdom had declined to accept orders from the Colonies because of alleged instructions from Whitehall that their output, or most of it, should be retained for the home market.[76] The list included tractors, tyres, agricultural machinery, metal piping, surgical equipment, electrical insulators and barbed wire. The Colonial Office, with final responsibility for dependent territories, was unique in Whitehall in being interested in virtually all commodities while having no voice in allocations. Its representatives protested that the directives were inconsistent with the accepted principle that the economies of the Colonies should be treated as integral parts of the United Kingdom economy. An inter-departmental committee was called, and it was agreed at the next meeting of the CCD that Colonial orders should be treated, in general, on equality with home orders.[77] The Colonial Office was invited to inform Departments of items of particular difficulty in the Colonies so that the supply position might be re-examined. The new United Kingdom situation indicated the need for machinery in the Colonial Office to ensure that supplies for the Colonies matched the finance provided, on the one hand, and that the Colonies played their part in United Kingdom policy, in particular the export drive and dollar shortage, on the other.

In January 1948, the Prime Minister asked the Secretary of State what progress was being made with arrangements for dealing with economic planning in the Colonies.[78] In a Note on Economic Development in the Colonies,[79] which was subsequently circulated to the EPC,[80] Mr Creech Jones, after outlining the organisation of work within the Economic Division, explained that

> the oversight of Colonial economic planning is the job of the whole Division, and, in order to ensure effective co-ordination between the work of the three Assistant Under-Secretaries of State and their various departments, a weekly meeting is held by the Deputy Under-Secretary of State at which the three Assistant Under-Secretaries of State, the Assistant Secretaries, the Chief Statistician, the Liaison Officers and the Director of Colonial (Geodetic and Topographic) Surveys are present. In addition to these weekly meetings, a monthly meeting of the Economic Division is held under the chairmanship of the Parliamentary Under-Secretary of State.

Since July 1948 a regular list of priority projects, mainly, but not entirely economic, has been kept in the Colonial Office in respect of the whole Colonial Empire. This list is revised each month at one of the weekly meetings of the Deputy Under-Secretary in the light of advice received from the various sections of the Office.

He raised three points in his Note to the Prime Minister, who replied as follows.[81] First, he supported, in principle, the proposals made by the Secretary of State for strengthening the Economic Division of the Colonial Office, and suggested that details should be settled with the Chancellor of the Exchequer. Secondly, he agreed that it would be useful if Conferences on economic development were held in East and in West Africa as soon as definite assurances of support were received. Thirdly, in answer to the request that the Secretary of State be authorised to give those attending the Conference 'an unqualified assurance that His Majesty's Government are going to extend to the Colonial authorities all the help in their power, not merely in money but also in the supply of materials and men', he suggested that CDWP should be asked to include among their recommendations 'a statement showing what assurances of our support could safely be given'.[82] As noted earlier, the main bottleneck in Colonial development was seen by CDWP to be in the shortage of steel, and the CDWP asked for at least an additional 100,000 tons of steel annually for the Colonies. However, the Production Committee had meantime agreed that external development schemes should have second claim for an allocation in the fourth quarter of 1948,[83] and the decision had to be reconsidered. As the Parliamentary Under-Secretary told the House of Commons in February 1948: 'When any African Governor dies the word "steel" is found written across his heart, because he realises that without steel nothing can be accomplished in Africa.'[84] The Materials Committee made the reallocation in July 1948, and thereafter specific quantities of both structural steel and also general and sheet steel were set aside for the Colonies.[85] The Committee on Colonial Development re-established the principle that Colonial requirements were to be considered on a par with those of the United Kingdom.

v. CONFERENCE OF COLONIAL SUPPLIES OFFICERS, 1949

In the early weeks of 1949, the Supplies Department of the Colonial Office was heavily engaged with the Import Programme Sub-

Committee of CCD in examining the import programmes of the Colonies, and formulating recommendations about supplies from the United Kingdom, hard currency ceilings and so forth. It was suggested that these exercises would be facilitated if Colonial Government officials concerned with import policy were summoned to London, in April or May, with the purpose of reviewing the results of the current exercise and of explaining to such officials the underlying policy constraints.[86] The Parliamentary Under-Secretary and the Secretary of State readily agreed.[87] In his Circular Telegram of 5 February 1949[88] the Secretary of State informed Colonial Governments of the intention of holding a Conference of officials. The objectives were threefold: (i) to review procedure followed in preparing and deciding on 1949 import programmes, and considering modifications in the procedure for 1950; (ii) to exchange information on important commodities in short supply; and (iii) to review the relative desirability of various countries as sources of supply. As far as possible, it was hoped that Colonial representatives should be officers concerned with the preparation of programmes of import requirements in each territory. Many of the Colonies were not well informed about the reasons for our restrictions on their imports from hard currency areas, or about the future supply position of some of the most important commodities. Also, it was not always easy for the Colonial Office to appreciate some of the requirements and problems of the Colonies. In preparing for the Conference, information was sought on supply prospects from North America.[89] It was reported that practically everything likely to be needed by Colonies was available at favourable prices. This situation was due to two main causes. First, the United States export control system had operated to protect the domestic supply position, so that export allocations had been allowed only after full consideration had been given to home needs. So there was no really serious backlog and manufacturers were interested in developing oversea outlets. Secondly, the boom days for exporters, which continued until 1948, were over as a consequence of the almost universal shortage of dollars, and there was a large volume of cancelled orders. Thus rice, of which there was a world shortage in 1946–47, had become a currency instead of a supply problem; flour, which was under strict control in 1947, was under general licence; lard and other fats were being offered, Jamaica reporting in March 1949, that the landed cost of prime tallow from the United States was one-third of the cost of Argentine tallow purchased through the Ministry of Food in 1948; meat had just become easier; agricultural machinery was thought to be in short supply largely because of large Colonial demands for crawler and track-laying types, which were mostly for specialised products but had lately showed signs of considerable improvement in deliveries. Among the difficult items were machine tools and drilling equipment, though because of export restrictions rather than production problems.[90] Consequently, it was thought the least said the better at the Conference as delegates would be sufficiently apprised of the situation.

The Conference opened on 8 June 1949, in London. Some forty Colonial delegates attended and officials of various Departments participated in the discussions. The Parliamentary Under-Secretary, Mr Rees-Williams, in welcoming the Colonial delegates, said the Colonial Office was anxious to be told if things were being done 'which in the view of the Colonies were wrong. Economic liaison officers had been appointed. It was to supplement the information which we had of conditions in the Colonies and to discuss certain specific important supplies problems' that the Conference had been called.[91]

The delegates were controllers of imports, not economic advisers, and were consequently concerned with the detailed working of the controls required by the United Kingdom authorities, rather than with general policy issues. Thus, papers which argued the case for continued membership of the sterling area by the Colonial territories were not central to their interest. They accepted membership without question. Nor was the broad strategy of HM Treasury of close concern. Colonial interests were quite naturally and properly parochial; rather surprisingly, the Colonial Office report to CDC on the Conference complained about this.[92] They wanted to know, for example, how luxuries from hard-currency areas which were excluded by, say, Kenya, could be imported into the United Kingdom and then offered for sale to agents in the Colonies. Suspicion was voiced that (i) the United Kingdom was not limiting hard-currency imports as strictly as the Colonies were required to do, and (ii) United Kingdom trade was using the restrictions in the Colonies to gain the profit on re-exporting to them goods originating in hard-currency countries as, for example, in the case of caustic soda from Belgium and paper from Canada, both via the United Kingdom to Kenya. While there was no wish to question the view that Colonial territories derived benefit from membership of the sterling area, or that the strength of sterling was of importance to the Colonies, the issue of price differentials was a real and vexatious one, as was for some the possibility of continuing their own entrepôt trading. This was aggravated by the fact that the delegates felt that it would be difficult to confine any additional licensing of hard currency imports within the sort of limit which

Whitehall would be happy to accept.

The Treasury official who addressed the Conference[93] explained that the occurrences instanced were liable to happen as the result of any of three arrangements. First, there was a token imports scheme which admitted a certain number of inessential American goods into the United Kingdom. In all cases these were goods which had been previously imported regularly in larger quantities. The scheme was felt to be a useful safety-valve for taking the steam out of the complaints of American exporters. Secondly, inessential goods, for example from Switzerland, sometimes had to be admitted under the terms of bilateral agreements. As the result of complaints, the Treasury undertook to consider whether these arrangements could be extended to Colonial importers. Finally, and of limited relevance to the Colonies, there was the arrangement whereby manufacturers in the United Kingdom could import supplies from hard-currency sources in order to produce goods for soft-currency countries, providing there was a 100 per cent uplift. It was doubtful whether this was justified and it was under review. In answer to a question, it was said that there were no political impediments to increasing trade with soft-currency areas, and the recent bilateral trade agreement with Poland indicated that such trade was being expanded. In reply to another delegate, it was said that Marshall Aid had not been used for pushing American exports of goods which were not wanted by the countries receiving aid. To some it seemed that there was more flexibility in the United Kingdom import policy than there was in Colonial policy, and it was suggested that they should be brought on to an equal footing. Others felt that the United Kingdom negotiators of bilateral and financial arrangements with third parties forgot that Colonial administrations had to convince majorities of unofficials that the policy followed was the right one, and that the negotiators were concerned with Colonial welfare. It was explained that arrangements had just been changed, so that Colonies could obtain some of the essentials included in bilateral agreements and dispose of some of their exportable surpluses of goods in the same category. The Colonial Office undertook to explore the possibility of providing the Colonies with more information on the background to negotiations so that the arrangements might be better understood.

At the final session on 17 June 1949, the Secretary of State emphasised that 'all concerned with the problem of obtaining essential supplies for the Colonies were most anxious to ensure that the essential needs of the Colonies were met.'[94] The problem was to achieve this with, on the one hand, differences in prices of imports from different sources and, on the other, the need to protect the gold and dollar reserves of the sterling area. He noted that 'all who had attended the Conference had remarked on the manifest desire of all Colonial delegates to co-operate in maintaining, and making more efficient, those controls which it had been necessary to impose, rather than to question the need for them.' He concluded that the Conference had been a great success, providing the Colonial Office with knowledge of problems and personal contacts which would help to improve the working of the controls. He hoped that such meetings could be arranged more regularly in the future. Delegates echoed these sentiments.

Yet one of the surprises of the Conference was that, while Colonial delegates took the opportunity to explain their own difficulties, most of the points raised concerned the machinery for co-operation between the United Kingdom Government and Colonial Governments. It was represented that hitherto enough had not been done to protect Colonial interests in, for example, bilateral agreements between His Majesty's Government and foreign countries. The Colonial Office undertook to pursue such matters with the Overseas Negotiations Committee, or direct with the Treasury and Board of Trade. This alone amply justified the calling of the Conference. The better briefing of those about to set Colonial dollar 'ceilings' for 1950 was a further advantage.

The *ad hoc* action over the Gold Coast's import requirements and the Conference just discussed should not be looked at as isolated events, but rather as illustrations of the problems of the period and of the general strategy of dealing with them. By the end of 1947, the Colonies were both failing to spend the funds available for development, and failing to fulfil their traditional role of net dollar-earners. By the middle of 1948, largely because of the concern with the Gold Coast, it was realised that the main reason for both these failures was that, in a period when virtually everything was subject to allocation, there was no machinery for ascertaining the essential requirements of the Colonies for steel, cement and so forth, nor any way of knowing what they were in fact obtaining. In the absence of requirements programmes, the import needs of the Colonies from the United Kingdom were in fact largely going by default. Development suffered, and more dollars had to be allowed than would otherwise have been necessary. The strategy, therefore, was, on the one hand, to ascertain requirements and persuade the relevant Whitehall Departments that reasonable allocations should be made to meet them; and, on the other, to persuade the Colonies that, provided their essential requirements were met, it was sensible of them, as members of the sterling area with their reserves in sterling, to restrict their purchasing from the dollar area.

vi. THE GENERAL SUPPLIES POSITION, 1948–1952

It has been noted that the most serious shortage was that of iron and steel supplies.[95] Before the war, the Colonies had imported between 350,000 and 450,000 tons of steel a year, of which some 175,000 tons came from the United Kingdom. In 1947, exports of steel from the United Kingdom amounted to 167,000 tons, which were barely sufficient to satisfy the requirements normally met by the United Kingdom steel industry. No provision was made for arrears of maintenance, new developments, or the shortfall from other suppliers. Additional supplies were therefore sought from the United Kingdom, and Colonies were asked early in 1948 as part of the CDWP enquiries to furnish details of their requirements of unfabricated iron and steel for 1948 and 1949. These turned out to be of the order of some 335,000 tons, and it was possible to raise the allocation for the fourth quarter of 1948 by 18,500 tons. A further enquiry of July 1948 revealed that requirements from the United Kingdom were over 500,000 tons; with the help of that evidence, a further 9000 tons of general and sheet steel was secured for the Colonies for the first quarter of 1949. The rate of flow of supplies from the United Kingdom was thus around 184,000 tons, including such surplus and discard steel as could be obtained by importers outside allocation. General and sheet steel totalled 140,000 tons and structural steel accounted for the rest.

A Working Party scrutinised the requirements notified by Colonies and accepted that some increase in 1949 was necessary. Colonies were advised to plan on the basis of supplies in the second half of 1949 of general and sheet steel rising to a level equivalent to an annual rate of 180,000 tons. The memorandum stated that: 'By the end of 1949, Colonies as a whole should be able to rely on getting from the United Kingdom a flow of steel of some 285,000 tons, of which some 45,000 tons would be structural steel and very approximately 60,000 tons surplus and discard steel.' Although the position was expected to ease in 1950, supplies would be necessary from third countries. Dollar ceilings were to be raised in so far as essential supplies were available from the United States, where prices were likely to compare favourably with the United Kingdom and the Continent.

This easier position with regard to Colonial supplies reflected the satisfactory progress that had been made in the relaxation of economic controls in the United Kingdom. During 1948 consumer rationing had been abolished for several commodities; control of manufacture had been abolished for some twenty commodities; all restrictions – other than import and export licensing – had been removed on the use of some materials, including chemicals; where the supply and currency position had permitted, the resumption of private purchase had been allowed; in many instances licences to supply and licences to manufacture had been revoked; control of freight rates had been removed except from the United kingdom coasting trade.[96] By July 1949, however, the seriousness of the dollar drain was evident. In a memorandum on the economic situation the Lord President of the Council, Mr Herbert, later Lord, Morrison, stated that: 'At this moment our last reserves of gold and dollars are vanishing at the rate of about £12 million worth a week. At the present rate they would be down to zero in just over 200 days from now, and in far fewer days than that our position will become untenable unless the fall can not only be stopped but reversed.'[97] Already Colonial Governors had been asked to suspend the issue of licences for imports from the dollar area, except where this would cause undue hardship.[98] Total savings of some 14 per cent on the 1949 dollar ceilings were reported to be possible, and for the whole of the West Indies and the Bahamas it was 18 per cent.[99] However, as the general basis for the sterling area as a whole was that dollar imports would have to be reduced for the year 1949–50 by 25 per cent, considerable further reductions were necessary if that reduction was to be secured.[100] The position was further complicated by the announcement in September 1949 that the dollar exchange value of sterling was to be reduced by 30 per cent. Amendments to dollar programmes to allow for the devaluation were made, as far as possible, in fixing dollar ceilings for 1950, this being helped by the greater competitive relation of sterling and soft currency prices. The proposed total ceiling of $167.8 million for 1950 turned out to be slightly above the actual expenditure of $159.7 million.[101] The ceiling proposed for 1951 was $155.6 million,[102] but again there were complications. The first of these was connected with price rises associated with rearmament in both the United Kingdom and the United States, and the war in Korea. Rearmament brought also the second problem, namely that of the shortage of supplies. In the summer of 1951 it was necessary to reduce the allocation of steel for direct import.[103] This was further reduced for the first quarter of 1952 at a Meeting of Ministers on 23 November 1951.[104]

The whole supply and production situation was reviewed at a meeting of Commonwealth Ministers in September 1951. Mr John

Dugdale, the Minister of State for Colonial Affairs, attended, accompanied by delegates from the Colonies. Since 1 January 1951, a token imports scheme had operated in the West Indies and the Bahamas whereby certain foods, textiles and consumer goods could be imported from North America, as was the case under the United Kingdom's own scheme.[105] At the Conference, the general need of the Colonies for consumer and capital goods was reiterated by several speakers,[106] the Minister of State arguing that the need for adequate supplies for the Colonies was as great as the need for adequate arms. While the Minister of Supply, Mr G. R. Strauss, sympathised with this view, he felt that the United Kingdom was not in a position to exercise a judgement between the claims of other Commonwealth and Colonial countries. It was proposed that officials might explore the possibility of evolving a system of agreed principles of priority between Commonwealth countries in regard to United Kingdom exports of steel and capital goods. However, the officials reported that 'it was not considered practicable to establish a system of agreed principles of priorities under which allocations between Commonwealth countries of steel and goods in short supply would be determined.'[107] The Conference agreed that the matter should be further studied in London with a representative of the Colonies taking part.

VII. THE BALANCE OF PAYMENTS OF THE COLONIAL TERRITORIES, 1950–1952

Mr Oliver Lyttelton, later Viscount Chandos, became Secretary of State on 28 October 1951, in the second Government of Sir Winston Churchill. On 19 November 1951 he addressed a memorandum to the Cabinet on the balance of payments of the Colonial Territories.[108] It was shown that, whereas the United Kingdom and other independent members of the sterling area had since 1950 been running into rapidly decreasing deficits in their current accounts with both the dollar area and the rest of the world, the Colonial territories had maintained and, if current trends and policies continued, would continue to maintain a substantial surplus. The principal figures are shown in Table 1.1. At the same time the sterling assets of the Colonies in London had topped the £1000 million mark, having grown by about £400 million during the previous eighteen months.

It was noted that part of the Colonies' surplus on current account was attributable to United Kingdom military expenditure in the Colonies and direct grants of one type or another to the Colonies. If

TABLE 1.1   Sterling Area Oversea Balance of Payments, 1950–1952

	£ million 1950 (actual)	£ million 1951 (partly forecast)	£ million 1952 (forecast)
United Kingdom current account	+221	−472	−540
Independent Sterling Area current account	+101	− 34	−355
Bahrain current account	+ 14	+ 23	+ 35
Colonies current account	+131	+212	+ 90
Total Sterling Area current account	+467	−271	−770

there had been no military expenditure and no direct grants, the Colonial surplus would have been reduced to £58 million in 1950 and to an estimated £124 million in 1951, whilst forecasts for 1952 showed a slight deficit. Statistical data for the period before were insufficient to enable a detailed comparison to be made between current figures and those of the early post-war years. However, it was considered that the probability was that, although there was an increase of some £100 million in the Colonies' sterling balances over the four years 1946–50, this was more than cancelled out by movements of capital in the opposite direction and by a moderate import surplus, so that the Colonies during that period may have had a moderate balance of payments deficit.

The situation since 1950, which stood out in marked contrast to earlier years, was caused by the exceptional increase in the earnings of the Colonies due to high prices, which resulted from rearmament and other world factors combined with a smaller increase in Colonial imports. While the value of exports trebled between 1948 and 1951, the value of imports only about doubled. The surplus was due to two main factors. First, part of the proceeds of the sale of Colonial products had been added to the reserves of Government, marketing boards and other organisations, partly for stabilisation purposes and partly because of the unavailability of supplies. Secondly, there was the world-wide shortage of capital goods, partly steel, and the reduction, since the end of 1950, in the quantities of the latter, which had acted as a severe break on the implementation of development programmes, both public and private, just as they had gained momentum.

It was submitted that steps should be taken, as far as it was within the power of the United Kingdom to take them, to secure a better flow

to the Colonies of the supplies which were required and on which they
should be allowed to spend their earnings, if discontent and severe
inflation, with all its dangerous possibilities, were to be avoided. This
was urged on grounds of Colonial policy, the United Kingdom having
a special constitutional responsibility for Colonial territories which it
did not have for other members of the sterling Commonwealth. It was
urged also in the interests of the United Kingdom itself; for increased
production in the Colonial territories of the foodstuffs and raw
materials which were so badly needed depended, partly, on direct
investment in their production and on the improvement of basic
economic services, such as communications, all of which required
capital goods; and partly on an improvement in the physique, morale
and willingness to work of Colonial peoples, all of which depended on
the availability of more consumer goods of the right type.

The Secretary of State did not ask his colleagues to take specific
decisions on his paper. It was pointed out that the allocation of steel to
the Colonies would be considered at a meeting to be held by the
Chancellor of the Exchequer, Mr R. A. Butler, later Lord Butler of
Saffron Walden, on the following day. Meantime, the Cabinet took
note of the Secretary of State's memorandum.[109]

The Ministerial Meeting was concerned to determine the allocation
of steel for the first quarter of 1952.[110] The Minister of State for
Colonial Affairs, Mr A. Lennox-Boyd, later Viscount Boyd of Merton,
showed that the proposed rate of export to the Colonies
would, if maintained throughout 1952, amount to rather less than 60
per cent of the 250,000 tons which was considered to be the minimum
necessary to satisfy their urgent needs. It was claimed that the high
Colonial and other surplus was due, not only to higher raw material
prices, but also to greater restraint in dollar purchases than either the
United Kingdom or other self-governing members of the sterling
Commonwealth had shown. It was added that any suggestion of a
sacrifice of Colonial needs for United Kingdom requirements would
provide a powerful theme for nationalist propaganda in the Colonies.

The Chancellor reminded the Meeting that the reduction in exports
to the Colonies had been much less than in exports to the rest of the
sterling Commonwealth. It was not possible to do more than agree to
consider an increase when greater supplies became available. There
were United Kingdom defence requirements under the three-year
programme to be taken into account, and also the need for some
reserve in order to provide the necessary latitude for the negotiations
with other Commonwealth countries at the forthcoming discussions
with Commonwealth Finance Ministers. The proposed allocation was

approved in principle. This situation lasted for some time. With the relaxation of controls and allocations in the 1950s, the problem of supplies merged into the perennial problem of sterling and the balance of payments.

SOURCES

1. EPC (48) 92, 1 Nov 1948, and 112, 7 Dec 1948.
2. EPC (49) 7, 10 Feb 1949.
3. Cmd 7433, June 1948, p. 1, para. 1.
4. File 19294/62, Economic General 1947–48 (CO 852/870), item 1: unnumbered Circular of 20 Aug 1947 from the Secretary of State to all Colonies.
5. Ibid., item 2: Confidential telegram No. 276 of 21 Aug 1947 from the Governor of the Seychelles, Dr P. S. Selwyn Clarke, to the Secretary of State.
6. Ibid., item 4: Confidential telegram No. 225 of 10 Sep 1947 from the Secretary of State to the Governor of the Seychelles.
7. Ibid., item 12: Confidential telegram No. 564 of 20 Sep 1947 from the Governor of Northern Rhodesia, Sir John Waddington.
8. Ibid., minute of 23 Sep 1947 by Mr H. A. Harding.
9. Idem.
10. Ibid., item 13: Confidential telegram No. 608 of 29 Sep 1947 from the Secretary of State to the Governor of Northern Rhodesia.
11. Ibid., item 17: 'The Economic Crisis in relation to East Africa', by Sir Charles Lockhart, dated 5 Sep 1947.
12. Ibid., item 18: Proceedings of Conference, Part II, Oct 1947.
13. Ibid., item 38.
14. Ibid., minute of 22 Nov 1947 by Sir S. Caine to Mr H. R. Butters.
15. Ibid., minute of 3 Dec 1947 by Mr H. R. Butters.
16. Ibid., minute of 5 Apr 1948 by Sir Charles Jeffries.
17. Ibid., minute of 9 Apr 1948 by Sir S. Caine.
18. Ibid., minute of 21 May 1948 by Sir Charles Jeffries.
19. Ibid., minute of 4 May 1948 by Mr J. B. Williams.
20. Ibid., minute of 4 May 1948 by Mr H. Beckett. Messrs G. Steel and J. M. Martin agreed – minutes of even date.
21. Ibid., item 34, letter of 6 May 1948 from Mr D. B. Pitblado to Mr W. L. Gorell Barnes.
22. Ibid., item 38, covering letter, para. 2.
23. Idem, para. 3.
24. Idem, para. 4.
25. Ibid., minute of 11 Oct 1948 by Mr H. T. Bourdillon.
26. Ibid., item 47, letter of 24 Aug 1948 from the Governor of Trinidad, Sir John Shaw, to Sir Thomas Lloyd. See also items 49, 52 and 55.

27. Ibid., item 50, letter of 15 Sep 1948 from the Governor of the Bahamas, Sir William Murphy, to Sir Thomas Lloyd.

28. Ibid., item 66, Secret letter of 21 Sep 1948 from the Governor of Kenya, Sir Philip Mitchell, to Sir Thomas Lloyd.

29. Ibid., item 67, letter of 26 Sep 1948 from the Governor of Kenya, Sir P. Mitchell, to Sir Thomas Lloyd. The cartoon by Illingworth was on p. 119 of *Punch* for 11 Aug 1948.

30. Ibid., minute of 5 Oct 1948 by Sir Thomas Lloyd.

31. Ibid., minute of 20 Nov 1948 by the Parliamentary Under-Secretary, Mr D. Rees-Williams.

32. Ibid., item 71, Personal and Confidential letter of 22 Nov 1948 from Sir T. Lloyd to the Governor of Kenya.

33. Ibid., item 72, Personal and Confidential letter of 6 Dec 1948 from the Governor of Kenya, Sir P. Mitchell to Sir T. Lloyd.

34. Ibid., minute of 4 Jan 1949.

35. File 17265, Economic (CO 852/801), item 7. Note of a meeting held on 5 Apr 1949 to discuss a report by Mr Gallagher on his visit to the West Indies.

36. Secret file GEN/174/012, May 1957, para. 52, p. 8.

37. *Report of the Commission of Enquiry into Disturbances in the Gold Coast, 1948* (Colonial No. 231 of 1948).

38. Colonial No. 231, para. 18.

39. Ibid., para. 20.

40. File 31312/2 Part I, West Africa, Gold Coast, 1948 (CO 96/795), item 10, telegram no. 147, 29 Feb 1948.

41. Colonial No. 231, para. 201.

42. Colonial No. 232, 1948.

43. File 31312/2D/1, West Africa, Gold Coast, Part I, 1948 (CO 96/796), item 43, secret memorandum of 29 June 1948 by Mr A. B. Cohen.

44. Colonial No. 232, p. 11.

45. Ibid., p. 12.

46. File 17265, Economic, Part I, 1948 (CO 852/801), item 1, immediate top secret telegram no. 923 from the Governor of Nigeria, Sir John Macpherson, to the Secretary of State, sent on behalf of Mr W. L. Gorell Barnes.

47. Ibid., item 1a, unnumbered savingram of 21 July 1948.

48. Idem.

49. Ibid., item 3, minute of 22 July 1948 by Mr G. L. M. Clauson.

50. Ibid., item 17, letter of 29 July 1948 from Mr P. Harris, Board of Trade, to Mr W. L. Gorell Barnes.

51. Ibid., item 5, immediate top secret telegram no. 610 of 24 July 1948 from the Governor, Sir G. Creasy, to the Secretary of State.

52. Ibid., item 20: notes of a meeting held in Mr Gorell Barnes' room on 30 July 1948.

53. Ibid., items 26/27: telegrams no. 678 and 877 of 31 July 1948 to Gold Coast and Nigeria.

54. Ibid., item 41, Secret telegram no. 666 of 11 Aug 1948 from the Governor, Sir G. Creasy, to the Secretary of State.

55. Ibid., item 61, telegram no. 926 of 13 Aug 1948 from the Secretary of State to the Governor, Sir G. Creasy.

56. CD (B.P.) 49/33, 16 Feb 1949: Committee on Colonial Development, Sub-committee on Import Programmes.

57. File 19298/63, Economic, 1947–8 (CO 852/871), item 1a, minute of 10 Nov 1947 by Sir S. Caine to the Secretary of State.

58. Ibid., minute of 20 Nov 1947 by Sir S. Caine.

59. Ibid., item 2, letter of 22 Nov 1947.

60. EPC (48), 18th Meeting, 6 May 1948.

61. File 19298/63, Economic 1947–8 (CO 852/871), item 17: CDWP/1/48 of 1 Jan 1948.

62. Ibid., minute of 23 Dec 1947 by Mr C. G. Eastwood.

63. Ibid., minute of 23 Dec 1947 by Sir S. Caine, who said he had added in a project of £10 million 'which has come to notice in the usual casual way'.

64. Ibid., item 31, Circular No. 10 of 27 Jan 1948.

65. Ibid., item 35, unnumbered circular of 3 Feb 1948.

66. File 19298/63/48, Economic (CO 852/874), item 6: priority savingram no. 461 of 31 May 1948.

67. File 19298/63, Economic 1947–48 (CO 852/871), item 51: 'Colonial Investment Programme in the Colonies', by Miss Nield.

68. Ibid., item 54, note of conclusions on capital investment by Mr A. F. Drake of CEPS, 27 Aug 1948.

69. Ibid., item 58, CDWP(48) 47, discussed at the meeting on 15 Sep 1948.

70. Ibid., item 59, letter of 16 Nov 1948 from Mr A. E. Drake to Mr R. W. Nicholson, enclosing Notes and proposing a meeting on 18 Nov 1948.

71. Ibid., minute of 19 Nov 1948 by Miss P. Deane.

72. Cabinet Office file 6/15/25 Part I, item 1, GEN 210/1st Meeting, 9 Jan 1948.

73. Ibid., minute of 16 Jan 1948 by Sir Norman Brook.

74. EPC 35(48), item 4, 9 Dec 1948.

75. CD (48) 1st Meeting, 21 Dec 1948.

76. CD (49) 1, 25 Jan 1949.

77. CD (49) 3, 28 Mar 1949.

78. Cabinet Office file 6/15/25 Part I, item 10, Prime Minister's Personal Minute Serial No. M 22/48 of 29 Jan 1948.

79. Ibid., item 12, Feb 1948.

80. EPC (49) 7, 10 Feb 1949.

81. Cabinet Office file 6/15/25, Part I, item 13, Prime Minister's Personal Minute No. 27/48, 15 Feb 1948.

82. Ibid., item 19a, Prime Minister's Personal Minute Serial No. M 38/48.

83. PC 8(48), minute 2.

84. H. of C. Deb., Vol. 447, col. 2093, 24 Feb 1948.

85. EPC 7(49), item 5, 10 Feb 1949.

86. File 18495/91, Economic, Part I, 1949 (CO 852/834), minute of 10 Jan 1949.

87. Ibid., minutes of 14 and 15 Jan 1949 by the Parliamentary Under-Secretary and the Secretary of State.

88. Ibid., item 1, Circular No. 16 of 5 Feb 1949.

89. Ibid., item 121, letter of 4 May 1949 to Crown Agents for the Colonies, Washington, DC.

90. Ibid., item 198, letter of 27 May 1949 from Crown Agents, Washington, DC.

91. File 18495/91/1, Economic Supplies 1949 (CO 852/834), item 22, minutes of a meeting held in Church House on 8 June 1949.

92. CD (49) 26, 28 June 1949, para. 4.

93. Ibid., item 23, 9 June 1949.

94. Ibid., item 32. File 18495/91/1, Economic Supplies 1950 (CO 852/1133), item 6, includes the full minutes of the Conference.

95. File 18495/91/1, Economic Supplies 1949 (CO 852/834), item 7, memorandum on iron and steel.

96. CP (49) 13, 17 Jan 1949, Appendix.

97. CP (49) 159, 21 July 1949.

98. Circular Telegram No. 53 of 4 July 1949.

99. CD (49) 30, 27 July 1949.

100. Idem.

101. CD (50) 3, 11 Jan 1950.

102. CD (51) 5, 2 Feb 1951.

103. PC (51) 17th Meeting of 20 July 1951 quoted in EPC (51) 19th Meeting of 31 July 1951, minute 6.

104. GEN 391/1st Meeting.

105. CD (51) 5, 2 Feb 1951.

106. CSP (51) 24: Confidential Minutes of Meeting of Commonwealth Ministers Concerned with Supply and Production, Sep 1951, pp. 31-2.

107. Ibid., p. 143.

108. C (51) 22, 19 Nov 1951.

109. CC 10(51) item 6, 22 Nov 1951.

110. GEN 391/1st Meeting, 23 Nov 1951.

2 Development and Finance, 1945–1951

1. THE OPERATION OF THE CD & W ACT, 1945

(a) Allocation

The need for and enactment of the CD & W Act, 1945, was examined in Chapter 15. The Act made available a total sum of £120 million over the ten years ending on 30 March 1956 for the same objects and territories as provided under the 1940 Act. A problem arose immediately as the 1940 Act defined Colonies for which grants might be made under the Act as those 'not possessing responsible government'. It was felt in 1945 that it would not be proper for the Secretary of State to make a scheme within the terms of the Act for Malta, in the knowledge that it would run on beyond the date of the grant of responsible government, as it was the Secretary of State's policy to restore responsible government to Malta as soon as the Maltese were ready for it after the end of the German war. When the Governor learnt the position, he was shocked, feeling that 'if an announcement of that sort were to be made in Malta at this time my position, and that of any Englishman in the administration, would become quite untenable.'[1] However, he was assured that it was intended to treat Malta as a separate problem. By the Malta (Reconstruction) Act, 1947, the advance of moneys from CD & W was permitted 'notwithstanding its possession at any time of responsible government'.

The object of allocating a share of the money to each Colony from the beginning was, in the first place, to ensure that all the money did not go to the earliest claimants and, in the second place, to give each Colony a firm figure for the amount of assistance on which it could rely.[2] Without that assurance it would be difficult, if not impossible, to draw up a realistic development programme. No single yardstick was used to make the allocation. A start was made with the figures of population, and then the result of that calculation was revised to take account of other relevant factors, such as existing commitments, the

prosperity or otherwise of the Colony and the like. In the end, the
smaller and poorer Colonies received much more than their share
would have been on a population basis. This point emerged clearly
over the allocation to Jamaica and its Dependencies, the Cayman
Islands and the Turks and Caicos Islands. When the question of the
allocation to be set aside for the two Dependencies from the £6.5
million available for Jamaica and its Dependencies was discussed in
the Executive Council of Jamaica, the Elected Members were averse
from making any allocation for the Dependencies which could not be
justified on a strict application of a per capita basis.[3] The resulting
allocations of £35,000 for the Cayman Islands and £32,000 for the
Turks and Caicos Islands were too small to finance even the limited
advance considered necessary, though the Governor felt it difficult to
contest the attitude taken by the Elected Members, which held that so
much needed to be done in Jamaica itself that they could not
contemplate 'allocating to the Dependencies more than their fair share
of the total amount available'. The Governor sought a supplementary
allocation of £371,000 for the Dependencies. The Secretary of State's
Development Adviser felt there should be 'no question of any special
allocation from the reserve at this stage', and stated that

> In my view the Governor of Jamaica should be informed in no
> uncertain terms that the final approval of D & W schemes rests with
> the Secretary of State and that he is responsible to parliament to see
> that the funds which they have voted are distributed in the Colonies
> according to need . . . Allocation on a mere count of heads is most
> undesirable. If this policy had been adopted throughout, Jamaica
> and its dependencies would not have received a sum amounting to
> anything like £6.5 million.

The Elected Members, he concluded, should be asked to think again.[4]
The Comptroller for D & W in the West Indies advised in similar
terms.[5] The Secretary of State wrote accordingly to the Governor of
Jamaica, agreeing with the needs of the Dependencies but regretting
his inability to make a supplementary allocation. He pointed out the
misunderstandings shown by the Executive Council in thinking the
Dependencies should be treated solely on a basis of population,
whereas, if that factor alone had been taken into account in
determining the joint allocation to Jamaica and its Dependencies, 'the
amount could not have been more than one quarter only of the £6.5
million which has, in fact, been allocated'. It was also pointed out that,
in addition to issues under the CD & W Act, the following had been

received by Jamaica since 1939: (i) for price stabilisation to March 1945, the latest date for which figures were available, £970,000; (ii) for banana guarantee to March 1946, with some repayments likely to be due, £3,499,357; (iii) for guarantee of minor commodities, £315,563 to March 1946; and (iv) for hurricane rehabilitation, £2,230,000. That gave a total of £7,015,820. So the Secretary of State did not feel, in the light of that total, that so much required to be done in Jamaica itself that the needs of the Dependencies were residual, but rather that 'the relative condition of the Dependencies of Jamaica calls for special efforts for their improvement'. He asked that the Executive Council be invited to reconsider the matter 'with a view to amended proposals being submitted which I could reasonably accept as giving just and proper recognition to the needs of the Dependencies in the employment of the joint allocation of £6.5 million'.

The Treasury was invited to comment on the proposed general allocation,[6] and stated it would have preferred to have seen a rather larger sum set aside as a reserve, although, in view of the difficulties encountered in making the allocation, it did not wish to press the point.[7] The Colonial Office agreed, both with the desirability of an adequate reserve and with the difficulties of arriving at an acceptable scheme of allocation, even with the reserves which it had been possible to set aside.[8] In February 1947, a Treasury official suggested to his colleagues that the Colonial Office be asked to warn Colonies that the allocation of 1945 should be regarded as provisional, and that where local revenues could be expected substantially to exceed the 1945 estimates it might be necessary to divert part of the original application to other territories less fortunately placed. It would, he argued, be unfortunate from every point of view if poor Colonies were kept from a larger share of the £120 million, because of the dog-in-the-manger attitude of the wealthier territories where CD & W grants might serve either to keep taxation unjustifiably low, or to swell surplus balances.[9] While there were obvious advantages in reallocating in the light of experience, the proposal being canvassed within the Treasury at the time was that there might be substantial interest-free loans from the Colonies to the United Kingdom from both (a) existing resources, including currency funds, and (b) the proceeds of taxation and local borrowing, which were in any case felt to be necessary in order to avert overspending. Any reallocation of CD & W funds should, it was suggested, be limited to what poor Colonies would be likely to use rather than to take away what rich Colonies were unlikely to use, which was a pointless exercise as the purpose was to limit Colonial expenditure.[10] As a result of this recommendation, it was accepted that the proposal to roallocate CD & W should not be taken up with the Colonial Office.[11] The latter regarded it as politically impossible to cut a Colony's allocation in any case.[12]

The allocation by groups of territories and purposes was shown in Chapter 16, Section i.

(b) Grant-aided Territories

The Treasury was anxious, following the passage of the 1945 Act, to negotiate a Concordat with the Colonial Office and the Dominions Office, in order to provide a working basis for determining the extent to which new expenditure in grant-aided, or otherwise Treasury-controlled, Territories should be charged against (a) revenue or (b) CD & W Funds. Until this was agreed in principle, it was obviously difficult to deal with proposals from the Colonies and Territories concerned for new expenditure. The Treasury interest was two-fold.[13] First, it was concerned to see that grant-aided Colonies did not obtain a 'hidden' increase, over the monies voted by Parliament under the 1945 Act, by over-loading the grant-in-aid. Secondly, it wanted to ensure, as far as possible, that the Colonies' CD & W allocations were spent on schemes which helped them to become self-supporting. It was realised that the Colonial Office and the Dominions Office would be anxious that the grant-aided Colonies, having no other resources, should be able to stretch their CD & W allocation as far as possible. To that end, it was realised that they would be expected to claim that some kinds of new expenditure, even where, under the most stringent definition, it might be considered developmental, should be charged against their grant-in-aid. The matter was discussed at a meeting of officials of the Treasury, Colonial Office and the Dominions Office on 26 September, 1946. A letter was subsequently sent to both Departments giving the views of the Treasury.[14] As far as capital expenditure was concerned, the matter was uncomplicated. The problems mainly concerned public works, and it was proposed that the charge against grant-in-aid should be based on the pre-1939 level allowing for (a) any actual increase in costs, and (b) maintenance costs of any service that was originally financed out of revenues. Apart from that, new work would be financed from CD & W funds, unless it could be shown that they were essential, not simply desirable, and should not obviously, as would a new hospital, for instance, come from CD & W sources. Matters relating to recurrent expenditure were likely to arise mainly in connection with personnel, either by way of increases in emoluments or of increases in establishments. Some of these would be unlikely to be services covered by CD & W, e.g. police forces, while others would be so covered, e.g. schoolteachers. It was suggested that the first kind should continue to be considered strictly on their merits. The rest, it was argued, should be considered according to whether they were confined to the period of the Act or were longer-term. In the case of those coming wholly within the period of the Act, CD & W provisions would be applied. Otherwise, it would be necessary to take account of the Colony's ability to finance the service when the Act was due to expire, as neither the continuance of the Act nor the transfer to grant-in-aid might be presumed. Even so, increases in recurrent expenditure should, it was stated, be accepted if they related to increases in the cost of living or to the provision of essential, rather than desirable, increases in establishments, e.g. of inspection of schools.

Given the assumptions, the Treasury proposals were reasonable but the Colonial Office was not at all happy about them. It was fearful that any formula would introduce a measure of rigidity and so increase rather than diminish difficulties.[15] In his unusually forthright minute, Sir Frank Stockdale, after accepting the need for a formula but fearing the impracticability of the one proposed, went on to list the data necessary to provide the basis for the proposed exercise and then added:

In the discussions with the Treasury, it might also be brought out that all costs have increased as in this country and that the diets in most Colonial hospitals and other public institutions are now costing double what they did pre-war. Many of these diets are of low nutritional values and should be improved but this is not contemplated in most Colonies because they cannot be put at a level which is so much higher than the normal dietary of the people, which invariably is much lower than is required for sustained and efficient work.

It should also be stated quite clearly that it is quite uneconomic to provide personnel for technical departments without adequate provision under 'other charges' for expenditure on execution and maintenance of works. No agricultural department for example is operating efficiently and economically unless there is provision under 'other charges' equal to the cost of the staff under personal emoluments. Similarly, when I was in Ceylon it was accepted that the personal emoluments of the Public Works Department should not be greater than 10 per cent of the total expenditure of the Department and we had another accepted percentage in regard to the irrigation department in respect of maintenance works. I think, but I am not quite certain, that it was 12 per cent.

The point I wish to make is that it is quite uneconomic to employ in a small Colony a Superintendent of Public Works at, say £600 per annum unless he has upwards of £6000 work to carry out during the year. The state of affairs in all the small Colonies which I have visited is deplorable. Buildings are dilapidated, there is insufficient provision for maintenance and quite inadequate provision for renewal of equipment and for replacement of buildings. It is well accepted in many Colonies that it is easier to get a completely new building than to get any repairs to an existing one. This should not be tolerated but it will persist in the grant-aided colonies unless a more liberal view is taken on the proper maintenance of existing services. Go to the West Indies. See the public buildings and their equipment. Look at the so-called school buildings, hospitals, etc. I defy anyone with any shred of pride not to be thoroughly ashamed at the whole picture. We know it. If we do not we should and we should take the stand for decency against pressure from those who control the purse strings. After all, when blame comes (and Colonial peoples have in the past been more than tolerant) it falls on the Colonial Office and not on the Treasury. Mr. Sidebotham and I saw something of this picture in St. Helena and I am glad to see that something was attempted and carried through. The same, but more, is required in many of the smaller West Indian colonies and we just cannot allow this 'public assistance' expenditure to be pushed on to the C. D. & W. vote.[16]

When the Colonial Office reply to the Treasury letter was received,[17] it was thought 'to be faintly tainted with the heresy that welfare is the main object'.[18] It wished to exclude several Territories from the exercise, not to be bound by past precedents, not to adopt a pre-1939 basis for capital expenditure, and to be able to spend more lavishly on the poorest Colonies. It wished to divide capital expenditure between administration on the one hand, and D & W on the other; it was anxious to be able to provide for 'minimum tolerable standards', even though residual recurrent finance problems would arise. It was, of course, this last point which led to the comment quoted. However, the Treasury was keen to arrive at an agreed basis, as the use of CD & W monies in grant-aided Territories had already been the cause of much dissension in the past.[19] Accordingly, the Colonial Office proposals, which were thought likely to prove more satisfactory than their own suggestions, were accepted with a few reservations.[20]

All Treasury-controlled Territories were to be included; past precedents were not to be binding, provided the need for consistency was accepted. The Treasury was not willing to accept the proposition that the raising of standards under CD & W implied a raising of the standard of minimum services for which grant-in-aid assistance could be claimed by a Colony which was not itself able to pay for these services. This was so because CD & W was not regarded as wholly a welfare measure; it was also intended to foster economic development. Consequently, it was considered by the Treasury that: 'An effective programme of development must have the result of diminishing the number of cases in which essential services require assistance out of grant-in-aid funds.'[21] 'If this did not happen sufficiently, then there will have been a failure to achieve a true raising of standards.' Hence, the Treasury wished to examine the ten-year programme of all Territories, and not merely those in receipt of grant-in-aid sub-ventions. The Colonial Office was quite pleased, believing, indeed, that any working arrangement was better than the stultifying deadlock of the past year.[22] It thought that the only difficulties likely to arise in accepting the Treasury view concerned the unwillingness to make exceptions for those Territories not wholly and obviously within the grant-aided category.[23] The territories involved were Nyasaland, Cyprus and the Far Eastern Colonies. It was accepted that 'the true object of development should be the raising of standards that can be maintained by the Colonies' own efforts'; it was felt that 'a measure' of educational and health services was often a prerequisite for economic development, and consequently 'that the combined result of both forms of development must be judged over the long term, rather than the immediate future.'[24] This was surely true, and it raised the further point as to which Territories were and which were not economically developable. But in 1947, if permanent pensioners of HMG were conceived by anyone, they were certainly not discussed between departments. A Treasury official merely minuted that he found the dictum that results should be judged 'over the long term' quite meaningless in the absence of a yardstick.[25]

At the time, the Treasury's main concern was to obtain agreement that all grant-aided and Treasury-controlled Colonies should be treated equally, and it expressed its disappointment that this agree-ment had not been forthcoming after nine months of discussion.[26] It was exasperated by the Colonial Office attitude, which ignored the principle that the United Kingdom taxpayer should not subsidise nor be liable to subsidise, as in Treasury-controlled but not grant-aided Colonies, from funds other than CD & W any services for which CD & W provision had been made.[27] It was appreciated that the position of

Treasury-controlled Colonies not in receipt of grants-in-aid was different from that of Colonies actually in receipt of grants-in-aid. But it was emphasised that any additional expenditure by the latter, financed by revenue or surplus balances, which might, sooner or later, involve calls on HMG should be regarded as coming within the general rules.[28] Naturally, if there were no residual liability for the Imperial Exchequer, such Colonies were free to spend on development projects. After further discussion, the terms of a telegram to the Leeward Islands, the Windward Islands and British Honduras were agreed; the telegram was sent on 9 October 1947.

In the telegram it was recalled that in the Despatch of 30 April 1940, the CD & W Vote was said to be 'generally speaking intended to be additional to, not in replacement of, the grants-in-aid included in the Colonial and Middle Eastern Services Vote'. The telegram proceeded thus:

3. Any assistance, therefore, from Imperial Funds which becomes necessary to maintain existing standards of Government in the Colony will be charged to the Colonial and Middle Eastern Services Vote and transfer of expenditure to Colonial Development and Welfare schemes will not normally be appropriate. To go beyond this, however, and meet from the Colonial and Middle Eastern Services Vote expenditure which falls within the purposes of the Colonial Development and Welfare Act would be contrary to the intentions of Parliament, which has set a definite limit to the total amount of assistance to be voted for the purpose covered by that Act.
4. It is therefore necessary to examine all proposals for expenditure in Treasury-controlled and grant-aided Colonies to ensure that a correct division is observed between expenditure to be attributed to local revenues, including the grant-in-aid on the one hand, and to the Colonial Development and Welfare Vote on the other. I think that it will be helpful to such Colonial Governments to have a statement of the procedure proposed in some detail and I, therefore, set this out in paragraph 5 of this telegram.

5. *A. Capital Expenditure*

(1) Local revenues or grant-in-aid should bear the cost of erection, repair, replacement, or enlargement of administrative buildings or other administrative works including e.g. prisons, post offices, etc., where expenditure on such works is accepted as essential.

(2) Local revenues or grant-in-aid should also bear the cost of repair or replacement, up to the same but not a higher standard, of buildings and capital work which are *prima facie* suitable objects for Colonial Development and Welfare assistance, e.g. schools, hospitals, roads, airfields, irrigation works, agricultural or veterinary stations, etc.

(3) The Colonial Development and Welfare Vote should bear other expenditure on buildings or works in category (2) above which involves an improvement in quality or extension in size over the standard of the existing buildings when new.

B. Personal Emoluments

(1) Local revenues or grant-in-aid will bear the cost of increases in establishment necessary to enable Government to carry out efficiently responsibilities not arising from the development programme, including all such posts as legal, police, etc. which are not regarded as eligible for assistance under the headings of Development or Welfare. Local revenues or grant-in-aid will also bear increases in emoluments of existing posts (other than those paid from the Colonial Development and Welfare Vote) due to general salary revisions.

(2) Colonial Development and Welfare Vote will bear the cost of new posts arising from the development programme.

(3) Posts under Colonial Development and Welfare schemes will normally be on contract terms but may be held on a pensionable basis when

   (a) Recruitment on a contract basis is found impossible; or
   (b) To avoid personal hardship to individual officers through long periods of secondment at salaries above their pensionable emoluments; or
   (c) The retention of the post on a permanent basis after 1956 can be justified.

C. Other Recurrent Expenditure

It will in general be necessary, in Colonial Development and Welfare schemes for capital expenditure, to ensure that provision is available under the Colony's Colonial Development and Welfare allocation to meet the additional recurrent expenditure arising out of the schemes until 1956. Recurrent expenditure arising from Development programmes will not be approved as a charge against local revenue except where, as in the case of certain Treasury-

controlled Colonies, sufficient funds are available for the purpose.
6. As I have indicated here, I appreciate that the position of
Treasury-controlled Colonies not in receipt of grants-in-aid is not
the same as that of Colonies actually in receipt of such assistance, but
the fact that Treasury control has to be exercised is evidence of the
existence of a contingent liability on the Imperial Exchequer. It is
also felt that it will be more satisfactory in the long run to place the
finances of such Colonies on a firm footing by restricting expenditure from local revenues on projects eligible for Colonial
Development and Welfare assistance so that Treasury control can
be dispensed with at the earliest possible moment. The above
procedure will, therefore apply equally to both classes of Colony.

These principles were later applied to problems of the incidence of
charges arising in other grant-aided or Treasury controlled Colonies.
    An issue arose over the incidence of recurrent charges. Following the
receipt of the Secretary of State's telegram of 9 October 1947, the
Administrator of St Lucia suggested that additional medical staff
employed by the St Lucia Government should not be made a charge
on CD & W funds until the local and medical establishment either
compared favourably with that of other West Indian Colonies, or had
at least passed a minimum level. The Colonial Office wished to adopt
the Administrator's interpretation of the principles laid down in the
telegram.[29] The Treasury insisted that the general rule should be that
in grant-aided, and Treasury-controlled, Colonies all expenditure on
purposes coming within the CD & W Act should be charged to the
CD & W Vote.[30] Any other basis was regarded as unjustified and
impracticable: development had to be accepted as 'Development', even if services were built up to no more than a minimum
standard.

II. COLONIAL LOANS

When each territory was informed in November 1945 of its allocation,
it was invited to draw up a ten-year plan of development, which was to
take into account not only the money provided under the Act but also
whatever contribution each territory could provide from its own
resources and from loans. By June 1948 seventeen ten-year plans,
involving a total expenditure of £180 million, had been received. Of
that total expenditure, almost one-third (£59.5 million) was to be

provided from United Kingdom funds and the rest from Colonial resources. When a plan was approved by the Secretary of State, individual schemes were submitted for approval. These showed the works to be undertaken, the appointments to be made, and the cost involved. This last was divided between the United Kingdom contribution in grants and loans, and the local contribution from revenue and borrowing, the latter divided between local loans and those on the London market. It was recognised that, as both the nature of schemes and the economic situation of Colonies varied, the method of financing had to vary appropriately. Once approved, the scheme, with its particular financial provisions, became the authority for expenditure and the basis of accounting.

In the summer of 1945 the problems of the raising of public loans had been presented to the Colonial Office in concrete form by Nigeria and, though with details less fully worked out, by the Development Commission in Cyprus. It was decided to take the matter up with the Treasury.[31] While it was agreed that Nigeria could bear the charges arising from the proposed loans, the general question of raising loans on London by overseas borrowers was under active consideration within the Treasury,[32] which had meantime suggested that all overseas borrowers should first borrow all they could locally, both in order to relieve pressure on the London market and 'to counter the obviously inflationary effects of a large local expenditure at a time when the supply of goods available for local consumption would continue to be limited'.[33] The Colonial Office was asked to provide the best estimates, or guesses, of probable Colonial demands for loans, over and above what was to be provided under CD & W. It turned out to be a sum of the order of £46 million for new money for development purposes during the five years 1946–50 inclusive, and a net amount, after allowing for sinking fund balances, of £25.7 million for the conversion of existing Colonial loans maturing during the same period.[34] A further attempt was made towards the end of 1946 again to estimate the probable net loan requirement of the Colonies for the same period as before. At £52,250,000, it came within the margin of error of the earlier guess, and, like it, was also made within the Office without consultation with Colonies, so as 'to avoid putting ideas into their heads'.[35]

While discussions continued with the Treasury, certain anxieties were expressed from several West Indian Colonies about the cost of local borrowing. Thus, the Economic Adviser in British Guiana, Mr Oscar Spencer, suggested the creation of a Colonial floating debt, and it was agreed that, despite the danger of borrowing on short term for long-term purposes, there was scope in some Colonies for the introduction of a system of Treasury bills for use for self-liquidating purposes.[36] In reply to Professor Cyril Beasley, the Colonial Office found it very difficult to lay down any hard and fast rules on the purposes for which loans should be raised, the amount that should be included in development plans, or on the method of calculating what a Colony could reasonably carry in loan charges.[37] In April 1947 the Comptroller for D & W in the West Indies, Sir John Macpherson, stated that his Economic Adviser felt that it was 'inappropriate, and embarrassing, to be asked to suggest terms for loans, unless he is made aware of Colonial Office policy', and an early statement of policy on the general issue of loans for development purposes was sought.[38] The Crown Agents were asked to comment, in particular, on the Comptroller's suggestion that a collective loan be raised in London and reissued as required to the smaller West Indian Governments.[39] The Secretary of State in his reply[40] stated that the long-term advantage of developing the financial resources of a Colony might well outweigh the higher cost, and the Treasury was unlikely to sanction borrowing on the London market unless local resources had been fully explored. On the idea of a collective loan, the advice of the Crown Agents was to the effect that it would be necessary to specify which Colonies were assuming the obligation, and to what extent each was involved, as in the case of an individual loan; interest charges would be payable from the date on which the loan was floated. Once a loan had been sanctioned, it was stated there would be no difficulty in arranging it – amounts of £500,000 being appropriate for ordinary public issue, while lesser amounts, for periods up to twenty years, could be handled by the Crown Agents, either directly or through brokers. The Secretary of State preferred to avoid local loans being issued on an income tax-free basis.

While the Colonial Office thus gave general guidance, those responsible for development plans could hardly feel assured that any external loan requirements would, in fact, be met. Mauritius provided a case in point. In February 1947 the Colonial Office enquired of the Treasury whether it would agree, in principle, to Mauritius eventually borrowing in the United Kingdom up to £3,750,000 for development, on the understanding that surplus balances would be drawn on before any loan was raised, and the actual raising of the loan would be deferred as far as possible by advances from the Joint Colonial Fund (JCF). It was accepted that some portion of the amount required would be raised before 1950.[41] The Secretary of State had approved the plan, subject to Treasury agreement concerning the provision of the loan funds, £1.5 million being expected to be required before 1950.[42] The Treasury was prepared to agree in principle, but felt it quite impossible to give any firm assurance as that would involve taking a view of the condition of the London market in 1949.[43] It was surmised that the position was unlikely to be difficult, because either Mauritius would not need an issue or the market might easily cope. Even so, this was stated 'without prejudice to the view which the Capital Issues Committee (CIC) may take of Mauritius requirements and that, in any event, it is not possible for us to give any indication at the moment of the actual size of any particular issue which Mauritius may be allowed to make, nor of a precise date for it.'[44] While it was realised that this would not be found 'particularly satisfactory' as any promise might not be possible to keep, it was suggested that the matter should be shelved until it was 'likely to become a really live issue'. By October 1947 the Crown Agents felt that, owing to the large reserve required to meet food shipments, a loan would be needed in 1948 rather than 1949,[45] and the Colonial Office enquired of the Treasury if this were possible, as a loan ordinance would in that case have to be made.[46]

The tentative nature of the assurances that the Treasury was prepared to give has been sufficiently indicated, and there is no need to repeat much the same story with reference to Trinidad, Northern Rhodesia or any other Colony.[47] It was strongly felt in the Office that approval of a ten-year development plan did commit HMG to permitting the borrowing that was provided for in the plan, and if it did not 'Colonial Governments have been sold a very mongrel pup'.[48] Following discussions with officials in the Central Economic Planning Staff and the Treasury, it was decided to take the general problem up with the Treasury. The latter was told that the arrangements for granting Colonial Governments access to the London market 'leave much to be desired and that we have been saved from considerable embarrassment only by the fact that physical shortages would force Colonies to proceed slowly with their development plans and have enabled them to defer raising loans.'[49] The Treasury was asked to confirm that the Colonies might raise up to £40 million on the London market by the end of 1950, and that more positive assurances should be given to Colonial Governments on which they could confidently base their financial policy. A guarded assurance over Sierra Leone's deep-water quay was not thought to be of value. It added that the consent of the CIC was 'not the obstacle it would appear to be'. However, at the official level, the Treasury was unyielding, arguing that the essence of the matter was to decide what projects were agreed and what sources of finance were available, for 'in the circumstances as they have developed over the past two years, the Colonial Office cannot assume that it will be possible for HMG to accept all the implications of each of the agreed ten-year development plans', as they remained 'blueprints, and as such liable to modification'.[50]

Clearly, the time had come for the Secretary of State, Mr Creech Jones, to take up the whole question of permission for Colonial Governments to raise loans on the London market with the Chancellor of the Exchequer, Sir Stafford Cripps. The Secretary of State was particularly disturbed by the reference to blueprints liable to modification, and the need to proceed on a hand-to-mouth basis, especially the latter.[51] For, as he said,

> We cannot tell the Colonies to plan ahead adventurously and at the same time refuse the very contribution towards that planning which depends upon ourselves. The great danger, which I have to face in pressing ahead with Colonial development on the economic side, is that our efforts may be interpreted in the Colonies as cynical exploitation for the sake of United Kingdom interests. Nothing is more likely to foster such suspicions than the impression that the United Kingdom Government, having encouraged Colonies to launch adventurous plans, and having led them to expect loan facilities in the process, then draws back at the point where those plans need United Kingdom support.

He asked for a general assurance that access to the London market up to a 'certain rough total' would be available when needed, and a similar assurance should be given to individual Colonial Governments. He noted that the Colonial Development Working Party (CDWP) had regarded the ten-year development plans as, in general, sound and well balanced, and had invited attention to the problem of the provision of London finance. Actually, in paragraph 7 of its Interim Report CDWP had said: 'We have not yet examined the plans in detail and would not suggest that the distribution of expenditure contemplated is necessarily the best possible. But we do not think it wholly unreasonable.' As the result of this strong representation, the Treasury signified its approval in principle to applications being made by Colonial Governments for loans on the London market up to a total of around £65 million, excluding conversions, in the period to 31 March 1952,[52] though later references quoted the amount as £60 million; there was no letter from the Treasury. A Circular Despatch on loan policy was sent to all Colonies on 19 January 1949, in which the upshot of the appeal to the Chancellor was explained and the early issue of loans in some urgent cases was promised.[53] In the case of Trinidad, expenditure had been undertaken in the expectation of local borrowing, which had not materialised, with the result that the Colony was running out of funds; the Federation of Malaya needed reconstruction finance urgently, while the East African High Commission sought finance for transport development.

The total of around £60 million was prepared from information in the Office for the consideration of the CDWP and received its blessing.[54] While it was intended as a provisional figure, it became clear over the following months that together with some CD & W grants, some private capital and the operations of OFC and CDC, the programme represented about the maximum diversion of United Kingdom resources. For it was not then possible to gauge the outcome of the Washington talks of the Secretary of State for Foreign Affairs, Mr Ernest Bevin, and the Chancellor of the Exchequer, Sir Stafford Cripps, or the effect of devaluation of sterling by 30 per cent as from 19 September 1949, or probable dollar export requirements. It was, clearly, in the circumstances, extremely unlikely that any worthwhile increase in the loan programme could be expected. Fortunately, it appeared highly probable that the £60 million would be sufficient to meet the needs of Colonial Governments for development until 31 March 1952. As the Circular Despatch of 18 January 1949, stated, finance was not then, in the case of most fields of development in most Colonial territories, the major limiting factor. However, owing to the difficulties of raising loans, several Colonies had, it transpired at a meeting at the Treasury on 25 October 1949,[55] committed their own resources to such an extent, for purposes of development, that the maintenance of their whole financial position depended on external borrowing. The Secretary of State was, he told the Governor of Kenya, aware that this was due, in part, to urging by HMG that local resources be utilised as fully as possible, and partly because of lack of access to the London market.[56] But he felt also that there was, perhaps, a further influence which had contributed to the situation, namely the tendency for the costs of development plans, more particularly the unproductive part of such plans, to rise so much that 'this spectacle of expanding needs having to be met from the facilities provided by a contracting market begins to assume the proportions of a nightmare.' The Treasury had warned that the state of the London market, especially in view of the approaching General Election, was likely to be even more difficult than it had earlier been feared. Without proposing any 'radical reversal of the present policy of Colonial development', he recommended that plans 'should be kept under review and, should be brought into effect as flexibly as possible, in the light of available financial resources'.[57] This guidance was accepted by the Governor of Kenya who, in a reply, noted the complexity of the problem, the most perplexing part of which concerned educational projects. Despite its long-term importance it was 'difficult sometimes to justify expenditure on education, especially primary and secondary education rather than technical training'.[58]

The dilemma was inescapable, as it became increasingly apparent that the capacity of the London market to absorb Colonial loans – a capacity that was far from unlimited under the most favourable conditions – had become seriously worsened. Thus, when the Government of Jamaica raised a loan on the London market early in January 1950, only about one-tenth of the amount issued was subscribed by the public. Later, it was necessary to reduce an offer on behalf of the East Africa High Commission (Railways and Harbours) from an intended issue of £10 million to £3 million, which was the amount of the Kenya Government loan falling due for redemption in May 1950. Subsequently, the remainder was issued, as was £2 million of a Uganda Government £3 million loan. So, although the Treasury assured the Colonial Office that 'the Colonial programme has not been forgotten, and is not being given less priority than its relative importance justified',[59] some postponement of Colonial borrowing was inevitable, with the corollary that development plans should be carried out as flexibly as possible. The Secretary of State explained the position as it had developed in a Confidential Circular Despatch of 15 June 1950.[60] In respect of resolving the dilemma, he advised that priority should be given 'to those projects which are most important, particularly from the point of view of strengthening future revenue'. However, that in itself was a poor second-best to more adequate borrowing facilities, and the Secretary of State drew attention, as had his predecessor, to the possibility of borrowing from the International Bank for Reconstruction and Development (IBRD).

Over the past year, the margin between the cost of borrowing on the London market and the cost of IBRD loans had narrowed to roughly one-half per cent, i.e. from just over $3\frac{1}{2}$ per cent on London to just over 4 per cent from the Bank. The virtual impossibility of borrowing from the IBRD to make purchases in sterling, or Colonial currencies, remained a major obstacle. The Secretary of State invited Colonial Governments to let him know whether, if that restriction were removed, they would wish to use IBRD loans, because, in that case, he, in turn, would proceed to take the matter further. The replies were such that the Colonial Office set about preparing information required for discussions with IBRD and, at the same time, provisional estimates of Colonial loan requirements for 1952–55.[61]

iii. COLONIAL STERLING BALANCES

The Treasury's somewhat equivocal policy over Colonial loans, and much besides, in the immediate post-war years must be seen largely in the light of the very real anxiety over the rate of liquidation of the wartime accumulation of sterling balances. In the present context, it is appropriate to concentrate attention on Colonial holdings of sterling liabilities.

The quantitative position was assessed in March 1945, both with regard to total holdings and to rate and extent of run-down.[62] Naturally, totals could be more precisely estimated than speed and extent of liquidation. In Table 2.1 the three columns of figures show respectively: (i) the estimated total holdings of sterling balances on 31 March 1945, were £711 million; (ii) the estimated extent of liquidation of these balances over the decade to 31 March 1955, was

TABLE 2.1 Colonial Sterling Balances, 31 March 1945 and 1946

Holding	Total £m	Estimated extent of liquidation 1945–1955 £m	Revised total (at 31 March 1946)[63] £m
1. Currency Funds			
(a) London boards	95 ⎫		106.4
(b) Other Colonial currencies	91 ⎬ 40		136.1
2. Crown Agents			
(a) Banking or liquid funds	61	45	97.7
(b) Non-banking or earmarked funds	113	10	138.2
3. Commercial banking liabilities	185	50	234.6
4. Loans to HMG	41	10	47.6
5. CD & W: ten-year liability	120	120	120.0
6. West Africa: cocoa profits	5	2	5.0
Total	711	277	885.6

expected to be of the order of £277 million; and (iii) the estimated total holdings of sterling balances was raised for 31 March 1946, to £885.6 million. The run-down of balances was not expected to be evenly spread over the decade but instead to rise to a peak of some £35 million by the end of the fifth year and then to drop to a level of around £20 million a year in the second half of the decade.

In addition to normal requirements, allowance was necessary for rehabilitation and reconstruction but, as Lord Keynes commented, 'Figures for reconstruction always are fanciful.'[64] At a meeting of Treasury, Colonial Office and Bank of England officials in Keynes' room on 20 February 1946,[65] it was agreed that 'for the next five years the problem was basically how to prevent accumulated sterling from being liquidated against imports'. Greater taxation, strict import controls and devaluation of Colonial currencies were all discussed and found, for one reason or another, unsatisfactory. It was felt that no expedient should be dismissed simply because of political difficulties 'in view of the seriousness of the situation'. The immediate concern was not due, except in the case of Palestine, to any sharp fall in balances, but rather because HMG had accepted, by Article X of the Anglo-American Financial Agreement, the obligation to endeavour to secure the early completion of agreements whereby part of accumulated balances were divided into three categories: (a) balances to be released at once and convertible into any currency for current transactions, (b) balances to be similarly released by instalments from 1951, and (c) balances to be 'adjusted', or written off. Apart from any relief deriving from an agreement over Colonial balances, it was considered that failure to deal with them would make arrangements with other creditors more difficult to come by. The Colonial Office insisted that, as not only the Secretary of State but HMG as a whole were trustees for the interests of Colonial Governments and peoples, who were unable to negotiate on their own behalf, HMG could not drive as hard a bargain as they reasonably might with Governments of more independent status, such as the Dominions or India or Egypt.[66] It was said that in any case, in view of obligations undertaken to develop the Colonies, 'it would be as impolitic as it would be immoral to take from the Colonies with one hand what we gave them with the other.'

Consequently, the need for drastic action with regard to Colonial balances would have to be demonstrably inescapable for any Secretary of State to consider it seriously. Two possibilities of such necessity were instanced: either the burden of Colonial balances was intolerable (a point which would be virtually impossible to demonstrate), or the absence of an agreement made the conclusion of agreements with other creditors impossible. It was further stated that, in the first place, it was not generally the case that the Colonial balances resulted from profiteering at the expense of the United Kingdom. In all cases the terms of trade had moved against the Colonies, especially in West Africa. In reply to an assertion that the increase of sterling balances itself indicated wartime 'profiteering' on the part of the Colonies, it was said:

> In any case, if profiteering is to be mentioned, it is we who are now open to the charge since, now that we are at last sending our exports in some volume to the Colonies, it is at prices between two and three times above 1939. If we are talking in terms of 'getting our own back', is not this the obvious and least troublesome way of doing it, instead of making public the startling conflict in policy between offering large gifts for Colonial development with one hand and taking away existing balances with the other?[67]

Secondly, United Kingdom expenditure in the Colonies had been direct military expenditure to a much lesser extent than in India or Egypt, and much more the continuance of normal pre-war purchases of produce at prices nearly always closely controlled and based on pre-war levels. Thirdly, sterling accumulations, at least in some cases, were the result of austerity and saving, as Colonies had restricted their imports and run savings campaigns. Those who responded by building up accounts in local Savings Banks hardly deserved penalising. Fourthly, there was a fairly large haphazard element about some of the constituents of the sterling balances, e.g. bank deposits by big United Kingdom firms engaged in Colonial trade figured indirectly in the totals if they were held locally but not if they were held at London head offices. Fifthly, concentration on the Colony–United Kingdom relationship could result in some inequities, as in some areas Colonial banks were more closely related to centres other than London where balances would be kept, e.g. West Indies and Canada, Fiji and Australia, Ceylon and India. Finally, in some areas, particularly in Palestine, some of the private balances were due to investments and gifts.

By way of positive proposals, if the special position of the Colonies could not entirely shield them from action, it was suggested that the choice lay between currency devaluation and the creation of a fiduciary proportion in Colonial currency funds without changing the exchange value of the currency.[68] While devaluation would discourage imports directly, it was realised that sterilising part of the currency cover would only have a contingent effect, apart from its obvious effect on the statistical balance. It was acknowledged from the Treasury that there was, in fact, no case for a devaluation of Colonial currencies in terms of sterling, because there was no 'fundamental disequilibrium' between the Colonies and the United Kingdom as required by the rules of the International Monetary Fund.[69] The Bank of England felt that the facts of the situation did not justify devaluation, except possibly in the cases of Palestine and Ceylon, nor was it acceptable on moral grounds; also, it would lead to a running-down of balances to a bare minimum.[70] The Colonial Office, for its part, was wholly opposed 'to any continuing general control of physical imports in order to keep down consumption'.

Lord Keynes, while agreeing with much of Mr Caine's 'very able' letter of 5 March, rejected 'the tacit underlying assumption, namely, that it would be improper to ask any of the Colonies to make any contribution whatever to the cost of the war', and suggested that something positive should be worked out which took full account of Mr Caine's arguments.[71] For political reasons, the Secretary of State felt unable to contemplate any drastic action for dealing with Colonial sterling balances, unless, as noted above, the necessity was demonstrably inescapable. However, some officials in the Treasury regarded the Colonial Office standpoint as untenable

in trying to give the Colonies all the privileges of neutrals during the war and of favoured children after the war. I could understand [Caine's] arguments better if they came from Eire, where they might meet with the sympathy they would deserve. But, at least, Eire does not participate in the Colonial Development and Welfare Fund. I think we must stand up for the oppressed taxpayer in this country, who has regularly contributed, e.g. to the relief of hurricane damage and similar calamities all over the Colonial Empire as need arose. This time *we* have had the hurricane.[72]

According to the same official, the Colonial Office was expecting the United Kingdom to reduce its standard of living for a generation in order to finance CD & W and the repayment of sterling balances and so raise standards in the Colonial Empire and 'It is this fundamental clash of policies which makes a solution so difficult. And we are bound by the Anglo-American Agreement. I do not see any solution at present. A theoretical one might revolve round annual interest-free loans from each Colony.'[73]

Lacking a general solution, the Treasury considered that it should collect details on each Colony, as their economic positions differed widely, before deciding what action should be taken.[74] But the Bank of England had no information on the distribution of ownership of the various sterling balances, nor was it able to obtain reliable information.[75] Nor was the relevance of such information, or that on population, trade, etc., to a decision on the problem of Colonial sterling balances understood by the Bank. It repeated its proposal that a portion of the currency cover should be allocated as a contribution to CD & W and, possibly, in addition some, or all, of the interest-free loans made by the Colonies during the war should be similarly allocated, though it was admitted that 'the sums thus removed from our immediate liabilities would not be considerable.'[76] The fear was that there would, as indeed in the case of Palestine there had been, a rush to liquidate balances. One official was inclined 'to guess' that the war had marked a third stage in economic demands of the Colonies: 'The first was for beads and mirrors; the second for cheap textiles and the like; we may now be seeing the demand for semi-luxury goods. If so, although much of the new balances may have accumulated with traders, they will certainly want to hold and finance much bigger stocks to meet the new requirements of the lower and lower-middle classes.'[77] The correctness of this view was shown in the Gold Coast, where the inability to procure sufficient supplies of some of the semi-luxury goods that had come to be wanted contributed to the unrest, which, in turn, set the scene for the disturbances of 1948. Sir David Waley, to whom the guess was addressed, minuted: 'We had better wait to see what information on this point Mr Kershaw gives us.' While the latter feared that the problem of the quick liquidation of the balances might arise, he never referred to the problem that Mr Rowe-Dutton raised.

A Working Party was set up in June 1946, with the Treasury, Colonial Office, Board of Trade and the Bank of England represented, to consider this matter. By the end of July 1946 a paper was prepared which set out the Treasury view that, because not more than £300–£400 million would be released up to the end of 1950, part of the existing balances ought to be cancelled.[78] The Colonial Office considered any such cancellation impossible, and submitted its own paper[79] to the Working Party. The broad political difficulty was obvious, because the exaction of any forced contribution was contrary to the repeated declarations of the intention of HMG to assist Colonial economic development as generously as United Kingdom resources permitted. Administratively, it was undesirable, as it would require legislation in several Colonies or, alternatively, an Imperial Act, which had not been attempted since 1776. Nor could a common formula be found, as the Colonies differed in economic condition, potential, and in ownership of balances. Finally, certain unfavourable responses were likely. Thus, Colonial Governments might drive harder bargains over the prices of their exports, or they might limit the flow of funds to London, or accelerate the liquidation of remaining balances. The Colonial Office pointed out that part of the balances, e.g., those of banks and trading companies, were not controllable. Only in so far as physical imports were concerned could 'targets' be set.[80] The Colonial Office deplored a policy of cancellation from the Colonial standpoint, believing, at the same time, it would be fundamentally unwise in the long-term economic and political interests of the United Kingdom itself. But the Chancellor of the Exchequer, Dr Hugh, later Lord, Dalton did not feel that it was politically impossible to ask the Colonies for a cancellation by way of a contribution to the overhead costs of the war. He minuted: 'We must not admit – till a very late stage, if at all, – that *any* sterling creditor can make no "adjustment".[81]

However, for whatever reason, no action arose from the Chancellor's minute, and the Colonial Office submitted its own proposals six months later.[82] It was suggested that, instead of asking the Colonies to cancel outright any of the accumulated sterling balances held by them, they should be asked 'as a gesture' to convert a part of their existing holdings into interest-free loans to HMG, which would be repayable only when required to meet certain specified obligations of Colonial Governments. The interest-free loans were to be of two kinds: (i) Colonial currency reserve funds and (ii) Colonial surplus funds. At the same time, Colonial imports would be restricted and Colonial Governments would be urged to raise taxes in order to absorb purchasing power, and to use the proceeds for development purposes. The suggestions were generally welcomed as on the right lines in the Treasury,[83] though there were phrases and points which some officials wished to alter. Thus, one wished to omit the phrase 'as a gesture', and to add the proceeds of extra taxation to the interest-free loans, financing development expenditure by CD & W grants and loans.[84] It was generally accepted that a special relationship existed with the Colonies, justifying more generous treatment than India and Egypt would have the right to expect.[85] The Bank of England saw the main aim was to guide Colonial policy so that it did not increase balance of payments difficulties in the sterling area as a whole, and consequently favoured economy on consumption goods and on expenditure on productive development programmes.[86] The Economic Secretariat of the Cabinet Office was more sceptical, feeling that 'the only part of the Colonial balances we need worry about would be that part held by commerical banks and private persons', though nothing was to be done about them.[87] A compulsory transfer of part of those funds to Colonial Governments and currency authorities was proposed. But there was no reaction to that proposal and the Secretary of State, Mr Creech Jones, accepted the general policy approved by the Working Party.[88] Dr Hugh Dalton, the Chancellor of the Exchequer, minuted: 'I am not sure about this. Anyhow we should postpone decision. H D.'[89]

The Colonial sterling balances were estimated to stand at £805.5 million as at 31 March 1947. During the second and third quarters of 1947, the net annual rate of fall was £92.8 million (i.e. from £805.5 million to £759.1 million in six months) and the gross rate, i.e. the rate at which those Colonies whose balances fell drew them down, was £113.6 million a year.[90] Available figures of these balances and of visible trade suggested that the Colonial Empire, taken as a whole, had been in deficit with the rest of the world since June 1946, and the dollar surplus of the Colonial Empire was less than it might have been. Although measures were taken in August 1947, to arrest the tendency, these were in the import field only. The Bank of England suggested that it should discuss with the Treasury (a) internal financial policy in the Colonies and (b) the conflicting claims of economy in the use of sterling balances and expenditure on development. The Colonial Office pointed out that balances were higher than they had been two years before, and felt that balances must at times be expected to fall, especially in an abnormal period, which it was claimed the six months April–September 1947 had been.[91] Also, the Colonial Office had encouraged Colonies to raise further taxation, although it was necessary 'to bear in mind the very great political difficulties of securing such action by Colonial Governments, having regard to the very rapid increase in their constitutional independence and the difficulty of persuading them that more taxation is required when their budgets are already comfortably balanced: 'The higher theory of budget surpluses is as yet very little appreciated by the Colonial legislators, who have to vote the taxes.' In fact, the Government funds of all Colonies, with the prominent exception of Ceylon and a few others, had not declined over the previous twelve months, which pointed to the importance of changes in private holdings.

In January 1948 it was decided to renew pressure for the adoption of the proposals that had been put to the Chancellor some six months earlier.[92] The new version concentrated on the proposal for interest-free loans from the Colonial currency reserves and other surplus funds.[93] But, as the Bank indicated, the proposal to freeze a quarter only of the cover of currencies did nothing to immobilise sight liabilities until, and unless, the currencies contracted by more than 75 per cent, which was highly unlikely.[94] So the problem centred round the Colonial Surplus Funds, where it was thought a Colonial Government had its only opportunity for embarrassing the United Kingdom by drawing on London funds. Otherwise, the Bank of England saw a contradiction in a policy, 'which, on the one hand, seeks to "freeze" Colonial sterling assets and, on the other hand, proposes to spend £120 million in the next ten years under the CD & W Act and to authorise the expenditure over an unspecified period of some £165 million on account of the Colonial Development and Overseas Food Corporations.' It was, therefore, suggested that it would be better if Colonies were asked to use their existing balances to finance development expenditure, or some part of it, and thus to postpone the need to supply new money from the United Kingdom. In the light of this comment and the restrictions imposed on Colonial imports and Colonial investment, the proposals being circulated were said to look 'even more like window-dressing' than they had in 1947.[95] However, it was quite rightly maintained that the exercise had not been planned for the sake of what it realised from the Colonies, but rather because, unless the Colonial balances were adjusted, the attempt to achieve an adjustment of the balances of India, Egypt, etc, would come to nought.[96] The proposals should, it was urged, be pressed, unless Ministers decided that adjustment should not be sought of any of the balances. Mr, later Sir David, Pitblado ended a long minute of 12 March 1948, with: 'Much depends on whether a plan of this sort is advantageous in our other Sterling Area negotiations.' A request for contributions from African Colonies in respect of defence was proposed. But, in view of the time which had elapsed and the failure to got any other large holders of sterling to cancel part of their holdings, the official who had drafted the original proposals felt, in August 1948, that they were not worth reviving and, in any case, the Colonial Office was said not to have regarded the scheme 'as much more than window-dressing' in the first place.[97] It was pointed out that while, from a Colonial development point of view, the use of balances to finance development expenditure was likely to accelerate growth, the expedient would be likely to involve increased unrequited exports from the United Kingdom, thus aggravating the balance of payments position, and so should be avoided.[98] In a discussion between the Economic Secretary to the Treasury, Mr Douglas Jay, and officials, that view was endorsed.[99]

However, the Treasury was now faced with demands from the Colonies for substantial commitments by way of loans, beginning with a loan of £12 million for Malaya, and totalling some £40 million by the end of 1950.[100] The total of loans which the Colonial Office would like to raise to March 1952 was £65 million.[101] A policy decision was required as to how those demands were to be met.[102] There were, in fact, three more or less distinct questions to be answered in order to come to such a decision.[103] First, whether it was useful to continue to consider cancellation, or 'adjustment', of Colonial sterling balances; secondly, whether Colonial loans could be raised on the London market when there was ample sterling locked up in their currency backing funds; and, thirdly, what was appropriate long-term policy to be pursued with regard to Colonial currencies. On the first of these, it was by now generally recognised that there was no convincing moral basis for cancellation, and that it would be indefensible to try, unless India and Egypt agreed to sizeable cancellations, which it was clear they would not. The same was true of alternative 'adjustments'. As regards the second question, the argument turned on what was likely to be the attitude of the Colonies themselves to their sterling holdings in the long run. Those who advocated allowing the Colonies to borrow in London were thought to be making 'a tacit assumption that the Colonies will be ready for evermore to take the highly unsophisticated and naïve view that they "need" to have sterling backing of 100 per cent, or even 110 per cent, of their note circulation. It is this assumption that the opponents of Colonial borrowing find so difficult to swallow.'[104] It was felt that, as they approached independence, Colonies would realise that backing of as much as 50 per cent with local securities would be just as acceptable as 100 per cent sterling backing, especially as 'most of their financial officials will have been educated at the London School of Economics anyway'. That led directly to the third question, namely the need to establish a sound doctrine appropriate to the needs of developing Colonial territories and consistent with Treasury requirements. An authoritative study was proposed but was not supported, for while it was admitted that some greater elasticity would be wanted than the automatic mechanism of the currency board system allowed, no satisfactory alternative was seen. In any case, an anti-inflationary system was not inappropriate at that time and, if expansion should be desired, it could be given by controlled use of sterling balances or borrowing on the London market. So it was thought better to leave the system alone while so much in the world was in a state of flux.[105] However, it seemed to some that the issue should be brought to a head, and a memorandum was requested 'setting out the problem, balancing the arguments and coming down in favour of borrowing in London'.[106] But it was not regarded as a practical problem of any urgency,[107] and the draft was not finalised until the end of May 1949. A copy was sent to the Governor of the Bank of England.[108]

It was agreed that cancellation was, as the Bank had said it had felt from the first, not possible, and that interest-free loans were not worth pursuing, especially as the Colonies were currently seeking higher earnings on their currency funds.[109] Nor did the Bank press for the use of currency funds for financing development. Consequently, there was nothing further to be done about Colonial sterling balances, and the Bank proposed that attention be directed instead to the need for a greater co-ordination of development programmes, Colonial borrowing and indirect Colonial demands on the London market. The Colonial Office also accepted the argument of the memorandum.[110] It was mentioned that, whereas many of the other holders of sterling balances had been allowed substantially to run them down, Colonial balances had increased since 1945. It was stated that the Secretary of State would be advised to resist any pressure for long-term interest-free loans from the Colonies because (a) some others had liquidated much of their balances, (b) there was a special relationship between HMG and the Colonial Governments which others would accept as a sufficient reason for not taking action over Colonial sterling balances should other holders be asked to agree to partial cancellation, and (c) the Colonial Office was not sure that Article X of the Loan Agreement applied to Colonial territories. Furthermore, the memorandum had not recognised that the rate of Colonial expenditure on dollar imports had nearly halved between 1947 and 1949. While the Colonial Office was impressed by the dangers inherent in any infringment of the sanctity of the 110 per cent cover for Colonial currencies, it wished to be able to consider any particular case on its merits. The memorandum was revised to allow for these suggestions, though not without some opposition in the Treasury.[111] When completed, it was already rather out-of-date and could not be passed to the Chancellor.[112] Instead, it was suggested it should form part of the report on the sterling balance problem as a whole, and any recommendations would have to be reconciled with those in the wider field. Meantime, the memorandum was put by until the upshot of the discussions with the United States on the general sterling balance issue was known.[113]

The matter remained dormant, it seems, until November 1951 when the Cabinet asked that consideration be given to the use of sterling balances to provide funds for investment in the Colonial

Empire, and to reduce the calls on the London market.[114] The point was made during the discussion of a memorandum by the Secretary of State, Mr Oliver Lyttelton, concerning possibilities of increasing the supply of Colonial foodstuffs and raw materials to the United Kingdom, that the Colonies were expected to draw on their sterling balances towards providing roughly half the total cost of the four-year development programme, which they were to find from their own resources.[115] It was suggested in the Treasury that consideration should be given to the way in which the larger Colonies intended to use their sterling balances as compared with the disposable balances available, i.e., after allowing for balances earmarked or otherwise unavailable.[116]

IV. THE COLONIAL ECONOMIC DEVELOPMENT COUNCIL

(a) The Council is appointed

In the Circular Despatch of 12 November 1945 (Cmd 6713) it was stated that 'the main purpose of development planning should be to ensure that all the resources available are used to the best advantage, and the whole field of possible development and welfare is surveyed, and that the sums to be devoted to each project are determined, so that the programmes form a well-balanced whole.' The Treasury feared that a tendency might develop for Colonies to devote their CD & W funds to those schemes which were least likely to yield a financial return so that 'a Colony's development programme, as a whole, may thus appear well balanced, without its proposals for using its CD & W allocation adequately reflecting the need for economic develop- ment.'[117] It felt that the intentions of Parliament in passing the CD & W Act, 1945, was 'undoubtedly' that Colonies should use their allocations evenly for both development and welfare, and it was proposed that the Colonial Office and the Treasury should 'act as watch-dogs in this respect'.[118] The Treasury asked to see the full programme of CD & W expenditure of the individual Colonies. The Colonial Office, accepting the point, agreed to let the Treasury see the individual Colony sketch-plans.[119] In this manner, the Treasury came to have a voice on the general development plans of Colonies, although formally its rights extended only to those of grant-aided Colonies and to the use of CD & W funds in general development expenditure.

However, the Colonial Office was not unmindful of the need to review the plans submitted and, in the Circular Despatch of 21 November 1945, had promised to give 'special attention to the best means of securing the most competent review of possibilities of economic development and the means to promote it'. As the result of that review of machinery, it was, as noted earlier, decided to appoint a Colonial Economic and Development Council (CEDC) 'to advise the Secretary of State for the Colonies on the framing and subsequent review of plans for economic and social development in the Colonial Empire, and on questions of general economic and financial policy'. The following were appointed members of the Council: Chairman – Lord Portal (Viscount Portal of Laverstoke, PC, Minister of Works and Planning, 1942–44; Chairman, Portals Ltd; Chairman, Great Western Railway); Members – Mr J Benstead (General Secretary, National Union of Railwaymen; President, International Transport Workers' Union), Sir Bernard Bourdillon (Governor, Uganda, 1932–35, Nigeria, 1935–43; Director, Barclay's Bank DCO and Barclays Overseas Development Corporation; Member, Colonial Economic Advisory Committee), Sir Graham Cunningham (Chairman, Triplex Safety Glass Co., 1935–41; Comptroller-General, Ministry of Supply; Chairman, Shipbuilding Advisory Committee 1944–60; Member, Economic Planning Board, 1947–61), Sir William Good-enough (Director, Barclays Bank, 1929–51, and Chairman, 1947–51; Member, Colonial Economic Advisory Committee) and Sir Drummond Shields (Labour Member of Parliament, 1924–31; Parliamentary Under-Secretary, India Office, 1929; Parliamentary Under-Secretary, Colonial Office, 1929–31; Public Relations Officer, General Post Office, 1944–49). A further four members were appointed in October 1946; they were Mr J. McFadyen (Director, Co-operative Wholesale Society), Dr W. Arthur Lewis (Reader in Economics, London School of Economics), Mr G. Wansborough (who had had financial experience overseas) and Dr R. B. Wellesley Cole (a medical practitioner in Newcastle upon Tyne who had had tropical experience).

At the inaugural meeting of CEDC on 7 October 1946,[120] the new Secretary of State, Mr Creech Jones, said that it was not sufficient for experts to go out to the Colonies to advise. What was wanted also was a high-powered Commission in this country to assist the Colonial Office in dealing with the broader problems of development, a body which included men who had to cope with problems of finance and industry in their daily work. The part of the Office most closely concerned was the Development Division, which was organised in three departments – Production, Research and Finance – and had the services of the Adviser on Development Planning, Sir Frank Stockdale, who would act as liaison between CEDC and the Office. So far, only the ten-year development plans for Nigeria, Kenya, Northern Rhodesia and Zanzibar had been considered. They had been studied by the Geographical Departments, by the Development Division and by the various Advisers to the Secretary of State, before being approved by the Parliamentary Under-Secretary of State and submitted to the Treasury. The Secretary of State felt it would be a waste of the Council's time to involve itself in the details of the individual schemes, many of which were very small. He saw instead the Council's main task, on the development side, to be the thorough consideration of the broad outlines of the ten-year plans as they arrived, and of the main details of the more important component schemes. He drew particular attention to the need to consider the problems of each Colony as a whole, trying to assess what were its fundamental needs and the best way of meeting them, believing that 'for this purpose, the breadth of outside experience which would be available on the Council would clearly be particularly valuable'. Certain allocations had been made for regional groups of territories in East and Central Africa and the West Indies, and the advice of the Council was sought on the problem of regional development. The Council would also be consulted on a wide range of problems of general economic policy, some of which had been studied by CEAC but on all of which more work was needed. These included problems of marketing, long-term contracts, mining royalties, currency and exchange. For this reason, CEDC might find it convenient to work through two committees, one dealing with development and the other with general economic policy, and so avoid making the Council itself unwieldy.

After discussion, the Council agreed to recommend that:

(*a*) the Economic and the Development Committees should be standing committees of members of the Office, empowered to call in outside advice but not to co-opt outside members;

(*b*) questions should be referred in the first place to the Council, which would decide whether to deal with them directly or to refer them to one or other of the committees;

(*c*) committees should give an account of their deliberations to the Council without reporting any conclusions;

(*d*) members of the Council should not be members of the committees or attend their meetings but the Adviser on Development Planning should act as Liaison Officer between the committees and the Council.

The Council usually met fortnightly, having 22 meetings by 25 August 1947, when owing to retirements and resignations it ceased to exist in its original form. The nature of the discussions that took place is shown by the following. At the second and fourth meetings, 21 October and 4 November 1946, the Council considered, at the request of the Secretary of State, the Report of the Groundnut Mission to East and Central Africa. It accepted and endorsed the principles of the scheme as being of great value to the United Kingdom and to the Colonies concerned. It was agreed that implementation was a matter of urgency, but doubted whether sufficient crawler tractors would be made available to begin work by February 1947. Sir Graham Cunningham expressed the view, from his experience at the Ministry of Supply, that control of the scheme by a Government department, either direct or on an agency basis, was inadvisable; a government-owned Corporation was the only practicable method. The Council recommended that such a Corporation be set up forthwith. Sir Graham Cunningham undertook to enquire into the availability of tractors.

At its third and fifth meetings on 28 October and 18 November 1946, the Tanganyika Development Plan was discussed. The discussion brought out the following points: (i) the effective limitation on borrowing was likely to be the extent to which the Treasury would authorise new borrowing on the London market rather than the size of the debt charge. In the Nigerian Plan, which had been drawn up and approved in 1945, the estimated cost was £55 million, of which Nigeria's allocation of CD & W funds was £23 million, £17 million was to be obtained by loan and £15 million from revenues and surplus balances. Restrictions on borrowing were, therefore, serious limitations to the implementation of a plan. (ii) The general objectives of any plan should be, first, to see the population was adequately fed and, secondly, that it was healthy; the next priority should probably be communications. To fit in with this scheme, education should be directed in the early stages towards improving standards of feeding and health. While these requirements were sufficiently met in the Tanganyika Plan, as far as the fundamental problem of finding sufficient manpower to implement the programme was concerned, it was felt that a manpower budget, covering both native and European labour requirements, was essential before the plan could be usefully examined in detail.

At its seventh meeting on 16 December 1946, it was noted that the response to Colonel Oliver Stanley's Despatch of 27 February 1945, which circulated a memorandum on the development of manufacturing industries in the Colonies and asked for comments and proposals, had been disappointing. A certain amount of inertia and opposition to industrialisation had to be overcome, and more positive directive was needed. The setting up in Nigeria, and elsewhere, of separate Departments of Commerce and Industries was regarded as a promising development. Although large sums would be needed to finance the proposed Development Corporations, and only part of this could come from CD & W, Sir William Goodenough, speaking from his experience of Barclays Overseas Development Corporation, said that the provision of finance should not be regarded as a deterrent as development was bound to be gradual, and it would be some time before large amounts of capital were needed. He stressed the importance of having research work done outside the proposed Corporations so as to avoid loading them with overhead charges. Even though it had practically no overheads, the Barclays Corporation did not expect to see any direct return on its capital for some time.

The plan for Mauritius was approved at the eighth meeting, on 30 December 1946, the Council suggesting that efforts should be made to develop secondary industries, particularly those using much labour and little land, and that smallholders should be helped to improve their methods. The plan for Jamaica was approved at the eleventh meeting, on 10 February 1947, subject to the provision of adequate research to improve the quality and quantity of local foodstuffs and to promote the development of local industries. Attention was drawn to the necessity of ensuring that, if freehold titles were given for land settlements, steps should be taken to prevent subdivision and a multiplication of land disputes.

The Council discussed at the thirteenth meeting, on 10 March 1947, a memorandum by the Chairman, proposing the setting up by Act of Parliament of a Colonial Development Corporation to promote increased Colonial production on an economic and self-supporting basis, intended in particular to encourage the production of foodstuffs and raw materials where supply, to the United Kingdom or sale overseas, would assist the balance of payments. The proposals were welcomed in principle. It was emphasised that the long-term interests of the Colonies should be safeguarded, and the Corporation should help to improve present agriculture and encourage industrial development. The memorandum was submitted, after revision, to the Secretary of State. For an account of the establishment and the working of the CDC see Chapter 6, below.

In discussing the plan for Uganda at the twenty-first meeting on 28 July 1947, the Council agreed with the shift of emphasis from academic to technical education made in the plan, but felt that the possibility of increasing provision for more general expansion of education should be reviewed. It also emphasised the paramount importance of ensuring that the allocation of consumer goods from the United Kingdom to the Colonies should be sufficient to provide growers with an incentive to produce the maximum output of raw materials, which were so urgently required, not only for industry in the United Kingdom but also for the world market.

In this period, the Council was, in effect, an Imperial General Staff for Colonial Development. In the light of hindsight, the views and recommendations are seen to have been well-founded and highly relevant. Such weaknesses as there were at this time sprang from a different source, namely the initial preparation of plans. Before the end of 1946, it was clear that the plans reaching London were usually brave essays in a technique which was, admittedly, still in its infancy in the United Kingdom also. In most cases, they had to be based on quite inadequate general information about the resources of the territories, and scanty, unreliable statistics. It was felt that Colonial Governments would profit enormously from the technical expertise of those who had detailed knowledge of development planning. The Treasury was asked to approve the appointment of up to four Development Officers, in substitution for four other posts, to carry out this job. As the work was not a normal function of the Colonial Office, but would be of direct benefit to the Colonial territories, the Treasury suggested it should be applied for via a specific CD & W scheme. A scheme was prepared for two officers in June 1947.[121] However, when it was realised in the Treasury that the officers would be expected to spend much of their time in the Colonial Office, filling in, as and when necessary, the posts of established staff when they visited Colonies, the scheme was disallowed as one for appointing relief staff in the Colonial Office.[122] By September 1947 the Colonial Office was prepared to drop the scheme owing to 'the pressing shortage of manpower'.[123] The proposal was later revived in a different form and four 'economic liaison' officers were appointed to the Economic Department of the Colonial Office.

The preparation of acceptable plans was least advanced in the West Indies, despite the existence there of the Comptroller for D & W and his staff of experts. The detailed scrutiny of local plans was but indifferently done and spared the Colonial Office no effort in checking. Of course, being usually relatively small, West Indian schemes were easier to criticise in detail and, being poor, it was necessary to ask for supplementary grants if the original proved insufficient. Lack of skilled

staffs, particularly in Public Works Departments, led to wide depar-
tures from the approved scheme, if scrutiny was not close. Even so, it
had been expected that the D & W Organisation would have helped
Colonies in planning and relieved the Colonial Office of much
supervision. Neither, it seems, was true. The Organisation was so
largely concerned with procedure, and the advisers were rarely settled
in Barbados long enough to study and comment on schemes before
passing them on to London. Such was the position to 1947.

(b) The Council is reconstituted

In August 1947 Lord Portal resigned from the Council, and so did Sir
William Goodenough on becoming Chairman of Barclays Bank, while
Mr Benstead was due to retire from the TUC in October 1947. So the
Secretary of State decided to reconstruct the Council.

The reconstructed Council met for the first time on 30 March 1948,
with the Parliamentary Under-Secretary of State, Mr D. 'Rees-
Williams, as Chairman *ex officio* and a membership of both officials and
unofficials. The members were: Dr Wellesley Cole, Dr Arthur Lewis
and Sir Drummond Shields from the original Council; Lord Faring-
don, Dr Rita Hinden, Dr Keith Murray, Sir John Waddington, and
Mr R. W. G. Mackay, MP, new unofficial members; Sir Sydney Caine
(Vice-Chairman), Mr Gorell Barnes, Mr C. G. Eastwood, and Sir
Gerald Clauson, official members, with Mr R. W. Newsam as
Secretary. Each specialist Advisory Committee of the Colonial Office
was invited to nominate a rapporteur to sit with the Council; as were
the two new Corporations (OFC and CDC) set up by the Overseas
Resources Development Act, 1948, the Treasury and the Central
Economic Planning Staff.[124]

In his address to the first meeting, the Secretary of State said that the
main function of the Council would be to advise on broad issues and to
work out a proper balance between the economic and social aspects of
Colonial development, for there had been much criticism that one side
or the other had been over-stressed. Of late, the tendency had been to
give undue weight to economic development and to forget that social
development must keep pace with it. He went on to say that 'the need
to integrate the economy of the United Kingdom more closely with
that of Europe and, in turn, to integrate the economies of the Colonies
more closely with the economy of the United Kingdom, should give
the Colonies opportunities which they might not otherwise have to
raise the standards of living and develop social welfare.' The Council
would be asked to examine and advise on development plans, to

suggest subjects which should be studied, and to discuss broad problems with the Secretary of State's Advisers so that they might appreciate the problems which had to be solved. The Secretary of State said that it would be arranged that, if the Council's advice was not accpeted, the grounds for not doing so would be explained, as would the way in which the Council's advice was incorporated in the plans considered.

The chairman said that the Council would be the focal point in the Colonial Office for all development projects. He stated that 'there were three main shortages in the development of the Colonies' – shortages of capital goods, of consumer goods and of staff. The policy of the Colonial Office was to concentrate on projects giving quick returns in view of these shortages, and to expand the existing proved projects, such as rice production and the Nigerian Railways, rather than to go in for large-scale new enterprises. The Council would be asked to advise on development of all sorts, including development undertaken by private enterprise, for all investments leading to development called on the United Kingdom for assistance, either in finance or in the provision of supplies. There were also some questions of a general character on which the Council would probably be asked to advise, such as the co-ordination of road and railway systems and the effect of large-scale mechanisation on the peoples of the territories concerned. It was hoped that, through the advice given by the Colonial Economic and Development Council, it would be possible to put the various more specialised Advisory Committees into the general picture of overall economic development in the Colonial Empire, which was important if the Advisory Committees were to do their work satisfactorily.

It was feared by some unofficials that, as the Council was considerably larger than its predecessor, it might function less easily. It was, however, pointed out that the Council was intended to be a general forum to survey broad problems, and to ensure an overall balance in the economic plans put forward. Matters relating to particular aspects of development would be referred to appropriate Advisory Committees, and it was not likely that more than a few of the members would wish to talk on any one item on the agenda.

In the discussion of subjects which should be considered by the Council, the question of loans from the International Bank for Reconstruction and Development was raised. It was mentioned that Mr Gorell Barnes had just come back from a visit to America where this had been discussed with Bank officials. The reaction of the Bank was favourable to the idea of loans to Colonial Governments for remunerative investments; not necessarily financially remunerative, but also in securing the production of goods in scarce supply in the world. The Bank's rate of interest, which was $4\frac{1}{2}$ per cent, was higher than the rate of $3\frac{1}{2}$ per cent at which loans could be raised in this country. For this reason it would only pay Colonial Governments to raise loans in the International Bank if that meant they would get capital equipment which they would not otherwise get so quickly, and there was going to be nearly as great a shortage in America of this type of goods, once the Economic Recovery Programme (ERP) came into operation, as in this country. The Bank was only prepared to loan dollars for dollar expenditure. It was argued that this was against the general principles of the Bank when it was created, although the Charter of the Bank permitted this discrimination. The Corporations were advised to go to the Bank at an early date to obtain finance for a considerable amount of their investment, though Colonial Governments should not do so until after further consideration.

At the second meeting, on 11 May 1948, the Council discussed a memorandum on the principles of economic planning, which was referred to a sub-committee for report, considered the interim report on the Colonial Development Working Party, discussed a paper on international Colonial collaboration and heard a statement by the Chairman on his visit to East Africa. It was decided to meet on the fourth Monday of each month but at the third meeting, on 28 June 1948, it appeared unlikely that it would be possible to provide an adequate agenda for meetings to take place monthly, owing to pressure of work in the Colonial Office. It was agreed that meetings should take place when fuller agenda were available. The discussion of the points arising from the Chairman's statement on his visit to East Africa was concluded, and a paper on road versus rail competition was discussed. The Secretary of State's Adviser on Inland Transport, Mr A. J. F. Bunning, was invited, after visiting East Africa, to prepare a paper on the principles which should influence Colonial Governments when assessing the relative advantages of road and rail transport. At the fourth and fifth meetings, on 21 September and 19 October 1948, the British Guiana ten-year plan was discussed. Several recommendations were made, mainly seeking information or suggesting that information be made available to the Colony. The Council agreed, after hearing the Governor, Sir Charles Woolley, and his Development Adviser, Mr Oscar Spencer, to recommend to the Secretary of State that the plan be approved subject to (a) sufficient provision being made to raise the level of peasant productivity, (b) further consideration being given to the question of hydro-electric power,

(c) inclusion of a fisheries section in the plan, and (d) priority being given to the reorganisation of rice milling.

(c) The Council is enlarged

The Council proceeded through seven meetings in 1948 and one in January 1949, after which the Secretary of State and his Parliamentary Under-Secretary discussed with officials the terms of reference, the composition and the future of CEDC.[125] The Secretary of State said that the Council should prove of value in that it would make available to the Office the point of view of important sections of lay opinion on Colonial development, and it could survey the whole field of development in the Colonies. It was, in any case, politically necessary to have a Council. The value of the contribution which could be provided by the unofficial members of the Council would be greatly enhanced if they could be brought to appreciate the practical difficulties experienced in each field of development. He felt that it would be desirable for experts in the various fields to address the Council on the problems which they had to deal with, and on the policy which they were following. These talks might be given by the Advisers, and a talk might also be given by the Director of Colonial (Geodetic and Topographic) Surveys, which might be accompanied by a tour over the headquarters at Bushey Park to see the work being done. These talks by individual specialists might be prefaced by a general talk on the new function of the Colonial Office, which would explain how it provided central services and advice for Colonial Governments. The Council might assist by making suggestions to the Colonial Office as to how it might improve these central services. After discussion, it was decided that (i) CEDC was still required, (ii) no change in the terms of reference was necessary, (iii) arrangements should be made for experts in the various fields to address the Council on the work they were doing, (iv) the Advisers should continue to be members, (v) the economic Assistant Secretaries should continue to be members, (vi) the Council should be brought into closer touch with industry, (vii) three members of Parliament should be invited to become members, and (viii) it should be arranged so that about one third of the unofficial members should retire each year. Accordingly, Messrs G. Woodcock, M. Watt and A. L. Butler became members as representatives of the trade unions and industry, while Sir Ralph Glyn, MP, and Mr C. W. Dumpleton, MP, reinforced the chairman from the Parliamentary side.

The enlarged Council met three times in 1949 and four times in both

1950 and 1951. Except for visits such as the Secretary of State had envisaged and addresses by various Advisers, the work of the Council continued much as before, being mainly concerned with the examination of development plans, though an increasing number of Office papers on various aspects of Colonial relations were circulated. Indeed, Sir Ralph Glyn observed, at the meeting on 12 December 1950,[126] that for some time past the Council's time had been devoted primarily to detailed study of the development plans of individual Colonial territories. He feared that, as a result, the Council was in danger of failing to carry out their other responsibility for reviewing the progress of development in the Colonies as a whole. There were many aspects of development planning which could profitably be studied on a regional or pan-Colonial basis, such as the production and allocation of raw materials and the recruitment and employment of technicians who, as well as assisting directly in development, would be able to train Colonial peoples in their crafts. A general examination of the results of development planning in groups of Colonies having similar economic conditions would draw attention to the laggards, and, perhaps, throw some light upon the particular reasons for their backwardness. There was a need for the fullest co-operation between neighbouring Colonies, so that their experience might be pooled to the advantage of all. The Chairman, Mr John Dugdale, MP, Parliamentary Under-Secretary of State, expressed his agreement with these views, but hoped that it would not be thought that the idea of consultation and co-operation between Colonies was in any sense a novelty. In the course of discussion it was said, on behalf of the Colonial Office, that for some time the best way of assessing the broad results of the activity which had resulted from the CD & W Act, 1945, had been under consideration. At the time, it was difficult to obtain a clear comprehensive picture of the nature and rate of progress being achieved, but a memorandum was being prepared on the matter. It was agreed that the memorandum should be circulated to the Council.

In the memorandum[127] it was stated that, provided a careful selection was made of the sort of facts which were relevant to an assessment of overall progress, it should be possible to discern the significant economic tendencies, the impact of development plans, as well as other major factors, on the economy as a whole, the fields in which progress was more or less rapid, and the territories in which progress was along sound lines. Indicators of productive capacity, of consumption and of certain subsidiary matters like retail prices, wage rates in representative occupations, rates of company dividend as published, and currency in circulation were suggested. After discussion, the Council agreed to recommend that experimental assessments of economic progress would be prepared along the lines proposed.[128] At the meeting of 5 July 1951, the Chairman promised a paper for the following meeting, giving the first two experimental assessments of the economic progress of selected Colonial territories.[129] However, after the General Election, Sir Winston Churchill's second administration took office on 26 October 1951, and the new Secretary of State, Mr Oliver Lyttelton, quickly decided to dissolve the Council. The assessments were never made.

(d) The Contribution of CEDC

It is perhaps a somewhat curious fact that Labour Governments were anxious to enlist the advice of businessmen and others in the consideration of problems of Colonial development whereas Conservative Governments were not. Lord Passfield has been quoted in his insistence on such a committee. Mr MacDonald planned to continue on the same basis. However, when in the course of the debate on the CD & W Act, 1945, it was proposed by Viscount Elibank that 'there ought to be an Economic Advisory Committee composed principally of business men who understand and have taken part in overseas business, who will appreciate all the snags and difficulties involved, and who should be supported by scientists and technicians such as engineers, medical men and so on . . .',[130] the Parliamentary Under-Secretary of State, the Duke of Devonshire, was wholly unconvinced. He replied: 'I really cannot see why various noble Lords have stressed the desirability of the Secretary of State being assisted by a board or committee of some kind. I really cannot see how a committee sitting in the Colonial Office or anywhere else would be an improvement on a department of the Office charged with a particular task.'[131]

However, the new Secretary of State, Mr George Hall, adopted the idea. The two reconstructions and the statement by Mr Creech Jones of March 1949 indicate that it was not easy to come by a wholly satisfactory arrangement. Even in the vetting of development plans the Council could add little to what the officials and the Advisers knew. The existence of the Council might well have strengthened the Office in dealing with Governors on development matters, while the appearance of Governors and Development Advisers at the meetings when their plans were discussed must have been to the benefit of both the Office and the Colonies concerned. Once the main plans had been vetted, the the Council became less effective, partly because it lacked, as Sir Ralph Glyn observed, an overall view, and partly because the provision of general guidance to Colonial Governments was hardly a function the Council was equipped to fulfil. Nor should it be left unsaid that the experiment of sitting officials around the table with some of the main critics of Colonial policy was certain to have shortcomings. [The late Dr Rita Hinden put the considered views of an unofficial on CEDC to the author on 10 October 1969. The author acknowledges with thanks her kindness in doing so.]

The Secretary of State invited members of CEDC to raise issues and, at an early stage, one member submitted a memorandum[132] in which it was stated that 'the key to rapid and effective Colonial development is mass adult education: education not just in literacy or even primarily in literacy, but in life – in agriculture, in hygiene, in domestic living, in cultural values, in democratic organisation, in self-help and so on.' The memorandum was automatically circulated to the Council.[133] The Secretary of State's Deputy Education Adviser, Mr W. E. F. Ward, though yielding to no one in his enthusiasm for mass education, was sceptical: 'Suppose', he minuted,[134]

you have a completely successful scheme of mass education – everybody eating fruit and vegetables as well as carbohydrates, composting and contour ridging, preventing hookworm with shoes and latrines and malaria with mosquito nets and DDT, rearing the children on Trudy King methods, reading the Bible and *The Times*, running co-operative shops, crèches and clinics, with dances and folksong, puppet plays and embroidery and everything that mass educators have ever thought of. I cannot see that all this is going to increase the country's economic wealth at all, unless it is claimed that a well-fed and contented miner in the Udi coalfield will raise more coal per shift than the miner of today, which may or may not be so. It seems to me that a great increase in output can be achieved only through capital investment: power stations, industrialisation, mechanised and fertilised agriculture, harbours and communications, and so forth; and the capital for these things is not to be found in Nigeria.

However, the Parliamentary Under-Secretary minuted that 'Mass education is our policy. We do not argue about its desirability, only the means of carrying it out.'[135] The memorandum was welcomed, and the important place which mass education must play in Colonial development was generally accepted by CEDC. The Colonial Office had, it was stated, for some years taken particular interest in the subject. Since the publication in 1944 of the Report of the Advisory Committee on Education in the Colonies, entitled *Mass Education in African Society*, a sub-committee of the Advisory Committee had been studying mass education projects in the various territories. The scope of mass education implied in the memorandum was accepted by the Council, which referred to to an *ad hoc* sub-committee, which reported that it agreed generally with the memorandum, though it did not consider that mass education or, as it might be called, community development, should take precedence over other forms of development as might be understood from the memorandum.[136] It was felt that too little attention had possibly been paid to mass education in existing development plans, and that the key to such development was the provision of trained staff, existing facilities for training appearing to be somewhat inadequate. The Council agreed to recommend that the proposals, as amended to take account of its views, should be communicated in a Despatch to African Governors, who should be asked to report on the position in their territories and to submit proposals.[137]

That illustrates one kind of activity pursued by CEDC, but the main effort was concentrated on the vetting of development plans. An interesting case was that of Dominica, which presented the problem of how best to set about developing a Colony which had entered the vicious circle of poverty and bad administration. The Colony had been Treasury-controlled since 1928, and, in most years, had received a grant-in-aid. It was unable to provide any local funds for economic development. There were several reasons for Dominica's plight: lack of roads and the uncertainty of markets had prevented the expansion of production of citrus, it had become uneconomic to transport produce to market by head-pack, coastal shipping had declined and external sea communications were inadequate, the cost of essential services had increased steadily after the war, the short-lived boom in vanilla had ended because producers were unable to compete with exports from Madagascar and Mexico to the United States. A spirit of apathy, frustration and cynicism was widespread amongst the inhabitants.[138] The Economic Adviser with the D & W Organisation felt that quite inadequate attention had been paid to the withdrawal of knowledgeable estate managers in accounting for the decline of the island economy.[139] According to him,

the Colony has reverted to an inert peasantry, with a very small nucleus of planter-shopkeeper control. The political growth of the last generation has resulted in this small nucleus being virtually in control of the legislature, either directly or through agents. Their outlook is definitely against the type of development policy which has elsewhere come to be accepted as worthwhile. . . . It is important to guard against the fallacy of thinking that there is a body of alert-minded enthusiasts awaiting for capital to develop the island. There is, in point of fact, nothing of the kind, and all the evidence I have gathered suggests quite definitely that the expenditure of funds in the manner suggested in the Plan will not in fact contribute materially to any alteration of the position in ten years' time, unless it is supplemented by schemes involving direct attempts to increase productivity on the ground plus a great improvement of government administration, especially in the way of financial control, and an injection of individuals of proved competence to carry out such schemes.

The Governor agreed with Professor Beasley's main thesis, saying that 'new money, new energy and skill will have to be imported if we are to achieve the Colony's rehabilitation.'[140] Professor Beasley's own prescription was a block grant for three or more years without the usual Treasury control, plus a Receiver, or Administrator, on the Newfoundland model, in order to ensure that the money made available by the block grant should not be wasted or even peculated.[141]

The Dominica ten-year plan and covering Despatch[142] emphasised that the underlying aim of the plan was to bring to an end the Colony's reliance on grants-in-aid. Yet, because of its poverty, it could not find local funds to supplement its CD & W allocation, even with loan possibilities, to a point where that aim could be achieved in the ten-year period, 1946–56. The Administrator and Acting Governor therefore requested special assistance for the Colony to enable a further sum, principally £890,000 on roads, which would bring the total planned expenditure to £1,765,840, instead of £5–600,000 as under the so-called 'Practical Plan', which still exceeded the total of the CD & W block grant and local borrowings, and excluded roads, which were a necessary, though not sufficient condition, for development. Officials agreed that the 'Practical Plan' would achieve nothing at all as it excluded roads. The aims of the Despatch were accepted in the Colonial Office as entirely reasonable, though it was thought that, perhaps, the probable deficit, if the full expenditure recommended was not forthcoming, might be exaggerated. On grounds of social justice, it was regarded as desirable to raise the 'social minimum' in Dominica to that of the rest of the West Indies. It was thought that this gave grounds for considering whether practicable means should not be found in the form of CD & W reserves, as special assistance for Dominica and other grant-aided Colonies. The Chief Adviser of the D & W Organisation was certain that any plan which did not take capital and entrepreneurial skill into the Colony would fail, and a Development Agency in association with CDC was suggested as a means for providing capital and entrepreneurship.[143] It was regarded by the Colonial Office as the best hope.[144] It was felt that any such scheme would require basic services to be given major emphasis and, as a consequence, expenditure on many social services postponed. Discussions with CDC were suggested to see whether their co-operation was likely. Meanwhile, owing to the fact that the provision of a skeleton main road system was accepted to be a *sine qua non* for both development and good administration, immediate initial work was authorised, and it was said that any proposals for improvement in quality of Colonial staff which were put forward with the overall aim of economic development would receive sympathetic examination.[145]

Further consideration in the Office led to the view that, politics apart, it would not be practicable, or reasonable, to cut the social services side of the Practical Plan in order to find some of the money needed for building roads.[146] So, broadly speaking, officials proposed the adoption of the Practical Plan together with a minimum road programme, involving an extra £450,000 for Dominica, which would come in part from additional borrowing (£190,000), and the rest from the Windward Island reserve (£20,000) and from the CD & W general reserve (£240,000).[147] The Parliamentary Under-Secretary, Mr Rees-Williams, disagreed, on the grounds that the islands were 'a bottomless pit. The inhabitants breed children at an enormous rate and expect the British taxpayer to keep them on a perpetual dole. In my view, if communications are as necessary to the Dominica economy as some of the minutes suggest, then this money should be obtained by recalling the original allocations in order to provide it, and not by a fresh grant.'[148] As there was a conflict in the Office, the Secretary of State, Mr Creech Jones, discussed the matter and, while appreciating the points made by his Under-Secretary, agreed with the plan formulated by officials, providing CDC agreed to become involved and neighbouring islands did not expect further allocations because of the Dominica solution. At the same time he realised it was something of a gamble.[149] As the Colony was grant-aided, the proposal had to be put to the Treasury, while the conditions made by the Secretary of State were put to the Governor,[150] who readily accepted them.[151]

At a meeting with CDC, the Chairman of the latter, Lord

Trefgarne, said that the Board had approved plans for citrus and orange plantations, a fruit packing shed, canning factory and hydro-electric scheme, all of which required roads.[152] The overall investment was of the order of £250,000. A long memorandum was then submitted to the CEDC setting out the whole position.[153] The Council after a full discussion approved the revised plan without significant revision.[154] Points raised included shipping facilities, teacher training, the development of forest industries, and the centralisation of hospital services. The Secretary of State's Adviser on Fisheries, Dr Hickling, proposed several fishery developments, which, it was agreed, should be mentioned to the Administrator in the Secretary of State's Despatch on the Plan.

The dissolution of CEDC necessitated a review of the procedures for dealing with development plans and revised plans submitted by Colonial Governments. The procedure as laid down in June 1951 placed the responsibility for directing action in the Office on the relevant geographical department, e.g. the West Indies Department.[155] Plans were automatically referred to other interested departments, e.g. Finance and Economic General, and to appropriate Advisers for their comments. The geographical department concerned prepared a memorandum in collaboration with the Economic General Department, which was considered by an Office meeting, usually chaired by Mr Gorell Barnes, which, in turn, approved submission to the CEDC under cover of a memorandum based on the discussion at the meeting. After the plan had been considered by CEDC, it was submitted to Ministers, with the comments of CEDC and a note of action proposed. Action rested with geographical departments, but the Economic General Department was responsible for reporting to CEDC, particularly if its advice had not been accepted. Following the dissolution of CEDC, it was decided that the Office meeting should be a more thoroughgoing affair, as the immediate purpose was to recommend a course of action to Ministers.[156]

v. FIFTH REPORT OF THE SELECT COMMITTEE ON ESTIMATES, SESSION 1947–1948

In a minute of July 1948, it was observed that the additional expenditure necessary to get Dominica and, probably, other grant-aided Colonies, out of the vicious circle of poverty was small and, in view of the Fifth Report from the Select Committee on Estimates, which had remarked on the underspending of CD & W money, the additional expenditure should be sympathetically considered.[157] Two points arise: the first is the nature of the Select Committee's findings and the departmental reply; and the second is the specific point of underspending. On the first, as both the Committee's report and the departmental reply were published[158] it is unnecessary to rehearse the views and comments made by either side. More profitably, some general comments might be offered, based in part on those made earlier by Sir Sydney Caine.[159]

The main general criticism voiced by the Committee, and the main general impression which was conveyed to the press and the public at large, related to the alleged lack of economic planning. The Committee made some sweeping general statements, but a careful reading of the Report shows that the Committee was confused as to what was meant by 'planning'. There were two unresolved inconsistencies. In the first place, it emphasised, at the same time, the importance both of consultation with local opinion and the necessity of close control from the centre. Secondly, it spoke in some places of a 'strategy' of economic planning, implying merely the laying down of certain general objectives, and in others of an allocation of resources, which it appeared from the context to conceive as something extraordinarily detailed and precise. Nowhere did it give any examples of the defects of strategy which were alleged to exist.

In the initial statement contained in the White Paper which preceded the 1940 Colonial Development and Welfare Act, three points are relevant here. First, the principle that the development envisaged was development for the good of the Colony itself; secondly, the emphasis on full local consultation; and thirdly, the insistence on the preparation of comprehensive long-term plans. The 1940 system was never tried in practice because the war intervened, but when the 1945 Act extended the amount and period of assistance to be provided, all these three principles were tacitly, or explicitly, confirmed. A valuable change introduced by the 1945 Act was the provision for elasticity in the expenditure of the funds provided.

The third stage in the growth of the idea of Colonial development was the emergence of the idea of integrated economic development of the Colonies and the United Kingdom as a dominating factor in development policy. This only emerged during the course of 1947 as a result of the realisation that the United Kingdom alone was going to have continued difficulty in balancing its overseas accounts, and that help could be obtained if Colonial production of certain scarce commodities could be developed sufficiently rapidly. It was only then that the need for a coherent policy of capital investment in the United Kingdom itself began to be felt at all widely, and it was therefore hardly surprising that the need for integration of capital investment between the United Kingdom and the very much smaller units of the Colonies had not previously been thought of as a necessity.

So far as Colonial Development and Welfare projects were concerned, the issue as to control from the centre was settled in 1945 by two decisions which were not decisions of any one Government, as they were taken provisionally by Mr Stanley and confirmed and implemented by his successor. They were, first, to divide up nearly the whole of the available funds in separate geographical allocations to individual territories, and secondly, to include, for purposes of long-term planning, the resources available from local revenues and borrowing power as well as the grants to be made by HMG under the Acts. As a result of this second decision, it had emerged that the contribution of HMG to the Colonial development programmes averaged no more than 33 per cent. Inevitably, the local authorities, who were putting up most of the money, would expect to have a large share of the control in determining on what it was to be spent. Consequently, the Secretary of State could, in the last resort, only influence, and not dictate, the form and content of the programmes.

Coming to the details of the actual long term plans drawn up, it was not surprising that the Select Committee had received no evidence to show that there was any strategy of economic planning behind them, because the Committee asked for no general information at all about these plans and the way they were compiled. There was in every case a very definite consideration of the possibilities of economic development of the territory concerned, and of what kinds of additional production it was desirable to aim at. They aimed at the improvement of existing industries; at the development of the background services – communications, health, education, etc. – which were essential for the growth of further industries; and at surveys and research as the foundation for longer-term development. These were undramatic objects, but no one who had seriously examined the issues was able to challenge the conclusion that they represented the best practical use of the resources available at the time. The Cabinet had, for instance, accepted the CDWP conclusion that the maintenance and development of existing industries should be the first charge on available materials.

The plans were, however, strategic in the proper sense. It was realised that circumstances were unlikely to permit the implementation of every individual project to a precisely laid down programme.

The 1945 Act included a far-sighted provision which allowed for elasticity in the spending of the money for this reason. A further decision in the strategic field was to establish the Colonial Development Corporation in 1948 to fill a gap which, it was thought, might otherwise have been left between the provision of general services by Government and the undertaking of individual productive enterprises by commercial concerns.

Turning from the strategic sphere to more detailed or tactical operations, it was again only during 1947–48 that the necessity for some closer control of, at least, certain kinds of capital goods had become apparent, and the machinery of planning in the United Kingdom itself had developed to the point where Colonial needs could adequately be taken into account in the allocation of such capital goods. By the creation of the Colonial Development Working Party in association with the Central Economic Planning Staff, by the various measures to strengthen the economic staff of the Colonial Office, and by the steps which were taken to secure specific allocations of individual classes of capital goods for Colonial needs, most of the practical measures which the Select Committee recommended had been initiated.

Sir Sydney Caine believed that

the Committee would have been perfectly satisfied if we had presented to them something like the Colonial section of the Monnet Plan, which the French had prepared. That is a grand and impressive statement of certain highly desirable objectives. It is, however, a gross misuse of language to call it a plan. It is simply a dream of what the authors would like to happen. We could have produced such a document easily enough if we had been prepared to devote ourselves to it instead of to other things, but I believe that to do so would have been both dishonest, and not merely futile, but positively mischievous, because it would have diverted energies from more practical activities. We have chosen the alternative course of taking a sober estimate of what resources we are really likely to have available, and have then set down what we think to be the best use we can make of those resources. Possibly our estimates of the resources available, small as they were, were even then not sufficiently sober, but to have set down a series of dreams of the French variety would merely have been to raise still further hopes, which would have been still more certainly doomed to disappointment. As tested by the practical results, I believe we can show that our method, which has been followed perhaps even more consistently by the Belgians, produces far better results than the French. At least, as a result of the policy actually pursued by His Majesty's Government in relation to Colonial matters, the Colonies today are yielding us a very large surplus of dollars, whereas the French Colonies are very heavily in deficit.

Secondly, it is a criticism of our planning in 1945 and immediately afterwards that it was too much in financial terms, that is, we were dividing out amongst the Colonies sums of money and not supplies of materials. I would admit that there was an underlying assumption at that time that availability of money would bear the same relationship to availability of goods as it used to do before the war. For reasons which are not pertinent to the present discussion but arising out of the condition of suppressed inflation in this country, that relationship has not, in fact, been fully re-established. In effect, it was the realisation of this new state of affairs which led His Majesty's Government on the wider plane, and us in the sphere of Colonial planning, to undertake the re-examination of arrangements for provision of material supplies which was started last autumn.[160]

Confirmation of this point of view was given in the Secretary of State's own comments on the memorandum circulated by the Chief of the Imperial General Staff, Field-Marshal Montgomery, following his tour of Africa. The memorandum was referred to earlier in Chapter 1 of this volume. Mr Creech Jones minuted as follows:

While I agree with the CIGS as to the importance of a quick and vigorous development of Africa as part of the Western world, I have the following comments on what he says:

(a) The imposition on the African Territories of a grand design, or master plan, by central control and direction from London would not be practical politics, and would conflict with our declared policy of devolution in the process of building up self-government, which is based on the experience of the history of the British Commonwealth. Such a course would not secure the co-operation of the local people, without which effective development cannot take place.

(b) We have a clear and well-understood general policy for political and economic development in Africa; in addition, all the African Territories have comprehensive ten-year programmes, and there are regional plans as well. These will be supplemented by the plans to be made under the Overseas Development Bill. The present problem is one of execution, not planning.[161]

VI. UNDERSPENDING, OVER-ALLOCATION AND THE ACTS OF 1949 AND 1950

In November 1946 it was necessary to decide on the amounts to be
included in the Estimates for 1947–48 in respect of (a) Research and
(b) Development.[162] In the case of (c), the decision was not difficult:
£600,000 was suggested, compared with an estimated expenditure of
£304,000 for 1946–47. In the case of (b), the estimate for 1946–47 was
£9,295,000, and already it was clear from the commitments up to 20
November 1946, of £5,427,849, that actual expenditure would fall
well below the estimate. Actual issues from the CD & W Vote during
the years ending 31 March were:

TABLE 2.2

Year	D & W	Research	Total
1945–46	£4,558,774	£ 93,306	£4,652,080
1946–47	£3,577,300	£169,388	£3,746,688
1947–48	£4,898,889	£427,389	£5,326,278

For political reasons, it was felt that the estimate for 1947–48 should
not be far below that for 1946–47 and a total of £8.5 million was
suggested to the Secretary of State. The latter agreed, but was
perturbed:

I wonder [he minuted] if Colonial Governments can tell us why they
have been slow in getting off the mark. Do some of them lack a sense
of urgency? I am all in favour of laying good foundations and
starting things well and not spending just for spectacular purposes.
But sometimes the excuse of staff and materials is too easy, and other
reasons exist. We shall get into serious political difficulties from all
sides of the House unless we can show an acceleration. When
estimates are published, we might give as suggested a comprehensive answer to an arranged Question.[163]

Some officials believed that exhortation would help, but the Secretary
of State was persuaded that drawing up plans, enlisting skilled staff,
and procuring materials, were the real causes of slowness.[164] He agreed
that the Treasury would be reluctant to see an acceleration of Colonial
expenditure, as it would increase the strain on our balance of payments
over the next two or three years.[165] He said that he would tell the
Chancellor that, as the Colonial Office was trying to avoid undue
embarrassment then, he should be generous later on.[166]

Sir David Serpell told the author on 25 November 1975 the background of those inter-departmental discussions. Speaking of the immediate post-war years, 1946–1948, when he was involved in CD & W matters, he said that, on the one hand, the Treasury was anxious to restore a financial control which had not been effective for most purposes for several years, while, on the other hand, the Colonial Office found itself responsible for the affairs of territories which had been affected in a strikingly different variety of ways by the war. As the chapter shows, neither Department was altogether certain of its 'touch'; neither was, or probably could be, altogether suitably staffed for the work they had to do together. On CD & W matters, the Departments, nevertheless, made an effort, which was perhaps unusual at the time, to 'get on with it' by holding regular meetings in the Colonial Office at which CD & W proposals were discussed and, as far as was possible, decided. Yet it was admitted that some of the issues taken up, particularly in the case of grant-aided territories, would seem to be rather trivial by today's standards.

To return to the concern with underspending, the matter was set aside until August 1948, when officials began to consider the formulation of a more positive policy. By that time, although expenditure on development was far below the maximum of £17.5 million allowed in any year by the Act, expenditure on research was near the maximum of £1 million, and there was a possibility that the ceiling might be reached by 1950.[167] It was agreed by officials that most Colonial Governments were still finding difficulty in spending their territorial allocations, partly owing to administrative inexperience in handling new and complicated projects, but mainly owing to the serious shortage of materials and manpower prevalent throughout the Empire.[168] It was felt that some means should be found to increase the rate of expenditure of CD & W funds, especially over the next few years. Obviously, the main object of attack should be the limitational factors – the supplies of men and materials – but, in addition, the stage had been reached by several Colonial Governments where their CD & W allocations, though still largely unspent, were fully earmarked for schemes, and so it was recommended that certain allocations should be made from the General Reserve of £9.5 million. Under the 1945 Act a Central Reserve of £3 million and a General Reserve of £14 million were established. By the end of 1948, the Central Reserve was committed to a total of £2.41 million (£2 million for Higher Education and £410,000 for the Teaching Hospital at the University College of the West Indies, Jamaica) but £9.5 million of the General Reserve remained available for allocation. The recommendations were, first, that £2.5 million should be earmarked for the Caribbean area, mainly in respect of the Evans Commission's recommendations regarding British Guiana and British Honduras. These involved the settlement of West Indians from the overpopulated islands to the two sparsely-populated mainland territories. At the meeting of CEDC on 21 July 1949, when the Council took note of the action being taken on the Report, Dr Rita Hinden recorded her disappointment at the slowness in acting on the recommendations. The Colonial Office blamed the natural limitations of the territories for failure to achieve spectacular results in the short period.[169] Included also were sums for rebuilding of Castries, St Lucia, and other items. Secondly, £1 million should be earmarked for North Borneo and Sarawak, which received meagre initial allocations though their needs were considerable. Thirdly, £1 million should be devoted to broadcasting. Fourthly, there would be £3 million for African territories, because 'African development is of fundamental impor- tance and the African case must not be allowed to go by default', although no specific schemes had been submitted. Fifthly, the remaining £2 million would be kept for unforeseen contingencies and for other territories.

However, as existing allocations were so largely unspent, it was recommended that Colonial Governments should be warned that if underspending were still evident in three years' time some part of the allocation might be diverted for general purposes, as required. Finally, it was recommended that an Office Committee be set up to watch CD & W expenditure, to consider any applications for the use of the Reserve and to make recommendations to Ministers as necessary.

The Parliamentary Under-Secretary, Mr Rees-Williams, was in general agreement, feeling, in particular, that Parliament should be asked to raise the research ceiling quite soon.[170] The Secretary of State felt that, largely on political grounds, it was necessary to give more help to the High Commission Territories. As a result of representations by the High Commissioner, who sought an allocation of some £6.5 million for the three Territories, the allocation was raised by £200,000 to a total of £2.5 million.[171] Also, Malaya posed a special problem. He directed that, until the research ceiling could be changed, commit- ments should be pruned of extravagant, purely abstract and theoreti- cal projects so that it was 'absolutely certain that the expenditure is realistic and profitable'. The five recommendations were agreed.[172]

The first three decisions were duly implemented. The decision as regards the Evans Commission's Report was announced in Parliament by the Secretary of State, and that regarding the Borneo territories was made public as part of the financial settlements with those territories. Plans were set on foot for the deployment of the sum of £1 million earmarked for broadcasting. As regards the fourth decision, which concerned tropical Africa, no immediate steps were required as it was intended that the decision should be a guide for future action, as necessary. Implementation of the other two decisions, namely the preparation of a Circular Despatch and the establishment of an official Office Committee, was held up owing to a change in the situation. As a result of a casual conversation with the officer in charge of CD & W work in the Nigerian Secretariat, it was realised that in Nigeria, and probably elsewhere, any proposal to recover part of the 1945 allocation would have a most unfortunate political effect.[173] It was considered that Nigeria's allocation, and all other allocations, had been announced in such a way that it amounted to a firm promise, whether or not it was carried out by 1956. It would be represented, not without a degree of plausibility, that the fault lay in the United Kingdom's failure to supply men and materials, and so it would be greatly resented if the United Kingdom then threatened to withdraw some of the funds promised. This was at a time when a sharp acceleration in the rate of spending of CD & W money, owing mainly to the improved supply position, became evident. The increased rate was reflected in the need to present a supplementary estimate of about £2 million on the CD & W Vote. While spending was not proceeding at the rate of £12 million – the average needed to use up the whole £120 million in ten years – and still less sufficient to make up for past arrears, the beginnings of an increased flow was clear. That there was such a sharp realisation of a change between late November 1948 and early February 1949 is not surprising once it is realised that in August 1948 it was possible for an official to minute as follows:[174]

> There are virtually no reliable statistics relating to schemes made under the CD & W Act. . . . It was agreed in February, 1947, that statistics should be compiled by Accounts Department. . . . I have discussed recently with Mr Bryant, and he tells me that he now has the staff and will shortly commence compiling statistics. In view, however, of the large backlog to be made good, he does not expect to have much useful information available before April next year. . . . The best information we have with regard to the growth in the rate of expenditure is contained in Appendix VIII to the annual return of schemes for 1947–48. This shows the actual issues, which are based on the quarterly telegrams giving revised estimates of expenditure on each scheme. . . . The Table shows a steady

growth of expenditure from 1940 to 1948 broken by a peak in 1945 followed by a dip in 1946. This peak and subsequent drop arises from the fact that most Colonies over-claimed in the first quarter of 1946, in an attempt to avoid expenditure on schemes then in progress being charged to their allocations which became effective from April 1, 1946.

Although it was realised in August 1948 that 'Expenditure in recent months has been going rather faster than was expected',[175] it was considered that the £15 million of underspending by 1956 which had been forecasted in November 1947, would still come about. It was only when the draft Despatch was being discussed with the Treasury[176] that the Colonial Office came to realise that the sharp acceleration of expenditure cast doubt on the likelihood of any substantial underspending over the following three years. The Treasury had independently come to the same conclusion, expecting a further rise in the rate of expenditure before long.[177] Consequently, the whole basis of the Despatch needed reconsideration.

Other developments caused further complications. Thus, at the time when the proposals were put to Ministers in November 1948, it was not realised that research expenditure during the ten years might substantially exceed the existing allocation of £7.5 million. The original allocation of £8.5 million had been reduced by £1 million when that sum had been transferred to the Geological Survey. It had been agreed in November 1948, that the ceiling would have to be raised. The Parliamentary Under-Secretary regarded it as only a question of timing, as all favoured a ceiling of £2.5 million. But the Secretary of State was not happy to see less available for economic and social expenditure in order to raise the ceiling for research, and he wished also to have further details of research allocations. A meeting was called, when it was agreed that, subject to Treasury approval, amendments should be proposed to the CD & W Act to raise the annual research ceiling to £2.5 million and the annual overall ceiling to £20 million.[178] The Treasury readily agreed to both ceilings being raised.[179] It was at the same time agreed that details of existing research schemes and major projected schemes would be laid before the Colonial Research Council.

The CD & W Bill, 1949, which raised both ceilings but did not make any other change in the CD & W Act, 1945, received its formal First Reading on 18 May 1949. The 1945 Act stipulated that no scheme, not being a scheme for promoting research or enquiry, should continue in force after 31 March 1956. It was envisaged at the time when the Act was passed that expenditure on research, up to the prescribed annual limit, might continue after that date. The implications of raising the prescribed limit to £2.5 million were recognised when the limit was raised.[180] The Bill was non-controversial, the main Opposition speaker, Mr Alan Lennex-Boyd, saying: 'We welcome the Bill: we have no quarrel with it at all, and we shall do our best to facilitate its quick passage through the House.' He continued: 'Many of us disliked the annual limitation of the amount of money that would be spent on research and development and we are very glad to see those sums increased. Personally, I am a little in doubt as to why it is still necessary to have an annual ceiling. It is extremely difficult to budget these things over a calendar year with any accuracy and, when the Government are taking a step to amend the previous limitation, I am sorry they have not gone the whole way and abolished the annual ceiling altogether'.[181] The Bill received the Royal Assent on 30 July 1949, as the CD & W Act, 1949 (12 and 13 Geo. 6, Ch. 49).

Meanwhile, in a memorandum of 25 May 1949 on the policy to be pursued in making use of funds provided under the CD & W Acts, it was shown that there would be the need before the end of the ten-year period for an additional allocation of some £6 million to £8 million for research schemes.[182] At the same time, it had become apparent that the allocation of £1 million for 'other Central Schemes', as well as the reserve for Central Schemes amounting to £3 million, were likely to be overspent by 1956.[183] In order to discuss the implications of these and other forecasts, it was decided to convene the official Office Committee, as agreed by the Secretary of State in November 1948. It became known not by its formal title of the 'CD & W Committee' but rather as the 'Lloyd Committee', as the Permanent Under-Secretary was prevailed upon to take the chair.[184] At the first meeting, on 27 June 1949, there was a total of fourteen Colonial Office officials, with one official from the Treasury and one from the CRO. The memorandum of 25 May 1949 became the first paper of the new Committee.[185] It was agreed to recommend to Ministers that two of the decisions of November 1948 be abandoned, namely the proposals to send a Circular Despatch and to inform Governors in Africa that £3 million was earmarked for further projects.[186] As funds were committed rather than spent, it was thought premature to talk in terms of a new Act, and so it was agreed that a paper should be prepared for submission to Ministers setting out the arguments in favour of an over-allocation of a specific sum, say 10 per cent in excess of the £120 million, based partly on the extra requirements of research. If such over-allocation was agreed by Ministers, it was proposed that extra allocations might be made to Research and to Central Schemes. However, on further reflection, it was realised that over-allocation which led to overspending was based on a presumption that Parliament would provide further funds. Reluctantly, it was realised that such action was constitutionally improper and, therefore, it was necessary for Parliament to be asked in the immediate future for further funds.[187] At a meeting of officials on 19 July 1949 it was agreed that there was much force in this objection to over-allocation, and that the position should be reported to Ministers, along with an indication of the alternative courses of action which appeared to be available.

Only about £25 million of the whole £120 million voted in the Act had been spent. Yet, after allowing for all announced commitments and for the agreed, but not announced, additional allocation of £3 million for Africa, the maximum available balance of CD & W money was £1.35 million and already there were some claims on that, e.g. £250,000 for the High Commission Territories. The real crux of the matter was research expenditure because balances were so small, a fact which had not been realised at the time of the meeting with Ministers on 10 March 1949.[188] However, the Parliamentary Under-Secretary thought the predicament 'must have been foreseen when it was decided to have ten-year plans, and deprecated any approach to Parliament for a few years.[189] The Secretary of State, while prepared to discuss, doubted whether application to Parliament was available and, with other detailed points, said: 'Surely it is time we got some lines of policy on research.'[190] It was concluded, when the Secretary of State discussed the issues with officials[191] that (i) in order to restore flexibility to our management of CD & W expenditure, it was desirable to be able to plan on the assumption that the CD & W Act would be extended, and the funds made available would be correspondingly increased; (ii) there was no question of introducing further legislation on that subject during the lifetime of the existing Parliament; (iii) meanwhile the Secretary of State should seek the agreement of his colleagues, and, if they agreed, of the Opposition leaders, to the introduction of the necessary legislation early in the next Parliament; (iv) as Ministers were either away or engaged in preparations for talks in Washington and as the emphasis was on economy in Government expenditure, it was better to postpone for at least two months a decision on the main issue. A circular telegram had been sent on 4 July 1949 to all Colonial Governments to explain the nature of the dollar crisis, to inform them of the arrangements being made to discuss the problem with Commonwealth Finance Ministers, and to ask for the suspension, as in the United Kingdom, of the issue of licences for imports from the dollar area, except in those cases where seriously adverse effects would follow.[192] On Sunday 18 September 1949 the Chancellor of the Exchequer, Sir Stafford Cripps, announced the devaluation by 30 per cent of the exchange value of sterling. This affected Colonies favourably or adversely, largely according to whether they were exporters to, or importers from, the dollar area: in the first category were Malaya and West Africa, particularly the Gold Coast, while in the second were the West Indian territories, most acutely British Honduras.[193]

Meanwhile officials considered the future form of assistance in preparation for a submission to Ministers.[194] It was agreed that, in any approach to the Treasury, it should be made clear that more emphasis was to be placed on economic development than had been the case. It was felt that, while this would assist in securing acceptance of the proposals put to the Treasury, it was justified in itself. For, while United Kingdom assistance towards social services would not be excluded, it was sound policy for Colonial Governments to pay for as large a share of that as possible from their own resources, leaving United Kingdom assistance to finance economic schemes which would enable Colonies to carry the burden of social services on their own. Concerning a proposal to bring the grant-in-aid system, whereby the Treasury provided funds to finance a minimum of local administrative services where local budgets were inadequate, under the umbrella of the CD & W Acts, which provided, without Treasury control, grants for specific purposes, there were considerable doubts expressed. Some felt it would reduce the funds available for specific purposes if, for example, general support had to be provided for an economy in recession, while others felt it would inevitably blur the greater emphasis it was hoped to give to economic development under CD & W if minimal services had to be supported from the same source. It was agreed that it had been necessary, on the occasion of the 1945 Act, to allocate the greater part of the sums available in order to secure the co-operation of Colonial Governments in using their own funds for development. However, that end having been achieved, in future, if only to avoid a repetition of the existing difficulties due to over-allocation, it was agreed that a smaller proportion should be allocated and there should be no hurry even to do that. Sir Thomas Lloyd said that he hoped that the Secretary of State would be prepared to approach his colleagues and the Opposition leaders, in order to secure agreement to the principle of five-yearly renewals of the CD & W legislation, leaving open whether or not further consideration was necessary before a figure was proposed. Both the Parliamentary

Under-Secretary and the Secretary of State rejected this advice. As a poor second-best, the Secretary of State might, he thought, seek agreement to the solution of the immediate difficulties by prolongation of the existing Act by a year, with a correspondingly increased provision, i.e. a further £12 million, being one-tenth of £120 million.

Following discussions with officials, the Secretary of State wrote to the Chancellor of the Exchequer on 19 November 1949,[195] explaining that the Colonial Office was in serious straits about the provision of money for research in connection with CD & W and that, if no further funds were forthcoming, the whole research programme would have to stop by about the end of 1950. The Secretary of State proposed that the Chancellor should agree in principle to his seeking legislation in the summer of 1950 for a further £12 million to extend the CD & W programme to 1956. At the time, officials at the Treasury were under instructions to explore with the Colonial Office the possibility of cutting down expenditure out of the existing £120 million, so the chances of getting a favourable wind for a further £12 million additional expenditure, which would probably all be used up before 1956, seemed slender.[196] However, it was admitted that to have only £2.5 million left, out of which to initiate new research and survey schemes between then and 1956, was a very unsatisfactory position for the Secretary of State.[197] The Colonial Office had convinced the Treasury that, in the absence of early indication that more money would be available, sanction would have to be refused for some highly desirable schemes and some existing schemes might have to be curtailed. In all the circumstances, the Chancellor was advised to give the assurance requested, the amount of money being left for later decision.[198] The Chancellor approved. The first beneficiary of the assurance were the High Commission Territories, which received a supplementary allocation of £250,000. There was, apart from exceptional backwardness, 'compelling political reasons for pressing on actively with their development', because the question of the transfer of the territories to the Union of South Africa had again become a very live and immediate issue, and the Secretary of State for Commonwealth Relations felt that 'in dealing with Dr Malan's request it is imperative, if we are to avoid grave and incalculable consequences, that we should have every possible shot in our locker'.[199]

In his letter of 19 November 1949 to the Chancellor, the Secretary of State, besides seeking a way out of the existing impasse, outlined proposals for new CD & W legislation to extend the 1945 Act by five years and considerably increase the financial provision over that period, subject to greater emphasis being placed on economic development than had been customary. Within the Treasury, it was thought useful to consider, particularly given the difficult economic situation, whether it was desirable to continue a system under which direct United Kingdom Government aid for Colonial development was settled for ten years ahead.[200] Despite changes in emphasis by the Colonial Office towards economic development and towards fuller development of the natural resources of the Colonies for the benefit of the sterling area, it was not thought to be timely to commit resources in ten-year programmes of Colonial development, for such commitments did not conform with the plan to concentrate on the first essential object of viability by 1952.[201]

The new Secretary of State, Mr James Griffiths, wished to extend the 1945 Act from 1956 to 1961 and have a further £100 million for the purpose.[202] The Chancellor felt that it was sufficient to deal with the immediate problem and, although the minimum assessed requirement was only £4.75 million, he offered £10 million, and promised to consider later, as a separate issue, what further provision would be justified for the period beginning April 1956.[203] It was felt in the Colonial Office that it was necessary to accept the more limited horizon until it was known how we emerged from Marshall Aid, but it was not felt that the Chancellor's offer of £10 million was adequate. The Secretary of State wrote to the Chancellor, pointing out that the £4.75 million mentioned merely covered the minimum forseen requirement in the specific fields of research and survey, which represented a fraction of the field.[204] An increase to £20 million was requested, largely because of the decreased purchasing power of sterling and the valuable dollar returns that would be obtained from increased investment in the Colonies. According to an early official Treasury view: 'The most significant thing about the Colonial Office's approach is that it is based entirely on the needs of the Colonies, and hardly at all on what either the Colonies or the United Kingdom could afford to spend.'[205] Meantime, the Lord President wrote to say that there was no chance of getting a CD & W Bill through before the summer recess, but a place would be reserved for a short Bill in the 1950-51 Session.[206] When the question of the new CD & W legislation was taken up between officials of the Treasury and the Colonial Office,[207] it was agreed that it would be wiser to postpone a final decision on the amount of the additional money that might be made available, above the £10 million already promised, until the United Kingdom's contribution to Colonies in South-East Asia, following the Conference at Sydney, was known. The Secretary of State accepted that view, providing legislation could be introduced in the following

Session, and that meantime urgent allocations could be made in the assurance that at least £10 million would be forthcoming.[208] The Chancellor agreed,[209] and the Lord President asked the Secretary of State to circulate a paper to the Economic Policy Committee so that policy approval might be obtained.[210] The memorandum stated how the need for funds had arisen and left the actual sum, somewhere between £20 million at most and £10 million at least, undecided.[211] In a brief for the Secretary of State,[212] it was emphasised that one of the main purposes to which the additional funds would be put was for the continuation up to 1956 of essential work in the fields of (a) economic research, (b) geodetic and topographical surveys, and (c) geological surveys. About £5 million, in addition to what was already available, was necessary to keep such work going on the scale in mind. One of the other principal purposes for which money was required was for agricultural development, particularly in Africa and the West Indies. There was the need both for basic services, such as roads, before commerical development was possible, and also to improve methods of farming by, for example, experiments in group peasant farming under central management. Officials assured the Chancellor that the additional money would be sparingly used on only the most urgent and important projects for economic development, and that 'welfare' would continue to be financed from existing allocations.[213] The proposals were endorsed by the Economic Policy Committee.[214] The Colonial Office, which was anxious to justify a total of £20 million, excluding £1,500,000 for Malta,[215] was warned that, in view of the rearmament programme, the Treasury would be tight over any further CD & W provision, while it was felt in the Treasury that, short of a major crisis, it was not worth while trying for £15 million. So the Colonial Office was asked to make do with £20 million, and told there would be no objection to raising the overall annual limit from £20 million to £25 million but the limit for research should be kept at £2.5 million.[216] The Minister of State, Mr John Dugdale, approved, believing that 'we already spend quite enough on research'.[217] When he sought the endorsement of the settlement by the Minister of State for Economic Affairs, Mr H. Gaitskell, Sir James Crombie stated: 'In view of the large number of meritorious projects in the Colonies on which money might usefully be spent, I think the Colonial Office have been very accommodating in agreeing to accept a figure of £20 million.'[218] The Minister agreed, asking that it should be ascertained that the sum was not too small in relation to commitments in South East Asia.[219]

Two further changes were referred to in the Schedule to the CD &

W Bill as drafted in September 1950.[220] One was the proposal to delete the words in the 1940 Act, which remained in the amending Acts of 1945 and 1949, limiting the Colonies eligible for CD & W assistance to those 'not possessing responsible government'. The reason for the change was stated at the time[221] to be that some Colonies that were receiving CD & W assistance, as for example the Gold Coast, might before 1961 attain a form of government which could be held to be 'responsible' and yet the Secretary of State might still justifiably wish to continue to grant the Colony concerned CD & W assistance for a further period, depending on circumstances. It was proposed to delete the reference to Colonies 'not possessing responsible government', although the Secretary of State would not thereby become obliged to make schemes for the benefit of all Colonies. Under the proposed new wording, he could continue to withhold CD & W assistance from, for example, Southern Rhodesia, and either continue or cease, as circumstances warranted, to make grants to Colonies attaining a large measure of independence. The second change concerned Malta. By the Malta (Reconstruction) Act, 1947, which gave Malta responsible government, it was specifically provided in Section 3 that Malta would nevertheless remain eligible for CD & W assistance, which the territory was still receiving. With the proposed revised wording of the CD & W Bill, that provision became unnecessary.

The Bill received its Second Reading in the House of Commons on 9 November 1950,[222] and was read a Third time on 16 November without amendment. It received the Royal Assent on 15 December as the CD & W Act, 1950 (14 and 15 Geo. 6 Ch. 4) and came into force on 1 April 1951.

The Secretary of State decided that the new money, together with the sum of approximately £1.5 million remaining in the existing reserve, should be divided as in Table 2.3.[223]

Only the first four allocations were firm: the rest did not represent public commitments, and were extended for general planning purposes within the Office. It was not intended to divulge either (6) or (7), while in the case of (5) it was to be included in the Commonwealth plans for the area as a whole, which were expected to be announced shortly. The purposes to which the new money was to be devoted were described by the Secretary of State in a circular telegram of 19 October 1950 to all Colonies, thus:[224]

In considering the types of need which, in present circumstances, can qualify for financial assistance under the Act, I have decided that priority should be given to basic services, primarily economic,

TABLE 2.3 Allocation of Existing Reserve and of New Funds under the C & W Act, 1950 (£ million)

(1)	Research – final allocation to 31 March 1956	5.5
(2)	Malta – announced in Parliament	1.5
(3)	Geodetic and Topographical Survey	1.25
(4)	Geological Survey	0.75
(5)	SE Asia – provisional earmarking for 'Spender' Plan	2.5
(6)	Area reserve for African territories – excluding High Commission territories	4.0
(7)	Area reserve for non-African territories and High Commission Territories	3.0
(8)	General reserve	3.0
	Total	£21.5

which, though not necessarily remunerative in themselves, are essential as a foundation for further economic development. No hard and fast distinction can of course be drawn between economic and non-economic services: provision of adequate social services, besides being most important in itself, is essential for economic well-being in the long run, and some of these services, such as technical education, will be of great service to economic progress in the immediate future. No rigid attitude in this matter is therefore possible. Nevertheless, I am convinced that the best use to which the further limited funds can be put is in assisting Colonial Governments to strengthen their revenue, in order that they may be able to carry the burden of their own social services in the continuing future. The problem of mounting recurrent commitments is one of the most serious problems arising from the implementation of development plans. I am appreciative of the efforts which Colonial Governments are making to meet this problem, and one of the main objects of my control of these further funds will be to help in this difficult task, where help is most needed. It follows from this that I should find it very difficult to justify giving any further assistance to those Colonial territories whose revenues are buoyant and are likely to remain so in the foreseeable future.

The Permanent Under-Secretary of State felt it necessary to warn Governors that, although Ministers were due to consider whether further provisions might be proposed for a period after 1956 and also the possibilities of an overlap with the existing Act, it was unlikely that there would be a decision before 1954.[225] He counselled Governors to proceed on the basis that no further CD & W money would be provided after March 1956, and that the money voted under the existing Act, together with the £20 million under the new Bill, would be the limit available for all purposes of Colonial development up to 31 March 1956. One Governor enquired whether any unspent balance in 1956 could be carried forward, as otherwise he would wish to put the whole allocation into educational buildings and irrigation works programmes.[226] While the future was officially shrouded in mystery and anything said was in the nature of guesswork, it was felt that 'the United Kingdom would have to be reduced to a very low ebb indeed before HMG would contemplate a cessation of the present policy of financial assistance towards Colonial development' as from the end of 1956.[227] Even if there were a cessation, the unspent balances would almost certainly be allowed, he thought, to be spent in later years. But if a new Act carried on the policy, there was no clear-cut answer to the Governor's question: if the CD & W allocation was used without a reasonable local contribution, there would be criticisms from London, while, providing there was such a contribution, further proposals would receive a sympathetic hearing.

VII. PRIVATE INVESTMENT IN THE COLONIES AND MARSHALL AID

(a) United States Private Investment

The Fifth Report of the Select Committee on Estimates acknowledged the leading part which commercial enterprise had played in the economic development of the Colonies, noting: 'it is the declared policy of the Colonial Office to encourage private enterprise, but private enterprise cannot play its proper part in development so long as the belief exists among the Colonial peoples that it is unfairly exploiting them.'[228] In the present context, it is appropriate to deal with this aspect in relation to private investment in the Colonies and the receipt of Marshall Aid under the European Recovery Programme of the United States.

As stated in the earlier section on Colonial Loans, during the first half of 1948 the Colonial Office held informal conversations with officials of the International Bank for Reconstruction and Development (IBRD), concerning the possibility of securing loans for Colonial development projects.[229] The Bank was interested in making loans for projects which were, either directly or indirectly, productive. Loans would be available only to meet expenditure on equipment from the

United States, and would be for up to thirty years; and the rate of interest, including the Bank's commission charge, would be $4\frac{1}{2}$ per cent. On consulting OFC, CDC, and Colonial Governments, it was found that, on the whole, they were not very interested in borrowing at $4\frac{1}{2}$ per cent when, if they were allowed to borrow on the London market, it would cost 3 to $3\frac{1}{4}$ per cent. Also, deliveries of capital equipment to the Colonies, available both in the United States and the United Kingdom, were just as slow, and sometimes slower, from the United States than from the United Kingdom.

In order to give the Treasury authority to guarantee loans made to Colonial Governments by the IBRD, which was required as Colonies were not eligible for separate membership of IBRD, it was necessary to introduce a Colonial Loans Bill. This was non-controversial and quickly enacted.[230] No decision had been taken as to whether IBRD loans should be sought, as that was dependent on the Colonies which acceded to the European Recovery Programme being assigned a share of Marshall aid. While the terms of ERP aid were not known precisely in July 1948, a rate of 3 per cent had been mentioned, which would make loan aid much more attractive than Bank loans. The Treasury had decided meanwhile that the United Kingdom might require all the ERP loan aid available, and that any Colonial capital require- ments should be met from borrowing from the Bank. The reason was that, while Colonies could, in principle, borrow from the Bank, the United Kingdom was unlikely to be considered eligible. In that event, it was clearly necessary to equalise the terms on which Bank loans were available to Colonial Governments with those on which ERP loans were available, by HMG paying the difference, otherwise the refusal to allow those Colonies which acceded to the ERP Agreement to share in ERP loans could not be justified. Even so, there might still, it was feared, be misrepresentation in the United States of the position as simply a selfish refusal by the United Kingdom to let participating Colonies share in the benefits of ERP.[231]

In view of the difficulties and uncertainties about ERP loan aid, it was thought better for the Secretary of State to say very little on the subject in his speech on the Colonial Office Estimates in the House of Commons. In the event, no statement was made, because the Secretary of State was unhappy about its terms, which, he felt,

seem to express the problem of foreign investment in Colonial territories in a way that will arouse resentment by the Colonial peoples and imply an almost completely *laissez-faire* economy of the Victorian sort. Big foreign shareholding in mining, manufacturing, and commercial enterprise involves a degree of economic control from external sources which increasingly disturbs the political movements in the Colonies. It implies a degree of dominance in social and economic policy, as well as a drawing of wealth from the territory to alien areas – factors which inflame local feeling and, in the case of peoples less economically and socially developed, may involve a check on their own fumblings in economic activities and growth. Certain conditions need to be fulfilled if we wish to avoid the creation of the kind of 'finance Colonies', which some of the Central American states have become. I understand that some of the American states have tried to modify their financial dependence by insisting on conditions governing the proportion of local labour employed, and conditions under which enterprise should be carried on in terms of labour conditions and welfare provisions. Moreover, it is not enough to guarantee for the territory a revenue by royalties and taxation – these powerful financial and economic interests can exercise an influence on the Colonial Government which is reflected in political and social policy as well as economic development.[232]

The Secretary of State concluded cautiously as follows:

While I feel that we may, in certain circumstances, be required to encourage foreign capital into our territories and to recognise the principle of non-discrimination, we ought to have regard as to whether there are no other ready British sources of such capital, to try to get what materials and capital goods are essential from Great Britain, to make clear that the investment will not be permitted to enjoy excessive interest rates or profits, to insist that it should fit into the economic pattern of development of the territory, and satisfy the long-term social development of the people and territory. It must also take its place in the economic life of the territory in respect of its claim on resources of labour, steel, machinery, transport and necessary materials.

While the Secretary of State appeared to fear a rush of American investment, the Economic Secretary to the Treasury, Mr Douglas Jay, who had consulted the Parliamentary Under-Secretary of State for the Colonies,[233] did not expect to see a great deal of American private investment, though he welcomed any that took place 'as enabling us to press forward with our already ambitious plans for development and for the resulting improvement in the welfare of the people'.[234] Pressures for a public statement on the attitude of HMG to the investment of external private capital in the Colonies had been growing. In its Interim Report, the Colonial Development Working Party had recommended that a statement should be made 'calling attention to the fact that the United Kingdom Government is favourably disposed towards external private investment on reasonable terms'.[235] When he communicated the substance of the Interim Report to Colonial Governments, the Secretary of State had stated that he was 'fully aware that in many Colonial territories' the investment of private loan and equity capital from foreign and Dominion sources was 'a matter of considerable political delicacy'; and he assured Colonial Governments that, in any public announcement, he would 'make it clear that this is a matter in which HMG in the United Kingdom can only provide guidance to Colonial Governments, with whom the ultimate decision in any particular case must rest'.[236] He promised also to state that, whilst no special obstacles should be placed in the way of foreign investment just because it was foreign, equally no special privileges should be extended which would not be extended to British private capital.

In the United States Economic Co-operation Administration's (ECA) Mission Report on the United Kingdom, 1949/50, and Long-Term Programme, it was stated that the programme should, in its view, have included a statement of the conditions on which foreign capital might invest in Colonial areas in order to expedite development programmes.[237] Somewhat more cautiously, the Interim Report of the Overseas Territories Working Group in Paris expressed the hope that the participating countries of the Organisation for European Economic Co-operation (OEEC) would be able to solve 'some, at least, of the exchange and supply problems which at present impede the flow of real capital resources to many of the Overseas Territories'.[238] These sentiments reflected, at least in part, a general campaign which the United States Administration was working out in 1948, to get reluctant American capital interested in overseas investment.[239] The State Department had for the same reason sought in May 1948 to know HMG's attitude to the investment of American capital in the Colonies.[240] As the result of a discussion, the views of HMG were given to the State Department.[241] The agreed memorandum said that HMG considered that

foreign capital would be useful and desirable, provided it were invested in productive, long-term enterprises whose operations would be of economic benefit to the Colonial territories and to the sterling area, provided the foreign investors did not expect guarantees of profits and provided it was understood that the enterprises would be subject to the same laws and regulations respecting the welfare of the inhabitants, and so on, as are public and private United Kingdom and Colonial enterprises in British Colonial territories.[242]

On 20 August 1948 a representative of the Chamber of Commerce of the United States enquired at the British Embassy concerning the attitude of HMG towards possible dollar investment in enterprises in British Colonies, especially in Africa.[243] The enquiry was prompted by the authorisation, under section IIIb of the Economic Co-operation Act, 1948, whereby the Administrator could take certain steps 'in order to facilitate and maximise the use of private channels of trade' in furnishing assistance to European countries and, in particular, he was empowered to guarantee, up to an amount of £300 million, investments in connection with approved projects. It was understood that ECA could guarantee such investments against inconvertibility of foreign currency into United States dollars, but not against business losses.

It was decided to provide, in reply, a fuller account of HMG's attitude towards American investment in the Colonies than had been given in May to the United States Embassy. A draft Despatch was prepared in the Colonial Office and sent by the Foreign Office with the concurrence of the Treasury.[244] After replying in turn to the seven questions asked, the Ambassador was requested to impress once more on the United States Authorities 'the extent to which political and financial control in the British Colonial Empire is already devolved upon the Colonial Governments themselves'. It went on to elaborate thus:

These Governments are not mere executive machines: they have their own Legislatures, sometimes with wholly elected Assemblies, as in Jamaica and elsewhere, and very often with elected unofficial majorities. While HMG in the United Kingdom can lay down the broad lines of general policy, the application of that policy in particular territories is the primary responsibility of the Colonial Government itself, and there are both political and constitutional limitations to the extent to which HMG would be willing, or able, to enforce it against local popular opinion, if that should prove in any particular case to be adverse.

The Chamber of Commerce of the United States enquired further of the Embassy in Washington as it was hoped to produce a pamphlet for the benefit of members of the Chamber on the possibilities of investment in Africa.[245] In the course of the reply, it was stated that United States investment would be particularly welcomed in those cases where the sponsoring United States companies had special technical knowledge, or equipment, or could secure access to supplies of capital goods required which would not otherwise be available in connection with development in British Colonies.[246] Reference was made to American companies which had recently been given facilities for prospecting, e.g. the Bethlehem Steel Corporation for prospecting iron ore in certain parts of Nigeria, and the Anaconda Corporation for prospecting gold in British Guiana. Interest in the subject was also shown by officials of the United States Government in connection with the implementation of Article V2 of the Economic Co-operation Agreement of 6 July 1948. By Article V2(b), the right of access of American citizens, or corporations, in the development of materials required by the United States, because of deficiencies, or potential deficiencies, in its own resources, was to be on terms equivalent to those received by nationals of the United Kingdom or of the acceding Colonies. The commitment to permit American undertakings to operate on equal terms with local concerns was confirmed in December 1948.[247] No discrimination was being practised at the time against any United States concerns.

Given the marked interest, official and otherwise, in the possibilities of foreign private investment in the Colonies, it was thought in the Colonial Office that a comprehensive memorandum on the whole subject would be worth preparing. The Secretary of State, Mr Creech Jones,[248] regarded such a statement as opportune in view of the discussions arising from President Truman's Inaugural Address of 20 January 1949, in which he declared as his Fourth Point: 'We must embark on a bold new program for making the benefits of our scientific advances and industrial progress available for the improvement and growth of underdeveloped areas.' Subsequently, President Truman sent a message to Congress asking for 45 million dollars as a first year's appropriation for technical assistance to underdeveloped countries, to be given partly under bilateral arrangements and partly through the United Nations programme of technical assistance. In the Secret Circular Despatch to all Colonies of 17 February 1949[249] events since the previous Despatch of 19 July 1948 were recounted, and the observations of Governors were invited on a draft note on capital investment by foreign private enterprise in British Colonial Dependencies.[250] The note stated that many foreign concerns already operated in various Colonies, that there was no discrimination against them and that there was no intention of introducing discrimination. It was confirmed that the operation of State-sponsored corporations, such as CDC and OFC, was not intended to exclude private enterprise. Any concern contemplating investment in particular Colonies was advised to familiarise itself with relevant local legislation and regulations affecting commercial activities, and warned that the marketing of certain Colonial products might be subject to various controls and, in some cases, exports of certain commodities were channelled through producers' organisations. Foreign exchange was said normally to be made available for the remittance of dividends, interest, and similar payments, though not for the repatriation of capital which had been invested in a Colony for less than ten years.

Thus the draft clearly described the existing situation as regards foreign investment. It was intended for the information of foreign Governments and potential foreign investors. The CEDC recommended that it should be given early publicity, and the Secretary of State proposed to make it available first to Parliament, in reply to an arranged written Question.[251] However, the Chancellor of the Exchequer, Sir Stafford Cripps, felt it should be approved by the Economic Policy Committee, saying at the same time he was not altogether happy about its form 'as it seems rather to overdo the Private Enterprise aspect and to neglect the Planning aspect'.[252] The proposed statement was circulated without any basic change. In the covering note, the Secretary of State explained the need for such a statement, a need that had been reinforced by the enunciation of President Truman's 'Fourth Point' with its emphasis on the role to be played by American private capital in the assistance given by America in developing the underdeveloped areas of the world.[253] In the words of the covering note, and with the qualifying clause underlined in the original

> The keynote of the statement is, therefore, that the United Kingdom and Colonial Governments welcome private investment, whether British or foreign, provided it is in harmony with the Colonies' Plans of social and economic development and is devoted to productive long-term purposes for economic benefit to the Colonies and the sterling area; provided also that the investors conform to the local laws and regulations governing commercial undertakings, particularly as they affect the welfare of the Colonial peoples.

Traditionally, policy had been of the 'open door' variety, enabling foreign enterprise to participate on equal terms with British private enterprise. The draft note described current practice as agreed with Colonial Governments. Only someone opposed to private enterprise as such could seriously fault enterprises which fulfilled the stated conditions. But the appropriateness of such a statement at that time was another matter. The Minister of State at the Foreign Office, Mr Hector McNeil, raised the point in reference to the discussions on the long-term relationship between sterling and the dollar due to take place in September 1949, when the long-term need for an expansion of American investment overseas would be an important aspect.[254] The Lord President of the Council, Mr Herbert Morrison, in a minute of 20 June 1949 to the Prime Minister suggested that HMG should be deeply interested in attracting United States investment for purposes of Colonial development. The Chancellor of the Exchequer agreed, pointing out that such investment should earn dollars, save dollars, or improve the general economic position of the Colonies involved, and so contribute to the solution of the dollar problem.[255] A great influx of American private investment was not expected, as the scope for such investment was said to be conditioned by the state of basic services, such as communications, power, housing and health. It was in these fields that the Treasury saw the greatest need for foreign investment.

The Cabinet considered the Secretary of State's memorandum together with one prepared by the Treasury on the encouragement of United States private investment in the United Kingdom and the Colonies.[256] The Treasury's memorandum recommended no change in exchange control policy to facilitate United States investors borrowing freely in sterling or repatriating their capital within ten years. In this, and other, respects the two memoranda were in agreement; further consultation between the Departments concerned was suggested by the Cabinet, which agreed to defer any further public statement on investment of foreign capital in the Colonies until the financial discussions due to take place in Washington in September were concluded.[257]

The major result of the tripartite talks between the United States, the United Kingdom and Canada was, in this area, to re-emphasise the importance of encouraging foreign private investment, particularly from North America, in the Colonies.[258] An official Working Group on Overseas Investment was formed for 'continuing joint study' in Washington. The Commonwealth Working Party on Development – the official title of the Washington Group – consisted of representatives of Australia, Canada, Ceylon, India, New Zealand and South Africa under United Kingdom chairmanship. In order to provide a basis, the whole problem of encouraging United States investment was examined by an Inter-departmental Committee under Treasury chairmanship, with representatives of the Foreign Office, the Colonial Office, the Board of Trade, the Commonwealth Relations Office, the Central Economic Planning Staff and the Bank of England. The Committee reported in January 1950.

Before dealing with its report, some other views that had meantime been expressed might be noted. The Colonial Office view that it was all the more necessary to press ahead with basic development was confirmed by the Chairman of CDC, Lord Trefgarne, who stated that: 'The provision of better roads, health and education services, power supplies, etc., will not only have the effect of relieving new enterprises of considerable expenditure which is strictly non-productive, but will also reduce some of the obvious risks of investment and so encourage private investment.'[259] However, at the Governors' Conference in the West Indies in November 1949, relaxation of the ten-year rule for repatriating capital was considered to be a firm requirement.[260] The Minister of State for Colonial Affairs, Lord Listowel, also regarded this as 'the essential point'.[261] Yet a visiting businessman reported that, while there were some misgivings over the rule, they were not as pronounced as he had been led to expect, partly because of the guarantee which, in certain circumstances, the Administrator of ECA was empowered to give, and partly by the Economic Co-operation Agreement of June 1949, which applied to British Colonies.[262]

The main recommendations of the Inter-departmental Committee were as follows:[263]

(a) The existing selective policy towards United States investment should be maintained, and should be based on the criteria of dollar saving or dollar earning, or increased productivity, having due regard to balance of payments considerations.

(b) It might in certain circumstances be desirable to borrow for more general purposes which did not satisfy the criteria. If the dollars so required were used to strengthen the reserves, they would help the immediate balance of payments difficulties. But a great deal would depend on the terms on which such borrowing was made. Departments should continue to interpret the criteria flexibly.

(c) There would be no basic change in the policy of minimising orders of capital goods from dollar sources, although there might be individual projects where a switch to dollar sources would be advantageous and that policy should be applied flexibly in the United Kingdom and the Colonies. The provision of United States

capital for India and Pakistan should be encouraged by all possible
means.

(*d*) The proceeds of nationalisation, etc., which were then blocked
should remain blocked. (In the case of future investment, the right
to repatriate would remove the fear of similar blocking.)

(*e*) The existing system of examining and approving proposed
American investments should be simplified and accelerated, and
Colonial Governments should be invited to take similar action.

(*f*) A full statement – giving as favourable an account of our policy
towards United States investment as possible – should be made by
the Chancellor of the Exchequer in the House of Commons. A
parallel but separate statement should be made by the Secretary of
State.

The main pressure for full statements had come from the Foreign
Office and the Treasury.[264] The Colonial Office had never been quite
as keen, as it was felt, firstly, that there were not large amounts of
American private capital seeking outlets in overseas territories and,
secondly, that the Colonies would not be attractive to American
investors while there were exchange and import licensing controls.
When the draft was prepared, the Minister of State minuted: 'The
more I look at it, the less need can I see for the House of Commons to
have to listen to a glorified company prospectus asking people to invest
in "British Colonial Empire Limited".'[265] He felt that such statements
might defeat their own purposes and asked the Minister of State for
Economic Affairs, Mr Hugh Gaitskell, whether some method other
than statements to the House might not be more appropriate.[266] The
latter suggested that both the Treasury and the Colonial Office
statements could be included in a letter from the Ambassador in
Washington to the United States Secretary of State.[267] Such a letter
could, it was said, be given the necessary publicity in the United States
and Canada, which were the audiences in mind. Although a mountain
of paper on HMG's attitude towards North American investors had
produced no more than a not very impressive mouse, the Colonial
Office was content. The policy pursued in respect of United States
investment in the Colonies was as stated in reply to a Parliamentary
Question on 28 June 1950, namely:

Our policy is, in general, to welcome American investment in the
Colonies. But we have to bear in mind that such investment
normally carries with it a dollar liability for remittance of dividends
or profits and an ultimate liability for repatriation of capital. So

long, therefore, as the dollar problem is with us, our policy must be selective and we must satisfy ourselves that any given project will either give a net earning or saving of dollars, or will be of such substantial economic benefit to the Colonial territory concerned as to justify any possible loss of dollars involved.[268]

In the course of the following year or so much action was proceeding, or was contemplated, in connection with procuring United States interest in investment in the Commonwealth.[269] Thus, the Commonwealth Development Working Party was brought into existence in May 1952, under Treasury chairmanship, to act as a forum for the discussion of various problems arising in Whitehall concerning the means to attract United States investment;[270] each Commonwealth country was due to prepare a report on 'the possibility within the limits of national policy of reducing the obstacles to the inflow of oversea capital for desirable purposes'; if other Commonwealth countries accepted the Working Party's report, the senior financial representatives of the Commonwealth in Washington would consider what might be done to stimulate United States investment; the Under-Secretary of State for Commonwealth Relations, Mr John Foster, had made a preliminary exploration in New York of the possibility of bringing into existence an informal body of influential American bankers and businessmen prepared to advise on all aspects of investment in the Commonwealth;[271] the Secretary of State for the Colonies, Mr Oliver Lyttelton, had asked the Office to prepare a conspectus of the capital needs of the Colonies, both in public and private sectors, on the basis of which he could suggest an approach to the Americans and other outside interests; certain members of the Conservative Party were pressing the Secretary of State for the issue of a White Paper on HMG's policy towards investment in the United Kingdom, the Colonies and Southern Rhodesia; a committee had been set up within the Department of State to examine ways and means of securing American investment in the British Colonial Empire. In May 1952 the Overseas Territories Committee of OEEC considered the problem of investment of private foreign capital in the overseas territories of member countries.[272] At the same time, the Secretary of State considered that HMG should announce its desire to encourage the investment of foreign capital on terms to be negotiated.[273] In any case, officials felt that a Circular Despatch on United States investment was worth sending to Colonies 'if only to clear ourselves from American criticism of dragging our feet'.[274] The Despatch stated that 'the question of ways and means of encouraging the flow of the right type of American private investment to Colonial territories' had been under consideration.[275] HMG's policy remained as stated in 1950. Colonies were encouraged to make their policy towards United States investment known, and to publicise both the general economic conditions prevailing and any specific opportunities. Officially sponsored surveys of investment opportunities were suggested as a means of determining investment possibilities.

The Final Report of the Washington Group was issued on 31 October 1952.[276] It recognised that 'the task of securing an appreciable increase in United States private investment is likely in any event to prove formidable', though the difficulties were not insuperable as was shown by the experience of Canada, which was admitted to be somewhat special in view of its vast unexploited resources.[277] The conditions for a large sustained inflow of United States capital into Canada had, it was stated, been (i) detailed knowledge of specific investment opportunities on the part of United States investors, (ii) higher returns than on corresponding domestic investment, (iii) confidence that capital and earnings were not exposed to non-commercial risks, and (iv) an environment of economic freedom with minimum Government control. The general conclusion which emerged was that it would be unrealistic, in existing conditions, to expect any substantial increase in worthwhile United States private investment over the next few years, though it was important that the Sterling Area should make every effort to create conditions favourable for the flow of such investment. In this instance, as was to be increasingly true in the 1950s, concern for Colonial economic development became merged into the wider considerations of the Sterling Area. At this point, it is, therefore, appropriate to return to an examination of policy concerning ERP and the Colonies.

(b) Marshall Aid

Earlier it was stated that the Treasury did not want the Colonies to receive ERP loan aid. This was partly because of the United Kingdom's need of ERP loans, and partly because the Treasury wished to avoid the 'further complication' of 'bringing the Colonies into the programming business'.[278] In return, it was accepted that the Treasury would 'make up the different rate of interest' on Bank loans. For it was felt that, as the United Kingdom managed the dollar pool, so she should also manage the counterpart fund arising from ERP and, as far as the agreed disinflationary use of counterpart funds was concerned, the need for alternative disinflationary measures was thereby lessened. These latter measures might well have involved the reduction of funds for overseas territories. So, all in all, it was accepted in the Treasury that the decision could be defended, if need be, on 'moral' grounds, as well as grounds of expediency, especially when the funds allotted by ECA for Colonial development projects had been abstracted from the ERP allocation, which was supposed to represent simply the measure of the Sterling Area's requirements to achieve the object of ERP.[279]

Receipt of Marshall Aid involved the establishment of a Special Account at the Bank of England for HMG to deposit sterling in amounts commensurate with the dollar cost to the United States Government of assistance provided on a grant basis.[280] Of the amount so deposited, 5 per cent was to be allocated to the use of the United States Government under Article IV(4) of the Economic Co-operation Agreement together with any further sums that were required for administrative expenditure incidental to operations under the Economic Co-operation Act (Article IV(3)) and for costs of transportation of relief supplies and packages (Article IV(5)).[281] Initially, it was understood that HMG would draw upon the account in order to cancel short-term debt, though other uses could be agreed later. The ECA suggested in October 1948 that sums should be allocated from the Special Account to finance new projects in the United Kingdom and Dependent Overseas Territories which were expected to contribute substantially to economic recovery.[282] However, the Treasury felt that real investment was limited both by considerations of inflation and by the availability of real resources, which at home meant primarily the building labour force and steel, and abroad involved primarily the steel that could be made available for direct exports and exports of engineering goods.[283] As resources were so fully engaged, any additional investment would involve a diversion from the existing programme, except in those cases where additional resources were made available. This latter was true in the case of American technicians whose sterling expenses were met while they were engaged in the investigation of strategic resources in the Colonial Empire. This involved the temporary employment of some 25 geologists and of 24 to 30 geodetic engineers for two to three years to assist the Colonial Geological Survey and the Directorate of Colonial Surveys. The Treasury argument was accepted by the ECA, though it was felt that, even at the cost of some diversion of resources, raw materials should be developed while, as far as the United Kingdom was concerned, some extra resources were to be received from the United States.[284]

The question had been raised at the Conference of Colonial Supply

Officers as to whether some proportion of the 95 per cent of the Special Account should be made available to the Colonies for the redemption of Colonial debt, or other approved purposes.[285] It arose from a discussion of the arrangements whereby dollar imports for the Colonies were financed from free dollars rather than ERP dollars. Delegates, with the exception of the Maltese delegates, had not questioned the wisdom of the arrangement, but suggested that, for reasons of administrative convenience, Colonial Governments were being precluded from building up a source of sterling finance in the counterpart fund which could be drawn on later for debt redemption or development purposes. The chief exponents of that point of view had been the delegates of Malaya and of Malta. The latter argued, on the basis of being both European and war-shattered, that ERP assistance should be made available for her new power station, and counterpart sterling should be available to assist emigration. It was regarded as unfair that an ex-enemy, namely Italy, should receive Marshall Aid when she did not. The Minister of Reconstruction in the Government of Malta, Mr Mintoff, and the Commissioner General for Malta in London, Mr Ellul, took part in an inter-departmental meeting of officials at the Treasury, seeking agreement to the principle that Malta, as a war-shattered European country, was entitled to receive the necessary sterling financial aid to carry out a long-term reconstruction programme to enable the Colony to achieve economic viability.[286] They envisaged something in the nature of a 'Cripps Plan for Malta'. It was agreed to lay the case before Ministers. The proposal was seen to be, in essence, a sterling problem, needing to be examined in relation to Malta's economic prospects rather than as a Marshall Aid operation affecting specific projects. As the result of discussions begun in this way it was finally decided that the whole of the sterling counterpart for Colonial Marshall Aid schemes should be put up through a Vote for American Aid Counterpart Funds, which would be part of the Treasury's Vote. The practice continued until 1 April 1953, when this Vote was abolished and the counterpart in respect of United States Technical Assistance and Overseas Development Pool Schemes was made chargeable to the Vote of the sponsoring Department.[287] Consequently, Colonies could not consider that they had any direct claim to counterpart sterling.[288] The Governor of Malta was informed that expenditure of counterpart funds for purposes other than debt retirement could only be effected through Votes of Parliament; that the possibility of meeting Malta's sterling needs from monies voted by Parliament could only be considered against the background of a knowledge of Malta's economic position; and that, if Parliament was willing to vote funds for additional assistance to Malta, the ultimate source of such funds would not be a concern of the Government of Malta.[289] Following the passage of the CD & W Act, 1950, £1.5 million was allocated to Malta for reconstruction.

In February 1950 there was a new development concerning counterpart sterling.[290] ECA officials in Washington had come to the conclusion that, though they themselves appreciated the case for continuing the existing anti-inflationary practice of using the whole of the counterpart funds, apart from 5 per cent for debt redemption, they could not defend it in Congressional hearings, and needed to be able to point to some more specific use of the funds for constructive purposes. They proposed, therefore, that a substantial part, say £100 million, of the accumulated counterpart funds should be transferred to a new fund, which HMG would set aside for the financing of development in overseas countries, including British dependent territories. The use of the balance of the counterpart funds for debt redemption would then, it was said, be approved. The ECA officials were prepared to accept both that the new fund might be used to meet expenditure which would have been incurred in any event, i.e. be used instead of, rather than in addition to, CD & W expenditure, and that the new fund would be used not immediately, but over a period of ten years. They were, in fact, concerned with what they regarded as the valuable political effect of the creation of a fund which could be represented as the United Kingdom's contribution to the board purposes of the Point Four programme. The Chancellor of the Exchequer, Sir Stafford Cripps, minuted: 'In my view, this should be most strenuously resisted as it means interference by USA Congress in all our Colonial Development.'[291] In reply to Washington, the resources argument was again expounded: 'The purpose of the Special Account is, therefore, to demonstrate in monetary terms the disinflationary impact of Marshall Aid on the economy as a whole; but it does not, in and by itself, provide new and additional real resources.'[292] It was thought better not to stress either the interference with the United Kingdom's budget or the political intervention in the United Kingdom's investment programme that the proposal involved, although both of these points were strongly held in London. In view of the forthcoming CD & W Bill, it was said that Ministers might, indeed, be prepared, when introducing the Bill in Parliament, to state that, but for Marshall Aid, the United Kingdom would not be in a position to spare additional resources for the development of the Overseas Territories on such a scale.

However, in June 1950 the Head of the ECA Mission to the United Kingdom, Mr W. J. Kenney, wrote formally to the Chancellor of the

Exchequer to request a modification of United Kingdom policy on counterpart funds, a modification which might involve the 'spending' of these funds on schemes of Colonial development. The Minister of State for Economic Affairs first discussed it with Mr Kenney and then wrote to him. A State of complete deadlock emerged, as the proposals by ECA had, after careful consideration, been found unacceptable. Any spending of counterpart funds would, it was said, have, in order to avoid inflationary repercussions, to be offset by a corresponding increase in the budgetary surplus and would, therefore, be 'highly misleading – to use no stronger term'.[293] It was possible to sustain this view because the United Kingdom's investment programme was as substantial as resources allowed, and any expansion would necessarily be inflationary. Under the same conditions, the same would be true of any Colony. But there was not, on the whole, the same degree of organisation in the Colonies as in the United Kingdom, in the sense that the distinction between approved investment projects, on the one hand, and additional investment projects, on the other, was a much more vague distinction than it was in the United Kingdom. Also, many Colonies possessed a margin of unemployed resources, which could be diverted to additional investment without great harm. This question of Colonial resources arose over the offer by the United States on an allocation of dollar consumer goods for Malaya, where the inflationary situation was particularly serious.[294] The Colonial Office suggested that it should share the counterpart paid by the Malayan Government between those Colonies that were in special need[295] and, for the reasons just stated, after enquiring whether the Malayan Government would object, the Treasury concurred. It was an exception which proved the rule concerning the application of counterpart funds. Marshall Aid to the United Kingdom was suspended as from 31 December 1950.

(c) American Assistance for Bauxite Mining in Jamaica

So much for issues of private investment in the Colonies, on the one hand, and of the use of Marshall Aid, on the other. The two were combined in various projects whereby grants and loans were made to obtain United States equipment to facilitate investment in bauxite mining in Jamaica, and the production of lead and copper in Tanganyika, cobalt in Northern Rhodesia, kyanite in Kenya and industrial diamonds in British Guiana. The biggest of these projects was the development of bauxite in Jamaica and, as it raised issues of policy, it requires consideration.

On 8 January 1949, the Governor of Jamaica, Sir John Huggins, was told by the Embassy in Washington that two members of the ECA, both members of the Stockpiling Division, would arrive in Jamaica on 20 January with representatives of the Reynolds Metal Company.[296] The ECA had been approached by the Reynolds Metal Company for a loan of between 8 million and 10 million dollars to start bauxite mining on their property near Ocho Rios, and the ECA representatives wished to visit the site. The ECA had been approached in the same month by the Aluminium Company of Canada, which was considering the erection of a plant to produce alumina on their property in Jamaica. But the ECA was interested only in stockpiling either aluminium or readily available bauxite but not alumina, because of difficulties of storing alumina.[297] Bauxite had been discovered in Jamaica in 1942 in the course of analysing samples of soil from land which was infertile.[298] The analysis had showed that the soil was almost pure bauxite, which set the landowner looking for someone to exploit it. In August 1942 the Aluminium Company of Canada started prospecting. After it had found considerable quantities of bauxite, options were taken over some 27,500 acres of land, which was later purchased. Shortly afterwards, the Reynolds Metal Company of the United States obtained options on land, which was also later purchased. German U-boats were sinking bauxite ships from British Guiana at the time when these options were secured, and the Canadian Aluminium Company was anxious to obtain a nearer source of supply. But the U-boat menace was fairly soon brought under control, and the Combined Aluminium Committee in Washington decided, that, in view of the poor quality of the bauxite in Jamaica and the amount of equipment required to work it, it was not advisable to develop the deposits as a war time proposition. Later, the technical difficulties of processing the bauxite were overcome and both companies wished to develop their deposits. There was, at the same time, a need for sound new industries in Jamaica and, in view of the expected world demand for aluminium, the mining of bauxite there came to be regarded as a good long-term proposition.

The Reynolds Metal Company intended to spend up to 10 million dollars in the production of bauxite for export to their aluminium plant in the United States. It was proposed that 7 million dollars should be provided from the Strategic Materials reserve of ECA and the balance, which would represent sterling expenditure, would come from the 5 per cent counterpart money at the disposal of ECA. Both Reynolds and Jamaica Bauxites Limited, the local subsidiary of the Aluminium Company of Canada, asked for various assurances and tax concessions from the Government of Jamaica. But, to begin with, it is necessary to say a little about ECA 'theology'.[299] The 5 per cent was allocated for the use of the 'United States Government for its expenditures in the United Kingdom' and was under its absolute control (Article IV(4) of the Economic Co-operation Agreement). The 95 per cent was in the possession of the United Kingdom Government, available only for purposes jointly approved by the two Governments (Article IV(6)). Had the 95 per cent been used, instead of the 5 per cent, a procedural problem would have arisen, as the funds then would have had to pass through a Vote, presumably a Colonial Office supplementary Vote. No further control over drawings would have been obtained, as 'permissions to withdraw' would only have been negotiated in the form of an agreement to give to the company the funds on exactly the same terms as under the 5 per cent position. It was proposed to make the loan under section 117a of the Act, which said that the Administrator 'in agreement with the participating country, shall . . . provide by means of funds made available for the purpose of the title, an increase in the production in such participating country of materials which are required by the United States'. By making the scheme a section 117a scheme, the United States required the agreement of the United Kingdom Government. The advantage of the section 117a procedure, from the United States point of view, was that the funds were made available without any counterpart being required. The grant of an ECA loan was perfectly in order, providing HMG agreed.

From the beginning, the Secretary of State, Mr Creech Jones, was worried over the environmental consequences, minuting that it would be 'a tragedy if, for immediate gain, an area is devastated and can never be restored. The permanent importance of agriculture must not be sacrificed.'[300] He wished, also, to be assured that, in return for the concessions and the rather limited contribution to employment, Jamaica itself was getting something out of the deal, regretting that 'the Jamaica Government cannot itself do its own exploitation, but the idea seems much too revolutionary'.[301] When the announcement by ECA of their contract with Reynolds was imminent, the Secretary of State enquired urgently whether the contract would safeguard the 'restoration of the countryside and soil and prevention of ugliness'.[302] The London Office of the Aluminium Company of Canada Limited explained the extent to which Jamaica Bauxites Limited was contributing to the agricultural economy of the Colony.[303] Productivity was being raised, tenant holdings had been increased, the properties were being utilised to produce beef cattle of good quality and dairy products, while citrus and food crops were being grown.

At the same time, HMG was at pains to ensure that Reynolds should not receive more favourable treatment than the Canadian subsidiary, after allowing for the differences in their respective projects, merely because Reynolds had the backing of ECA.[304] The proposed arrangement with ECA was regarded as in itself unexceptional and, provided ECA did not make its assistance available at unfairly low rates of interest, no charge of discrimination in favour of a United States company was seen to arise. The ECA's early proposal that their loans to Reynolds, both in dollars and in sterling, should be interest-free and repayable by shipments of bauxite was welcomed by the Treasury, because the payment of interest was expected to perpetuate the 5 per cent fund, which was not desired.[305] It was, at the same time, stated that no less favourable terms should be extended by ECA to other companies, of whatever nationality. By June 1949 ECA had firmly agreed to assist both the Canadian subsidiary and Reynolds and to do so on equal terms.[306]

In the covering letter to the draft agreement between ECA and Reynolds, it was confirmed that ECA would treat equally with the Canadian subsidiary, to which it was prepared to advance 3.5 million dollars in United States currency and 3.5 million dollars value of sterling counterpart from the 5 per cent funds.[307] It was proposed that each advance should bear simple interest at the rate of 4 per cent per annum from the date of the advance, the full amount of such interest becoming due and payable twenty years from the date of the agreement.[308] This latter proposal was said to be a concession to the firm because the payments of principal had been 'heavily stepped up' for the earlier years.[309] However, it was feared in London that this might well place Reynolds in a favourable competitive position as compared with British companies operating in the same field in British Colonial territories. It was, therefore, proposed that interest be made payable annually, instead of after twenty years.[310] The proposal was not accepted in that form, but it was arranged that the value of each delivery should be split as between repayment of principal and simple interest on that amount of principal, so interest would be paid at the time of each delivery.[311] It was decided that the payment of interest would not perpetuate the 5 per cent counterpart fund, as once money had been withdrawn from it that was the end of the matter.

The only major question between the Government of Jamaica and Reynolds that caused difficulty concerned exchange control procedure. The normal procedure involved remittance to Jamaica of United States dollars for the full value of bauxite shipped to the United

States and for net profits, after provision of taxation, royalty and depreciation reserve to be remitted to the United States in US dollars.[312] On the recommendation of the Governor of Jamaica, an alternative procedure was agreed, whereby bauxite would be shipped free of payment and remittance effected in US dollars to Jamaica to cover wages, taxation, royalties and operating expenses, the latter to include a depreciation reserve. However, Reynolds did not wish to hold the depreciation reserve in Jamaica, and, eventually, that was agreed on condition that (a) normal import licensing procedure would apply, i.e. replacements would be obtained from the sterling area, if reasonably available, and (b) the Government of Jamaica would not provide any dollars to meet the company's future replacement needs.

The proposed agreements with Reynolds and Jamaica Bauxites, the local subsidiary of the Aluminium Company of Canada, were unprecedented, and required not only tripartite discussion between London, Jamaica and Washington but also much inter-departmental discussion, which was complicated in some important directions, e.g. the building of an ore-carrier from ECA funds when only seriously incomplete information was available until a late stage. Both ECA and Reynolds came to press for an agreement by the end of 1949. When it became clear that legislation in Jamaica to give effect to the proposed concessions could not be introduced during 1949, it was suggested by ECA that the Government of Jamaica should issue a letter to the Company stating that the appropriate legislation would be prepared with a view to its introduction at the forthcoming session of the Legislature.[313] The Executive Council, which had all along been eager to settle and pressed the Governor to accede, agreed that the request should be granted. The Secretary of State confirmed that, as soon as the two points at issue concerning the ore-carrier and exchange control were settled, HMG would be in a position to approve the Reynolds contract, providing that the contract contained a saving clause that the agreement would not come into force until the necessary legislation had been enacted in Jamaica.[314] However, as the grant of the various concessions did not affect ECA's attitude to the agreement, although ECA made it clear that it would like to see Reynolds obtain the concessions as the Company would be operating on a narrow margin, the Governor of Jamaica suggested that the inclusion of the saving clause should not be insisted upon.[315] Also, it was not proposed to submit the ECA contracts with the two bauxite companies to the Legislature; instead a single Bill was to be submitted to the new Legislature in January, providing for the grant by the Executive Council to any suitable applicant of customs duty and tonnage tax concessions, as specified in the Bill. The Governor explained this on the grounds that ECA contracts were not directly of concern to the Government of Jamaica. One Colonial Office official minuted his irritation with the Governor's reply in these words: 'My only comment on all the above is that I have no confidence in this kind of deal, which may put difficulties in the way of British investors in future, and I am sorry that Jamaica has apparently thought it necessary to sacrifice everything to the immediate object of seeing Reynolds in production at the earliest moment.'[316] A similar feeling arose over one feature of the agreement with Jamaica Bauxites. HMG stated evenly that it would agree that the Government of Jamaica should wish to afford the Company generous treatment in the matter of obtaining equipment from dollar sources if even a small delay in delivery from the sterling area could be shown to inflict hardship on the Company.[317] However, it was not thought to be reasonable to give the Company *carte blanche*, even within agreed maxima, to import from the United States and Canada for, although it was admittedly improbable that more than 32 per cent of total expenditure could be spent in the United Kingdom, it was regarded as important to preserve the principle that licences for imports from dollar sources were only granted if the goods in question could not be obtained on reasonably competitive terms, as to delivery and price, from the sterling area or soft currency sources. Instead, the Secretary of State offered to arrange for approval in advance of the category of goods which would be licensed from the United States and Canada, as was done in the case of Reynolds. The Company was not happy with that arrangement, because it alleged that it would delay plans if it was necessary to list equipment, especially as much of the mining and washing machinery was required at an early stage, while the specialised Canadian equipment could not be readily obtained elsewhere. The Company felt that the breaking-down of its dollar imports into broad categories for advance approval would involve serious delay. The Governor asked for bulk licensing to be sanctioned, and that was agreed.[318] The issue of import licences within the agreed totals was left to the Governor's discretion. It was agreed that an omnibus licence should be granted for the period of construction of plant, and that the licence would not be revoked so long as the licensee observed and performed his obligations under the licence, excepting only in circumstances beyond the control of the Government of Jamaica.[319]

This was a new departure in exchange control procedure. There had already been a firm refusal to provide CDC with a ration of dollars for use as it wished. While it was accepted that it was a sensible expedient during the construction period for Jamaica Bauxites,[320] when its renewal was sought, in the order to facilitate the expansion of the plant, certain criticisms were made of the technique.[321] On the one hand, it was a technique which could cause jealousy if other large importers in the Colonies heard of it even though the technique of import licensing was largely a matter for the Government of Jamaica, rather than HMG. On the other hand, the technique made it impossible for the Colonial Office to relate bauxite company expenditure to the annual basis used for approving each Colony's dollar imports. At the same time, advance approval of dollar spending, and the way in which the requirements for Jamaica Bauxites were taken out of the ordinary procedure of annual programming in Jamaica, might be thcught to provide the Company with an unfair advantage over other Colonial importers. Yet, all this was unavoidable, once the Governor urged: 'While I realise fully the importance of preserving principles involved in licensing dollar imports, I consider that, in this case, any small saving of dollar expenditure would not warrant inconvenience and delay which would result from adoption of the Reynolds procedure.'[322] As the result of pressures from Jamaica, HMG thus consented to the bestowal of unique concessions on the bauxite companies in that Colony. It was because of the preferential treatment involved that officials in London had reservations about the agreements.

(d) Insistence on Non-discrimination

An example of official insistence on non-discrimination arose in 1964 when the possibility of further CDC investment in an American firm in Trinidad appeared probable. The High Commissioner looked with disfavour on CDC money going to finance non-British enterprises.[323] As it happened, two of the three CDC investments in Trinidad were in that category and, although they were profitable in contrast to some other CDC investments in the area, the disguised nature of the contribution to the territory's development was resented by the High Commissioner. However, in the reply from the CRO, it was made clear that this view did not at all square with HMG's policy, which was to encourage investment in the Commonwealth from non-Commonwealth sources.[324] This policy was set out in paragraph 3(iii) of *The United Kingdom's Role in Commonwealth Development* (Cmnd 237 of July 1957) in these terms: '. . . the Commonwealth does not possess, within its own boundaries, all the capital required to carry out development on the scale or at the pace which its peoples seek. It is therefore right that additional capital should be sought from outside, both from the non-sterling capital markets of the world and from international institutions. Well-conceived expansion thus financed will result in an increase in general economic activity which benefits the Commonwealth as a whole.' In pursuance of that policy, CDC had made a number of investments in international projects in various parts of the Commonwealth and, although it was unfortunate that CDC – and the United Kingdom – were, in some cases, receiving no public recognition for their participation, there was, it was stated, no bar to CDC investment in international concerns simply on the grounds that non-Commonwealth capital was involved. However, in this particular case of Federation Chemicals, the company meantime raised the extra capital in the United States.

SOURCES

1. File 19277/34, Economic 1945 (CO 852/591), items 7 and 8, letters of 30 Apr and 11 May 1945, between the Governor of Malta, General Sir Edmund Schrieber, and Sir Arthur Dawe.

2. Treasury file IF 36/01, Part A, letter of 2 July 1945 from Mr J. B. Williams to Mr A. J. D. Winnifrith.

3. File 19275/65/42, Economic 1946 (CO 852/590), item 3, Confidential Despatch, 3 May 1946, from the Governor of Jamaica to the Secretary of State.

4. Ibid., minute of 4 June 1946 by Sir Frank Stockdale.

5. Ibid., item 6, Confidential Despatch of 7 June 1946 from the Comptroller for D & W in the West Indies to the Secretary of State.

6. Treasury file IF 36/01, Part A, letters of 23 and 31 Oct 1945 from Mr J. B. Williams to Mr A. J. D. Winnifrith.

7. Ibid., letter of 13 Nov 1945 from Mr A. J. D. Winnifrith to Mr J. B. Williams.

8. Ibid., letter of 14 Nov 1945 from Mr J. B. Williams to Mr A. J. D. Winnifrith.

9. Treasury file IF 36/01, Part B, item 18, minute of 22 Feb 1947 by Mr D. R. Serpell.

10. Treasury file OF 25/145/01, Part A, minute of 3 Mar 1947 by Mr N. E. Young.

11. Treasury file IF 36/01, Part A, minute of 5 Mar 1947 by Mr L. M. Helsby.

12. File 19275/95, 1946–48 (CO 852/863), minute of 24 Aug 1948 by Mr H. T. Bourdillon.

13. Treasury file IF 36/08, minute of 25 Sep 1946 by Mr D. R. Serpell, pp. 1–3.

14. Ibid., pp. 21–3, letter of 16 Nov 1946 from Mr A. J. D. Winnifrith to Sir C. Dixon.

15. File 19275/92 of 1944–47 (CO 852/861), minutes of 26 Oct 1946 and 1 Mar 1947, by Mr J. B. Williams and Sir Frank Stockdale.

16. Ibid.

17. Treasury file IF 36/08, pp. 27–33, letter of 24 Mar 1947 from Mr J. B. Williams to Mr L. N. Helsby.

18. Ibid., pp. 43–4, minute of 1 May 1947 by Mr L. N. Helsby.

19. Ibid., p. 39, minute of 26 Apr 1947, by Mr D. R. Serpell.

20. Ibid., pp. 47–50, letter of 3 May 1947 from Mr D. R. Serpell to Mr J. B. Williams.

21. Idem.

22. File 19275/92 of 1946–47 (CO 852/861), minute of 5 June 1947 by Mr A. Mackintosh.

23. Treasury file IF 36/08, pp. 51–3, letter of 18 June 1947 from Mr H. A. Harding to Mr D. R. Serpell.

24. Idem.

25. Ibid., pp. 58–9, minute of 21 June 1947 by Mr I. P. Bancroft.

26. Ibid., pp. 69–70, letter of 31 July 1947 from Mr D. R. Serpell to Mr H. A. Harding.

27. Ibid., p. 75, minute of 1 Sep 1947 by Mr D. R. Serpell. Also letter of 3 Sep 1947 from Mr D. R. Serpell to Mr H. A. Harding, item 24, file 19275/92 of 1946–47 (CO 852/861).

28. Treasury file IF 36/08, p. 85, minute of 11 Sep 1947 by Mr I. P. Bancroft.

29. Ibid., pp. 112–15, letter of 24 Dec 1948.

30. Ibid., pp. 116–17, letter of 7 July 1949.

31. File 19275/71, Economic 1945 (CO 852/551), minutes of 9 and 11 June 1945 by Mr J. B. Williams and Sir Frank Stockdale. Also Treasury file IF 231/603/01, 1945–1950, Part A.

32. Ibid., minute of 7 July 1945 by Mr J. B. Williams.

33. Ibid., item 5, letter of 21 July 1945 from Mr A. J. D. Winnifrith to Mr J. B. Williams.

34. Ibid., item 10, letter of 21 Aug 1945 from Mr J. B. Williams to Mr A. J. D Winnifrith.

35. File 19275/71, Economic 1945 (CO 852/591), letter of 21 Aug 1945 from Mr J. B. Williams to Mr A. J. D. Winnifrith.

36. File 19275/71, Economic 1946 (CO 852/591), item 25, Confidential Despatch No. 187 of 28 Nov 1946 from the Secretary of State to the OAG, British Guiana.

37. Ibid., item 24, letter of 11 Dec 1946 to Professor C. G. Beasley.

38. File 19275/71/64, Economic 1947 (CO 853/861), item 1, Telegram No. 156 of 26 Apr 1947 from the Comptroller for D & W to the Secretary of State.

39. Ibid., item 2, letter of 12 June 1947 from Mr J. B. Williams to Mr H. F. Downie.

40. Ibid., item 5, telegram No. 424 of 29 July 1947 from the Secretary of State to the Comptroller for D & W.

41. File 19275/71, Economic 1947 (CO 852/860), item 6A, letter of 24 Feb 1947 from Mr A. Emanuel to Mr D. R. Serpell.

42. Ibid., item 11, letter of 29 July 1947 from Mr W. G. Boss to Mr J. L. Rampton.

43. Ibid., item 13, letter of 8 Aug 1947 from Mr J. L. Rampton to Mr W. G. Boss.

44. Idem.

45. Ibid., item 15A, letter of 10 Oct 1947 from Mr A. H. Hicks to Mr W. G. Boss.

46. Ibid., item 15, letter of 11 Nov 1947 from Mr W. G. Boss to Mr J. L. Rampton.

47. File 19275/71, Economic 1948 (CO 852/860), minutes of 8 and 15 Mar 1948, by Mr H. A. Harding and Mr W. G. Boss.

48. Ibid., minute of 29 March 1948 by Sir Sydney Caine.

49. Ibid., item 6, letter of 14 May 1948 from Mr H. T. Bourdillon to Mr D. B. Pitblado.

50. Ibid., item 12, letter of 21 July 1948, from Mr D. B. Pitblado to Mr H. Bourdillon.

51. Ibid., item 13, letter of 20 Aug 1948, from the Secretary of State to the Chancellor of the Exchequer. See also Treasury file IF 231/01, Part A, of 1945–50.

52. Ibid., minute of 3 Dec 1948 by Mr J. N. A. Armitage Smith.

53. Ibid., item 20, Confidential unnumbered Circular Despatch of 18 Jan 1949 from the Secretary of State to Colonial Governors.

54. File 19275/71, Economic 1949 (CO 852/860), item 33, Note of 14 Oct for Sir Thomas Lloyd's impending discussion with the Governor of Uganda.

55. Ibid., item 45, letter of 9 Nov 1949.

56. Ibid., item 68, letter of 25 Nov 1949 from the Secretary of State to the Governor of Kenya.

57. Idem.

58. Ibid., item 75, letter of 17 Dec 1949 from the Governor of Kenya to the Secretary of State.

59. File 16516, Economic 1950, item 45, letter of 28 June 1950.

60. Ibid., item 39, Confidential Circular Despatch of 15 June 1950 from the Secretary of State to all Governors.

61. Ibid., item 70, letter of 15 Dec 1950 from Sir H. Poynton to Sir H. Brittain (Treasury).

62. Treasury file OF 25/10/2, letter of 15 Mar 1945 from Mr S. Caine to Sir Wilfrid Eady.

63. Ibid., item 25, Revised Total from *Bank of England Quarterly Report*, as quoted in the letter of 24 June 1946 from Mr S. Caine to Sir David Waley.

64. Ibid., minute of 23 Mar 1945 by Lord Keynes.

65. Ibid., Note of an informal discussion on 20 Feb 1946. Following this discussion Ministers agreed to refer the topic to officials – see minute of 17 May 1946 by Sir David Waley, ibid.

66. Ibid., letter of 2 Mar 1946 from Mr S. Caine to Sir David Waley.

67. Ibid., item 58, letter of 12 July 1946 from Mr R. N. Kershaw of the Bank of England to Sir David Waley.

68. Ibid., Private and Confidential letter of 5 Mar 1946 from Mr S. Caine to Sir David Waley.

69. Ibid., minute of 23 Mar 1946 by Sir David Waley.

70. Ibid., letter of 9 Apr 1946 from Mr R. N. Kershaw to Sir David Waley.

71. Ibid., minute of 17 Mar 1946 by Lord Keynes to Messrs Rowe-Dutton and Bolton.

72. Ibid., minute of 30 Mar 1946 by Mr E. Rowe-Dutton to Lord Keynes. Italics in original.

73. Ibid., minute of 20 May 1946 by Mr E. Rowe-Dutton to Sir David Waley.

74. Ibid., minute of 22 May 1946 by Mr A. T. K. Grant; minute of 24 May 1946 by Mr R. W. B. Clarke; letter of 24 May 1946 from Mr R. W. B. Clarke to Mr R. N. Kershaw, Bank of England.

75. Ibid., letter of 30 May 1946 from Mr R. N. Kershaw to Mr R. W. B. Clarke.

76. Idem.

77. Ibid., minute of 27 May 1946 by Mr E. Rowe-Dutton.

78. Ibid., item 76, Colonial Sterling Balances SAN (COL) 11.

79. Ibid., item 77, Submission by the Colonial Office – SAN (COL) 12 – enclosure with letter of 26 July 1946 from Mr S. Caine to Mr O. L. Williams.

80. Ibid., item 83, letter of 6 Aug 1946 from Mr S. Caine to Sir David Waley.

81. Ibid., item 79, minute of 9 Aug 1946 by the Chancellor of the Exchequer on the submission by the Working Party.

82. Treasury file OF 25/145/01, Part A, letter and enclosure of 20 Feb 1947 from Mr S. Caine to Sir David Waley. The paper was circulated on 14 Mar 1947, to the Working Party on Colonial Sterling Balances as SAN (COL) 14. After a discussion on 15 Mar 1947 the paper was revised and circulated as SAN (COL) 16.

83. Ibid., minute of 21 Feb 1947 by Sir David Waley.

84. Ibid., minute of 22 Feb 1947 by Mr N. E. Young.

85. Ibid., minutes of 26 Feb 1947 by Mr L. M. Helsby and R. W. B. Clarke, though Mr A. T. K. Grant disagreed.

86. Ibid., letter of 4 Mar 1947 from Mr F. F. Powell to Sir David Waley.

87. Ibid., letter of 17 Apr 1947, from Mr J. M. Fleming to Mr O. L. Williams.

88. Ibid., letter of 27 May 1947 from Sir Sydney Caine to Mr E. Rowe-Dutton.

89. Ibid., minute of 5 June 1947 by the Chancellor of the Exchequer.

90. Ibid., letter and memorandum of 11 Nov 1947 from Mr C. F. Cobbold to Sir Wilfrid Eady.

91. Ibid., letter and enclosure of 21 Nov 1947 from Sir Sydney Caine to Sir Wilfrid Eady.

92. Ibid., minute of 19 Jan 1948 by Mr O. L. Williams.

93. Ibid., letter of 22 Jan 1948 from Mr O. L. Williams to Mr J. Rootham, Bank of England.

94. Ibid., letter of 1 Feb 1948 from Mr J. Rootham to Mr O. L. Williams.

95. Ibid., minute of 21 Feb 1948 by Mr O. L. Williams to Mr N. E. Young and Mr D. B. Pitblado.

96. Ibid., minute of 23 Feb 1948 by Mr N. E. Young.

97. Ibid., minute of 7 Aug 1948 by Sir Sydney Caine, now Third Secretary in the Treasury.

98. Idem.

99. Ibid., minute of 4 Sep 1948 by Mr A. T. K. Grant.

100. Idem.

101. Ibid., minute of 23 Dec 1948 by Mr A. T. K. Grant.

102. Ibid., minute of 6 Sep 1948 by Mr E. Rowe-Dutton to Sir Henry Wilson Smith.

103. Ibid., minute of 30 Dec 1948 by Mr R. W. B. Clarke.

104. Idem.

105. Ibid., minute of 3 Jan 1949.

106. Treasury file OF 25/145/01, Part B, item 1, minute of 4 Feb 1949.

107. Ibid., item 11, minute of 18 May 1949.

108. Ibid., item 19, letter and enclosure of 30 May 1949 from Sir Henry Wilson Smith to the Governor of the Bank of England.

109. Ibid., item 24, letter of 23 June 1949.

110. Ibid., item 43, letter of 17 Aug 1949.

111. Ibid., item 47, minutes of 30 Sep, 4 Oct and 7 Oct 1949.

112. Ibid., item 48, minute of 19 Oct 1949.

113. Ibid., item 49, minute of 17 Nov 1949.

114. CC 9(51) item 3, 20 Nov 1951.

115. C(51)14, 12 Nov 1951.

116. Ibid., item 89, minute of 22 Nov 1951, by Sir Herbert Brittain.

117. Treasury file IF 36/01, Part A, letter of 8 Dec 1945, from Mr A. J. D. Winnifrith to Mr J. B. Williams.

118. Idem.

119. Treasury file IF 36/01, Part B, minutes of discussion of 14 Feb 1946 between the Colonial Office and the Treasury on development plans

120. CEDC, 1st Minutes – only copy with Library and Records Section, F & CO.

121. CDWAC No. 899.

122. Treasury file IF 36/03, item 17, letter of 17 June 1947 from Mr I. P. Bancroft to Mr H. A. Harding.

123. Ibid., item 21, letter of 25 Aug 1947 from Mr J. B. Williams to Mr D. R. Serpell.

124. File Economic 19286/3, 1948 (CO 852/866), item 6, CEDC(48), 1st Meeting.

125. File Economic General 97326/62, 1949 (CO 852/1040), item 7, note of a meeting held on 18 Mar 1949.

126. File Economic General 97326/62, 1950, item 24, minutes of the meeting of 12 Dec 1950.

127. File Economic General 97326/63, 1951, item 6, CEDC(51) 5, 15 Feb 1951: 'The Assessment of Colonial Economic Progress'.

128. File Economic General 97326/62, 1951, item 8, minutes of meeting of CEDC held on 17 Apr 1951.

129. Ibid., item 22.

130. H. of L. Deb., Vol 135, col 963, 10 Apr 1945.

131. Ibid., cols 965–6.

132. File Economic 19286/7/1, 1948 (CO 852/867), item 1, memorandum of 2 Apr 1948 by Professor W. Arthur Lewis: 'Principles of Economic Planning'.

133. Ibid., item 3, CEDC(48) 1, 11 Apr 1948.

134. Ibid., item 5, minute of 21 Apr 1948 by Mr W. E. F. Ward.

135. Ibid., minute of 10 May 1948, by the Parliamentary Under-Secretary, Mr D. Rees-Williams.

136. File 19286/3, 1948 (CO 852/866), item 31, CEDC(48) 5th Meeting of 19 Oct 1948.

137. Ibid., item 42.

138. File 64932, 1948, Dominica (CO 321/424), item 35, letter of 12 Nov 1948 from the Governor of the Windward Islands, Mr (later Sir Robert) Arundell to the Secretary of State.

139. Ibid., item 30.

140. Ibid., item 35.

141. Ibid., minute of 3 Mar 1948 by Mr J. C. Morgan.

142. Ibid., item 13, Despatch of 28 June 1948 from the Acting Governor of the Windward Islands with 'A Plan of Development for the Colony of Dominica'.

143. Ibid., item 27, telegram No. 422 of 12 Oct 1948 from the Chief Adviser to the Secretary of State.

144. Ibid., item 37, Savingram of 21 Dec 1948 from the Secretary of State to the Acting Governor, Windward Islands.

145. Idem.

146. File 64932 of 1949 (CO 321/424), minute of 4 Mar 1949.

147. Ibid., item 8, Memorandum of 9 Mar 1949 on the Dominica ten-year plan.

148. Ibid., minute of 10 Mar by the Parliamentary Under-Secretary of State.

149. Ibid., minute of 18 Mar 1949 by the Secretary of State.

150. Ibid., item 11, telegram No. 127 of 22 Mar 1949 from the Secretary of State to the Governor, Windward Islands.

151. Ibid., item 13, telegram No. 201 of 23 Mar 1949 from the Governor, Windward Islands, to the Secretary of State.

152. Ibid., item 20, minute of ninth meeting of 14 Mar 1949 with CDC.

153. Ibid., CEDC(49)18, 10 May 1949.

154. Ibid., item 37, minutes of the second meeting of CEDC in 1949, on 23 May.

155. File 97253/63, Economic General 1951, EOD 20/51, 1 June 1951.

156. Ibid., minutes of 18 Dec 1951 and 17 Mar 1952.

157. File 64932 of 1949, West Indies (CO 321/424), minute of 21 July 1948 by Mr Douglas Smith.

158. Fifth Report from the Select Committee on Estimates, Session 1947–48, *Colonial Development*, HC 181, 30 July 1948.

159. File 19260/78, Economic 1948 (CO 852/855), item 4, Note of 14 Mar 1948 by Sir Sydney Caine to Sir T. Lloyd.

160. Idem.

161. Cabinet Office File 6/3/5, Part 4, item 15/1.

162. File 19275/95, Economic Finance 1946–48 (CO 852/863), minutes of 21 and 26 Nov 1946 by Messrs H. A. Harding and S. Caine.

163. Ibid., minute of 30 Nov 1946 by the Secretary of State.

164. Ibid., minute of 20 Feb 1947 by Sir Sydney Caine to the Secretary of State.

165. Ibid., minute of 20 Feb 1947 by the Secretary of State.

166. Idem.

167. Ibid., minute of 11 Oct 1948 by Mr W. L. Gorell Barnes.

168. Ibid., item 8A, draft minute of 6 Nov 1948 for the consideration of Ministers.

169. File 97326/62, Economic 1949 (CO 852/1040), item 14.

170. Ibid., minute of 15 Nov 1948 by the Parliamentary Under-Secretary of State to the Secretary of State.

171. File 19275/65/63, Economic 1945, items 6 and 7.

172. File 19275/95, Economic Finance 1946–48 (CO 852/863), minute of 23 Nov 1948 by the Secretary of State.

173. File 19275/95, Economic 1949 (CO 852/863), item 15.

174. File 19275/95, Economic Finance 1946–48 (CO 852/863), minute of 16 Aug 1948 by Mr H. A. Harding.

175. Ibid., minute of 24 Aug 1948 by Mr H. T. Bourdillon.

176. File 19275/95, Economic 1949 (CO 852/863), item 11, letter of 19 Jan 1949.

177. Ibid., minute of 19 Feb 1949, on meeting with the Treasury on 17 Feb 1949. Also item 16, letter of 8 Mar 1949.

178. File 19275/113, Economic Finance 1949 (CO 852/113), item 5, Note of a meeting held in the Secretary of State's room on 10 Mar 1949.

179. Ibid., item 9, letter of 14 Apr 1949.

180. Ibid., item 50, Brief for Lord Listowel for Second Reading in the Lords on 19 July 1949.

181. H. of C. Deb., Vol. 465, col. 1619, 27 May 1949.

182. File 19275/95 of 1949, Economic (CO 852/863), item 22, memorandum of 25 May 1949 on policy to be pursued in making use of funds provided under the CD & W Acts.

183. Idem.

184. Ibid., minute of 23 May 1949.

185. CDWC(49) 1.

186. Ibid., item 33, minutes of the first meeting of the CD & W Committee held on 27 June 1949.

187. Ibid., minute of 12 July 1949.

188. Ibid., minute of 20 July 1949.

189. Ibid., minute of 21 July 1949 by the Parliamentary Under-Secretary.

190. Ibid., minute of 26 July 1949 by the Secretary of State.

191. Ibid., record of a meeting on 12 Aug 1949 between the Secretary of State and officials.

192. CD (49) 30 of 27 July 1949: 'The Colonies and the Dollar Standstill'.

193. CD (49) 39 of 22 Oct 1949: 'The Alteration in the Sterling Dollar Exchange Rates – Implications for the Colonies'.

194. File 19275/95 of 1949, Economic (CO 852/863), item 46, note of a meeting held on 14 Oct 1949.

195. Treasury File IF 36/638/04, p. 1, letter of 19 Nov 1949 from the Secretary of State to the Chancellor of the Exchequer.

196. Ibid., minute of 21 Nov 1949.

197. Ibid., p. 38, minute of 14 Jan 1950.

198. Idem.

199. Ibid., item 53, letter of 3 Jan 1950, from the Secretary of State for Commonwealth Relations, Mr P. J. Noel-Baker, to Mr Creech Jones.

200. Treasury file IF 36/638/04, pp. 68–70, minutes of 31 Jan and 16 Feb 1950.

201. Ibid., pp. 104–5, notes of a discussion on 24 Feb 1950.

202. File 19275/95 of 1950, Economic Finance, Part I, items 3 and 4, letter of 3 Apr 1950 from the Secretary of State to the Lord President of the Council in reply to an enquiry of 28 Mar.

203. Ibid., item 7, letter of 5 Apr 1950 from the Chancellor of the Exchequer to the Secretary of State.

204. Treasury file IF 36/638/04, pp. 138–42, letter of 19 Apr 1950 from the Secretary of State to the Chancellor of the Exchequer.

205. Ibid., pp. 151–7 minute of 4 May 1950.

206. File 19275/95, Economic Finance 1950, Part I, item 10, letter of 18 Apr 1950 from the Lord President of the Council to the Secretary of State.

207. Treasury file IF 36/638/04, p. 164, note of a discussion on 5 May 1950.

208. Ibid., pp. 175–6, letter of 18 May 1950 from the Secretary of State to the Chancellor of the Exchequer.

209. Ibid., p. 175, minute of 19 May 1950 by the Chancellor of the Exchequer.

210. File 19275/95, Economic Finance 1950, Part I, item 15, letter of 14 June 1950 by the Lord President of the Council to the Secretary of State.

211. Ibid., item 19, EPC(50) 72, 7 July 1950.

212. Ibid., item 20, Brief of 11 July 1950.

213. Treasury file IF 36/638/04, minute of 12 July 1950 by Mr A. Mackay.

214. File 19275/95, Economic Finance 1950, Part I, item 21, EPC(50) 18th meeting, 13 July 1950.

215. Treasury file IF 36/638/04, letter of 12 July 1950.

216. File 19275/95, Economic Finance 1950, Part II, item 23, letter of 29 Sep 1950, from Sir J. Crombie to Sir H. Poynton.

217. Ibid., minute of 1 Oct 1950, by the Minister of State.

218. Treasury file IF 36/638/04, p. 103, minute of 4 Oct 1950 by Sir J. Crombie.

219. Ibid., p. 104, minute of 9 Oct 1950 by the Minister of State for Economic Affairs.

220. File 19275/95, Finance 1950, Part II, item 22.

221. Treasury file IF 36/638/04, p. 105, note of 16 Oct 1950.

222. H. of C. Deb., Vol. 480, cols 1135–251, 9 Nov 1950.

223. File 19275/95, Economic Finance 1950, Part II, item 32, CDWC(50) 7, 11 Dec 1950.

224. Ibid., item 31, Secret unnumbered Circular (2) of 19 Oct 1950 from the Secretary of State to all Colonies except Bahamas and Bermuda.

225. Ibid., item 35, Secret and Personal letter of 5 Dec 1950 from the Permanent Under-Secretary of State to all Governors, except the Governor of Bermuda.

226. File 19275/95, Economic Finance 1951, item 2, Secret and Personal letter of 27

Dec 1950 from the Governor of Mauritius to the Permanent Under-Secretary of State.

227. Ibid., item 13, Secret and Personal letter of 16 May 1951, from the Permanent Under-Secretary of State to the Governor of Mauritius.

228. HC 181, 30 July 1948, para. 128.

229. File 19309, Economic 1948, item 6, minute of 7 July 1948 on International Bank Loans by Sir Sydney Caine.

230. H. of C. Deb., Vol. 458, cols 749–93, 19 Nov 1948, for Second Reading debate.

231. File 19309, Economic 1948, item 6, minute of 7 July 1948 on International Bank Loans by Sir Sydney Caine.

232. Ibid., item 7, minute of 13 July 1948 by the Secretary of State.

233. Ibid., minute of 29 July 1948 by Mr D. Rees-Williams.

234. H. of C. Deb., vol. 453, no. 152, cols 226–7, 6 July 1948.

235. File 19309, Economic 1948, Interim Report, CDWP, para. 54.

236. Ibid., item 16, Circular Despatch of 19 July 1948.

237. Ibid., item 17, Document ER(L)(48) 173 of 17 Nov 1948.

238. Ibid., item 18 OEEC, CE(48) 119 (Rev) of 8 Dec 1948.

239. File 19309/64 of 1948, Economic, item 11, letter of 20 May 1948 from Mr W. L. Gorell Barnes to Mr A. T. K. Grant.

240. Idem.

241. Ibid., item 19, letter of 12 June 1948 from Mr W. L. Gorell Barnes to Mr W. Stratton Anderson, Jr, US Embassy.

242. Ibid., item 18, Revised Memorandum of 30 May 1948, enclosed with letter of 4 June 1948 from Mr W. Stratton Anderson, Jr, to Mr W. L. Gorell Barnes.

243. Ibid., item 31, Confidential Despatch No. 1138 (1780/2/48) of 31 Aug 1948 from HM Ambassador in Washington to the Secretary of State for Foreign Affairs.

244. Ibid., item 46, Confidential Despatch No. 1470 (UR 6146/4995/98) of 14 Oct 1948 from the Secretary of State for Foreign Affairs to HM Ambassador in Washington.

245. Ibid., item 49, letter of 14 Oct 1948, from Mr J. W. Taylor to Mr E. Berthoud.

246. Ibid., item 57, letter of 4 Nov 1948 from Mr E. E. Sabben-Clare to Mr C. F. Martin.

247. Ibid., item 59, letter of 23 Dec 1948 from Mr T. L. Rowan (Treasury) to Mr T. Finletter, Chief of the United Kingdom Mission of ECA.

248. File 97351 of 1949, Economic, minute of 29 Jan 1949 by the Secretary of State.

249. Ibid., item 17, Secret Unnumbered Circular Despatch of 17 Feb 1949, on Capital Investment by Foreign Private Enterprise in the Colonies.

250. Idem, Annexure G.

251. Ibid., item 27, letter of 31 May 1949 from the Secretary of State to the Chancellor of the Exchequer.

252. Ibid., item 28, letter of 1 June 1949 from the Chancellor of the Exchequer to the Secretary of State.

253. Ibid., item 35, EPC(49) 74 of 5 July 1949: 'Investment of Foreign Capital in the Colonies' – Memorandum by the Secretary of State.

254. Ibid., item 37, letter of 18 July 1949 from the Minister of State for Foreign Affairs to the Secretary of State.

255. Ibid., item 39, Memorandum on Dollars and Colonial Development prepared for the Chancellor of the Exchequer.

256. EPC(49) 92.

257. CM 51(49), item 1, 29 July 1949.

258. File 97351, Economic 1949, item 57, Foreign Investment in the Colonies, 25 Oct 1949.

259. Ibid., item 59, letter of 9 Nov 1949 from Lord Trefgarne to Sir Hilton Poynton.

260. File 97351/62, Economic 1949, item 29, telegram No. 483 of 7 Nov 1949 from the Chief Adviser, D & W Organisation, to the Minister of State for Colonial Affairs.

261. Ibid., minute of 2 Dec 1949 by the Minister of State for Colonial Affairs.

262. Ibid., item 35, report of 29 Dec 1949.

263. File 97351/68, Economic 1950, Part I, item 39, 'Report of the Interdepartmental Committee on United States Investment in The Sterling Area': GEN 303/18 (Finch), 5 Jan 1950.

264. Ibid., minute of 30 May 1950, to the Minister of State, Mr J. Dugdale.

265. Ibid., minute of 26 May 1950 by the Minister of State.

266. Ibid., item 88, letter of 8 June 1950 from the Minister of State for Colonial Affairs to the Minister for Economic Affairs.

267. Ibid., item 94, letter of 27 June 1950 from the Minister of State for Economic Affairs to the Minister of State for Colonial Affairs.

268. H. of C. Deb. Vol. 476, cols 2258–9, 28 June 1950.

269. File 97351/68, Economic 1950, Part I, item 117, letter and enclosure of 29 Apr 1952.

270. Ibid., item 126, draft letter of 15 May 1952.

271. Ibid., item 122, note of 7 May by the Under-Secretary of State for Commonwealth Relations.

272. Ibid., item 128, note of a meeting on 12 May 1952 of the Overseas Territories Committee of OEEC.

273. Ibid., minute of 22 May 1952, by the Secretary of State.

274. Ibid., minute of 13 Aug 1952, by Sir H. Poynton.

275. Ibid., item 190, Confidential Despatch No. 835/52 of 22 Aug 1952 from the Secretary of State to all Colonial Territories.

276. File 97351/68, Economic 1952, Part II, item 237, Confidential FM(D)(W) 6 Final: 'Commonwealth Working Party on Development (Washington Group): United States Investment in the Sterling Area: Final Report'.

277. Idem, para. 35.

278. Treasury file IF 616/01 Part A, page 3, minute of 6 July 1948 by Mr T. L. Rowan.

279. Treasury file IF 616/01, Part C, pp. 17–18, minute of 7 Nov 1949.

280. Treasury file IF 616/01, Part A, pp. 4–7, letter of 25 Aug 1948 from Mr W. L. Hebbard (US Treasury) to Mr E. G. Compton (UK Treasury).

281. Idem.

282. ER(ECA)(48) 13th meeting of 6 Oct 1948.

283. Treasury file IF 616/01, Part A, pp. 61–3, letter of 9 Dec 1948 from Mr T. L. Rowan to Mr T. K. Finletter (ECA Mission).

284. Ibid., pp. 63–4, letter of 28 Dec 1948, from Mr T. K. Finletter to Mr T. L. Rowan.

285. Treasury file IF 616/01, Part B, pp. 189–91, Note of a meeting held on 3 Aug 1949 to consider the possibility of allocating counterpart funds to the Colonies.

286. Ibid., pp. 196–8, Note of a meeting held with representatives of Malta on 3 Aug 1949.

287. Treasury file IF 616/01, Part D, p. 261, letter of 14 July 1952.

288. Treasury file IF 616/01, Part C, pp. 63 and 99, minutes of 10 and 26 Jan 1950.

289. Ibid., p. 109, Secret telegram No. 28 of 4 Feb 1950 from the Secretary of State to the Governor of Malta.

290. Ibid., pp. 124–5, Confidential frame No. 517 of 11 Feb 1950 from the Ambassador in Washington to the Foreign Office.

291. Ibid., p. 123, minute of 13 Feb 1950 by the Chancellor of the Exchequer.

292. Ibid., pp. 135–9, Secret frame No. 958 of 17 Feb 1950 from Foreign Office to Washington.

293. Treasury file IF 616/01, Part D, pp. 142–3, letter of 18 Aug 1950 from the Minister of State for Economic Affairs, Mr H. Gaitskell, to the Head of the ECA Mission to the United Kingdom, Mr John Kenney.

294. Ibid., pp. 120–2, Note of a meeting on 2 Aug 1950 between the Secretary of State, Mr J. Griffiths, and the Head of the ECA Mission to the United Kingdom, Mr J. Kenney.

295. Ibid., pp. 176–7, letter of 24 Jan 1951, referred to in the minute of 30 Jan 1951.

296. File 19677/42 of 1949 (CO 852/942), Economic Production, Part I, Confidential telegram No. 120 of 8 Jan 1949 from the Ambassador in Washington to the Governor of Jamaica.

297. Ibid., Confidential frame No. 251 of 13 Jan 1949 from the Ambassador in Washington to the Foreign Office.

298. Ibid., item 36, Colonial Office of 11 Mar 1949: Jamaica Bauxite.

299. Ibid., item 37, minute of 14 Mar 1949 by Mrs E. M. Chilver.

300. Ibid., minute of 4 Mar 1949 by the Secretary of State.

301. Ibid., minute of 25 Mar 1949 by the Secretary of State.

302. File 19677/42 of 1950, Economic Production, Part I, minute of 30 Dec 1949 by the Secretary of State.

303. Ibid., item 93, letter of 29 Mar 1950.

304. File 19677/42 of 1949, Economic Production, Part I, item 63A, letter of 7 Apr 1949 to the High Commissioner in Ottawa, Sir A. Clutterbuck.

305. File 19677/42 of 1949, Economic Production, Part II, item 98, letter of 2 May 1949.

306. Ibid., item 113, minute of 17 June 1949 by Sir G. L. M. Clauson.

307. Ibid., item 116, letter of 1 Aug 1949.

308. Ibid., item 116, Article 1(b) of draft dated 1 Aug 1949, and item 138 for revised draft of 16 Aug 1949.

309. Ibid., item 117, Confidential telegram No. 3850 of 5 Aug 1949, from the Ambassador, Washington, to the Foreign Office.

310. Ibid., item 150, Confidential telegram No. 2920, Saving, of 5 Sep 1949 from the Foreign Office to Washington; and item 210, letter of 11 Oct 1949.

311. Ibid., Part III, items 250 and 251, Confidential telegrams Nos 5310 and 5320 of 11 and 12 Nov 1949, from Washington to the Foreign Office.

312. Ibid., item 132A, Secret telegram No. 747 of 29 Aug 1949 from the Secretary of State to the Governor of Jamaica.

313. File 19677/42 of 1949, Economic Production, Part III (CO 852/942), item 288, Saving Telegram No. 1286 of 30 Nov 1949, from the Governor of Jamaica to the Secretary of State.

314. Ibid., item 335, Confidential telegram No. 1089 of 26 Dec 1949 from the Secretary of State to the Governor of Jamaica.

315. Ibid., Confidential telegram No. 1032 of 29 Dec 1949 from the Governor of Jamaica to the Secretary of State.

316. Ibid., minute of 2 Jan 1950.

317. File 19677/42 of 1950, Economic Production, Part I, item 119, Confidential telegram No. 268 of 3 May 1950 from the Secretary of State to the Governor of Jamaica.

318. Ibid., item 147, Confidential telegram No. 367 of 15 June 1950, from the Secretary of State to the Governor of Jamaica.

319. Ibid., item 161, Confidential telegram No. 452 of 28 July 1950, from the Secretary of State to the Governor of Jamaica.

320. File 19677/42 of 1951 (CO 852/1177), Economic Production/Marketing, minute of 23 Nov 1951.

321. Ibid., minute of 11 Dec 1951.

322. File 19677/42 of 1950, Economic Production, Part I, item 146, Confidential telegram No. 351 of 9 June 1950 from the Governor of Jamaica to the Secretary of State.

323. File 2 – WID 20/202/1, CDC Activities in the West Indies, item 8, letter of 22 July 1964 from the High Commissioner in Trinidad.

324. Ibid., item 13, letter of 30 Sep 1964.

3 The West Indies, 1945–1952

1. CD & W ALLOCATIONS AND SKETCH-PLANS

In the communications from the Secretary of State to Governors in the West Indies during the early summer of 1945 there were references to the impending notification of individual allocations under the CD & W Act, and intimations that consideration of some applications would have to be deferred until sketch-plans had been submitted. In these circumstances, the Comptroller for D & W in the West Indies, Sir John Macpherson (since March 1945), felt that the help of his Organisation could be effective 'only if the approach to our common problems is made from the two angles of sketch plans and allocations'.[1] He felt that any other approach would be likely 'merely to intensify the loss of mutual confidence', which he and his Advisers found so distressing. He was seriously concerned to find an apparent lack of understanding of the nature of the sketch plans required, most sketch-plans then being conceived being 'little more than catalogues of projects to be financed wholly under the Act, without any attempt to estimate expenditure or to indicate the extent to which local funds will be available'. Governors generally seemed to be making heavy weather of preparing them. What he thought necessary was, firstly, guidance as to the nature of sketch-plans required from each Colony and, secondly, early appointment of a successor to Dr Benham as Economic Adviser to assist in the preparation of surveys of the economic and financial prospects of Colonies, such as Barbados, which needed and sought his help. As regards allocation, the Comptroller did not see, despite his predecessor's unique knowledge of the area, how equitable allocations could be made in London until sketch-plans had been considered. He assumed that some 25 per cent of the West Indies allocation would be placed at his disposal, partly for central schemes and partly as a reserve. Indeed, it had been agreed at an official meeting in the Colonial Office in July 1944[2] that, instead of receiving their individual allocations, West Indian Colonies should work within the total figure available to the whole area, the Comptroller being responsible for the broad allocation of funds to each Colony within that total. Had this been carried out, it would have produced something like the Fund that had been recommended for the area by the Moyne Commission. However, it was not to be, though on nearly every point the Comptroller's views corresponded closely with the terms of a draft Despatch that was about to be submitted to the Secretary of State.[3] Claims on funds were such that it had proved impossible to set aside a special West Indian reserve, apart from a small allocation to the Comptroller for regional schemes.

The Secretary of State, Colonel Oliver Stanley, approved Sir Frank Stockdale's proposed allocation of CD & W money on 18 June 1945. As stated in the telegram of 9 June, the allocations included £15 million to the West Indies. Communication of the allocations to Governors was held up until a Despatch was drafted, and so there was time to consult the Comptroller further. Two comments were made. First, it was felt that the West Indies General allocation of £750,000 was far too small and that the severe curtailment of expenditure on regional schemes was regrettable, particularly at a time when Federation was under consideration.[4] Secondly, it was suggested that the allocation to British Guiana of £2,350,000 should be increased at the expense of the allocation of £1 million for Trinidad, because when British Guiana had met the cost of drainage and irrigation works and of the development of the interior, there would be little left to supplement local expenditure on the improvement of existing social services.[5] At the same time, after regretting that a central reserve could not be established, the Comptroller felt that everything depended on the effectiveness of the sketch-plans, stating that 'if they are soundly composed, and funds are fully allocated in advance, a considerable part of the present functions of this Organisation will have been discharged.' A welcome readiness was being shown, it was said, by most Governors to invite the Organisation's views before sketch-plans were crystallised.

A limited reallocation was made so that British Guiana's share was raised to £2.5 million, and that of the West Indies General to £800,000, while it was proposed that Trinidad's should be reduced to £800,000.[6] At the same time, the Comptroller was invited to send any further comments. He replied that his main quarrel was with the decision that loans counted against allocations in the same way as grants, though he realised that was not an issue that could be re-opened.[7] He felt it would be preferable that assistance to compara-tively wealthy Colonies should be restricted to grants of interest, or guarantees of interest, on loans and, for that purpose, £800,000 would be generous for Trinidad. But no further changes to meet these points were possible, except that a line was inserted to the effect that loans had to count against allocations.

However, the Governor of Trinidad, Sir Bede Clifford, complained about the smallness of his Colony's allocation;[8] and, for reasons not disclosed, officials in the Colonial Office decided that allocating less than £1 million was a mistake, although done on the Comptroller's advice.[9] It was, therefore, proposed to allocate £200,000 from the general reserve to maintain Trinidad's share. The Comptroller, consulted as a matter of courtesy, took the matter up with the Governor, was unimpressed by the arguments, and was confirmed in his earlier view that Trinidad's needs were less than elsewhere in the West Indies, and that the allocation was regarded locally as merely a useful addition to the financing of elaborate development schemes in a period of peak expenditure. He did not regard the earlier allocation as in any way 'mistaken' but, providing no other Colony was penalised, he agreed to the extra £200,000 going to Trinidad.[10] An official, sympathising with the Comptroller's viewpoint, noted that the trouble with the put-money-where-there-really-is-something-to-develop argument was that the Colonial Empire could not be treated as a whole, in the sense that the Leewards would not benefit much if a commercial success was made of Trinidad.[11] But there was an alternative point of view, for another official thought the Comptroller's argument was too much influenced by the assumption that CD & W money was mainly to be regarded as a form of benevolence to the poorer Colonies, rather than a stimulus to development.[12] He feared that the Comptroller's argument would only lead to the situation where the poorer Colonies would be unable to finance their recurrent expenditure when the Act lapsed. The Parliamentary Under-Secretary, Mr Creech Jones, was not happy about the proposal:

> I dislike the raid on the Reserve money to supplement the Trinidad allocation, on the ground that, comparatively, the West Indies has been better treated than other regions, that Trinidad is relatively prosperous, that she has resources which no other West Indian Colony has, that she has reserves herself, and little direct taxation, and so on. Desperate needs elsewhere have also had to be jettisoned. We have also treated most inadequately territories like the H.C. Territories in Africa.[13]

He adopted the recommendation in the hope that the request for better planning would be heeded. The Secretary of State, Mr George

Hall, approved without comment. The Treasury was not keen either, stating that their chief doubt was whether it was wise to increase individual allocations from the reserve at that stage but, with propriety, added that if the Colonial Office was so disposed 'we will not, indeed cannot stand, in your way'.[14] Trinidad was consequently mollified.

The Secretary of State in the Caretaker Government, Colonel Stanley, did not feel that he should determine in the summer of 1945 the allocation of CD & W funds for the ten years commencing 1 April 1946. While he was appreciative of the propriety of the delay thus arising, the Comptroller was exercised as several Colonies were pushing ahead with the preparation for sketch development plans.[15] Consequently, he felt obliged to circulate a note giving suggestions for the development of sketch-plans in advance of receiving instructions from the Secretary of State.[16] In the note, it was suggested that each Colony might begin the preparation of a development programme by dividing the programme in two parts. First, there would be an outline of all development projects which were considered desirable, including projects not eligible for CD & W assistance, e.g. the construction of new government offices, police stations and the like. The purpose was to ensure that no desirable project was overlooked. Secondly, there would be a financial statement. This would provide, on the revenue side, (i) an estimate of any budgetary surplus over the period 1946–56, (ii) an estimate of any additional revenue that could be obtained by additional taxation or changes in the tax system, (iii) an estimate of the amount that could be raised by loans and (iv) when available, the Colony's CD & W allocation. On the expenditure side, there would be a selection of projects from those listed, which would absorb the whole of the estimated revenue under the four categories listed. It was realised that the estimates would be 'most approximate', and it was suggested that the financial programme should be left 'as flexible as possible'.

ii. THE ROLE OF THE D & W ORGANISATION, 1947–1949

The Comptroller visited London in July 1946. The notes prepared in Hastings House for the visit reviewed the role of his Organisation.[17] The work of the Organisation had increased steadily in volume over the previous two or three years, and also changed considerably in character. The Secretary of State's Despatch of 30 November 1940 to

Governors in the West Indies had stated that the object of the
Organisation was 'to provide a body of experts in a position to
undertake a constant review of the needs of the West Indies, and to
advise Colonial Governments and the Secretary of State regarding
development schemes'. It was further stated that 'schemes should be
framed by West Indian Governments and the Comptroller in
collaboration'. That definition of the functions of the Organisation was
reaffirmed in the Secretary of State's Despatch of 22 November 1944,
in which he requested Governors to arrange for the preparation of
sketch-plans of development. During the years 1940-45 no Colony
knew the CD & W allocation it could expect to receive under the 1940
Act, and applications for financial assistance were often submitted, it
was thought at Hastings House, without regard to overall planning.
There was a tendency to regard the funds provided under the Act as
'easy money' and the Comptroller as a benevolent Father Christmas.
In the circumstances, the Comptroller and his staff played a useful role
as a screening medium, which recommended assistance for only those
projects which were of real importance and would not involve an
undue burden on the Colony's budget in future years.

However, the Secretary of State's Circular Despatch of 12 November 1945 had changed the position. For the first time, each Colony
knew its CD & W allocation. Each Colony was requested to review its
financial resources, and to draw up a ten-year development plan
showing how the resources and CD & W allocation could best be used.
The plans, when approved by the Secretary of State, would contain
only projects which had been accepted as desirable in principle. The
Comptroller had the limited duty of ensuring that each individual
application for financial assistance accorded with the development
plan, that the passage of time did not necessitate any changes in that
plan, and that the details and estimates of the application were in
order. Experience had already shown that the necessary financial
checks were being applied in London, with considerable attention to
detail.

The second principal function of the Organisation as envisaged in
1940 was to provide advice, which was provided for over five and a half
years on almost every conceivable subject. While the presence of a
body of Advisers in the area was valuable, the major need in mid-1946
was seen to be the encouragement and assistance of West Indian
Governments to implement the recommendations already made to
them, which involved executive action rather than advisory functions.
Indeed, the work performed by the Organisation had become
increasingly unconnected with the CD & W Act and progressively

non-advisory. Some of the work, e.g. the organisation of the West Indian Conference of 1944 and the 'follow-up' of the recommendations of the Conference of 1944 and 1946, sprang from the fact that the Comptroller was also the British Co-chairman of the Caribbean Commission. However, much of the work had arisen because the Organisation was the first governmental agency in the West Indies with regional functions and a regional outlook. It had been called upon, in addition to arranging conferences on D & W matters, to organise conferences on such normal administration matters as the supply of oils and fats, currency, priority passage arrangements on British West Indian Airways (BWIA), for example, simply because there was no other suitable convening body for regional conferences. Even so, some problems, such as the administration of BWIA, the posting of staff within the area, and telecommunications, could have been handled better by a properly constituted and recognised regional organisation. Equally, it was felt that the execution of past recommendations would be facilitated if the Advisers were not confined to advisory functions.

It was recognised that the West Indies were too advanced politically to accept a governmental regional agency with executive functions. Indeed, the Organisation held that 'the basic factor (which is perhaps not fully recognised in England) is that the West Indies are *now* ripe for Federation'.[18] In support of that view, it argued that, quite apart from the fact that most of the West Indian legislatures, including the Legislative Councils of Barbados and Jamaica and the House of Representatives in Jamaica, had already welcomed the statement of policy on Federation contained in the Secretary of State's Despatch of 14 March 1945 to Governors of West Indian Colonies[19], there was 'a general realisation of the need for a common approach to West Indian problems'. The successful establishment over recent years of the following was instanced: the British West Indian Sugar Association, the Incorporated Chambers of Commerce of the British Caribbean, the Caribbean Labour Congress and the Federation of Civil Service Associations. War conditions, BWIA, and the Organisation itself were seen to have contributed to the trend towards regionalism, which the press had reinforced with greater regional coverage. 'All that is required is a positive lead to action – a lead which can only be given from London.'[20] It was suggested that this might be given by taking up a proposal made by several of the West Indian legislatures in their debates on Federation. It was that a conference should be convened in the West Indies to discuss the matter, with elected members from each legislature and under the chairmanship of the Secretary of State, or of the Parliamentary Under-Secretary. It was further suggested that the conference should be invited to: (*a*) set up a committee to make recommendations for Federation from the constitutional angle, (*b*) ask His Majesty's Government to establish an organisation to deal with the administrative problems, and (*c*) set up a committee to collaborate with the administrative organisation. The memorandum finally proposed that the D & W Organisation should be given limited executive powers, and should act as the administrative organisation once the proposal had been endorsed by the 'Federation Conference'. The Conference was held in 1947 at Montego Bay, Jamaica.

For the time being, there was no other effective regional organisation, certainly not the Caribbean Commission if many shared the views of the Governor of Barbados, Sir Gratton Bushe, on that body.[21] The attitude of suspicion and of thinly-veiled hostility to the Commission and the West Indian Conference of British officials was said by the Governor to be due to lack of precise information as to the aims, objects, functions and scope of the Commission and of the Conference; a belief that, as far as the Americans were concerned, the primary purpose of the two was to cloak American political and commercial penetration into the Caribbean at the expense of local government and to expose the British as the oppressors and exploiters of subject peoples; the excessive work thrown on overburdened Secretariats; the defective organisation of the two; and the apparent infringement of the 'sovereignty' of the local Governments by the West Indian Conference. The Governor, after elaborating each of these points, concluded that the Commission should be seen as 'the child of the need for co-operation – a means to an end and not an end in itself – and that it is to be the servant of Governments and not their master'. The Governor's elaboration of the point concerning American intentions is reminiscent of the report by Mr P. Hewitt-Myring, Public Relations Adviser to the Comptroller, of a conversation with the American co-chairman of the Commission, Mr Charles Taussig. It went as follows:

'You know, Charles', said that Englishman, 'within half a dozen blocks of where we are now [in Washington, DC], there's enough work to be done on behalf of the down-trodden Negro to keep you busy for the rest of your life. Why don't you get on with it and leave the British to work things out in their own way?' 'Ah', said Taussig, 'I can't do anything about our people.' He gave his most engaging smile. 'But I can about yours.'[22]

The Governor's letter was sympathetically received in the Colonial Office, where his main points had been covered, as far as the Colonial Office could manage to do so, in the drafting of the Executive Agreement of the Commission.[23] At the same time it was felt that the Governor had left out 'some of the wider considerations which we have to take into account'.[24]

The Comptroller complained in January 1947 concerning the attitude of some in the West Indies to his Organisation, largely repeating the substance of his Organisation's own memorandum of 1946.[25] It was felt that the matter should be carefully re-examined, especially as the Comptroller was expected to move to a Governorship early in 1948 and an appropriate successor would have to be appointed. However, at an Office meeting it was decided that, as the longer-term position of the Organisation was so closely bound up with the question of Closer Union between the Colonies in the West Indies, no radical reorganisation was desirable for the time being.[26] Neverthe-less, the Comptroller was reminded of the changed economic situation in the West Indies since the Royal Commission reported, partly as an unexpected result of the war.[27] Local resources had emerged as an important and, in some cases, dominant factor in the financing of development programmes. As a result, Colonial Governments wished to have more control over development plans, and this wish was reinforced by the development of local political control. Conse-quently, it was considered in the Colonial Office that there was 'no future for a D & W Organisation as something exercising even the most tenuous share of the Secretary of State's authority over Colonial Governments' and for the future a different conception was needed.[28] It was suggested, rather, that the Organisation should function as a corps of first-class experts available, as required, to give advice to Colonial Governments in the area, both in the planning of develop-ment and in the framing of policy, even where no CD & W funds were involved. Most of the points made in the memorandum and in Mr Caine's letter appear in the first ten pages of the Report by the Comptroller: *Development of Welfare in the West Indies, 1945–1946* (Colonial No. 212, 1947).

The Comptroller replied on 22 April 1947,[29] enclosing notes by his Education Adviser and his Economic Adviser. The Education Adviser argued the case for a combined unit of investigation and information – a West Indian Commission–with the right of information from West Indian Governments and, virtually, the functions of a standing Inspectorate-General. The Economic Adviser agreed that the existing role of the Organisation was untenable and needed changing. He thought the early lack of definition of the functions of the Organisation more responsible than the 1945 Act for the existing position, though it was not a matter for complaint:

> The circumstances which called into being the original post of Comptroller demanded speedy action and the measures accepted were palliative and opportunist, without necessarily being the worse for that. . . . It has now become increasingly clear that in so far as its original function is concerned, namely to deal with schemes involving expenditure under the Act, this Organisation has a negligible part and one which is bound to be a source of friction with individual Governments.

He contended that the usefulness and effectiveness of an advisory organisation depended, not on the technical power of sanction involving finance, but rather upon the status which was accorded to its advice, and that the D & W Organisation suffered from the lack of a clearly defined status. In order to make the Organisation effective, he felt it should be accorded the status of being the primary source of advice to the Secretary of State upon such general matters as were not the special responsibility of individual Governors. He, too, thought that a right of information and to initiate investigations were essential. While Mr Caine believed that jealousies had arisen because individual Governors had feared that the Comptroller was an embryonic Governor-General, the Economic Adviser had come to the view that 'probably the majority of the senior officials, including Governors, are plainly antagonistic to the policy of the Secretary of State in this matter of development and welfare, and since a successful Governor cannot very well say this, he, by an understandable deviation of object, fixes upon the Comptroller and his works as the object of his antipathy.' He concluded by noting that existing West Indian administrations were weak and needed considerable help, particularly if real progress was to be made towards a federal organisation.

The Comptroller stated that he would have raised the issue of the Organisation's status and future sooner had he not decided to await the outcome of the Closer Association Conference due later that year. He had long felt that the Organisation could best help by working for a representative West Indian body rather than as 'a vague and shadowy projection of the Colonial Office'. He assumed that the minimum result of the Conference would be the establishment of a Council, of which the Organisation's staff, but not the Comptroller, would become part, and the Parliamentary Under-Secretary of State would become chairman. So he was somewhat surprised to find that Mr Caine had raised the question of the Organisation's future *per se* with Federation merely as a possible complicating factor. He agreed that the root of the problem lay in setting up the Royal Commission's Organisation without its Fund to administer, though he did not quarrel with the decision not to accept the Royal Commission's recommendation to set up such a Fund. 'We thought', he wrote, 'of several quotations that might suitably have been used on the title page of our Report for 1945–46, but discarded the idea. One suggestion was to quote from Fowler's *Modern English Usage* under the heading COMPTROLLER: ". . . not merely archaic but erroneous".' He, like his predecessor, had warned the Colonial Office of the problems that the Organisation faced because of failure to define its purpose and of local opposition. He did not, however, believe there was as much resentment as Mr Caine seemed to think. Much turned on the personal predilections of Governors – for 'there *is* no common policy in the British West Indian Colonies.' He said that he would welcome any statement that the Organisation was a purely advisory body, although he shared his Advisers' doubts concerning a corps of experts on tap unless, and until, there was an imposed common policy in the area, because Governors tended to solicit the assistance of Advisers in fields of activity about which they were personally enthusiastic, but were disposed to eschew advice on other subjects, e.g. some Governors wanted no advice on housing and slum clearance and social welfare. Unless a policy was laid down and responsibilities defined, he believed that the services of experts of high quality could not long be retained. Meanwhile, he advised that any change in the status or functions of the Organisation should await the Conference in September.

The Comptroller's letter and enclosures were discussed by officials at the Colonial Office on 30 May 1947.[30] It had already been agreed that the 'Comptroller' idea, i.e. financial control, should be abandoned, but the problem remained of defining the precise future functions of the Organisation. While there was general agreement that the Organisation should be preserved for its advisory and fact-finding uses, the advisability of any quasi-Inspectorate status was disputed. Sir Frank Stockdale insisted that, whatever decision was reached, the Colonial Office should not appear, at any rate in the West Indies, to be abandoning the Report of the 1938–39 Royal Commission. Mr Caine proposed, as a result of the discussion, to write to the Comptroller again on the following lines: (i) complete emphasis should be placed on the advisory position of the Comptroller's Organisation; (ii) Advisers could receive power or authority only from some existing, or future,

West Indian constitution, for it could not be imposed by the Secretary of State; (iii) reorganisation would be limited to the period when West Indian federation was being worked out; (iv) the Secretary of State would be advised to announce at the Montego Bay Conference the intention to maintain the Comptroller's corps of advisers in the West Indies and to fit it into the West Indian Council, or whatever body emerged from the Conference. It was thought that the position of Comptroller also needed consideration. Views differed over the suggested abandonment of the Organisation's detailed scrutiny of individual development schemes, though it was realised that the position would change once the ten-year plans had been approved. It was later realised that there was little purpose in writing to the Comptroller in this way just before the Montego Bay Conference. An official discussed with him instead on the basis that the Organisation might be helped if it were publicly announced that it functioned by advice rather than control.

The future of the Organisation was not discussed at Montego Bay, but a decision was required on its relationship to the Standing Closer Association Committee (SCAC) which that Conference set up. In particular, it was a matter of some urgency to decide the relationship between the successor to Sir John Macpherson, if any, and the Chairman of SCAC, and between the staffs of both. It was felt in the Colonial Office that the two offices should be kept separate, the Comptroller being a civil servant but the Chairman not; while, in any case, the Comptroller was fully employed in his existing dual roles of Comptroller and Co-chairman of the Caribbean Commission. At a meeting at the Colonial Office, attended by Sir John Macpherson, it was agreed that the Comptroller should be separate from the Chairman and inferior to him in status, that he should be replaced by the Chairman as Co-chairman of the Caribbean Commission and be 'simply the leader of a team of specialists'; and that the Education Adviser, who was then Acting Comptroller, might be confirmed in his post.[31]

The Secretary of State agreed[32] with these proposals, under which the Comptroller's staff would become a corps of advisers, divested of any political or administrative functions, while SCAC would take over the Organisation's regional non-CD & W functions and perhaps administer its CD & W schemes also – although it was suggested that these latter might become the responsibility of individual West Indian Governments.[33] This last, however, never came to pass. The title 'Comptroller' lapsed for two years. Major-General Sir Hubert E. Rance became at the same time Chairman of SCAC, Chairman of the

D & W Organisation and Co-chairman of the Caribbean Commission, while Mr Hammond, as Chief Adviser, handled the day-to-day work of the Organisation. [General Rance, GCMG, CB, CBE, had been Major-General in charge of Civil Affairs, Burma, 1945, and Governor of Burma, 1946; he became Governor of Trinidad in 1950.]

As the Colonial Office files 71357 West Indies for 1948 and 1949 have been Destroyed Under Statute, it is unfortunately impossible to trace the evolution of the Organisation while Sir Hubert Rance was Chairman, except through published sources. Sir Hubert Rance published a *Report on the Organisation for 1947–49* (Colonial No. 264, 1950). As from 1 May 1950, the title of 'Comptroller' was revived, and Sir George Seel became both Comptroller and British Co-chairman of the Caribbean Commission.

III. EARLY STEPS TOWARDS FEDERATION

The tentative wartime moves towards a policy on Federation in the West Indies have been examined. Briefly, the Secretary of State, Mr Oliver Stanley, wrote to Governors in the West Indies on 25 July 1944 to suggest that the time was ripe for a declaration of policy on the question. The draft enclosed for comment was couched in political terms, because Federation was regarded by the Secretary of State principally as a vehicle of political advance for the smaller Colonies. The Comptroller urged that to confine the Despatch to political considerations could result in opposition 'from what may be described as capitalistic interests and an increase in the professed lack of confidence'.[34] He went on to say:

It seems to me that it would be desirable to take the opportunity of the publication of the Despatch to guide public opinion by stressing the need for Federation on economic and administrative grounds. It might, with advantage, show that co-operative action on economic and administrative issues may well be found necessary, either by the British West Indies as a whole or by the Eastern Group, whether or not political federation was achieved.

The Secretary of State told the Comptroller that he appreciated the points made, 'especially the desirability of stressing the need for federation on economic and administrative grounds'.[35] The final version of the Despatch, dated 14 March 1945, incorporated this latter suggestion. It proposed that a Conference might be called to consider the formulation of proposals for closer association.

The Despatch was debated by Legislative Councils throughout the West Indies and, on the basis of the reports received, the Permanent Under-Secretary of State felt that 'there is no doubt that opinion in the West Indies has become much more favourably inclined towards Federation.'[36] However, some reservations had been expressed. The Acting Governor of Jamaica, Mr, later Sir Hugh, Foot (who became Lord Caradon), reported that: 'The idea of federation, though steadily gaining strength, is still in its infancy in Jamaica politics. It seems to me to be important not to attempt to press for conclusion on the issue too soon.'[37] Following a conversation with Mr Alexander Bustamante, a member of the Executive Council and the leading politician, Mr Foot reported that caution in the approach to federation was advisable until more was known about its implications. Meanwhile, it was accepted that it would be a serious mistake if the Jamaica Government did anything to obstruct or retard the movement.[38] This message caused no surprise in the Colonial Office.[39] The Legislative Council of the Bahamas was unanimously against federation.[40] Unofficial opinion in British Guiana's Legislative Council was unfavourable, showing 'very evident distrust of a centralised machine in the Islands'.[41] When the debate was resumed after an adjournment, the Governor and Acting Attorney-General managed to convince the Council that discussion of the issues with the Islands was a better approach than outright condemnation.[42] It was accepted in the Colonial Office that the Bahamas would not participate; and that membership by the two mainland territories was doubtful.

The proposals in the Despatch had been 'quite deliberately vague' as officials had felt that, tactically, it was better to get Legislatures to commit themselves to the aim of federation, and build further from that, than to risk dissension by putting concrete proposals to them in the first place.[43] This was probably wise but, in accepting the Permanent Under-Secretary's advice to proceed, the Parliamentary Under-Secretary expressed his anxiety that 'we should become a bit more concrete about this vague idea of Federation – what we mean by it and whether we can prepare in draft for discussion some principles and proposals.'[44] The Secretary of State was in general agreement, and a memorandum was drafted, which proposed an initial Conference on Closer Association and, as a basis for discussion, a federation on the Australian model.[45]

In a comment on the memorandum, the Comptroller's Education Adviser held it was

necessary to show clearly the ponderable advantages that would result to the West Indian peoples, against the increase in governmental expense, political and administrative delays, and the burden of paper, which a Federal Government of the form proposed might entail, apart from the complexity of legislation necessary to bring it into being *vis-à-vis* existing Colonial legislation.

He hazarded a guess that federation 'among those who think about it at all, is commonly felt to be vaguely desirable as a means of unity, but that objections to it when they arise will be sharply realised. The financial issue alone will be crucial . . . An obligation of a metropolitan country to aid her Colonies is understandable. An obligation of Colonies to aid each other is less clear. If the reason is that they were British, why should the obligation be confined to the West Indies? If the reason is regional, why should it be confined to the British Colonies?' His positive contribution was to suggest that the initial Conference might establish a West Indian Council, with members from all Colonies, under the chairmanship of the Parliamentary Under-Secretary of State, and with a Secretariat and advisers drawn in the first place from the Comptroller's Organisation. The Council as such was not intended to have either sanctions or authority, but its chairman was expected to be able to influence Colonial Governments because he was a Minister of the United Kingdom Government.[46] The proposal was discussed by the Comptroller at a meeting with officials at the Colonial Office, where it was well received.[47] In the Comptroller's opinion, the essential advantage of the proposal was that it provided for Ministerial authority on the spot; and, while the Council would probably be left-wing in its opinion and might even at times be embarrassingly radical, that was inevitable and need not be regarded as a matter of concern. It was decided to incorporate the proposal in a memorandum, which would explain both the hard facts of the existing position of West Indian Colonies and also the case for closer association and the various forms it could take. A Memorandum along these lines was published in May 1947, together with a Despatch of 14 February 1947 which reviewed the debates on the Federation Despatch of 14 March 1945 and outlined the kind of Conference proposed for September 1947.[48]

A small 'working party' was set up in the Colonial Office to draft briefs for the Chairman of the Conference, which it was decided to hold in Montego Bay, Jamaica. At the same time, the Colonial Office was anxious to avoid prejudicing the deliberations of the Conference by submitting a complete set of detailed proposals for one or other form of closer association, even if such a course were possible in advance of some indication of the sort of line which the Conference was likely to take.[49] The Comptroller believed that it was desirable for the Secretary of State to lay down the principles upon which Treasury assistance would be offered in certain types of closer association,[50] as paragraph 23 of the Memorandum (Cmd 7120) caused uncertainty and apprehension. The paragraph ended: 'Any direct assistance to the Federal Government other than that given through specific schemes under the Colonial Development and Welfare Act of 1945 would appear to entail some restriction of that Government's authority.' Indeed, at the St Kitts Conference on Closer Union of the Leewards and Windwards, the Economic Adviser had felt it would have helped if a definition had been given of the 'extra expenses of federation' which the Treasury was prepared to meet for a period of years. Yet it is difficult to see how this could be done in advance of a clearer definition of the issue. In any case, the Treasury was not represented on the working parties nor at Montego Bay nor, it seems, was the Treasury consulted over either.

When the Comptroller was told of the decision to prepare a series of briefs for the Chairman of the Montego Bay Conference, the official added a handwritten 'personally personal postscript'. This included the question

> whether we do not harp too much on the strain of not wanting to force local opinion, and whether it would not pay dividends if the Colonial Office went to the Conference with a definite purpose, viz. to secure the setting up of an Office which would combine the functions of Governor-General and Comptroller, with the re-alisation that we may have to accept, as an interim second-best, someone who would combine the functions of Comptroller and permanent Chairman of a West Indian Council à la Hammond.[51]

This, however, was a minority view in the Office. More representative was the view expressed by Sir Sydney Caine, when he said that 'even assuming the best possible result from the Conference, it would still be some fairly considerable time before any effective machinery of closer association were set up in the West Indies.'[52] While he admitted this might be unduly pessimistic, he was surprised by the Comptroller's apparent expectation of either 'an effective federation or other machinery of closer association might come into being quite quickly'. The Comptroller marginally commented rather astringently: 'If the Colonial Office is defeatist, they are hypocrites!' In reply to Mr Seel's thoughts, he agreed that, at some stage, it might be highly desirable for the Office to take a fairly positive line, though he felt sure that it would be 'quite wrong to *start* by making it known that the Colonial Office had any definite purpose that was short of full federation'.[53] He endorsed the line taken in the memorandum in the White Paper, namely that the Conference should be free 'to go all out for a full Federal Constitution', as he believed that any attempt 'to fob the delegates off at the start with a *pis aller* would have a very adverse reception'.

The *Memorandum on Closer Association in the West Indies* which accompanied the Secretary of State's Despatch of 14 February 1947, i.e. Part II of Cmd 7120, showed that there were means other and less drastic than federation, among them the formation of a West Indian Council without legislative powers, by which some degree of closer association might be attained. However, these suggestions were put forward without much conviction. At the Conference, which opened at Montego Bay, Jamaica, on 11 September 1947, the delegates quickly adopted the view that they had assembled to examine the possibility of setting up nothing less than a Government of the West Indies.[54] In his opening address, the Secretary of State, Mr Creech Jones, quoted with approval from the published Memorandum that

> possibly the most important reason of all for the view that closer association is necessary lies in the fact that it is clearly impossible in the modern world for the present separate communities, small and isolated as most of them are, to achieve and maintain full self-government on their own. . . . On the other hand, a community of well over two million people in the Caribbean area, with much that is homogeneous in their culture, could reasonably hope to achieve real self-government, and to be strong enough to stand against economic and cultural pressure and to formulate and carry through a policy and way of life of its own.[55]

At the same time, the Secretary of State pledged the continuance of CD & W assistance and a contribution from CDC when it was established. Mr W. A. Bustamante questioned the benefits of federation on the grounds that he had 'never heard that in joining with bankrupts one can become successful or prosperous'.[56] He asked what power the federal government would have and, on finance, stated that 'although we of the West Indies are all alike, to me Jamaica and Jamaica's interests come first.'[57] He explained that he was not opposed to federation which would come 'one day', though he was unable to envisage 'the possibility of walking with a group of creeping and non-creeping persons'.[58] Another Jamaican, Mr N. W. Manley, who attended as a member of the British Section, Caribbean Commission, answered this argument.

> Federation by itself [he said] will not bring prosperity, but federation will enlarge the area of action and enlarge the possibilities of winning that prosperity which we West Indians alone can, and certainly must, create for ourselves. If the West Indies cannot produce a team of men in a federal cabinet that can see these lands of ours, and in some of them these teeming populations, and work out the beginnings of some regional plan of development which will give us the hope of being able to tackle the problem of unemployment, give us the hope of being able to find what sort of civilisation is possible for us and how it may be achieved, and set to work to make that plan effective, then all we deserve, each and all of us, is to be reduced back to the status of Crown Colonies.

It is one of the ironies of history that this protagonist of federation should, eleven years later, when the arguments on finance of his political opponent, Sir Alexander Bustamante, were pressing, bring about the collapse of the young Federation by holding a referendum on the issue: 'Should Jamaica remain in the Federation of the West Indies?'

At Montego Bay the representatives of the territories agreed, with one reservation to the first resolution, to fifteen resolutions in all.[59] In the first, it was resolved: 'That this Conference, recognising the desirability of a political federation of the British Caribbean territories, accepts the principle of a federation in which each constituent unit retains complete control over all matters except those specifically assigned to the federal government.' So any federation would be on the Australian, rather than the Canadian, model, i.e. the units would retain the 'residual powers'. The delegation of British Guiana registered its reservation, on the grounds that they had no mandate from their Colony to accede to it in the name of British Guiana. It was more remarkable that all the rest were prepared so to resolve. In the second resolution, they set down the condition on which they had done so, namely: 'That this Conference believes that an increasing measure of responsibility should be extended to the several units of the British Caribbean territories, whose political development must be pursued as an aim in itself, without prejudice and in no way subordinate to progress towards federation.'

As the interest here is not in West Indian federation as such, all the remaining resolutions, with one exception, may be passed over at this place. The others concerned: shipping and other communications; establishing a central body of primary producers; setting up a Trade Commissioner Service, a Customs Union enquiry and a Regional Economic Committee (the last to report on matters of common economic significance); adoption of recommendations on currency and a common financial year; recommendation that HMG should consider changes in the method of Treasury control of grant-aided Colonies and the possibility of substituting a block grant for three years to aid such territories; setting up an enquiry into the unification of public services in the area. The exception, Resolution 6, laid down what the next step should be. The Conference recommended: 'the immediate constitution of a Standing Closer Association Committee, composed of delegates appointed by the Legislatures of each unit in the British Caribbean . . . and of a Chairman and Secretary appointed by the Secretary of State.' The SCAC was requested to consider, and make recommendations, on (a) the assimilation of tariffs and of the legislation of the territories, (b) the unification of the currency of the territories, (c) the unification as far as was practicable of the public services of the territories, (d) the form of a federal constitution and federal judiciary 'most likely to give effect to the aspirations of the people of such territories', and (e) the means of financing the operation of all federal services, 'regard being had to all proposals in relation to this subject made to the Conference . . . at Montego Bay. . . .' The SCAC was to consist of seventeen West Indian representatives, two each from the five largest territories – Barbados, British Guiana, British Honduras, Jamaica and Trinidad and Tobago – and one each from the other seven territories – Antigua, Montserrat, St Kitts, Dominica, Grenada, St Lucia, St Vincent. The Conference, realising that the Chairman of SCAC would also be in charge of the D & W Organisation, recommended 'that the headquarters of the above Committee be in Barbados'. As stated earlier, Sir Hubert Rance became Chairman of SCAC, Chairman of the D & W Organisation in Barbados and Co-chairman of the Caribbean Commission. In a minute on the Montego Bay Conference to the Prime Minister, Mr Attlee, the Secretary of State, reported that 'the progress made was good, though some years must pass before federation can be made a reality'.[60]

Some Governors in the West Indies felt left out in the cold when the Montego Bay Conference was convened with political representatives from the territories to discuss the administrative structure, for which Governors were still responsible.[61] It was suggested, therefore, that the idea of a Governors' Conference should be considered and should take place before the proposed SCAC got down to work. All the Governors endorsed the idea of a meeting except the Governor of Jamaica, Sir John Huggins, who feared that 'even an informal Conference would arouse suspicion and might well jeopardise the smooth working of the Standing Closer Association Committee'.[62] However, it was agreed to proceed with the Conference.[63] An appropriate date was very hard to come by. The Minister of State, Lord Listowel, who was to preside, suggested 7 November 1949 as the opening date.[64] He was concerned that it should be announced early enough, in order to avoid the impression that it would consider the Report of SCAC without regard to what Legislatures might decide to do about that Report.[65]

After taking up his appointment, the Chairman of SCAC made a tour of the area (except for British Guiana, where the visit had to be postponed).[66] He was convinced that the key to any wide federation lay in Jamaica. He felt that Mr Bustamante's true feelings were those given in his first speech at Montego Bay, and that the attachment of Mr Manley and the People's National Party to federation made it hard for him to accept the same views, even if he wished to do so. Mr Manley pointed out the weakness of any regional economic development without a controlling executive body, which body, he said, could best be provided by federation. At the same time, Mr Manley admitted that, in his opinion, the smaller Colonies were not ripe for self-government, adding that even Jamaica's political consciousness was a growth but ten years old. The Chairman doubted whether SCAC would get far, or fast, with political federation. While he hoped to be able to set up an executive body with power delegated by the separate governments to run customs union, trade commissioners, unified services, etc., he realised that federation was anything but a burning issue. A few politicians were keen on it, but that was about all: 'We are not riding a tide of public feeling, and I don't know that the tide is even approaching us. We shall have to push our boat to the water.'[67] He stated that the amount of real thinking about the practical implications of Federation was negligible.

In answer to the Minister of State's request for guidance for his visit to the various West Indian territories prior to the Governors' Conference, the response was rather discouraging.[68] First, he was told that the fact had to be accepted that there was a widespread and probably ineradicable distrust of the motives of HMG. As a result, any policy strongly urged by the HMG was *ipso facto* suspect. Thus, the Secretary of State's statements at Montego Bay that HMG would support a federated West Indies caused some, particularly in Jamaica, to infer that HMG would be less well disposed to an unfederated West Indies. So it was thought to be desirable not to appear to 'push' federation, but to emphasise that the decision was one for the West Indians themselves. Secondly, misconceptions abounded as to the nature of a federal structure, and the widespread ignorance was used by some who did not wish openly to oppose the idea. It was accordingly advised that 'the omens were *against* the acceptance by the region of *any* proposals that the SCAC might put forward at that time'; it was, therefore, necessary to take a long view, as a 'now or never' basis was certain to mean 'never'.[69] The immediate contribution of the Report of SCAC was seen to be educative.

After four sessions, the SCAC agreed on its Report in October 1949.[70] The approach of the SCAC to its task was typified by the following sentences in paragraph 9 of their Report:[71]

We start from the assumption that the main underlying purpose of our task is to seek the shortest path towards a real political independence for the British peoples of the region, within the framework of the British Commonwealth – what is meant in fact by 'Dominion Status', . . . While we reaffirm the view expressed at the Montego Bay Conference that the political development of the units must be pursued as an aim in itself, we are satisfied that the sheer force of circumstances of the modern world makes independence on a unit basis a mirage. Independence or self-government as a Federation is however a practical possibility, and we have framed our proposals with this specific objective in view.

The full details of the Report hardly require repetition here. It is sufficient to note that a British Caribbean Federation of the territories represented was recommended, with an executive and legislative structure comprising a Governor-General, a Council of State of 14 members and a legislature of two Chambers, viz. Senate of 23 members and a House of Assembly of 50 members. According to Professor Beasley, there was an instruction that the Australian model should be followed in the relation between unit Governments and the Federal Government so that residual powers were left with unit Governments, but there was never any suggestion that the Australian arrangement of subjects should be followed as closely as had taken place.[72] Among other recommendations, it was proposed that, for a period of ten years, HMG should make to the Federation an annual grant equivalent to the average annual amount paid to units over the preceding five years, by way of grant-aid, and that on the establishment of Federation units should look, in the first place, to the Federation, not to HMG, for any grant-aid they might require. It was agreed that command of a specific source of revenue was necessary if the Federation was to enjoy the internal and international status required to enable it to discharge its function. It was proposed that Federal revenues should consist of not more than one quarter of the customs revenues of the Federation. The Federation would, in effect, be a customs union and free trade area.

The Chairman came to believe that Mr A. Gomes of Trinidad and Mr V. C. Bird of Antigua were probably the only two members of the Committee who were genuinely interested in Federation for its own sake.[73] He thought that the main strength of the Report, on the general policy side, was the clear demonstration of the financial and economic situation of the region in relation to constitutional realities. The acceptance of the situation was largely due, the Chairman said, to the efforts of Professor Beasley at the second session in Trinidad. The Minister of State had earlier been advised that the argument that self-government must be in step with financial stability might be used to a chosen audience. But he was warned that to some West Indians such an argument was anathema: 'they believe, like the Irish, that HMG is perpetually in debt to the West Indies for errors or omissions of the past three hundred years. The sum mentioned, in all seriousness, to liquify this debt is astronomical. . . .'[74] The Chairman expected that the recommendations would be assailed from both sides and might be rejected by some Legislatures, probably on the matter of representation in the House of Assembly. At the same time, he was unable to conceive of any body of recommendations which would achieve immediate and unanimous acceptance. Certainly there was no quick response in the territories.

Governors had received copies of the Report for their own confidential information by the time the Governors' Conference was convened in Barbados on 7 November 1949, and it was discussed at the morning session on the last day of the Conference, 11 November.[75] The Governor of Jamaica said that reaction in Jamaica depended largely on the outcome of the December elections, but it was possible to proceed with some interim steps, such as common customs legislation and tariffs, though this pre-federal action could not extend to the establishment of any central authorities for customs or other purposes, except the Regional Economic Committee to which Jamaica had already agreed.[76] The Acting Governor said there was in Trinidad no coherent opposition to federation, though the unpopularity of the chief advocate of federation, Mr A. Gomes, could become an important obstacle. There was a strong desire to postpone a decision until the new constitution was in being, which would be around the middle of 1950.[77] The Governor said there would be a strong majority against federation in British Honduras. The voting provisions proposed in the Report were likely to cause difficulty, 'owing to the antipathy between the people of British Honduras and Jamaica, and the large preponderance of votes which the latter would have in the federation'.[78]

The Governor of the Windward Islands thought that, for the smaller islands, there would be difficulty in securing a sufficient number of suitable candidates for office in a federal parliament as well as in the local legislature.[79] An official said that the Report was rightly based on the ambitions of the West Indies to become self-dependent, though it was impossible to make any assumption that the area could become self-dependent financially and economically. As the Report had to be submitted to Legislature for debate, there would be perhaps two years before the prospects of federation were known.[80] The Chairman of SCAC said that nothing less than full federation had been contemplated, but a form of federation of the Eastern Caribbean would be feasible if Jamaica, for example, did not accept the idea of federation. No right of secession was provided for in the Report.[81]

In May 1951 it was felt in the Colonial Office that the attitude of Jamaica was crucial in that, if Jamaica decided in favour of federation, the way forward would be clear.[82] It was wondered once again whether HMG could give a lead effectively in favour of federation. Sir Hubert Rance, now Governor of Trinidad, repeated his view that HMG should take no part in trying to force federation on the Colonies – though a lot of good could be done by an occasional letter asking those Colonies who had not debated the SCAC Report, when it was proposed, to do so.[83] The new Comptroller in Barbados, Sir G. Seel, stated that 'As far as we are concerned, our efforts from Hastings House must, so long as the Secretary of State's attitude is one of studious neutrality, be confined to encouraging as much as possible active participation in the Regional Economic Committee and Customs Union. Either or both of these may turn out to lead to federation by a side passage while the front gate remains locked.'[84] The Governor of Jamaica, Sir Hugh Foot, realising that progress towards Federation was delayed largely as a result of Jamaica's failure to make a move, endorsed the view presented by the Governor of Trinidad, as he believed that 'if the Secretary of State made a public appeal to the outstanding West Indian Legislatures to give early attention to this question more harm than good would be done.'[85] When the issue was discussed in the Executive Council in Jamaica the Opposition, led by

Mr N. W. Manley, was extremely critical of much of the SCAC
Report, with the consequence that Ministers were anxious to avoid the
need to defend the whole Report against the attacks.[86] However, it was
resolved to accept the aim of West Indies federation, to accept the
Report as a basis of achieving Dominion Status, and to propose that a
Conference of West Indian representatives should be held in London
to consider the financial aspect of federation.[87] The Comptroller
commented in September 1951: 'There seems to be a certain
awakening in Jamaica it is true, due partly to the fact that we have a
Governor who is interested in the matter and partly to local political
tactics. Elsewhere 1951 has seemed to me disappointing.'

The Secretary of State had no objection to the proposal for a
London meeting[88] and, on 6 February 1952, his successor, Mr Oliver
Lyttelton, published a Despatch on the proposal, which showed that
he was prepared to proceed in the direction of Federation.[89] But, as in
a chess tournament, moves were only made after a respectable
interval. On 16 June 1952 Mr W. A. Bustamante, the Majority Party
leader, announced that he was in favour of a Federation of the British
West Indies, although he added that 'Jamaica will not be railroaded
into a Federation without full and indisputable evidence that a BWI
Federation will benefit this island and the region as a whole'.[90] In
order to maintain interest in federation, the Executive Council of
Jamaica suggested in August 1952 that a date, preferably in late
March or early April 1953, should be announced.[91] The Governor of
the Leeward Islands warmly endorsed this suggestion.[92] However, the
Secretary of State doubted whether it would be wise to hold a London
Conference until a preliminary meeting between representatives of
Governments had been held in the West Indies to consider the
situation resulting from (a) the decision of British Guiana and British
Honduras not to participate in federation, and (b) the declared
intention of the Jamaica Legislature to press for substantial change in
the SCAC plan.[93] But the Governor of Jamaica feared that, in a
Conference in the West Indies, more extreme and unrealistic views
would prevail over more moderate ones, whereas this would not be so
likely to occur in London.[94] Mr A. Gomes of Trinidad and Mr J. A.
Renwick of Grenada argued strongly along the same lines and the
Governor and Secretary of State accepted the view.[95] Accordingly, he
suggested that the holding of a Conference in London in late March or
early April should be announced; the date eventually fixed for the
opening of the Conference was 13 April 1953.[96]

Meantime, doubts were growing in the West Indies on the value of a
federation on the lines proposed in the SCAC Report. The Under-

Secretary of State, the Earl of Munster, found during his tour of the territories during the spring of 1952 that doubts had been expressed, in particular, on the availability of suitable federal civil servants and of suitable federal legislators, as these latter would, under the terms of the SCAC Report, be excluded from local legislatures.[97] The Comptroller was no less doubtful whether the proposals of the SCAC Report were on the right lines: there appeared to be no popular urge for federation and little understanding of the full implications of political federation. Most of the smaller islands were, he thought, approaching a state of bankruptcy and the SCAC proposals for their representation in the federal legislature would not be acceptable to the larger Colonies. Professor Beasley argued that the small islands could not carry the overheads involved in 'double-decker' legislatures and the paraphernalia of administration that went with them. He felt that the balance of advantage lay in external pressure towards a Customs Union, which represented the only way, short of federation, by which the British West Indies could attain a recognised international status in, e.g., commercial negotiations and on international economic and financial matters. Also, it would bring the Colonies together in their common interest, providing a realistic approach to some of the common problems of the area. However, the Colonial Office found Professor Beasley's statement on the financial issues involved in West Indian federation a 'disappointing document' which did 'no more than gild the SCAC's lily'.[98] It was suggested that the D & W Organisation should instead circulate its own conclusions on the financial issues in the light of such information as was available, with indications of the practical implications.

iv. THE ROLE OF THE ORGANISATION, 1949–1953

This latter proposal implied a positive pre-federal role for the D & W Organisation. The development of such a role followed naturally from the Montego Bay Conference and the setting up of the SCAC. It was further encouraged by the Governors' Conference. A memorandum on the possible future functions of the Organisation was prepared by the Chief Adviser on the basis of memoranda by each of the Advisers, and circulated to the Colonial Office and Governors in the West Indies prior to the holding of the Governors' Conference in November 1949. The Social Welfare Adviser thought that the Organisation 'should fill the gaps in local administration as judged by modern standards. It should control some funds in order to ensure that the social services do not fall below a decent minimum owing to poverty. . . . It should not be limited by Governors' concepts of administration but should be a repository of high and enlightened standards.'[99] It was thought better not to tell the Governors this. The Assistant Adviser for Agricultural Education felt that, as schemes were usually received by D & W in their final form, the Organisation always appeared in the role of destructive critic rather than that of a colleague in construction. Similarly, when faced, on visiting territories, with gross mismanagement of schemes involving large sums of British taxpayers' money and clearly doomed to failure, D & W had no *locus standi* to suggest ways of improvement. He suggested that, in all matters relating to development expenditure, whether of British or local funds, D & W should be recognised as the agent of the Colonial Office, so that applications to spend funds would proceed to the Colonial Office *via* the Organisation and all Colonial Office comment would pass through the Organisation.[100] The Administrative Secretary put forward the following points for consideration: (*a*) the Organisation might play a more considerable part in the review of development plans than it had done in their initial formulation; (*b*) the basic strategic task, being mainly economic in nature, required a strengthening of the economic side; (*c*) the emphasis on in-service training of officials should be endorsed, and Governments advised to make the utmost use of it; (*d*) copies of applications for CD & W assistance, or for the extension or variation of schemes, should continue to be sent to the Organisation; (*e*) the practice of consulting the Organisation at an early stage on proposals should be extended; and (*f*) Governors should be invited to comment on the usefulness of each and every advisory post and whether any additional subjects should be provided.[101] The Construction Engineer thought the pooling of information in his field should be encouraged,[102] while the Building Research Officer wanted the Organisation's responsibilities towards schemes in progress laid down and suggested there should be closer relations with local development committees.[103] These notes were distilled into a series of questions, as it was feared that some Governors would not otherwise read the memorandum and, in the process, at least one justification for the Organisation was dropped in the interest of good relations,[104] namely that: 'Any force which tends to moderate the twin curses of West Indian administration – opportunism in politics and discontinuity in administrative personnel – is worth using.' In acknowledging a copy of the memorandum, it was pointed out from the Colonial Office that there was no more CD & W money left unallocated and that that, together with the economy breeze which was beginning to blow, was not going to make it easy to get additions to staff.[105]

At the Governors' Conference, it was agreed that the Organisation provided a useful service and should be continued. It was hoped that the services it provided would be taken over and maintained by any federal organisation that might be established.[106] It was agreed that assistance from the Organisation would be useful and would, as appropriate, be sought, both in the preparation of Development Plans, where these had not already been approved, and where reviews were undertaken. It was agreed that the help of the Organisation's Advisers in reviewing departmental policy might usefully be sought from time to time by Governors. It was agreed that any defects in the administration of a D & W scheme should be made known to the Governor and, if there was any divergence of view in a matter of importance between a Governor and an Adviser on the staff of the Organisation, the Secretary of State should be informed, usually by the Governor or, if he so decided, by the head of the Organisation. The arrangements for holding regional conferences were agreed to be satisfactory, and the services rendered by the Organisation in that connection were warmly appreciated by Colonial Governments. If funds were available, it was agreed that it would be useful to have both a Statistical Officer and an assistant to the Economic Adviser. So the Organisation received the commendation and support that it sought from Governors. It had become in integral part, on the economic side, of the apparatus of Colonial development in the area.

This was not thought to be true of the Caribbean Commission, either by the Organisation or by the Governors. When a Colonial Office brief on the Commission was discussed by D & W Organisation officials, it was agreed that there was no problem of 'overlapping' between it and the Commission, as the latter was 'not a fruitful source of useful advice or assistance on anything'.[107] At the Governors' Conference, the difficulties of setting up an international organisation with purely advisory and consultative functions were appreciated, but disappointments was expressed with the nature of its contribution, which had not been commensurate with its cost to HMG.[108] However, it was accepted that the Commission had fulfilled a purpose in the field of international co-operation in the area in that, otherwise, the Dependent Territories Division of the United Nations Organisation might have concerned itself more with the affairs of the British West Indies. As HMG had agreed to support the strengthening of international co-operation to deal with regional, social and economic problems, there was no question of withdrawing from the Commission, though the British Section would be expected to encourage economy and ensure that the work of the Commission was directed towards, and confined to, such projects as would provide a real service and be of direct benefit to the area. It was agreed that HMG should support the Caribbean Research Council which, although it had been set up in 1946, had held meetings only in December 1947 and May 1949. Although the Committees of the Council had not met at all, they were being reorganised; it was hoped that, with the team of members nominated by the British Section, it should be possible to ensure that future activities would be confined to essentials.

As from 1 May 1950, when Sir George Seel became head of the Organisation, there was a reversion to the title of 'Comptroller'. He wrote to the Colonial Office after six weeks' tenure of the appointment to say he had not found a great deal to do.[109] He went on: 'I have not the equipment of special knowledge or experience to enable me to figure as a Stockdale and, in any case, I think the time for that in this particular organisation is past. There is a definite lull in SCAC and the subject of Caribbean Commission correspondence between us is not, as you will agree, particularly edifying.' If there were no revival of activity on the federation front, he said he would plead before long to be recalled to the Colonial Office. But he assumed there would be a revival and, in any case, felt that to abolish the Organisation 'would look unutterably silly and might strike quite a resounding blow against what remains of the United Kingdom's general prestige in these parts'. According to the *Barbados Advocate* of 10 January 1952, at the time of the Governors' Conference 'there was a very keen anti-British sentiment in the area' which had since been largely dissipated. Those who persisted were alleged either to admire Russian imperialism or to wish to denounce Britain's mistakes in the area in order 'to feather their own unsavoury nests'.[110] He recommended that the post of Chief Adviser be discontinued now that the Comptroller was not involved in SCAC matters. In an accompanying memorandum on staffing needs, the Comptroller's main points were, first, that the Advisers should work to a co-ordinated plan and, therefore, a senior administrative officer should be in charge and, secondly, the chief function of the Organisation was becoming that of a regional co-ordinating agency, which was necessary in the absence of any political association of the Colonies or the embryo of a federal organisation, if political association should come about.[111] A case was put forward for reviving the posts of Engineering Adviser and Labour Adviser and creating the posts of Statistical Adviser, Assistant Public Relations Adviser and Adviser on Public Services, the last being intended for the existing Chief Adviser. The memorandum was accepted in the Colonial Office as 'a most valuable and authoritative piece of work'[112] and proposals on staffing were put to the Treasury, which readily agreed.[113]

Meantime, the Comptroller's suggestion that the Organisation should be regarded as the local centre for regional co-ordination had been taken seriously, and he was 'a little staggered' by what it could mean in practice. Apart from the Caribbean Commission, he was expecting to have to accept the titular overlordship of the Directorate of Aeronautical Telecommunications, and possibly of the Meteorological Services and of Civil Aviation, as well as the organisation for emigration from the islands to British Honduras, and the Regional Economic Commission.[114] In view of the 'somewhat untidy' result of the Trinidad elections, he thought it would be a useful step to enlarge the scope of the Organisation as a regional co-ordinating body.

Thus, in the period 1949 to 1950, satisfaction with the Organisation was expressed by the Governors and by the Colonial Office, both for its past contributions and in its new regional role. However, this was not so in the area, particularly in the smaller islands. In January 1951 two Colonial Office officials toured the area, receiving an impression which the West India Royal Commissioners of 1938–39 would have readily recognised and appreciated: 'The principal impression which [we] had of Antigua was of dilapidation and disrepair. St Lucia, with its lack of agricultural tradition and its mendicant attitude, filled us with an even deeper and more insidious gloom. St Vincent . . ., in spite of its deteriorating finances, we found in certain remarkable respects stimulating and encouraging.'[115] The main problem was still, as it had been in 1938–39, the pressure of increasing population on small, isolated territories with slender agricultural economies and virtually no industry. Despite years of spending on so-called 'balanced' development plans, it was found that, with notable exceptions, the policy had failed. One symptom of the failure was recurrent costs growing faster than local revenues. It arose from the tendency to provide in development plans for social improvement, regardless of the degree of economic, i.e. income and revenue-raising, advance. This was sometimes alleged to be justified on the ground that the improvement of social conditions was a necessary basis for economic progress. However, the fundamental social problem was seen to be over-population in relation to resources. Accordingly, the officials concluded that 'a resolute concentration on the development and utilisation of economic resources is the only policy which, apart from maintaining financial stability, can hope to strike at the root of the social evil.' Despite the efforts of the past decade, the basic problem was no nearer solution; for the future an emphasis on economic development was regarded as essential.

This emphasis had been placed already by the Secretary of State in informing Colonial Governments of the new CD & W Act. It was realised that, with the rise in import prices, to which sterling devaluation had contributed, the growth of recurrent expenditure was not entirely avoidable, and the Windwards and Leewards would require larger grants-in-aid of administration. It was recognised to be unwise to resist urgently necessary wage and salary increases, and even food subsidies, on the grounds that local resources were inadequate. It was said that it was 'easy to see, against the background of unrest already occurring in Grenada, and perhaps not far below the surface on other islands, where such a policy could lead'. Already the policy had caused such a deterioration in the standard of administration that day-to-day problems were being neglected, and there was, therefore, little hope of coping with development problems or, without consider-able cost, making good the physical deterioration to assets. While not true of all the islands, it was said to be outstandingly true of Antigua, where HMG would have to accede to some increase in grants-in-aid if there was to be avoidance of frustrating, with one hand, the development that it was hoped to promote with the other. It was thought that the arrears in maintenance of works in Antigua was, at least partly, due to past indifference engendered by the knowledge that when the building fell down or the capital got burnt out HMG would have to provide a replacement.

While it was realised that condemnation came easier than reform of the system, it was proposed that the grant-in-aid should be assessed on the basis of a review of the probable requirements over the next three years and, barring catastrophes, kept at that level for the full three years. At the Montego Bay Conference, HMG was invited to consider the possibility of effecting changes in the methods of Treasury control of grant-aided Colonies (Resolution 12) and to consider, as an experimental measure, the advantages of substituting a block grant for three years to aid such territories, while freeing them of direct year-to-year budgetary control for the three years covered by the grant (Resolution 13). The Report of SCAC included a proposal for a block grant for ten years to Treasury-controlled West Indian Colonies administered by the proposed federal authority. The proposals were passed to the Treasury on the basis of a block grant for five, not ten, years. The problem of estimating was admitted to be difficult for, if 'contingencies' were included in the figure, it might well weaken the main purpose of instilling a sense of responsibility and initiative, but if there were no allowance for such contingencies further false economies might be unavoidable. A minimum working reserve was suggested to cover the possibility and avoid the drawbacks of either alternative. Assessment of the need on a three-year basis should, it was suggested, be carried out by officials from the Colonial Office and the Treasury. Even if the scheme was not adopted, it was thought to be useful for a team of officials to visit the area during the year to study the problems at first hand.

The issue of Treasury control was a perennial source of annoyance and irritation in the West Indies. In 1947 the Governor of British Honduras told his Colonial Secretary that the repeated delays in approving the Estimates – the final approval was received on 23 August for the financial year beginning on the previous 1 January – not only caused considerable losses at a time when prices were rising but also 'made our attempts to educate the local Legislature in financial responsibility appear insincere'.[116] The view was heartily agreed in the Colonial Office, where it was felt that Treasury control 'gets worse every day'.[117] The Governor felt that if the goodwill of 'this very loyal Colony' was to be retained, some simplification of Treasury control was necessary. At the Montego Bay Conference in September 1947 delegates from grant-aided Colonies expressed the exasperation which was being increasingly felt over the delays in securing approval of their Estimates, and the general impotence of the local Legislatures, with rare exception, to dispose of revenue derived from the pockets of the people of the Colony. However, there was another side to the issue: where Parliament had voted monies in aid of Colonial revenues, the first duty of the Accounting Officers and Departments of HMG was to ensure that the funds were applied to the purpose for which Parliament intended them.[118] Whether this could be achieved without the existing detailed scrutiny and control over each item of a Colonial budget needed exploration. Certainly the possibility was held out, in connection with the proposals for Closer Association of the West Indian Colonies, that assistance could be provided without the existing kind of scrutiny. The Treasury was asked to discuss the possibility with the Colonial Office;[119] and, as Hong Kong, the Western Pacific – where the Governor, Sir Brian Freeston, was 'as a newcomer . . . deeply disturbed at the delays in approval of Annual Estimates . . . and the absence of any approved deveopment policy'[120]– and North Borneo were also presenting difficulties, the Colonial Office was in turn invited in January 1948 to consider the matter in a broader context than the West Indies, in order to evolve a new basis for Treasury control.[121] Six months later the Treasury expressed the hope that it would be found possible to 'work the substance, as distinct from the form of Treasury control, on very much the same lines as . . . for financial relations with the African Colonies'.[122]

The financial devolution referred to arose from the deliberations of the Conference of African Governors, held in November 1947, which recommended that, where assistance from United Kingdom funds was not involved, the Colonial Office should concern itself with financial detail only as required to secure the Secretary of State's interest in the major issues of policy, such as measures against inflation, fiscal policy, exchange and currency control, development finance and loan policy.[123] It was concluded that, in the Tropical African Territories, the Secretary of State's interest in these major issues could most effectively be secured by consultation and discussion between the Colonial Office and the Governments concerned. In accordance with these principles, the Secretary of State decided that formal control over the finances of those Territories whose finances were not under the control of HM Treasury – and the only African territory receiving a grant-in-aid was British Somaliland – would in future be exercised only through the Secretary of State's function of advising His Majesty on the assent to the Appropriation and Supplementary Appropriation Ordinances and other legislation of a financial character. Other types of formal control were discontinued, except where payments by HMG were involved, e.g. as under the CD & W Acts.

As the ball had been set rolling by two Resolutions of the Montego Bay Conference and as the political ill-effects of Treasury control had been most apparent in the West Indian territories, the deliberations in the Colonial Office continued to have particular reference to the West Indian area and be conducted in conjunction with the West Indian Departments.[124] For some of the other grant-aided territories this hardly mattered, because it was stated that 'with staffing and other arrangements as they are at present in these places [the Gilbert and Ellice Islands, the British Solomon Islands Protectorate and the New Hebrides] whose capitals have hardly been built yet and whose staffs generally are working under considerable difficulties, [it was] . . . very doubtful whether we could expect to get the arrangements working satisfactorily for a couple of years at least.'[125] After high expectations and the usual lengthy round of memoranda, letters and discussions, the results were somewhat disappointing. They amounted to little more than a speeding-up of machinery, on the basis of advance surveys to be received not later than 15 October each year of the general financial position, revenue and expenditure.[126] This was, however, an improvement, and the Treasury's handling, even before the institution of the new arrangements, of the estimates for 1949 of

British Honduras, St Lucia and Dominica was heartening.[127] More-over, it was still being considered, as stated in the Despatch, whether more sweeping modifications could be made, though officials were divided as to whether or not the Office should pursue the matter further with the Treasury before the new technique had been tried.[128] It was instead agreed, first, to give the new arrangements a trial over the following 'Estimates season' and, secondly, to circulate a note on Treasury control to the West Indian Governors' Conference. The note asked whether, in the light of recent improvements, any more radical changes were required.[129]

The Governors' Conference returned a fairly emphatic affirmative answer to this question, and reverted to the suggestion for a block grant over a period of three years, with the further suggestion that Financial Advisers might be appointed by HMG to ensure that HMG's money was wisely spent.[130] It was generally agreed that the block grant system was highly desirable because of the financial incentive it would provide to the Governments concerned, besides eliminating a great deal of unprofitable administrative work in London. Delay was not the main criticism, though some of the delay was quite unnecessary. Thus, it was found that Treasury officials had interpreted 'non-disallowance' as synonymous with 'approval' and until non-disallowance of an Ordinance had been signified the Ordinance in question could not be put into effect.[131] While the removal of delay through the new arrangements had helped officials, it had not contributed to the appeasement of the unofficials, who resented both the external control and the lack of financial initiative, which was the crux of the matter. The Governor of British Honduras stated that, in his view, political opinion in British Honduras would resent control by a West Indian Federal Authority more than by HM Treasury and the block grant proposal in the Report of the SCAC might act as a deterrent to political federation in his Colony.[132] Treasury control was not efficient, being a negative hindrance rather than a positive incentive. Financial advice could only properly be given on the spot, as had been realised in India, Burma and Egypt, where HMG had appointed Financial Advisers when British money had been at stake. The Conference stressed that such Advisers should not be attached to the D & W Organisation.

This last point was due to the recognition of the difference between general policy advising and the day-to-day administrative handling of financial matters. While the first could – and should – emanate from the D & W Organisation, the other was necessarily locally based. The D & W Organisation was considered as having an essentially consultative role, which could best be applied in relation to individual schemes at the formative stage. However, the Colonial Office remained doubtful whether the proposal to appoint Financial Advisers would work smoothly in practice. It was feared that local politicians would resent, and try to by-pass, the Adviser, and HMG would then be involved in supporting him – assuming that suitable men were available for the unenviable job. The idea of substituting a system of CD & W grants for the grants-in-aid had to be abandoned because there was insufficient CD & W money to proceed and at the same time to assist the poorer Colonial territories in undertaking basic development work on which the whole economic future might depend.[133]

Still, the role of the Organisation necessarily changed over time. As the memorandum of October 1947 stated: 'it is the case that during the war the Comptroller had certain powers in regard to the variation of schemes, but with the return to more normal conditions regard has to be paid to the fact that he has, and can have, no such inherent powers as a matter of principle.'[134] Later, the Organisation came to be regarded as virtually a pre-federal organisation. The Treasury took exception to this, following the visit of one of its officials to the area. While not suggesting that the tendency towards the provision of regional services was 'necessarily a bad thing', doubt was expressed whether, if a new organisation was being considered, it would be felt proper to put the cost on HMG.[135] The Treasury roundly asserted that the West Indies did not get sufficient value out of the Organisation for D & W purposes to justify supporting it for such purposes and, therefore, the Organisation should be reduced to the size and structure necessary to cope with its new tasks. It might be noted that the burden of the Colonial Office visit in 1951 was the serious shortcomings of the system of Treasury control, while the upshot of the Treasury visit in the same year was the doubt on the new role of the D & W Organisation and a request for its budget to be reduced by around 10 per cent in the year 1952–53. Even if one's sympathies are more with the Colonial Office view than with that of the Treasury, it cannot be denied that the latter was not without justification, even though somewhat narrowly based. It is likely that a joint Colonial Office and Treasury team would have come up, in the circumstances, with a more balanced view as the result of some useful mutual education on the nature of the West Indian problem.

Be that as it may, the Comptroller was instructed to suggest economies that would reduce his current budget from £59,950 to £57,200, and his next budget to about £55,000.[136] According to the Report by the Comptroller for 1953, the total cost of the Organisation for 1952–53 was £62,776 and the estimate of expenditure for 1953–54 was £62,860 (Colonial No. 310 of 1954, para. 34, p. 13). In complying, the Comptroller asked, quite reasonably, whether the contributions to the less productive Caribbean Commission were also to be reduced.[137] In addition to these immediate budgetary cuts, the Colonial Office had been asked by the Treasury to review, over the longer term, the purposes and scope of the D & W Organisation. The Comptroller, for his part, reiterated his view that the Organisation had gradually ceased to be able to participate with the local Governments in long-range development planning or to undertake regional planning of development and welfare schemes. For, as political responsibility was extended, Governments inevitably wished to deal direct with the Colonial Office.[138] The Organisation was, instead, providing a much appreciated pool of first-class technical consultants, and servicing regional conferences on particular matters. The smaller islands found the assistance of the Advisers indispensible while, as the only neutral body in the area, the Organisation provided an essential focus for non-political regional interests. Though, strictly, it was admitted, Colonial Governments should refund expenditure on conferences, this was not practicable until the position concerning Federation was clearer. This statement reads rather oddly when compared with a minute concerning the first meeting of the Regional Economic Committee in May 1951. It read: 'It is to be hoped that nothing more than a clash in personalities between the Comptroller and his Economic Adviser is reflected in the Committee's tendency to break away from the control of the Development and Welfare Organisation, and this in turn is matched by the Comptroller's view that any services which the Organisation renders must be on a payment basis.' The official added: 'If this tendency persists, it will not be conducive to the building up of the Organisation into a future federal secretariat, if that is the intention.'[139] The Comptroller's general view was accepted in the Colonial Office, where the Organisation's work as a functional regional body was regarded, not as a change, but rather as a logical extension of the original functions of the Organisation in that they were directed towards the same objectives of planned and co-ordinated economic development and social betterment.[140] It was agreed, between the Colonial Office officials and the Comptroller, that the time for a further review of the Organisation's future would come either when a Federal Government was being set up or when it was known that the movement towards federation had failed. Until then, it was thought to be quite indefensible to abolish certain advisory posts, as had been suggested by the Treasury. It was also agreed that the

Comptroller's role was primarily diplomatic, and, as such, could be expected to explain and further HMG's policy in the area. While this was undoubtedly true, it might be wondered whether the change of emphasis from developmental, i.e. economic and social, to diplomatic was not, at least in part, because of the lack of technical qualifications of the Comptroller, who had said in his letter of 12 June 1950: 'I have not the equipment of special knowledge or experience to enable me to figure as a Stockdale. . . .' It is possible, in other words, that, if the Comptroller had been technically qualified, rather more developmental work could still have been undertaken by the Organisation in association with local Governments.

The Parliamentary Under-Secretary of State for the Colonies, the Earl of Munster, discussed the functions of the D & W Organisation with the Comptroller and his Advisers during a visit to Hastings House on 16 April 1952.[141] Discussion turned on the problem presented by the waste of funds made available under CD & W grants, and the means of ensuring that, in the existing crisis, the United Kingdom's taxpayers' interests were safeguarded. There were thought to be two main ways in which the Organisation might be concerned. First, there might be a failure to make use of the advisory services of the Organisation, leading to the preparation of ill-considered schemes. Secondly, Advisers might be in a position to advise on the execution of schemes in which waste of funds was taking place. As in the case of the school building programme of Trinidad, it was stated that, if consulted early enough, the Organisation was often in a position to supply information and advice based on its regional experience which would lead to better use being made of D & W grants. Mr Hammond was of the opinion that there were two main reasons for the failure to make the best use of CD & W funds. One was the technical weakness of Government departments in the area; this was being improved by training schemes. The other was the administrative weakness of the departments, which was more difficult to improve. The Minister agreed, believing that the building of effective administrations was a long-term task.

Naturally, the position was most acute in the Leeward and Windward Islands, where it seemed likely that within the following year or two none, with the possible exception of St Kitts, would be solvent. In St Lucia alone it was estimated that total calls for assistance might arise to a total of £1 million per annum. One solution would be to put the Islands in commission, but this was probably impracticable because of obvious political difficulties. The Comptroller, while in full agreement with his Advisers' views as to the need for action to avoid wastage of United Kingdom funds, considered that the existing constitutional position made it virtually impossible for the Organisation to intervene effectively unless it was invited to do so. It was reluctantly accepted by the meeting that there was no immediate prospect of finding a solution to the unsatisfactory state of affairs concerning the execution of large-scale projects.

To return to the Comptroller's discussions with the Colonial Office as to the Organisation's future role, both he and the Colonial Office were convinced that the Organisation should carry on with its D & W work and with its regional functions, and that these necessitated an establishment of much the size that then existed. The Treasury was so informed[142] and agreed in general with that view, though it sought economies as and when regional functions were taken over by Colonial Governments.[143] HMG was, at the time, committed to a policy of severe economy in public expenditure, and the Treasury was under instruction from its Ministers to scrutinise every item of Government expenditure with great thoroughness. However, after consulting the Comptroller, it was only found possible to dispense with the Assistant Economic Adviser and the Assistant Public Relations Adviser.[144] The Treasury's main grievance was that the Organisation was financed from the Colonial Office Vote rather than 'as it properly should be financed, from either CD & W funds or by the Colonial Governments concerned'.[145] The Colonial Office was 'not very happy' about this revelation of the Treasury's attitude towards the Organisation. The Permanent Under-Secretary of State at the Colonial Office found the 'constant sniping by the Treasury at the Organisation both irritating and a waste of time. . . . The Moyne Commission definitely recommended that its costs should be borne by HMG direct and outside any finance for development and welfare.'[146] If it persisted, he intended to take the matter up with Sir Edward Bridges himself. Nothing further appears to have been heard of the point, possibly because Mr S. E. V. Luke undertook, after he had settled in at Hastings House, where he was due to become Comptroller on 1 May 1953, to discuss the role and performance of the Organisation with Governors and others in a series of tours. The upshot of his visits in the area was that he felt that, while federation remained a possibility in the area, it would be a grave mistake to change drastically the functions and, therefore, the structure of the Organisation.[147] If federation was rejected or postponed *sine die*, then it would be necessary to work out some alternative arrangements for regional consultation short of political federation, and to transfer to that locally-financed body as many as possible of the regional functions exercised by the Organisation. The Colonial Office was in full agreement with his assessment of the value of the Organisation and his views on its immediate future.[148]

Although it might be concluded from the Treasury's anxiety to hive off regional functions on to regional bodies that these latter existed in number and maturity, the Regional Economic Committee (REC) was in 1953 the only alternative body to which such a transfer could have been made. The REC arose out of the deliberations of the Montego Bay Conference of September 1947. It was a prolonged and difficult task to assemble the Committee, which held its first meeting at Hastings House, Barbados, from 16 to 25 May 1951, under the chairmanship of Professor C. G. Beasley. Apart from discussing its own status, organisation and functions, it discussed the proposed Trade Commissioner service in the United Kingdom, the Customs Union Commission Report, external trade matters and regional economic matters. The Chairman concluded his report to the Colonial Office by saying that 'in spite of difficulties, I think something was achieved and there is no doubt that the Committee has powerful backing in the region. The changed attitude of Jamaica was particularly noticeable and may exert much influence, at least towards the formation of a Customs Union.'[149] In the opinion of the Comptroller in October 1953, the REC had still 'to find its feet as an effective regional organisation' and owed much of its rather limited contribution to 'the constant help and advice that it and its secretariat had received from the Comptroller and his staff'.[150]

Indeed, the implication of the Comptroller's report on his visits was not that it was timely to devolve regional functions, but rather that the Organisation itself needed strengthening in order to carry through its new exercise of CD & W responsibility. It was required to prepare a regional assessment of needs for the West Indies, and to advise upon, and dovetail, the local territorial assessments. The Colonial Office proposed that a Financial Adviser should be added to the Comptroller's staff,[151] but the Treasury opposed any such appointment.[152] Certainly, the Colonial Office was aware that it could not make out a strong case.[153] The main reason given for the appointment was the need for assistance in connection with the new CD & W Act but, by the beginning of March 1954, the immediate work in the West Indies had been completed. Bids for money under the new Act had been prepared with the help of the Comptroller's staff and the rest of the work was to be completed in the Colonial Office by mid-July. In fact, with the falling off of D & W applications under the existing Act, the Comptroller's work on D & W schemes was expected to fall.[154] Accordingly, it was decided to accept the dropping of the post for the current round.[155] It would, perhaps, have been better to have argued the case in the first place on the continuing inability of Professor Beasley to cope alone with all the economic matters arising – which was, in fact, the Comptroller's essential worry.[156]

Apparently rather unexpectedly, Governors in the West Indies were informed in 1952 that the Secretary of State was considering the question of regional co-ordination of defence planning in war and the position of the D & W Organisation in relation to war planning in the West Indies.[157] Governors were reminded that the United States Government had accepted responsibility for the general defence of the area, while the main responsibility for local defence planning rested with Colonial Governments. Co-ordination would, it was stated, be required between the Colonial Governments in matters such as economic controls, supply and shipping problems and other civilian war measures. During the 1939–45 war, a Schooner Pool had been organised for the distribution of commodities and probably the same would, it was suggested, be needed again. Here was a field where the Secretary of State felt that the D & W Organisation could be of assistance, and he enquired of Governors what aspects of civilian defence planning might best be undertaken on a regional basis and be handled by the D & W Organisation.

During the 1939–45 war the bulk of the essential foods and other commodities required for the Caribbean area had been obtained from the United States and Canada through the British Colonies Supply Mission in Washington. If the same sources of supply were again involved, a similar organisation in Washington would be necessary. Local co-ordination in inter-Colonial trade and shipping would require the revival of the Schooner Pool by the D & W Organisation. Some Governors went no further,[158] some not as far.[159] The Governor of Jamaica alone envisaged a major role for the Organisation in regional co-ordination concerned with (i) the submission of the import requirements of the British West Indian territories; (ii) the making of export and shipping arrangements with the United Kingdom; (iii) the organisation of internal trade and shipping within the West Indies; (iv) the collection of statistical data; and (v) the planning of regional production in the best interests of the whole area.[160] With that notable exception, the replies did not contemplate any wide assumption of new activities on the part of the Organisation. Indeed, as the Comptroller remarked, there were 'traces . . . of an anxiety to circumscribe in advance the role which this Organisation could play'.[161] Developments such as the REC were, as he noted, ignored. The Comptroller felt that it was 'inconceivable' that HMG should not use the regional co-ordinating services of the Organisation. After making the point that the extent to which co-ordination was possible depended on the authority of the co-ordinator, the Comptroller reminded the Colonial Office that the Organisation was being less, rather than more, used as a regional co-ordinating agency. Thus, it had not been called in over the Jamaica hurricane, or over the setting up of a Faculty of Agriculture at the University College, or over the 1950 CD & W allocations to Colonies. So, unless the emphasis was changed for purposes of wartime co-ordination, the Comptroller foresaw the Organisation's role 'limited to co-ordination in a purely routine secretarial capacity'. He hoped that the Secretary of State would wish him to convene and preside over regional conferences between HMG and West Indian Governments on defence planning. If the Americans wished to use the Caribbean Commission machinery for regional co-ordination purposes, it would increase the importance of the D & W Organisation as a link between HMG and West Indian Governments, on the one hand, and the Commission, on the other. It was naturally accepted that the introduction of a federal government would change the whole picture.

The interest here in this enquiry concerning the non-military side of defence planning lies in the attitude it reveals towards the desired role of the D & W Organisation, which, with the exception of the regionally-minded Governor of Jamaica, was conceived generally to be a rather lowly one. In 1952–53 the Organisation appears to have reached a rather low ebb, both in current functioning and in views of its likely future role. This contrasts markedly with the upshot of the deliberations of the Governors' Conference in 1949. It seems likely that the inability wholly to parry the economy thrusts by the Treasury, together with the Governors' conception of minimal functions in wartime and the depressed tone of the Comptroller, all sprang in 1952–53 from the decline of the Organisation's traditional duties with development planning and social welfare, on the one hand, together with the slowness with which federal sentiment crystallised after the Report of the SCAC was completed, on the other. Any organisation that is compelled to dawdle publicly at the crossroads is bound to lose both external support and its own self-confidence. The Chairman began his report for 1947–49 with the relaxed statement that the Organisation could be regarded 'as an outstanding example of British adaptability to changing circumstances or, alternatively, as a demonstration of the British tendency to muddle through'.[162] By 1953, the Comptroller's report was focusing attention on the various regional bodies with which the Organisation was concerned – the Regional Economic

Committee, the Oils and Fats Conference and the Regional Labour Board – and various meetings of representatives from the West Indian Governments that were held under its auspices, including a meeting concerning British West Indian Airways Limited and several meetings on technical matters.[163] Indeed, the only positive statements concerning the Organisation itself were of the replacement of Sir Stephen Luke for Sir George Seel as Comptroller, and the reduction in the staff.[164] In fact, the Comptroller and the Colonial Office were trying to maintain the *status quo* until the fate of the latest federal scheme was determined. By 1953–54 that was the key to the Organisation's future role.

SOURCES

1. File 71357/1 of 1945–46, West Indies (CO 318/471), item 1, telegram No. 253 of 18 May 1945 from the Comptroller for D & W to the Secretary of State.

2. D & W Headquarters file 57 of 1943–52, item 16, Note of a meeting on 21 July 1944 of Mr T. Lloyd, Sir Frank Stockdale, Mr Beckett, and Mr Rogers.

3. File 71357/1 of 1945–46, West Indies (CO 318/471), item 2, Secret telegram No. 286 of 9 June 1945 from the Secretary of State to the Comptroller. The telegram was based on a minute of 2 June 1945 by Mr P. Rogers, ibid., who favoured the idea of withholding 25 per cent as proposed by the Comptroller, subject to the views of Finance Department, which, presumably, was unable to agree.

4. Ibid., item 4, Secret telegram No. 333 of 27 June 1945 from the Comptroller to the Secretary of State.

5. Ibid., item 6, telegram No. 654 of 4 July 1945 from the Governor of Jamaica for the Comptroller to the Secretary of State.
   of State.

6. Ibid., Secret telegram No. 372 of 19 July 1945 from the Secretary of State to the Comptroller. It incorporated the proposals in Sir Frank Stockdale's minute of 13 July 1945, in ibid.

7. Ibid., item 9, Carib. No. 100, Secret telegram of 25 July 1945 from the Comptroller to the Secretary of State.

8. File 19275/65/48 of 1946, Economic, items 1 and 2, telegrams Nos 1420 and 65 of 6 Dec 1945 and 1 Feb 1946, from the Governor of Trinidad to the Secretary of State.

9. Ibid., minute of 12 Apr 1946 by Mr J. B. Williams of discussions between Mr S. Caine, Sir Frank Stockdale and himself.

10. Ibid., item 9, telegram No. 225 of 30 Apr 1946 from the Comptroller to the Secretary of State.

11. Ibid., minute of 10 May 1946 by Mr J. E. Marnham.

12. Ibid., minute of 16 May 1946 by Mr J. B. Williams.

13. Ibid., minute of 28 May 1946 by the Parliamentary Under-Secretary of State.

14. Ibid., item 14, letter of 30 July 1946 from Mr A. J. D. Winnifrith to Mr J. B. Williams.

15. File 71357/1 of 1945–46, West Indies (CO 318/471), item 18, letter of 19 Oct 1945 from the Comptroller to Mr T. I. K. Lloyd.

16. Ibid., item 18, letter of 19 Oct 1945 from the Comptroller to the Governor of the Windward Islands.

17. Secret D & W Headquarters file 57 of 1943–52, item 22, memorandum on 'The Future of the Comptroller's Organisation'.

18. Idem, para. 8.

19. File 71295 of 1945, West Indies (CO 318/466), item 5.

20. Secret D & W Headquarters file 57 of 1943–52, item 22, para. 8.

21. File 71321/7/1 of 1946, West Indies (CO 318/470), item 31, secret letter No. SI 30/S.2/23 of 24 June 1946 from the Governor of Barbados to the Comptroller.

22. Unpublished official 'History of the Development and Welfare Organisation in the West Indies' by Mr P. Hewitt-Myring, p. 71.

23. File 71321/7/1 of 1946, West Indies (CO 318/470), minute of 9 July 1946 by Mr A. Macintosh.

24. Ibid., minute of 11 July 1946 by Sir A. Dawe.

25. Top Secret (Pouch) File 71357 of 1947, item 1, letter of 14 Jan 1947 from the Comptroller to Mr G. F. Seel.

26. Ibid., item 14, note of meeting on 26 Feb 1947 in Mr Caine's room.

27. Ibid., item 7, letter of 13 March 1947 from Mr S. Caine to the Comptroller.

28. Idem.

29. Ibid., item 15, letter of 22 Apr 1947 from the Comptroller to Mr S. Caine.

30. Ibid., item 19, minutes of a discussion on the future of the Organisation of the Comptroller for Development and Welfare in the West Indies on 30 May 1947.

31. Ibid., item 25, note of a meeting held on 30 Oct 1947 to discuss the future of the Comptroller's Organisation and the appointment of the SCAC.

32. Ibid., item 26, minute of 4 Dec 1947 by Mr G. F. Seel.

33. Ibid., minute of 10 Dec 1947 by Mr J. C. Morgan.

34. D & W Secret file 00301, Part 1 of 1944–1950, item 5, secret and personal telegram of 17 Nov 1944 from the Comptroller to the Secretary of State.

35. Ibid., item 7, letter of 22 Nov 1944 from the Secretary of State to the Comptroller.

36. File 71295 of 1945, West Indies (CO 318/466), minute of 21 Nov 1945 by Sir George Gater.

37. Ibid., item 80, Confidential Despatch of 6 Nov 1945.

38. Ibid., item 90, telegram No. 1255.

39. Ibid., minute of 29 Dec 1945 by Mr P. Rogers.

40. Ibid., item 67, Despatch No. 107 of 27 July 1945 from the Acting Governor, Mr D. G. Stewart, to the Secretary of State.

41. Ibid., item 78, letter of 25 Oct 1945 from the Governor of British Guiana, Sir Gordon Lethem, to the Permanent Under-Secretary of State.

42. Ibid., item 89, Despatch No. 202 of 30 Nov 1945 from the Governor of British Guiana to the Secretary of State.

43. Ibid., minute of 26 Nov 1945 by Mr P. Rogers.

44. Ibid., minute of 21 Nov 1945 by the Parliamentary Under-Secretary of State.

45. Secret D & W File 00301 of 1944–50, Part I, item 28, 'Federation in the West Indies' by Mr P. Rogers.

46. Ibid., item 31, letter of 11 Dec 1946 from Mr S. A. Hammond to Mr F. Kennedy.

47. Ibid., item 30A, note of a discussion in Mr Seel's room on 26 Sep 1946 of a proposal by Mr S. A. Hammond for a West Indian Council.

48. *Closer Association of the British West Indian Colonies* (Cmd 7120, May 1947).

49. Secret D & W File 00301, 1944–50, Part I, item 48, Personal and Confidential letter of 8 May 1947 from Mr G. F. Seel to the Comptroller.

50. Ibid., item 49, letter of 13 June 1947 from the Comptroller to Mr G. F. Seel.

51. Ibid., item 48, Personal and Confidential letter of 8 May 1947 from Mr G. F. Seel to the Comptroller.

52. Secret D & W Headquarters File 57 of 1943–52, item 33, Private and Confidential letter of 3 May 1947 from Sir Sydney Caine to Sir J. Macpherson.

53. Ibid., item 35, letter of 5 June 1947 from the Comptroller to Mr G. F. Seel.

54. *Conference on the Closer Association of the British West Indian Colonies, Montego Bay, Jamaica, September 11–19, 1947. Part 2: Proceedings* (Colonial No. 218 of 1948).

55. Ibid., p. 9.

56. Ibid., p. 24.

57. Ibid., p. 25.

58. Ibid., p. 27.

59. *Conference on the Closer Association of the British West Indian Colonies – Part I: Report* (Cmd 7291, Jan 1948).

60. File 71295 of 1947, West Indies, Part II (CO 318/483), item 220, minute of 22 Sep 1947 from the Secretary of State to the Prime Minister.

61. File 71295/14/1 of 1948, West Indies, minute of 10 Dec 1947 by Mr G. F. Seel.

62. Ibid., item 16, Personal and Confidential letter of 25 Jan 1948 from the Governor of Jamaica to Mr G. F. Seel.

63. Ibid., minutes of 9 and 12 Mar 1948 by Sir Sydney Caine and the Secretary of State.

64. Ibid., item 62, letter of 10 Jan 1949 from the Minister of State for Colonial Affairs to the Chairman of SCAC.

65. D & W Secret file 00301 Part I, item 61, Secret and personal letter of 17 May 1949 from the Minister of State to the Chairman of SCAC.

66. Ibid., item 55, letter of 15 Sep 1948 from the Chairman of SCAC to the Minister of State.

67. Idem.

68. Ibid., item 65, letter of 5 Sep 1949.

69. Idem.

70. Ibid., item 67, Secret and Personal letter of 26 Oct 1949 from the Chairman of SCAC to the Secretary of State.

71. *Report, British Caribbean Standing Closer Association Committee, 1948–49* (Colonial No. 255 of 1950 and Advocate Co. Ltd, Barbados).

72. D & W Secret file 00301, 1951–52, Part II, items 22A and 22, note by Professor

Beasley enclosed with Confidential letter of 19 Oct 1951.

73. D & W Secret file 00301, 1944–50, Part I, item 67, Secret and Personal letter of 26 Oct 1949 from the Chairman of SCAC to the Secretary of State.

74. Ibid., item 65, letter of 5 Sep 1949.

75. File 71503, 1949, West Indies (CO 318/496), item 96, record of meetings of the British Caribbean Governors' Conference held at Government House, Barbados, 7–11 Nov 1949.

76. Idem, p. 34.

77. Idem, p. 35.

78. Idem, p. 35.

79. Idem, p. 35.

80. Idem, pp. 35–6.

81. Idem, p. 36.

82. D & W Secret File 00301, 1951–52, Part II, item 6A, Personal and Confidential letter of 22 May 1951 to the Governors of Trinidad and of Jamaica.

83. Ibid., item 8, Personal and Confidential letter of 5 June 1951 from the Governor of Trinidad.

84. Ibid., item 1, letter of 21 Mar 1951 from the Comptroller of D & W.

85. Ibid., item 9, Personal and Confidential letter of 25 June 1951 from the Governor of Jamaica.

86. Ibid., item 11, Secret and Personal telegram of 30 July 1951 from the Governor of Jamaica to the Secretary of State.

87. Ibid., item 20, letter of 22 Sep 1951.

88. Ibid., item 13, telegram of 4 Aug 1951 from the Secretary of State to the Governor of Jamaica.

89. Ibid., item 39, Despatch No. 61 of 6 Feb 1952 from the Secretary of State to West Indian Governors.

90. Ibid., item 56A, *The Gleaner*, Kingston, Jamaica, 16 June 1952.

91. Ibid., item 68, Savingram No. 62 of Aug 1952 from the Governor of Jamaica to the Secretary of State.

92. Ibid., item 74, Personal and Confidential telegram No. 882 of 25 Aug 1952 from the Governor to the Secretary of State.

93. Ibid., item 73, telegram of 2 Sep 1952 from the Secretary of State to the Governor of Jamaica.

94. Ibid., item 75, telegram No. 69 of 5 Sep 1952 from the Governor of Jamaica to the Secretary of State.

95. Ibid., item 81, Personal and Confidential telegram No. WICIR 43 of 22 Sep 1952 from the Secretary of State to Governors in the West Indies.

96. Ibid., item 96, Confidential telegram No. WICIR 68 of 31 Dec 1952 from the Secretary of State to Governors in the West Indies.

97. Ibid., item 40, extract from Note on Discussion with Lord Munster at Hastings House on 16 Apr 1952.

98. Ibid., item 59, letter of 7 June 1952. For Beasley's draft and the covering letter of 28 Apr 1952 from the Comptroller, see item 45.

99. D & W File 00251/1, item 1, Governors' Conference: Role of the D & W Organisation.

100. Ibid., item 2.

101. Ibid., item 3.

102. Ibid., item 4.

103. Ibid., item 5.

104. Ibid., item 6.

105. Ibid., item 10, letter of 7 Oct 1949.

106. File 71503 of 1949, West Indies (CO 318/496), item 96, Record of Meetings: British Caribbean Governors' Conference, 7–11 Nov 1949, pp. 22–9.

107. D & W File 00251/1, minute of 1 Nov 1949 by the Administrative Secretary.

108. File 71503 of 1949, West Indies (CO 318/496), item 96, Record of Meetings: British Caribbean Governors' Conference, 7–11 Nov 1949, pp. 17–21.

109. File 71357 of 1950, West Indies, item 11, manuscript letter of 12 June 1950.

110. File WIS 74/01 of 1951–54, item 6.

111. File 71357 of 1950, West Indies, item 11, Memorandum, pp. 20 and 22.

112. Ibid., item 15, letter of 26 Aug 1950.

113. Ibid., item 17, letter of 1 Sep 1950.

114. Ibid., item 19, extract from a personal letter of 21 Sep 1950.

115. File 19275/95 of 1951, Finance, item 5, Confidential Report of 4 Apr 1951 on a visit to the West Indies (19 Jan–27 Mar 1951): CDWC(51) 2.

116. File 71295/17 of 1947, West Indies (CO 318/488), item 1, minute of 8 Sep 1947 from the Governor of British Honduras, Sir Gerald Hawkesworth (on leave), to the Colonial Secretary of British Honduras.

117. Ibid., minute of 26 Sep 1947 by Mr H. Beckett.

118. Ibid., item 4, draft memorandum of 12 Nov 1947 by Mr G. F. Seel.

119. Ibid., item 12, letter and note of 24 Dec 1947 from Mr G. F. Seel to Mr D. B. Pitblado.

120. File 16400/2 of 1948, Economic Finance (CO 852/766), telegram No. 37 of 4 Feb 1948 from the Governor to the Secretary of State.

121. Ibid., letter of 12 Jan 1948 from Mr D. B. Pitblado to Mr G. F. Seel.

122. Ibid., item 13, letter of 24 July 1948 from Mr D. B. Pitblado to Mr H. T. Bourdillon.

123. Ibid., item 11, Circular Despatch No. 4 of 16 June 1948 from the Secretary of State to Governors of Colonies in Africa.

124. File 16400/2 of 1948, Economic Finance (CO 852/766), minute of 18 Dec 1948 by Mr H. T. Bourdillon.

125. Ibid., minute of 20 Dec 1948 by Mr J. B. Sidebotham.

126. Ibid., items 28–30, despatch of 16 Dec 1948 from the Secretary of State to the Governors of British Honduras (No. 114), the Windward Islands (No. 155) and the Leeward Islands (No. 101).

127. Ibid., minute of 18 Dec 1948 by Mr H. T. Bourdillon.

128. File 16400/2 of 1949, Economic (CO 852/766), item 3, minute of 9 Mar 1949, appended to Note on Financial Relations with the West Indian Colonies.

129. Ibid., item 9, note of Oct 1949 on Treasury Control, para. 8.

130. File 71503 of 1949, West Indies (CO 318/496), item 96, pp. 12–13.

131. File 16400/2 of 1948 (CO 852/766), Economic Finance, item 9, note of 6 May 1948 by Mr H. T. Bourdillon of a discussion with Mr D. B. Pitblado and Mr D. R. Serpell.

132. File 71503 of 1949 (CO 318/496), West Indies, item 96, p. 12.

133. File 1600/2 of 1949, Economic (CO 852/766), items 29–31, semi-official letter of 31 Oct 1950 from the Permanent Under-Secretary of State to Governors of Trinidad and British Guiana and the Acting Governor of Jamaica.

134. Top Secret (Pouch) file 71357 of 1947, West Indies, item 20, para. 17.

135. File WIS 74/01 of 1951–54, West Indies, item 1, letter of 10 Dec 1951.

136. Ibid., item 3, telegram No. 454 of 21 Dec 1951 from the Secretary of State to the Comptroller.

137. Ibid., item 4, telegram No. 512, of 24 Dec 1951 from the Comptroller to the Secretary of State.

138. Ibid., item 8, report of 21 Jan 1952 of a discussion with Sir George Seel on the future and scope of the D & W Organisation.

139. File 71295/15/3, Part II of 1951, West Indies (CO 318/507), minute of 14 June 1951.

140. File WIS 74/01 of 1951–54, West Indies, minute of 22 Jan 1952.

141. D & W File 123/3, item 54A, note on discussion with Lord Munster at Hastings House on 16 Apr 1952.

142. Ibid., item 13, letter of 23 May 1952.

143. Ibid., item 16, letter of 5 Aug 1952.

144. Ibid., item 22, letter of 1 Oct 1952.

145. Ibid., item 25, letter of 13 Nov 1952.

146. Ibid., minute of 17 Nov 1952 by the Permanent Under-Secretary of State, Sir T. Lloyd.

147. Ibid., item 30, Confidential letter of 20 Oct 1953 from the Comptroller, Sir Stephen Luke, to the Permanent Under-Secretary of State, Sir T. Lloyd.

148. Ibid., item 32, letter of 8 Jan 1954 from the Permanent Under-Secretary of State to the Comptroller.

149. File 71295/15/3, Part II of 1951, West Indies (CO 318/507), item 105.

150. File WIS 74/01 of 1951–54, West Indies, item 30, Confidential letter of 20 Oct 1953 from the Comptroller to the Permanent Under-Secretary of State.

151. Ibid., item 31, Confidential letter of 4 Jan 1954.

152. File WIS 43/01 of 1954–1956, West Indies, item 1, letter of 16 Jan 1954.

153. Ibid., minute of 6 Mar 1954.

154. Idem.

155. Ibid., minute of 18 Mar 1954 by Sir Charles Jeffries.

156. File WIS 74/01 of 1951–54, West Indies, item 30, para. 15, letter of 20 Oct 1953 from the Comptroller to the Permanent Under-Secretary of State.

157. D & W Secret file 00280 of 1952, item 1, Secret Despatch of 17 Apr 1952 from the Secretary of State to OAGs in the West Indies.

158. Ibid., items 3, 6 and 10, e.g. Governor of British Guiana, Trinidad and the Governor's Deputy, Leeward Islands.

159. Ibid., items 4 and 7, e.g. Governor of British Honduras was not interested in the schooner pool; and Governor of Barbados mentioned the continued existence of the pool.

160. Ibid., item 8, Secret Despatch No. 976 of 28 July 1952 from the Governor of Jamaica to the Secretary of State.

161. Ibid., item 9, Secret letter of 9 Aug 1952.

162. *Development and Welfare in the West Indies, 1947–49* by Major-General Sir Hubert Rance, Chairman of the Development and Welfare Organisation in the West Indies (Colonial No. 264 of 1950). The introductory part of the report was drafted by Mr P. Hewitt-Myring, the Public Relations Adviser. There were several adverse comments on the style in which the report was drafted, including the sentence quoted which, it was thought, 'might well be construed into an admission that we are muddling along with development in the West Indies, with its obvious reflections not only on the organisation itself but also on the Colonial Office and the Secretary of State', according to a minute of 8 May 1950 by Mr N. L. Moyle in West Indies file 71320/1 of 1950 (CO 318/508). Sir H. Rance was generally content, however – see letter of 16 Mar 1950 from him to Mr G. F. Seel at item 4 in ibid.

163. *Development and Welfare in the West Indies, 1953* by Sir Stephen Luke, Comptroller for Development and Welfare in the West Indies (Colonial No. 310 of 1954), Chapter 1.

164. Idem, paras 32 and 33. The posts involved were those of Assistant Economic Adviser, Assistant Public Relations Adviser and Sugar Agronomist.

4 The World Food Shortage: Oils and Fats

1. NATURE OF THE PROBLEM

At the Cabinet meeting of 31 January 1946 the Prime Minister, Mr Attlee, was invited to consider what special machinery should be established to supervise action by Government Departments to meet current difficulties arising from the world shortage of food.[1] The Prime Minister proposed the setting up of a Ministerial Committee on World Food Supplies (WFS), under his chairmanship, to keep the situation under review, to co-ordinate action and to focus on the major issues calling for decision by the Cabinet or international bodies concerned.[2] The panel of Ministers was: Lord President, Foreign Secretary or Minister of State, Chancellor of the Exchequer, Secretary of State for India and Burma, Secretary of State for the Colonies, Secretary of State for Scotland, Minister of Agriculture, Minister of War Transport, Minister of Food, Chancellor of the Duchy of Lancaster. Other Ministers were to be invited as necessary. At the third meeting, on 19 February,[3] the Committee discussed a memorandum by the Minister of Food, Sir Ben Smith,[4] drawing attention to the considerable deterioration during the previous few months of the oils and fats situation. It was a picture of unrelieved gloom, in which stocks were dangerously low, supplies were well below earlier estimates, new demands had arisen,the fat ration had been cut, and further cuts were unavoidable unless supplies could be increased. The significant details were as follows. The agreement reached in the spring of 1945 with the Governments of the United States and Canada provided for the running down of United Kingdom stocks during 1945 from 672,000 tons of crude oil to 350,000 tons, and then to 325,000 tons by 30 June 1946. Before the end of January 1946, they were approaching the minimum level below which distribution difficulties would arise. As regards supplies, three wartime sources had been reduced. Wartime stocks of whale oil had nearly been exhausted, and as the combined result of a very late spring in the Antarctic, atrocious weather, and the catch consisting largely of fin whales, which yield only half the oil of blue whales, a shortfall of 25,000 tons of oil was probable. Supplies of American lard, which at one time in the war reached 200,000 tons per annum, fell to 79,000 in 1945, and the cessation of Lend-Lease in August 1945 had led to further curtailment while Indian exports of groundnuts were first reduced and then cut off completely.

Three major changes had occurred which falsified all previous estimates. The first was on the side of demand. The Far East, which pre-war contributed some 1,750,000 tons of oil to world supplies, had become a net importer. Demands amounting to 70,000 tons had been presented for Burma, Hong Kong, Malaya and British North Borneo, mainly in the form of Indian groundnuts, and the total requirement for 1946 was expected to be in excess of that figure. On the supply side there was, in addition to the deficiency of whale oil already mentioned, a gloomy outlook for Indian groundnuts. In December 1945, the Government of India had to reduce the export quota because of heavy crop damage in Madras caused by drought and a subsequent cyclone. In January 1946, the prospect of acute food shortage in India made it necessary to cut exports further. At the same time, production of palm kernels and palm-oil in British West Africa had fallen off sharply.

The announced reduction of one ounce in the weekly fats ration would save 70,000 tons of oil in 1946 but, without greater supplies, the reduced ration could still not be maintained. The Minister of Food, therefore, proposed that (i) the prices of Nigerian palm products should be increased and the increase passed on to the producers; (ii) the whaling season might be extended; (iii) there should be purchases of American lard if it was available; and (iv) the Combined Food Board should be asked to reallocate oils and fats for 1946 to take account of the new situation. These proposals were agreed. Sir Leslie Monson told the author on 2 September 1975, that his personal involvement at the time as head of the Production Department in the Colonial Office was concentrated on the price paid for Nigerian palm products by the Ministry of Food and, though there are references to the issue in the narrative, they do not reflect the acerbity of the argument as he remembered it. On the one side, there was the Director of Oils and Fats in the Ministry of Food, Mr Jasper Knight, who was obdurate that the way to get more was to offer the producer a higher price. He was – and this was consequential – equally obdurate in his opposition to any part of his Ministry's price being taken for price stabilisation funds. For what seemed a long time, his Minister supported him and carried more weight in Ministerial circles apparently than the Secretary of State for the Colonies. On the other side, officials in the Colonial Office and the Government of Nigeria, besides their doubts about the validity of Mr Knight's arguments and their fears of the inflationary consequences if they were proved valid, were concerned about the political consequences of the Ministry paying substantially less for Nigerian palm products than they did for similar produce from elsewhere, as this would lead to charges of 'Colonial exploitation'. They felt that this could be averted if the surplus, above what was paid direct to the producer, was paid, as had taken place for several years in the case of cocoa, into a price stabilisation fund. It was this consideration even more than that of giving confidence for the future to producers that, if he remembered aright, Sir Leslie believed lay behind the proposal for a stabilisation fund. Mr Knight's refusal to accept local advice interestingly fore-shadowed his future role in the East African Groundnuts Scheme. Before the war he had been the chief buyer for Unilever on the London market, and in African affairs had an alternative source of advice in the United Africa Company (UAC), a subsidiary of Unilever. Sir Leslie said that he had no evidence that Mr Knight drew on the advice of the UAC in this particular controversy and did not for a moment suggest that he used his position in the Ministry improperly on behalf of the UAC. On the contrary, the point is that Mr Knight genuinely believed that market men understood those things and that civil servants, whether in Whitehall or Lagos, were deceiving themselves if they thought they did.

The WFS Committee[5] invited the Parliamentary Under-Secretary of State for the Colonies, Mr Creech Jones, to impress on Governors of the West African Colonies the seriousness of the world situation and invite them to make more foodstuffs available for export.

The Committee invited the Parliamentary Under-Secretary also to advise on the steps necessary to increase West African supplies and, in particular, to comment on the Minister of Food's proposal that the price of Nigerian palm products should be increased and the increase passed on to the producers. However, the Governors advised that, so long as the supply of consumer goods, in particular cottons and household goods, was short, an increase of price would be more likely to decrease than increase production.[6] In addition, it was advised that producers required security as regards future prices if production was to be expanded; it was proposed that a fund should be accumulated to provide price stabilisation, which would receive the revenue from an export tax to be paid by purchasers of palm kernels through a corresponding rise in price. The WFS agreed not to pursue the proposal of a price increase, noted with approval the alternative proposal made by the Governor, and invited the Parliamentary Under-Secretary of State to discuss with the Board of Trade the provision of consumer goods for West Africa and provide a memorandum on this point.[7]

By 12 March, when the WFS held its sixth meeting, the oils and fats situation had deteriorated still further.[8] A White Paper, *The World Food Shortage*, was published in April 1946 (Cmd 6785) setting out the facts. The situation in India was given particular attention (paragraphs 16–18) as was the situation in South-East Asia (paragraphs 25–9 and 71–6) but Africa was only mentioned (paragraph 38). The Government of India had prohibited further export of groundnuts and rapeseed and was expected to prohibit the exports of linseed. In total, nearly 200,000 tons of oil were involved. At the same time, the marketing of West African palm products had declined sharply. The Minister of Food still blamed low prices, with further difficulties arising from inadequate local transport to marketing centres in Nigeria. A Committee on Food Supplies from South-East Asia (SEAF) was constituted by CP(46)52 'to concert action by United Kingdom Departments with a view to increasing the supplies of rice and other foodstuffs in South-East Asia'.[9] At the fifth meeting, its terms were extended 'to cover other countries outside South-East Asia in which were similar difficulties in increasing the export of foodstuffs'. The chairman of SEAF, Lord Nathan, the Parliamentary Under-Secretary of State for War, was a member of WFS. The WFS invited the Under-Secretary of State for the Colonies and the Parliamentary Secretary to the Ministry of Food to arrange for the stimulation of exports from West Africa to be further discussed by SEAF. When, at the eighth meeting of WFS, measures to stimulate the exports of oils and fats from Africa were further discussed,[10] Lord Nathan reported that the lack of transport, which seemed to be the main obstacle to increased exports, had been investigated. It had been found that there were twenty-four surplus locomotives which might be suitable, although some of them were pledged to the Australian Government, which might, however, waive its claim. The military authorities had been asked to assist in repairing such locomotives as required repairs and were to be asked also whether demobilised army drivers could be encouraged to become lorry drivers.[11] Later the GOC West Africa proposed the formation of a special transport company to help the Nigerian Government to move accumulated stocks of palm kernels down to the ports. He estimated he could move 450 tons a week out of the total stocks of approximately 24,000 tons.[12] The Secretary of State, Mr George Hall, said that 500 lorries were being shipped to West Africa at the rate of 50 a week, while the Parliamentary Secretary to the Board of Trade, Mr J. Belcher, said that his Department was giving urgent consideration to the question of consumer goods for West Africa. The matter was taken up by SEAF on 2 April 1944[13] where, on the one hand, the Colonial Office representative argued the problem was mainly one of transport and partly one of providing incentives to producers while, on the other hand, the Ministry of Food representative said the production of groundnuts in West Africa appeared to be satisfactory as did transport to the coast for up-country stocks, which were not excessive, but the marketing of palm oil and palm kernels had declined significantly over the last three or so months and producers needed inducements to gather the crops. To the Board of Trade, it seemed that special 'priorities' assigned to particular countries for particular purposes would either be ineffective or result in similar problems arising elsewhere; it recommended reliance on 'the normal commercial mechanism, which should be freed and kept free from regulatory obstacles'.[14] The Colonial Office, which had consulted the Board of Trade, foresaw difficulties in applying controls to increase supplies to West Africa.[15] There seemed a danger of becoming involved in a vicious circle for, unless adequate supplies of consumer goods could be directed or attracted to certain food-producing countries, world supplies of food could not be increased and, unless world supplies of food were increased, the production of consumer goods would decline. The Lord President, Mr H. Morrison, was asked to arrange for the Board of Trade to consider with the India Office ways and means of increasing supplies, particularly of cotton goods, to countries from which increased exports of food might be secured.[16]

At the ninth meeting of SEAF,[17] production and transport were again discussed in the light of a memorandum by the Director of Oils and Fats at the Ministry of Food, Mr J. W. Knight.[18] On British East Africa, it stated that local consumption had increased enormously, practically the whole of the groundnuts being consumed locally. The West African crop was said to be above normal in both Nigeria and Gambia and, although railings from Kano were slow owing to 'the war-weariness of the Nigerian railroads', the crop was expected to be cleared by the time the new crop was coming forth. The Governor's stock estimate was said to be 'unduly pessimistic'. But the decline of sales in West Africa was felt to be an absolute disaster, requiring an increase of prices and the removal of restrictions on lorry transport. Governors had already been authorised to increase the price paid for groundnuts, but the Governor of Nigeria felt that the motor transport regulations were essential to ensure that maximum use was made of lorry transport.[19] No explanation was given for this view. The Committee took the view that there was advantage in increasing the rate of railings from Kano. It was a matter of evacuating stocks: the Secretary of State reported that no additional supplies of groundnuts could be made available from Nigeria. Indeed, he went on to say – and this has an obvious interest in the light of later developments – that: 'The only African territory where groundnut cultivation could be increased was Tanganyika but that was a long-term question and, moreover, there were considerable technical difficulties'.[20] The Director of Produce Disposal in Nigeria, Mr R. S. Mallinson, reported that Nigeria had received six locomotives from the Gold Coast and 15 were due to arrive from Canada in December, and evacuation was not badly behind schedule. The palm-oil and kernels position was less satisfactory, mainly, he thought, because of the accumulation of money by producers, who marketed less and wished to buy more consumer goods. Any attempt to introduce mechanical methods would require considerable supervisory personnel, which was not available.[21]

Meanwhile, the situation with regard to edible oils in the Far East and South-East Asia was causing grave concern. Hong Kong badly needed supplies, but difficulties of procurement and high prices made supplies from China prohibitive and the Ministry of Food was still unable to provide an allocation.[22] Burma, too, had a desperate need for groundnut oil and sought sesame or other oil from Siam[23] and groundnut oil from India.[24] The position became desperate, as the promised 9000–12,000 tons were not received as promised. The Governor found it 'quite impossible effectively to encourage rice cultivation unless we can supply cultivator with essential goods, of which cooking oil is chief need'.[25] In Malaya, a potential source of supplies, the ruling that each export transaction involving coconut oil had to be referred to London had the effect of halting authorised exports and diverting supplies to the black market, largely for Hong Kong. The Ministry of Food was prepared to negotiate a contract to the end of 1950 to buy all copra and coconut oil, as was negotiated with Ceylon.[26] It also proposed that margarine allocated to Burma should be sent to the United Kingdom, and groundnut oil intended for the United Kingdom sent instead to Burma.[27]

II. MISSION TO WEST AFRICA

The oils and fats situation was so serious by May 1946 that the Secretary of State for Foreign Affairs, Mr Ernest Bevin, who was particularly concerned over the plight in the Far East and South-East Asia – total exports of oil from the Far East, including Malaya, were not expected to exceed 381,850 metric tons as compared with 1,651,550 metric tons before the war[28] – felt that everything possible should be done to relieve the position. Accordingly, he proposed that a Mission should visit West Africa to make sure that everything was being done there to increase supplies.[29] The proposal was discussed by SEAF on 20 June 1946.[30] The problem was thought to have three aspects, namely production, collection of crops, and transport, and the Mission needed suitable expertise in these fields. A sub-committee accepted this view, and proposed the following terms of reference: 'to investigate and report, in consultation with Colonial Governors, on the possibilities of increasing during the period of the immediate world food shortage, the exportable surpluses of vegetable oils and oil seeds in West Africa; and to recommend means of securing the maximum production of these commodities, including the provision of the necessary transport and other facilities for their speedy movement to ocean ports.'[31]

The circumstances of the appointment of the Mission were rather peculiar. The Colonial Office was not convinced of its necessity but, because of a series of events which brought a temporary difficulty over transport in Nigeria to the attention of WFS and SEAF, the Secretary of State was strongly pressed by the Prime Minister and the powerful Mr Bevin and felt obliged to agree.[32] By the time the Mission's Report was presented, the emergency had passed and 'quite frankly the Report has fallen pretty flat'.[33] The Governor of Nigeria had impressed upon the Colonial Office that *in the end* the means of increased production were the provision of European staff, loco-motives and road transport, equipment and consumer goods of all kinds.[34] At a private meeting with Mr H. A. Tempany, the Secretary of State's Agricultural Adviser, on 7 August 1946 the latter told Sir Bernard Keen that 'the Nigerian Government was doing the maxi-mum possible in the conditions and had done so for years. It was highly unlikely that a short-term mission would be able to put its finger on any omissions, even if they existed.' (Sir Bernard Keen's Diary, p. 2.) However, even if the Mission did no more than confirm the difficulties that the Governor had stated and stimulate efforts to meet them, the Secretary of State thought it would be justified.[35]

Dr, later Sir, Bernard A. Keen, FRS, of the Rothampstead Experimental Station was appointed Chairman with Mr J. McFadyen, Director of the English and Scottish Joint CWS, as business member and Mr C. E. Rooke, former General Manager of

Nigerian Railways, as railway member. Mr R. S. Mallinson, Director of Supplies, Nigeria, was secretary. A briefing meeting was held at the Colonial Office on 14 August at which officials of the Ministry of Supply and the Board of Trade took part, along with representatives of the Association of West African Merchants. Owing to the Destruction Under Statute of File 19606/9/4 of 1947, no official record of this exists. The account given is taken from page 2 of the Diary of West Africa Tour, 1946, kept by the chairman of the Mission, Sir Bernard Keen, with his permission. The task to be undertaken was regarded as essentially short-term, i.e. 'to get more, if possible, out of existing acreages', especially from the next crop of groundnuts with more palm-kernels and oil in 1947–48. The official of the Ministry of Supply, Mr Spark, explained that consumer goods – primarily cotton goods of all kinds – were the most difficult to supply and, at the same time, the essential incentive. The world allocation fixed in Washington was sub-allocated among the West African Colonies by the West African Governors' Conference, which similarly divided other kinds of imports. India was heavily reducing her allocation of cotton goods to the pool, with adverse effects on West Africa's share. Oil output, which was 409,000 tons in 1944, fell to 368,000 in 1945. According to a note to the Colonial Office from the Association of West African Merchants, the fall was the combined result of (a) shortage of consumer goods, (b) increased local consumption of oil and oil seeds, (c) controls and restrictions on normal transport, (d) low prices ruling for palm-oil and kernels 10–12 years previously had destroyed any incentive to thin out seedlings and tend mature trees, (e) increased tapping of trees for palm wine, (f) more attention to the cultivation of food crops, because of the high price of imported foods, (g) wartime recruitment of labour, (h) the drift of young men to the towns, and (i) Army allowances to African wives which removed the incentive for them to crack nuts. Throughout West Africa, palm kernels were the women's perquisite, providing 'pin-money'. In the absence of more consumer goods, raising the price of oil tended to reduce the number of kernels cracked. The Mission saw lots of uncracked kernels lying about (Sir Bernard Keen's Diary, page 8). The suggested remedies were to increase the quota of consumer goods, abolish transport controls, increase the supply of hand-presses for palm-oil and institute more propaganda on their advantages, to encourage the planting of selected seedlings in place of 'wild' trees and, rather than to advance prices further, to increase the supply of silver currency, which was regarded as a consumer good. In reply to a request for suggestions for improving the production of oil seeds in Nigeria, Mr F. Samuel of the United Africa

Company mentioned, besides consumer goods, 'the introduction of silver as against alloy coinage might well prove to be a potent stimulant towards the greater production of primary products' as the silver coins would be hoarded and therefore 'tantamount to the introduction of desired consumer goods'.[36] However, this was not thought in the Colonial Office to be practicable sufficiently quickly to affect the immediate supply problem.[37] When he met the Mission, Lord Nathan said he regarded the prime object as being 'to ensure that the authorities in West Africa were seized of the urgency of the matter'[38]

The Mission spent thirty-one days in Nigeria and briefly visited the Gold Coast, Sierra Leone and Gambia. Its Report[39] was divided into four sections, the first of which dealt with Agriculture. It explained that farming was on a peasant basis, with food as the primary crop. Oil-bearing crops were secondary and the amount produced depended on the price and availability of consumer goods. It was the practice to clear the bush on land intended for farming and to allow the bush to return when the land was exhausted. Farms were small and mechanisation and artificial manuring would be difficult to introduce. Population increase had resulted in land being kept in cultivation too long and there had been soil erosion. There had been a tendency to concentrate on cash crops. An agricultural survey on these matters was advised for Nigeria and Sierra Leone. Groundnuts were grown in Nigeria and also Gambia. Manuring and weeding would increase yields. Palm-oil and kernels were produced, mainly in the coastal area, from wild trees whose yield was lower than in the East Indies. Fertilisers were advised. Benniseed was grown in Nigeria, preferably on poor land.

The second section discussed Production and Development. In Nigeria, the maximum possible area was already sown in the Northern Provinces and increases would have to come from raising the yield per acre. Development in the Bornu Province by large-scale farming methods was not advised as evacuation would be difficult. While the basic price had been raised by £4 to £16 per ton, the minimum price had been raised only £2 to £11. If this affected the volume marketed, it was recommended that the difference between basic and minimum should be restored to £3 by increasing the minimum a further £2. In Sierra Leone, groundnuts had not been exported before the war but production had increased during the war so that there was an exportable surplus. Extension of acreage was not encouraged because the hillside cultivation involved would lead to erosion. It was recommended that the Government should buy this surplus, publishing a price each February, by which time local demand would have been satisfied. The exportable surplus of groundnuts in Gambia came in roughly equal amounts from local producers, farmers from the neighbouring French Colony who rented land annually, and from imports from the French Colony – the second and third categories being attracted by the availability of consumer goods, the supply of which it was important to maintain. Large areas could be brought into production though, owing to the labour shortage resulting from considerable under-population, mechanisation would be necessary, and, once launched, the project could be taken over by the Farmers' Co-operatives. The river provided easy means of evacuation.

The third section considered commercial and economic aspects. Since 1942 the West African Produce Control Board had bought, through agents recommended by the Governments, all oilseeds available for export. It was recommended that this should continue; maximum prices should be exhibited at buying stations; prices should be increased despite the argument that this might reduce food crops and that, if consumer goods were not available, output might fall; part of the price increase might be withheld for creating a stabilisation and development fund. In view of the rise of the Nigerian cocoa price, an early decision on price was urged. As native traders were ignoring price controls and making exorbitant profits, greater supplies of goods together with the formation of consumer co-operatives were recommended. Native chiefs should, it was suggested, be paid bonuses for collecting quotas of kernels, as was done in Sierra Leone.

The final section dealt with transport. In Nigeria, irregularity of ocean shipping had slowed evacuation by causing overcrowding of transit sheds, holding of lighters and railway wagons under load and running of road transport at reduced capacity. Given a steady flow of ships, clearance capacity of the port of Lagos exceeded the capacity to feed it. On the railways, there was a serious lack of European staff owing to the inadequacy of salaries, which should be raised. Africans needed training before they could take over many of the posts held by Europeans. Lack of engines limited traffic, although traffic per engine was greater than before the war. Lack of staff and spare parts delayed repairs and reduced maintenance. Engines, wagons and spare parts should be given priority rating in the United Kingdom. Road transport also needed spares and new vehicles. The Mission did not favour the lifting of the road transport control.

As was expected, the Mission confirmed what was known rather than indicating anything new of significance. The conclusions, given in order of importance, were: (a) only small increases of exports were possible, (*b*) the ex-German property in the Cameroons was capable of considerable increase, if they could get the machinery, (*c*) there were good opportunities for power and hand-presses and kernel crackers, (*d*) the price of benniseed needed raising, (*e*) consumer goods should be increased, and (*f*) the bad transport situation required attention. (Sir Bernard Keen's Diary, pp. 71–2.) It was stated in the Diary that 'the bottleneck in palm products is evacuation. At low river, the rafts must be broken and man-handled; at high river the launches must be warped. But consumer goods are even more essential: kerosene, cloth, bicycles. Evacuation to the river was by bicycles; although roads are plentiful and the motor is used, it is not really economic' (pp. 57–8).

Sir Bernard Keen told the author on 21 July 1970 that the Mission was not invited to discuss its findings at the Colonial Office and, owing to the destruction of the two relevant files, it is not possible to assess reactions to the Report in the Office.[40] It is known that the Secretary of State, Mr Creech Jones, addressed Despatches to all four Colonies on 23 June 1947, referring to earlier telegrams, which are not available.[41] The Governors' attention was directed to some of the Mission's recommendations, while they were asked for their views on other recommendations. In the only reply available, that of the Governor of the Gambia, Sir Andrew Wright, it was reported that (i) arrangements had been made, as recommended, for the posting-up at buying stations of written notices with full particulars of buying prices, though their value was conditioned by the illiteracy of the farmers; (ii) consideration was being given to the timing of the announcement of the price of groundnuts in the Gambia in relation to the announcement of the price in the neighbouring French Colony; and (iii) the payment of commission to district, or village, heads or to native authorities was inadvisable, as likely to reduce further the existing low level of food production and be otherwise objectionable.[42] The Mission's proposal of a bonus to native chiefs had particularly interested the Ministry of Food, which felt in 1947 that the need to explore every possible means of increasing the export of oilseeds from West Africa was 'even more urgent now than it was a year ago'.[43] But the Governor's advice against introducing such bonuses was reluctantly accepted.[44]

iii. THE EVACUATION PROBLEM

The Mission provided a vivid account of the transport situation in West Africa, with particular reference to the state of the Nigerian Railways. It remarked that the repeated and vigorous representations of the Nigerian Government on matters of supplies and staff 'all make very strange reading when measured in the light of circumstances and the high priority of oilseeds supply to the United Kingdom.'[45] The evacuation problem was crucial for the maintenance of the fats ration in the United Kingdom. The Secretary of State assured the House of Commons, in answer to a question on the Mission's report, that the question of alleviating the transport situation in West Africa was receiving his personal attention and that everything possible was being done to speed up delivery of the large and various requirements.[46] The position was considered at length by the Select Committee on Estimates which visited Nigeria in March–April 1948. The chairman of Sub-Committee B, which visited West Africa, was Sir Ralph Glyn, MP. In its report, it gave the following succinct account of the position:

87. The Nigerian Railway is owned by the Government, and is managed by a separate department, which presents its annual budget to the Finance Committee of the Legislative Council separately from the main Government Budget. The railway was designed over forty years ago to carry a maximum of 1,480,000 tons of goods traffic per annum. Before the war, the highest tonnage reached was 1,200,920, in 1937–38. Since 1943, the designed maximum has been regularly exceeded. In 1944–45 1,709,690 tons were hauled and in 1946–47, the latest year for which figures are available, 1,742,880 tons, the highest figure yet reached. At the same time, the engine mileage, which was originally envisaged at about $5\frac{3}{4}$ million per annum has fallen by about $\frac{1}{2}$ million from the 1944–45 peak figure of 7,076,660. Thus, in spite of a decreased engine mileage, the railway has managed to carry a larger load.
88. Nevertheless the increase in tonnage which the railway has been able to carry by the intensive use of the rolling-stock has not kept pace with the increasing output of produce in the Northern Provinces. In the seasons 1942–43 and 1943–44, when the ground-nut crops for export amounted respectively to 101,000 and 172,000 tons, the railway was able to clear the whole amount to the coast by the beginning of the next season. In the 1944–45 season, the export crop rose to 211,000 tons, and at the beginning of the next season 5,216 tons had not been carried. By November, 1947, the stock uncleared amounted to 92,148 tons, and at the beginning of November, 1948, when the next season's crop will begin to arrive at railhead, there is likely to be a balance of 175,000 tons of old crop waiting to be moved from the Kano area. This would be enough to

provide an ounce of margarine a week for the population of the
United Kingdom for a year.

89. This situation is due to no fault of the management of the
railway. As has been shown, the total tonnage hauled has been
steadily increased in spite of a decreasing engine capacity. Nor was
there any failure to provide for replacements. As far back as
October, 1943, the Ministry of Production had received from the
Crown Agents a list of Colonial railway requirements for 1945
which included 11 main line locomotives for Nigeria, and in the
following July these locomotives were given a place in the United
Kingdom programme of production for 1945. In November, 1944,
the order was allocated by the Ministry of Supply to a manufacturer
whose works were not capable of making engines of the required
design, and it was not until August, 1945, that a suitable manufacturer was found. At the same time, the Nigerian Government asked
for the order to be increased to 20 engines. It now became a question
whether the Nigerian order could be placed in the United Kingdom
programme of production for 1946. The Colonial Office, supported
by the Ministry of Food, strongly urged the Nigerian claim on
account of the importance of moving not only the groundnut crop
from the Northern Provinces, but also the palm products. At this
point it was discovered that the firm finally selected to carry out the
Nigerian order had begun work on an order of between 30 and 64
engines for the London and North Eastern Railway, which had
never been authorised in the official programme of production, and
that it was too late to stop it. As a result, the Nigerian order was put
back for delivery to August, 1947. The 20 engines were eventually
shipped on 12th May, 1948. In the meantime, in June, 1947, 14
engines arrived from Canada, 13 months after the placing of the
order.

90. The foregoing account makes it plain that the present accumulation of groundnuts in Northern Nigeria was due not to the
shortage of engine-building capacity, but to a complete breakdown
of the organisation in London for arranging priorities.

91. The 20 engines which have now been despatched represent only
a small part of what is needed. There is an equally acute shortage of
wagons and other rolling-stock. Fifty coal wagons indented for in
October, 1944, were shipped in May and June, 1948. With the help
of these and a supply of springs to maintain existing wagons, it will
be possible to increase the movement of groundnuts from 17,000 to
30,000 tons a month. Even so, as has been mentioned, there is likely
to be a balance of 175,000 tons of old crop at the beginning of

November. At this rate, arrears will not be cleared until 1952, assuming that future export crops will be no higher than they were in 1947–48. If the arrears are to be cleared by November, 1949, an additional 9 locomotives and 160 25-ton wagons must be delivered this year.[47]

In Appendix 7 of the Report, the chairman of the Kano Committee of Groundnut Buying Agents stated that the railway never recovered its previous level of efficiency after the strike of August 1945. This might have been due, in whole or part, to the influence mentioned by Mr C. E. Rooke, former General Manager of the Nigerian Railways, in his Note appended to the Keen Mission's report. This influence was of a 'politico-racial' nature, provoked by agitators and stimulated by the press (Colonial No. 211, p. 54).

However, it was not 'a complete breakdown of the organisation in London for arranging priorities', as stated in paragraph 90, but rather the lack of priority rating that accounted for the delays and shortages. After the fuel crisis of the winter of 1946–47, the Prime Minister directed that 'in deciding between competing demands on available resources of labour and materials, we must for a time give precedence to projects which will increase our supplies of coal, gas and electricity.'[48] The Ministry of Food and the Colonial Office both took steps to improve the transport situation in Nigeria, and both failed. The Ministry, encouraged by the Keen Mission's report, discussed the possibility of securing existing locomotives, or altering any in process of construction to meet Nigerian requirements, with the Board of Trade and the Ministry of Supply. A progressive diminution of capacity from the middle of 1948 was feared if wagons were not renewed or, at least, well and quickly repaired.[49] Failing all else, better storage was suggested, for 'if we lost 50,000 tons of groundnuts, or more, in West Africa, it would neutralise everything that is being done in the first year in East Africa.'[50] In 1947 it was much more difficult to arrange an allocation of cotton for the manufacture of tarpaulins than in previous years.[51] The Foreign Secretary, Mr Bevin, drew the attention of the Chancellor of the Exchequer, Dr Dalton, to a letter by Mr Walter Fletcher, MP, in *The Times* of 21 August 1947 in which it was alleged that some 200,000 tons of groundnuts were lying 'apparently immovable' in the Kano area. The Chancellor minuted to the Secretary of State, Mr Creech Jones, that, if anything approaching that total was in fact lying idle, both the Foreign Secretary and he were anxious that every effort should be made to ship them, trusting that 'nothing will be left undone to get these groundnuts moved at once'.[52] A few days later, the efficacy of the system of allocating steel was questioned at a Cabinet meeting.[53] The Cabinet was informed that, owing to the drop in steel production on account of the fuel crisis, the allocations exceeded the actual supply and the allocation system was being overhauled. The Cabinet declined to give overriding priority to the production of agricultural machinery or to increase the allocation of steel for that purpose.[54] When it passed on to consider a memorandum concerning the possibilities of increased production of dollar-earning commodities in the Colonies,[55] it was informed that 100,000 tons of groundnuts were held up at Kano awaiting the supply of locomotives to the Nigerian Railways. Unlike the memorandum from the Ministry of Agriculture, the Colonial Office memorandum did not ask for super-priority, although there was little hope otherwise of solving the evacuation problem in West Africa. Instead, rather weakly perhaps, the Prime Minister said that immediate steps should be taken to ascertain whether the railway equipment required for the development of Colonial primary products could be made available from surplus War Department stock. The matter was taken up, at the suggestion of the Secretary of State for Foreign Affairs, by the Foreign Office with other Departments concerned. From the replies received, it became clear that most of the serviceable surplus locomotives were returned to the United Kingdom for the reconstruction of the railway system here.[56] There was, in view of the large demand for additional locomotives in this country, therefore, virtually no prospect of any of these surplus locomotives being available for the Colonies.[57]

However, long before the Cabinet discussion, Mr Creech Jones had written personal letters to the Minister of Supply, Mr J. Wilmot, concerning delays in the supply of railway equipment for the Nigerian Railways.[58] He wrote again in August 1947, because the delays were also affecting locomotives for East Africa and wagons for Malaya, suggesting that there might be 'some risk of the fact being overlooked that locomotives for groundnut production in East and West Africa, for example, are also a matter of direct interest to the United Kingdom'.[59] It was hoped in the Colonial Office that the Ministry of Supply would give this higher or at least equal priority compared with home demands.[60] In his reply, the Minister of Supply made two points: first, the fuel crisis had delayed the whole programme of production by between four and five months and, secondly, the Prime Minister's list of priorities did not include any work for export.[61] So Colonial orders were to continue to take their turn in the queue.

The existing system was that the Colonies received a portion of the Board of Trade's allocation of steel for export, a share which had settled down at around 15 per cent of the total allocation, then amounting to 140,000 tons, although it was adjustable if a sufficiently strong case was presented.[62] Even so, locomotives for Nigeria had no priority and this appears to have been the crux of the matter. The firm making the locomotives for Nigeria was unable to guarantee delivery as forecast, because of uncertainty over the delivery of materials.

In September 1947, the managing director of the Vulcan Foundry Limited reported to the Crown Agents that the Ministry of Supply had declined to take any action on the question of material priorities and 'in consequence export locomotive material has no priority today although, in addition to being valuable as an export, many of our locomotive orders are sponsored by Government Departments for railways concerned with the movement of food.'[63] Accordingly, the Parliamentary Under-Secretary of State, Mr Rees-Williams, asked the Minister of Supply, Mr G. Strauss, 'to extend special facilities to the Vulcan Foundry Limited for the necessary material for these locomotives.[64] A copy of the letter was sent to the Minister of Food, Mr J. Strachey, who supported the plea in a letter to the Minister of Supply in which he emphasised that the precarious fats ration largely depended on the movement of groundnuts from Kano to the coast for shipment: 'A month hence there will still be about 100,000 tons of groundnuts from the 1946 crop awaiting railing and, from then onwards, the new crop of probably 300,000 tons will be arriving at the rail-head.'[65] The Minister capitulated as the result of representations from four different quarters, with the result that the delivery of steel to the company was improved.[66] But this was a unique occasion, not a precedent, and so not repeatable.

The Colonial Office official who had initiated the steps leading to the appeal to the Ministry of Supply wished to secure some measure of priority for locomotives and rolling stock for Colonial railways generally, in view of their relevance to schemes for Colonial economic development. He felt that, unless steps were taken to secure a general priority, 'we may be open to criticism at some time or other in the future'.[67] In fact, the Vice-Quartermaster-General had discussed the problem with the Nigerian Government on behalf of the War Office and at the request of the Minister of Food in November 1947.[68] The Army could not repeat its offer of 1946 to supply motor vehicles, owing to its own shortages. The proposal to use landing craft was impracticable, as was the use of aircraft which, if available, would cost 2/6d per ton mile. So rail evacuation was the only possible means and required the earliest possible supply of twenty locomotives, one hundred and fifty hopper wagons and sixteen boilers. The VQMG agreed to report this to the War Office and stated that 'every endeavour would be made at Cabinet level to obtain the insertion of these items in the Prime Minister's list'. A special meeting was held at the Ministry of Supply on 12 January 1948 under the chairmanship of Lieutenant-General Wrisberg to discuss the requirements but there was little success.[69]

The evacuation problem of West Africa was not the only Colonial transport problem. The official involved had minuted in November 1947 that: 'We are receiving such pressure in the way of supply of all types of railway material because of the importance of the East African groundnut scheme.'[70] By February 1948, it was clear that: 'In the last analysis, East African groundnuts *do* compete with West African groundnuts for all sorts of supplies and facilities.'[71] There was also a general backlog problem in the Colonies. For example, the Governor of Mauritius reported that existing rolling stock included five engines dating from 1865 and eleven with over fifty years' service; there were fifteen boilers which had been in use for over twenty years and, while seven had been ordered, delivery had been promised for only three in 1949.[72] The General Manager of the Gold Coast Railways, Mr J. Salkield, stated that 75 per cent more traffic was being carried, although this was less than was offered, and the old material being used could fail at any time.[73] However, it was felt in the Colonial Office that the Central Economic Planning Staff and the Supply Departments could not be expected to give really serious attention to Colonial requirements unless, and until, they were given a fairly complete picture of these requirements, and regular progress reports on the extent to which requirements were being met. In the case of Colonial railways, it was not felt that the selection of particular items was satisfactory as the maintenance and improvement of the whole railway system was necessary, if breakdowns were to be avoided.[74] When the Secretary of State asked the Secretary of State for War in December 1947 whether qualified Royal Engineer officers could be loaned 'to help in carrying out urgent civil engineering tasks in the Colonies', he mentioned both East and West Africa as areas where difficulties of transport and technical supervision were holding up 'vitally important schemes of production'.

The general situation with regard to priorities was changed in October 1947 when the Prime Minister's Directive of March was modified. The effectiveness of the Directive had inevitably caused difficulties elsewhere, particularly in implementing the new programmes for expanding home food production and exports. A review of the system of priorities was to be made by CEPS, but, meanwhile, the necessary requirements of agriculture and of export were added to the priorities of fuel and energy equipment.[75] The Ministry of Food was told that overseas food production schemes sponsored by HMG were to receive equivalent priority.[76] In April 1948 the Production Committee of the Cabinet agreed that industrial building at home should have first claim on the increased allocation of steel, while 'the external development programmes, particularly those for Colonial and oil development' should come next.[77]

Priorities did not always solve problems, however. The Ministry of Supply was directed to make arrangements to expedite the completion of the twenty Vulcan locomotives destined for Nigeria, but the makers still found delay in steel deliveries.[78] Yet when the Gold Coast ordered one passenger-type locomotive, it was delivered.[79] Again, under the new system of allocating steel,[80] the Board of Trade was allowed only a very small quantity of steel for priority issues to clear bottlenecks and itself decided whether priority steel should be allowed in any particular case. Neither the Colonial Office nor the Special Section of the Ministry of Food liked the Board of Trade alone to determine the distribution of steel earmarked for export, and tried to arrange for regular inter-departmental meetings.[81] The matter was discussed at the meeting of the Colonial Development Working Party's Sub-Committee on Railway Requirements, where it was stated that the estimates for Colonial requirements were too low, involving a big shortfall to be carried forward to 1949. It was agreed that the Iron and Steel Board would consider the matter further.[82] By the end of July 1948, Colonial Governors were told that productive capacity for railway locomotives was completely allocated for 1949 and manufacturers' order books for 1950 delivery were rapidly filling up, so that orders for 1950 and 1951 should be placed immediately.[83]

Thus, despite the acknowledged urgency of the evacuation problem, Nigerian railways did not receive special treatment. Indeed, they suffered further as a result of the attempt being made to develop railways in East Africa to carry groundnuts, and of the allocation of steel to the Overseas Food Corporation (OFC). As regards the first of these, it was reported that the Chief Mechanical Engineer of Tanganyika Railways was visiting Basra to select items from surplus rolling-stock for the East African groundnuts project.[84] As regards the second, the Chairman of the OFC, Mr L. A. Plummer, assured the British Supply Office in Washington in November 1948 that the shortage of steel was not a significant part of the Corporation's problem: 'We are treated generously by the Government on the matter of steel for root cutters, root rakes, etc. Some items we have difficulty over, for example, tool steel for workshops. But this only amounts to 300 tons a year.[85]

This was the subject of sharp comment by the Colonial Development Working Party in its Interim Report but, before considering that, it is well to take account of Sir Sydney Caine's comment of March 1948 concerning the specific complaint made by the Fifth Report of the Select Committee on Estimates, Session 1947–48, which has been referred to for its general assessment in Chapter 2, Section V, of this volume. On the complaint of bad planning in respect of rolling stock for the Nigerian railways, Sir Sydney Caine argued:

It would be a valid criticism of lack of planning if the Nigerian requirements had been neglected simply because there was no authority concerned at all with the allocation of railway supplies. That however is not shown. What does emerge is that, at various stages, the Nigerian requirements were set aside as of less urgency than the requirements of other railway material. Naturally enough, we in the Colonial Office questioned the wisdom of those decisions, but they are, in the first place, not the result of lack of planning and, in the second, not necessarily wrong merely because they failed to give Nigeria all it wanted. I have little doubt that a case could be made out to show that at the relevant times the other requirements which were given precedence over Nigeria's appeared even more urgent. Indeed, it is quite likely that they not merely appeared to be so, but were more urgent. It is well known that the British railway system has been stretched very near to the limit in the last two winters, and there was great anxiety last autumn as to whether there might not be a second fuel crisis, owing to lack of rolling stock to transport coal. I should not like to argue that it would have been worth while enabling Nigeria to move its groundnuts at the cost of preventing coal being moved in this country. I do not say that was necessarily the choice when the decision was taken to postpone the Nigerian orders, but it is the kind of choice which any planning organisation has constantly to be making. It is easy to criticise afterwards, and particularly easy to point out how certain requirements have not been met, but it is not so easy, as we discover time and again in the meetings of allocation committees, to reach any agreement on what ought to have been sacrificed in order to meet the particular requirement which is being championed.[86]

To return to the Interim Report of the CDWP,[87] which was concerned to discover the current and prospective hindrances to production in the Colonies: it showed that sterling finance was not hindering development. The real difficulty was the continuing shortage of goods and services. While it was not suggested that no new schemes should be started until all arrears of maintenance had been cleared, it was stated that major new developments could not successfully be undertaken unless basic facilities, such as transport, were available. The dangers of ignoring this aspect and neglecting small schemes, which would give quick returns, in favour of ambitious projects with a long gestation period, were illustrated thus:

At Kano, in Northern Nigeria, there were at the end of October 1947 immense tarpaulin-covered pyramids containing 92,000 tons of groundnuts. These would be available to help maintain our fats ration if they could be moved to port, but for lack of railway materials the pyramids are likely to grow to at least 145,000 tons by the end of October 1948. Had part of the effort devoted to starting the East African groundnut scheme been put into obtaining supplies for the existing Nigerian railway, we believe they would have yielded larger short-term results.[88]

When the report was considered, Ministers agreed that the first need, and the most profitable use for scarce resources, was to make good the productivity of existing facilities, notably railways and communications.[89] However, there was no mechanism whereby this could be effected. It was a matter of providing priorities within a system of priorities. The Minister of Supply noted, in his letter of 28 August 1947 referred to earlier, that the Prime Minister's list of priorities 'did not, of course, include any work for export'.[90] When this was allowed for, there was no super-priority for the Nigerian railways. Equally it was true, as Mr Creech Jones assured the House of Commons, that there was 'no question of East Africa getting priority'.[91] Because of supply problems, particularly in respect of heavy land-clearing equipment, the Overseas Food Corporation was unwilling to start operations in Northern Rhodesia in 1947.[92] Yet there was a tacit acceptance in the Colonial Office of the attraction of supplies to East Africa. As early as November 1946 it was felt that it was unlikely that any immediate action could take place on the report of the Keen Mission, because of the heavy commitments in East Africa.[93] It was realised, as early as May 1947, that any new schemes for mechanised food production in West Africa would have to rely on dollar supplies, because military surpluses would have been used up for East Africa.[94] Meanwhile, the Opposition persistently questioned the Government about the evacuation problem. Ministers frankly acknowledged the transport bottleneck, giving from time to time information on the despatch of locomotives. Thus, Mr Creech Jones stated that fourteen Canadian locomotives had been despatched to Nigeria in 1947 and twenty British locomotives were being manufactured;[95] by June 1948 twenty of the sixty-three locomotives on order had arrived in Lagos[96] and the number delivered to West Africa since the end of the war now came to fifty-eight.[97] At the time, it was not realised in the Colonial Office that engines were usually withdrawn when new engines were received. This information came as a shock after the first 78 engines were delivered and it was found that 76 had been withdrawn.

The requirements of Colonial railways were examined by the Colonial Railways Sub-Committee of the Colonial Development Working Party.[98] A carry-over to 1949 was regarded as inevitable, and the possibility of varying the sequence of orders placed with manufacturers was said to be limited. Attempts by special action to get equipment for one Colony, say Nigeria, to prevent a breakdown were held to be likely to create equally serious difficulties elsewhere. So the only real possibility of accelerating deliveries was said to be in an expansion of the output of the industry making rolling stock. The Ministry of Supply disagreed with this view because by volume exports of locomotives and wagons were running at 229 per cent and 236 per cent respectively of the monthly average for 1935–37. Such a rate of demand was not likely, it was added, to be maintained for very long.[99] Possibly with the evacuation problem in mind, the report stated flatly: 'The date of the orders rather than the urgency of needs determines the rotation in which orders are now placed on behalf of the Colonies. No opportunity now occurs for considering priorities.'[100] Sequence planning operated in rolling stock production; stock being produced to specification could not easily be switched to expedite another order. It was, as a result, rarely possible to bring forward appreciably the delivery dates scheduled by manufacturers.[101] Yet it was accepted that the lack of wagons was the cause of the evacuation problem, and the accelerated delivery of some of the wagons, particularly the 150 hopper wagons ordered by the end of 1946, was very necessary.[102] It is not easy to reconcile this last statement with the previous declaration that priorities could not be considered. It seems that, when the Prime Minister said that steps should be taken to seek rolling stock from surplus War Department stock, he should have required that a sufficient minimum of rolling stock should be made available, without delay, to the Nigerian Railways from a combination of surplus stock and new production. Lacking such a directive, Ministers and officials had to operate within a congested and somewhat unpredictable system. The CEPS investigated the position in 1948 with officials of the Colonial Office, Ministry of Supply and the Crown Agents, and officials from the Ministry of Supply visited the works of the manufacturers concerned. The enquiries showed that no award of special priority at that time could accelerate deliveries. The Treasury authorised dollar expenditure on ten Canadian locomotives, but the delivery date for Canadian wagons did not justify such expenditure. The Chancellor of the Exchequer concluded that 'the lesson to be drawn from this unhappy business is, of course, that plans for orders such as these, which involve a fairly long cycle of production and are in a field where the order book is likely to be congested, should be laid well in advance and the Colonies should now be working out their needs for the early 1950s.'[103] The Secretary of State had, in fact, anticipated this by advising the Governor to over-order.[104] When delays in delivering raw materials suddenly nullified the special steps taken to bring forward the delivery of locomotive boilers for Nigeria, the only positive suggestion made in the Colonial Office was that there was need for a 'proper "chaser" who would go down to the works and find out precisely why nothing can be done, if that is really the case'.[105] The Ministry of Supply and the Crown Agents sent officials to investigate together but the delay was found to be unavoidable, as the sequence of material production at the steel mills did not correspond with the sequence required for the building programme.[106] At the Nigerian end, railings declined sharply in September and October 1948, because of unduly large railings of livestock in connection with the Mohammedan Festival.[107] An inter-departmental meeting, presided over by the Parliamentary Under-Secretary of State, Mr Rees-Williams, considered the alternative possibilities for improving evacuation, and came to the same conclusion as had the VQMG, namely that the only solution was the despatch of sufficient locomotives and wagons.[108]

The CEPS was anxious that everything possible should be done to maximise the use of existing facilities meanwhile, and proposed that an expert should visit Nigeria to advise on wagon turnround and rail traffic problems generally.[109] The Office knew of no one to send, felt that the VQMG had fully covered the ground, and held that turnround depended on the number of locomotives in service.[110] The Governor was assured that the Nigerian Railways were 'the first concern' of the Office.[111] When the Economic Secretary to the Treasury repeated the proposal made earlier by CEPS,[112] the Office still felt reluctant to adopt it.[113] The Minister of Food asked the

Secretary of State to reconsider it[114] and the Economic Secretary approached the Parliamentary Under-Secretary again.[115] Despite some doubts in the Office, the Parliamentary Under-Secretary felt everything possible should demonstrably be done to meet the situation[116] and the Secretary of State agreed 'because of the political and psychological value at this end'.[117] The Economic Secretary to the Treasury, after discussion with the Transport Commission, put forward the name of the Assistant Divisional Superintendent at York, Mr H. F. Pallant,[118] who reported that the main reason for the delay in the movement of traffic was the shortage of engines and wagons.

The notification of a shortfall on estimated railings for April 1949, due to unexpected engine breakdowns and the arrival of wagons without bogies or coupler springs,[119] shocked both Ministers. The Parliamentary Under-Secretary felt there had been a lack of follow-up of production in the United Kingdom by both the Office and the Crown Agents, and held that the technical staff in Nigeria was undermanned and overworked. Neither the Office nor the Nigerian Government had put forward fresh ideas to cope with a situation, which was 'week by week falsifying their expectations'. In part, this was due to the inability of officials in the Colonial Office to appreciate technical matters and the Crown Agents were asked to supply more easily understood monthly reports.[120] However, the Parliamentary Under-Secretary believed that the Foreign Secretary would support a plan to use the RAF, now that the Berlin airlift had ended.[121] The Secretary of State was no less disturbed, particularly as three Ministers had made statements and promises in the House of Commons. Immediate enquiries were to be put in hand and the Minister of Food's suggestion of Conference was to be adopted.[122] He informed the Acting Governor of Nigeria of his deep concern and worry over a question which was arousing considerable interest in the House of Commons.[123] There were faults at both ends, the United Kingdom and Nigeria, with the result that railings had pursued an erratic course over two and a half years. The backlog on 31 October 1949 was unlikely to be less than that of the previous year, amounting to 155,000 tons, and would not be cleared before March 1950, instead of by January 1950 as earlier forecast. The inter-departmental meeting again explored all possibilities of improving the evacuations. Air transport was ruled out by the doubling of the cost of the groundnuts that would result. As before, it was concluded that the only effective method was to concentrate on all possible measures for increasing clearance over the Nigerian railways.[124] Persistent efforts at both ends resulted in monthly railings exceeding 40,000 tons for the first time in

October 1949.[125] The actual figure was 42,317 tons. It had been as low
as 23,000 in April. It seemed at last possible that, with the improved
railway clearances and the probable lower crop in 1949–50, the
evacuation problem would be solved.[126] By March 1950, the Colonial
Office was again worried by the low railings, and seeking a review of
the position.[127] Defective wagon bogies, water shortage, locomotive
spares, port congestion at Apapa, wagon shortage and the need to
transport 4000 rams, all contributed to this.[128] The Secretary of State's
Adviser on Inland Transport discussed the situation in Lagos in
December 1950, and reported the need for more realistic forecasting of
railings, defects in new rolling stock and declining productivity on the
Nigerian Railways. No remedy was seen for the third malady.[129]
Maintenance was, by the end of 1950, the crux of the problem.[130] The
workshops were turning out work inferior to those of the Gold Coast.[131]
Even so, the accumulation of groundnuts was dispersed. The balance
of the 1948–49 crop was cleared by June and all the 1949–50 crop,
which was a small one, was cleared by October 1950.

iv. THE PROBLEM IS SOLVED, 1951–1960

At the end of May 1951 the Minister of Food, Mr Maurice Webb,
wrote in some anxiety to the Secretary of State, Mr James Griffiths,
because the railings were down to half of the expected requirements for
the 1951–52 crop and maintenance of the margarine ration required
regular receipt of some 6000 to 7000 tons of groundnuts per week. He
asked for everything possible to be done to ensure this.[132] The
Governor of Nigeria reported that the tonnages of groundnuts, cotton
lint and cotton seed which the Nigerian Railway should be able to
carry over the period November 1951 – December 1952 inclusive were
respectively 330,000, 18,000 and 20,000 on the basis of three
assumptions. These were that there would be no serious labour
troubles and the output of the workshops would not deteriorate
further, seven locomotives would be delivered and in service by June
and various spares on order would be received, and railings of French
groundnuts would be restricted to 2500 tons a month. He further
advised that the appointment of expatriates to new posts of foreman
status would be resented on political grounds and could precipitate a
strike throughout the Railway, but vacancies in established posts
should be filled quickly.[133] The Minister of Food was assured,
providing the programme was achieved.[134] By January 1952, his
successor as Minister of Food, Major G. Lloyd George, later Lord

Tenby, was seriously concerned with the effect that the continuing labour troubles in Nigeria were likely to have on the programme, as any shortfall would either have to be made up by non-sterling purchases or lead to a reduction in the fats ration.[135] A drastic cut in imports of oils and fats from non-sterling sources, owing to the acute balance of payments problem, meant that the maintenance of the programme was essential, if the supply of oils and fats was not to be imperilled.[136] It was indicated to the Governor of Nigeria, Sir John Macpherson, that the continued failure of the Railway to expand its carrying capacity was not only an embarrassment to HMG and a limitation on supplies of oils and fats to the United Kingdom, but would also place limits on the development of the agricultural economy of Northern Nigeria.[137] In an editorial comment on the situation, *The Times* (11 July 1952) quoted a Nigerian official who said 'Either Nigeria decides the future of its railways or the railways decide the future of Nigeria.' At that time, the likely size of the 1952–53 crop was not known, although it had been reported from Nigeria that 'the fertiliser campaign, the efforts being made to increase the output of cotton and the attractive producer prices being offered by the Marketing Boards, make it reasonable to expect that the average annual output will rise in the course of the next few years to 400,000 tons of groundnuts and 100,000 bales of cotton.'[138] The Secretary of State, Mr O. Lyttelton, was warned that, unless something drastic could be done, there was 'every prospect of bigger and better pyramids from now on'.

Officials were unable to explain why the Nigerian Railway did not do better, although it was thought that improvements in management might follow the change of the Railways and Harbours Administration from a Government Department into two statutory Corporations. The Secretary of State was asked to impress upon the Governor, during his forthcoming visit, the need for even ruthless measures to improve the efficiency of the Railway.[139] He discussed all aspects during his visit of May–June 1952, telegraphing to London instructions to expedite the delivery of locomotives and various spares on order.[140] On his return, he asked the Minister of Food to support any representations made to the Minister of Supply, Mr Duncan Sandys, later Lord Duncan-Sandys, to allocate more steel to the makers of locomotives, so that the longer-term building programme might be advanced.[141] At that time, the percentage of engines out of order was around forty, and the carry-over in October 1953 was estimated at about 200,000 tons.[142] The Ministry of Supply was approached by the Ministry of Food to consider measures for expediting the delivery of locomotives to

Nigeria, but, at an inter-departmental meeting, the Ministry of Supply official in the chair indicated that a good case could be made for every order being undertaken by the two firms. It was agreed that it was impracticable to alter the production programmes of locomotive manufacturers. Delivery of the locomotives for Nigeria was possible only if supplies, especially of plate, could be improved.[143] In the short term an improvement in carrying capacity could only be obtained by getting better use out of the Railway's existing locomotives, which meant increasing efficiency in the running-sheds and workshops.[144] The Nigerian Minister of Transport, Chief Bode Thomas, stated that all engines on order would be needed to transport groundnuts in 1953. If engines could not be provided from the United Kingdom, they should be sought elsewhere; and, if better delivery dates were offered elsewhere, the Railway should consider whether it should cancel existing contracts.[145] It seemed to one official that it would be better for the United Kingdom to import more steel rather than lose orders to the Continent[146] but it is not clear whether this suggestion was pursued. The Nigerian Government did place a considerable number of orders on the Continent but somewhat lower prices did not always mean better deliveries.[147]

A bumper crop of groundnuts of 400,559 tons in 1951–52 was followed by another record crop of 401,370 tons in the 1952–53 season, leading to an estimated carry-over of 168,000 tons. This latter was partly due to the increased claims on the Railway, owing to the steadily increasing volume of internal freight and import traffic. Cotton production was increasing, and the Cotton Marketing Board was also involved in losses due to delays in transport, while cottonseed was liable to spontaneous combustion in open storage. No appreciable improvement in railings was possible until locomotives, rolling stock and specialist staff were provided on the required scale. That, at best, meant until 1954, according to an appreciation of the groundnut railment position as at 31 May 1953 by the Department of Marketing and Exports, Lagos.[148] The Nigerian Railway was convinced that retarded delivery dates and failure to recruit personnel were the basic cause of the problem.[149] Officials in the Colonial Office were convinced that everything possible was being done to supply these deficiencies.[150] The matter was drawn, in the strongest terms, to the attention of the Minister of Supply, Mr D. Sandys, by the Lord President, Lord Woolton, on 3 October 1952, by the Minister of Food, Mr G. Lloyd-George, on 13 October and by the Secretary of State, Mr Oliver Lyttelton, on 17 October.[151] According to the answer to a Parliamentary Question, the following number of locomotives were supplied to the Nigerian Railways: March to December 1945 – 11; June and July 1947 –14; March to May 1948 – 26; November 1948 to September 1949 – 12; April 1949 – 10; February 1949 to June 1950 – 43; March 1951–9; September 1952–7. On 19 February 1953 there were 120 locomotives in running order; 31 were in workshops.[152] Clearly, new locomotives were largely replacing existing locomotives, rather than adding to the stock.

In April 1953, the Colonial Office was disturbed to learn from the Crown Agents that the locomotives on order would be delayed until November 1954, owing to the serious shortage of steel. The chairman of the inter-departmental committee was told that, unless the situation was improved, the matter would be raised in the Cabinet.[153] The Ministry of Food supported this reaction.[154] The Ministry of Supply replied that everything within its power had been done to remove the steel bottlenecks by giving the firm the necessary allocations 'but it had not been possible to get corresponding deliveries against the paper allocation'.[155] The firm reported in September 1953 that their main supplier of boiler plates short-delivered in each of the first three quarters, by 72, 28 and 272 tons respectively, and the firm remained severely handicapped.[156] Despite the efforts made, the Secretary of State recognised that the outstanding orders simply could not be expedited, and warned that he would ask the Minister of Supply to intervene, if there was any sign of the dates slipping.[157]

The financial implications of holding large stocks were serious, as the capital needed to finance both current purchases and unrailed stocks absorbed the bulk of the reserves of the Nigeria Groundnut Marketing Board. At the end of March 1954, the Board had some £15 million tied up in stocks, largely of the 1953–54 crop. Prolonged storage involved the Board in heavy additional costs, due to loss in weight and quality, debits, tarpaulin costs, pest infestation measures and losses through deterioration. These losses came to about £3.15.0 per ton, or £1.5 million on a 400,000 ton crop.[158] Delays in delivering locomotives and rolling stock continued to be regularly reported throughout the period 1954–56.[159] Railings exceeded 50,000 tons for the first time in the month of November 1957,[160] and, in view of the clearing of the previous two seasons' crops, the Secretary of State no longer required monthly railing figures.[161] By January 1960, quarterly returns were also dispensed with.[162] The evacuation problem was solved at long last.

This chapter was written with a threefold purpose in mind. First, it was thought to be necessary to show the great severity of the world food shortage, with special reference to oils and fats, with which Mr Attlee's

Government had to cope. The fuel crisis of the winter of 1946–47 compounded the situation, leading to the Prime Minister's directive of March 1947 giving priority to the coal, gas and electricity industries, which inevitably brought about bottlenecks elsewhere. Secondly, the essential purpose behind the endeavours, apart from Mr Bevin's concern with the plight of South-East Asia and the Far Eastern Colonies, was the maintenance of the fats ration in the United Kingdom. The benefits to Nigeria were incidental to this and largely consequential. The presupposition of 1940 that Colonial development should be wholly for the benefit of Colonial peoples was abandoned in the face of the overriding requirements of the world food shortage. Thirdly, the detailed account of the evacuation problem was intended to show, as concretely as possible, the overloaded state of the United Kingdom economy, and the imperfection of the system of controls, which attempted to allocate scarce materials in accordance with a tight priority. When Ministerial pressures were at their greatest, with the ultimate threat of taking matters to the Cabinet, the chairman of the inter-departmental committee had, in May 1953, to admit that 'it had not been possible to get corresponding deliveries against the paper allocation'.

Yet the evacuation problem was essentially a short-term matter, one of moving supplies that were available. The requirements were rolling stock and engineers. It was a matter, to use Churchill's words, of giving Nigerians the tools to do the job. A new dimension was added when it was attempted, as it was to be in both West and East Africa, to expand Colonial production. In the following section, the production problem in West Africa is discussed while, in the next chapter, the East Africa Groundnuts Scheme is treated.

v. WEST AFRICA: THE PRODUCTION PROBLEM

During the war, the United States and the United Kingdom purchased and allocated food supplies on behalf of the United Nations. As early as 12 June 1942 the United States Economic Defense Board had pressed for further attention to Nigerian supplies of palm oil and palm kernels as 'some claim that, properly handled, the present production could be increased by 50 per cent or more'.[163] A Memorandum of Understanding was the basis for purchasing and allocating oils and fats, and when the Combined Food Board was established it adopted the same basis for continued collaboration.[164] An Oils and Fats Committee was set up. At its ninth meeting, the

United States group proposed a reduction of the lard allocation to the United Kingdom. In the discussion, various suggestions were made as to what alternative sources might be secured in British West Africa. It was agreed that the British representatives would make a study and report to the Committee what merchandise was needed to obtain larger supplies, as higher prices alone would not be sufficient to do so.[165] The estimated export of groundnuts from West Africa was around 200,000 long tons.[166] It was agreed to apply for locomotives for use in hauling West African groundnuts to port.[167] The matter was revived again in the discussions over the 1946 allocation. The desperateness of the situation at that time has been described. Here it is sufficient to record that current consumption of soap and edible fats in the United Kingdom was already one-eighth below the wartime level and, therefore, any further reduction of the tentative 1946 allocation was being vigorously resisted.[168] Instead, it was proposed that the United States, Canada and the United Kingdom should agree to parity of *per capita* consumption of edible visible fats during 1946. The United States administrators did not regard that as possible, and rejected the view that, whenever a world deficit arose, American consumption should be questioned. As part of a general review, both uses and sources of supply were to be considered. Among the sources, was the United Kingdom's procurement in West Africa. The United Kingdom representatives undertook to examine whether any cuts could be made in United Kingdom inedible consumption and whether anything could, in the short or long run, be done to speed up procurement in West Africa.[169] The Americans refused to be hurried and, it was suspected, that it was hoped in this way to stimulate action on the part of the United Kingdom to increase supplies from Malaya, New Guinea and West Africa on the basis that 'America helps those who help themselves'.[170] The Minister of Food, Sir Ben Smith, reported to his Permanent Secretary, Sir Frank Tribe, that in all discussions with American officials 'we are confronted with accusations that we are not taking all possible measures to increase our own supplies'. He concluded that no appeal, at whatever level, would obtain much help from the United States 'until we are able to show that we have obtained maximum quantities from the sources available to us'.[171] In reply to a request for much fuller information on the steps being taken to maximise supplies from Empire sources, the Ministry of Food referred to the consideration of West African supplies by Lord Nathan's Committee.[172]

The Keen Mission was the immediate result of these deliberations. Meantime, there was a political wave of decontrol in the United

States, which put the United Kingdom at considerable disadvantage as she was a large importer and continued price and ration controls. The Head of the British Food Mission wrote gloomily, asking for instructions and a visit by the Head of the Oils and Fats Division of the Ministry of Food to deal with the 1947 allocation.[173] The United States Secretary for Agriculture was acknowledged to be subjected to continual pressure, arising from allegations that in the Dutch, French and British Colonies efforts to rehabilitate production had been less vigorous than was possible.[174] When the Committee on Fats, Oils and Foods of the IEFC met on 20 December 1946, the American delegate contrasted the slow recovery elsewhere with American expansion at home and the successful rehabilitation of copra production in the Philippines. The British delegate did not accept the comparison, mentioning the setting up of the Cabinet Committee on World Food Supplies, assistance in rehabilitating the Norwegian whaling fleet, rehabilitation of Burma's rice production and the launching of the East African groundnuts project.[175]

On 28 January 1947, a Memorandum was received from Messrs Lever Brothers and Unilever on the expansion of world production of oils and fats.[176] It was divided into three parts. Part I set out briefly the world situation as estimated for 1947 and 1948 compared with 1939, and considered the world's future needs. Part II made suggestions for possible short-term developments, while Part III was confined to long-term policy. On the assumption that by 1956 the average *per capita* consumption throughout the world could be raised from the 1938 level of 21.4 lbs to 25 lbs, and assuming an annual increase in population of 1 per cent, it estimated that the world would have to produce nearly 25 million tons of oils and fats to satisfy that demand, which meant an increase of 10 million tons over the 1946 level, and 7 million over the 1938 level. So the problem was massive in its dimensions. In the short run, reliance had to be placed on rehabilitating existing sources of supply of groundnuts, sunflower seeds, rapeseeds, linseed and sesame seed, although it was recognised that this would not by itself provide the necessary supply. Measures that would yield results after ten or so years were also considered to be essential. These involved the development of palm-oil plantations, which was said to be one of the cheapest and most useful oils to produce. No data on cost was included in the Memorandum. It was discussed, along with the Report of the Keen Mission, at an inter-departmental meeting held at the Ministry of Food under the chairmanship of Mr A. E. Feaveryear on 2 April 1947.[177] The Agricultural Adviser to the Secretary of State, Mr G. F. Clay, thought that large-scale production of oilseeds might be possible in the Northern Territory of the Gold Coast and Gambia. It was agreed that a Mission might be sent to investigate. He also suggested that a valuable increase in production might be secured in Nigeria by the development of mechanised cultivation, based on the village units. It was agreed that this intermediate stage between the traditional cultivation by the hoe and the highly capitalised mechanisation being used in East Africa should be investigated. The Ministry of Food was prepared to support a submission by the Colonial Office to the Treasury along these lines. At the same time, the Agricultural Adviser felt it should be possible to expand considerably the output of existing producers, mainly small peasant producers. He put forward the idea of fixing fair prices, which would be revised annually according to an agreed formula, such as the cost of living or import price indice.

Already in February 1947 Mr Geoffrey Heyworth of the United Africa Company (UAC) had proposed to the Secretary of State the mechanical production of groundnuts in the Northern Territories of the Gold Coast and in suitable areas in Sierra Leone. The suggestion was stated thus:

From a cursory examination of reports, it would appear that an area of not less than one million acres in the Northern Territories of the Gold Coast could be developed for groundnut cultivation on lines similar to those of the East African scheme. This area is partly tsetse-infested and consequently unpopulated, or thinly populated. [Later trials showed that the Damongo area lacked adequate rainfall for the large-scale cultivation of groundnuts. Mr Heyworth's 'not less than a million acres' agrees with the Mission's estimate of about 1,250,000 acres in Western Gonja, but as Mr Heyworth did not specify precisely where his area was, it is not possible to be certain that it included the Damongo area, though it seems highly likely to have done so.] A large-scale development and the prospect of appreciably higher values of groundnuts for a long time to come, compared with pre-war prices, would overcome the high costs of evacuation to the coast and would open up a large new area. Sierra Leone also appears to offer good possibilities. There are sizeable areas available within reasonable distance of the railhead, which appear to be entirely suitable for the cultivation of groundnuts.[178]

But the Office was unable, owing to lack of information, to form a firm view on the proposal and had to start from scratch.[179] It was thought that, while some areas were lightly populated, others were densely populated, although suitably-sized areas might be found which would not seriously interfere with local farming or tenure. It was not known whether such tracts of land would be suitable for groundnuts, although, for the sake of the future of the territory, it was hoped that they would be. The Acting Director of Marketing suggested that a price sufficiently high to stimulate production should be announced, providing a buying organisation and transport could be assured. While the extra output might be relatively small, it would be available quickly, whereas the mechanical production scheme could not help for years.[180] As far as Sierra Leone was concerned, development along lines being worked out in Tanganyika could not be contemplated, because there were no available sizeable areas near the railways; groundnut farming on Tanganyikan lines 'would only be possible after the most serious interference with local farming and tenure'.[181] The former Director of Native Production in East Africa stressed the urgency of getting increased supplies, and suggested Governors should be asked to advise on the price necessary to stimulate peasant production.[182]

The possibility of developing large-scale mechanised production of groundnuts in the Gold Coast was discussed between Ministry of Food and Colonial Office officials on 3 and 4 April 1947. The Minister of Food was anxious to urge the Secretary of State that a survey party should be sent to the Gold Coast; Colonial Office officials accepted that there was a case for further investigation.[183] The Secretary of State, Mr Creech Jones, agreed[184] and telegrams were sent to the Governors of the Gold Coast and Nigeria, and repeated to the Governor of The Gambia.[185] They were informed that, in view of the likelihood that shortage of oils and fats would continue 'for many years to come', His Majesty's Government was surveying possibilities of developing groundnut production in new areas by mechanised methods, providing the necessary organisation and equipment could be made available without retarding full development of the East African plan. It was hoped to send a Mission comprising men of agricultural, transport and business experience whose terms of reference would be: 'to investigate the suitability of conditions in the Northern Territories of the Gold Coast, Northern Nigeria and The Gambia for large-scale mechanised production of groundnuts for export, and if conditions are considered suitable to make recommendations as to the methods of production to be adopted, due regard being paid in any such recommendations to the social and economic effects on the territory concerned.'

The Governor of the Gold Coast, Sir Alan Burns, replied that it was not an opportune time for such a mission 'since widespread and lively fear of reputed design of non-African interests to secure an economic stranglehold, promoted by Cocoa Board legislation, Abortive Concessions legislation, European share of timber industry and the Association of West Africa Merchants' share of commerce, has still to be dispelled.' It was suggested that the mission's work should be divested from the outset of 'any appearance, however fallacious, of being an instrument of non-African economic domination or exploitation', which might influence the choice of personnel and the terms of reference.[186] From Nigeria, the Governor, Sir Arthur Richards, later Lord Milverton, stressed the unanimity between his advisers and the Keen Mission of the impracticability of large-scale production in Bornu Province, and referred also to the uncertainty of rainfall in the Province. He added that further production in the Northern Province would require an immediate solution to the evacuation problem.[187] The Governor of The Gambia, Sir Andrew Wright, agreed to the proposals and the terms of reference.[188] Meantime, Mr Samuel of the UAC had spoken about the proposals to the Minister of Food, Mr Strachey, who wrote to the Secretary of State urging the sending of a Mission to the Gold Coast and The Gambia. Nigeria was excluded, because of the views of the Keen Mission.[189] But, as Northern Nigeria was then the chief groundnut-producing area of British Africa, the Secretary of State decided to include it. The terms of reference were amended to meet the points raised by the Governor of the Gold Coast. They were: 'to investigate the suitability of conditions in the Northern Territories of the Gold Coast, Northern Nigeria and The Gambia, for large-scale mechanised production of groundnuts for export, in accordance with a programme covering a fixed term of years and, if conditions are considered suitable, to make recommendations as to the methods of production to be adopted so as to ensure the full co-operation of the local inhabitants, due regard being paid in any such recommendations to the social and economic effects on the territories concerned.'[190] Yet anxieties remained over the Mission in the Colonial Office, for while it was felt that the Gold Coast Government would be able to calm any agitation that might arise, providing it was sufficiently categorical on such matters as private enterprise, or at least the UAC, and land and European settlement, this was not so in Nigeria, where it was feared that distorted rumours might whip up anti-British feeling. An early announcement was strongly urged.[191] Mr A. B. Cohen agreed that there would be grave local political objections to a mechanised groundnut scheme run by UAC or private enterprise. In fact, he thought it would be 'impossible'.[192] The three Governors were told on 19 May that the members selected were the Secretary of State's Agricultural Adviser, Mr G. F. Clay, a member of the Development Division of the Office, Mr, later Sir Leslie, Monson, and a member of the London Passenger Transport Board, Mr McKenna. A fourth member with knowledge of mechanised agriculture and unconnected with commercial interests in West Africa, Mr Frank Sykes, was added later. In the announcement of the Mission, it was emphasised that the Keen Mission of 1946 had drawn attention to the prospect of mechanised production in The Gambia and this Mission was investigating on a wider basis.[193] The Mission left for West Africa on 5 June and returned to London on 20 July 1947. On the outward journey, Mr Sykes studied the *Plan for the Mechanised Production of Groundnuts in East and Central Africa* (Cmd 7030, February 1947). According to Mr Monson, Mr Sykes was a 'Doubting Thomas about the East African scheme, which he thinks is unjustifiably optimistic in the estimate of yields, in the low number of tractors, etc., employed, and in the belief that weeding can be avoided. In fact, he has said here that groundnuts is not really a good crop for mechanisation at all.'[194] The point is taken up further in the next chapter, on the East Africa scheme.

A report by the Department of Agriculture of the Gold Coast claimed that at least one-third of the Northern area possessed soils suitable for the mechanical production of groundnuts but they were in scattered areas.[195] Climatically, it was just within the region known to be suitable for large-scale groundnut production, as indicated by experience in Nigeria and The Gambia. The Southern area was too elevated and rainfall was wrongly distributed for groundnuts. But the Mission was doubtful whether the soil types of the Northern Territories and Northern Ashanti were suitable for mechanised cultivation. It was found that the physical position in The Gambia was not as reported by the Keen Mission. The two areas investigated did not carry elephant grass but orchard bush; one area consisted of outcrops of hard rock, which would hamper mechanised production, while the other was settled by migrants from over the French border.[196]

At a meeting with the Governor's Deputy and other officials in Lagos, it was stated that, while the main concern of the Mission was long-term development, substantially increased yields were possible in existing areas if phosphatic fertilisers were applied.[197] Two possible areas for mechanised production had been found, which should first be cleared with the assistance of paid labour and then converted into a system of village settlements. It was assumed that the railway supply and staff difficulties would be solved by 1949, and that it was possible to expand current capacity to carry an additional 200,000 tons per annum on a single-line working. The projected extension of the Apapa wharves would render port facilities adequate. The Mission did not estimate either capital requirements or production costs. As plantation operations by private enterprise were not acceptable in West Africa and local finance for a public corporation unlikely to be available, a member of the Mission thought one of the projected United Kingdom Corporations, either the Overseas Food Corporation (OFC) or the Colonial Development Corporation (CDC), might be an appropriate institution. The Governor's Deputy favoured a local Corporation, on the lines of the Cameroons Development Corporation, which had been well received in Nigeria. By placing management in the hands of a local body with African representation it would find favour locally. In a further discussion with the Chairman of the Mission next day, the Governor's Deputy stressed that the first requirement would be for labour, which, for political reasons, should be found as far as possible within Nigeria. It was estimated that every five production units would require 100 tractors and that the 75 Bornu units would, therefore, represent a tractor strength of 1500. These, together with ancillary equipment, would require a considerable technical staff of drivers, mechanics and fitters, presenting an opportunity for the employment of numbers of Southern artisans and trained ex-servicemen. Sir Leslie Monson told the author that all the advice received by the Mission from the Governor's Deputy and the officials in Lagos was to the effect that the introduction of labour from Southern Nigeria into the North would have political repercussions there; the only division of opinion was between those who thought that it should be ruled out on these grounds and those who thought it should be put into effect, despite local opposition, in the wider interests of Nigeria as a whole and of the United Kingdom. Because of this divergence of view, the Mission avoided a recommendation on the point.

It was thought that the exclusive use of the road services operated by the Railways for evacuation would arouse opposition and, therefore, either the less economical African-owned transport would have to be allowed to participate or the managing corporation would have to operate its own motor transport.

In its Report,[198] the Mission stated that there were five areas in West Africa in which the large-scale production of groundnuts and other crops would be practicable by semi-mechanised means. The total acreage of these areas exceeded 5 million, of which some 2,750,000 were expected to be cultivated. The areas were, in the Gold Coast,

(a) in Western Gonja, (b) in Northern Ashanti; in Northern Nigeria, (a) in Bornu round Damaturu, (b) in Kontagora; and in The Gambia, an area of about 35,000 acres. Each of the first four areas covered about 2000 square miles, i.e. 1,250,000 acres, and were thinly populated. It was proposed that these four areas should be developed by local Development Corporations, using, in part, local capital and labour. The small area in The Gambia should, it was suggested, be developed by either the OFC or the CDC. Owing to variable topography and soil types, complete mechanisation was not practicable and hand labour would have to supplement machines. The small Gambia area could be developed over a few years to produce 1500 tons of groundnuts a year, but elsewhere immediate large-scale development was not considered practicable and development in each of the areas should, it was advised, be on the basis of pilot projects involving 12,000 acres, i.e. 20 tractor units. It was further recommended that cultivation should continue for three crop years before any further development was undertaken and, meantime, transport problems could be given attention. It was expected that the quantities of shelled groundnuts available for export would be:

TABLE 4.1 Forecast of Shelled Groundnuts
Available for Export from 1949
(tons)

1949	5,500
1950	10,000
1951	20,500
1952	30,500
1953	55,500
1954	95,500
1955	135,500
1956	165,500
1957	195,500
1958	225,500

and thereafter remain at the 225,000-ton level.

In addition, a considerable amount of cereals would be produced each year, rising to a maximum of 85,000 tons of millet in each area. It was hoped to build up a livestock industry to make use of the grass ley. In both Nigeria and the Gold Coast labour requirements were expected to be 550 supervisory and some 54,000 subordinate staff with 19 and 1200, respectively, in The Gambia. The all-in f.o.b. (free on board) cost of producing groundnuts was expected to be in the range of

£19. 10. 0 to £25. 0.0 a ton, and that of millet at local centres from £12. 17. 8 to £15. 3. 10. According to a minute of 9 January 1948, the Minister of Food, Mr Strachey, said at a meeting that morning that he had been told the previous evening by a director of UAC that, in the latter's own estimate, groundnut prices would not fall below £30 a ton over the next ten years. Whether this was c.i.f. (cost, insurance and freight) or f.o.b. was not clear, the difference being around £5. 10. 0; if it was c.i.f. London, it would approximate the maximum cost of production given in the Report.[199]

The Mission had concerned itself, not so much with the question of an immediate increase in groundnut production, but with the general pattern of development by native producers in Africa. It proposed a system which, with the aid of mechanisation, could break the existing bottlenecks in hand-cultivation and lead to a considerable expansion of output. It coincided with the view, expressed by the Governor of Kenya, Sir Philip Mitchell, and others, that progress in Africa involved the establishment of new social communities, modernised and efficient, as a demonstration, before the mass of African peasants could be persuaded to change.[200]

The Report was approved by the Colonial Advisory Council of Agriculture, Animal Health and Forestry, which saw no alternative to the methods proposed.[201] The Secretary of State discussed the Report with the Mission on 25 November, but no record of the meeting appears to exist.[202] At a meeting of officials, it was thought that the machinery requirements would be extremely difficult, if not impossible, to satisfy over the following years; it was agreed that an open mind should be kept on the Report until the West African Governments and the prospective financing bodies had been consulted.[203] After further discussion in the Office, Confidential Despatches were sent to West African Governments on 4 February 1948.[204] The Secretary of State, Mr Creech Jones, dealt with four aspects. First, he enquired whether Governors considered that the CDC should be invited to participate in the financing, possibly totalling £25 million, and management of the projects. Secondly, while in 1948 and 1949 agricultural tractors and implements could be supplied in the numbers required, there was difficulty in supplying clearing equipment. Thirdly, it was tentatively estimated by the Ministry of Food that f.o.b. groundnut prices per ton would decline progressively over the years 1948–50 to 1956 from £35 to £20, whereas the Mission's all-in f.o.b. cost was £19. 10. 0 to £25. The latter did not take account of other crops and livestock production. Even so, as the Mission suggested, it might be still better to grow sunflowers in some of the areas, cotton in one or two areas, or possibly some other crop. The Agricultural Economist in the Gold Coast was reported to have concluded that the true f.o.b. price was £50 a ton[205] but Mr Frank Sykes was prepared to stand by the Mission's costings on the ground that land clearing would not be as expensive as in East Africa and unmetalled roads were adequate.[206] Mr D. McKenna agreed with Mr Sykes.[207] Finally, Governors were asked whether imported labourers would be likely to settle in the new areas, what form of community should be developed, and whether such a community could in time be expected to take over the projects.

The Governor of the Gold Coast, Sir Gerald Creasy, was in general agreement with the proposals of the Report, including the pilot schemes in the Northern Territories and in Northern Ashanti, which he regarded as of crucial importance for the future not only of groundnuts but of mechanised agriculture throughout the Gold Coast.[208] Steps were being taken to select suitable sites for the two schemes. In reply to the Secretary of State's Despatch of 4 February 1948, he feared local opposition to control by the CDC proportionate to its capital contribution, and intended to establish an Agricultural Development Corporation, financed mainly locally, to deal with agricultural expansion. In an article in *West Africa* (15 May 1948) the Governor stated he was 'determined that, despite the large amount of assistance which will be required from the C.D.C., there shall be a minimum of control exercised from outside the Gold Coast'.[209] Groundnuts could be controlled through a subsidiary company, whose equity capital would be mainly local while expatriate funds would be in the form of debentures. Eventually, co-operatives of the settlers would, he expected, buy out the company, so that the whole concern would be owned and controlled by the growers themselves.

The Governor's Deputy, Mr Hugh Foot, welcomed the Mission's proposals as far as they referred to Nigeria, but thought the Damaturu area (Bornu) should not be proceeded with, because of shortage of water and problems of evacuation.[210] He proposed instead a pilot scheme in the Kontagora area, which the Mission also recommended. However, doubts were expressed on the Mission's proposals for developing a healthy and prosperous agricultural community, because there would be political opposition to introducing agricultural labour on a large scale to the Northern Provinces from elsewhere in Nigeria, and the labourer who would be attracted by paid employment would not usually become a settled farmer. A scheme modelled on that employed by the Sudan Plantations Syndicate was, therefore, favoured, and two officers were sent to visit the Gezira scheme. The full participation of the CDC was welcomed as necessary, detailed arrangements being left for later discussions in London. As a result of the study of the Gezira scheme, it was proposed (a) that the land on which the scheme was to be undertaken should be taken over by the Government, not leased out to a local Corporation or to CDC, and (b) the need to convince the local population that its effective participation was essential was said to require that the local advisory committee be given powers in matters, such as housing, community projects and welfare services, where local knowledge was of dominant importance.[211]

The Gambia part of the Report was abandoned in favour of a scheme to produce eggs and poultry, or, as one minute read, 'The Gambia proposal died when the egg scheme was hatched.'[212] Mr Sykes insisted that if there was to be only one pilot scheme, it should be in The Gambia.[213] However, while the quality of samples collected in the field was high and their contents of oil and extractable protein satisfactory when compared with samples grown elsewhere, examination of the crop as it was marketed in the United Kingdom apparently revealed some time later an exceptionally low quality.[214]

The Gold Coast, with its greater specialist staff, was the first Colony to submit a Plan for the mechanised production of groundnuts. The memorandum, addressed to the CDC, provided a full assessment of the implications of adopting the Mission's recommendations. The estimated capital cost had been raised to £29,098,290, as against the Mission's figure of £12,717,800, while the estimated cost of production per ton of shelled groundnuts, f.o.b. Takoradi, was approximately £43, as against £25 in the Mission's report.[215] The Chairman of the CDC, Lord Trefgarne, replied that there was little likelihood that the CDC would participate in the project as presented, because (a) it would have to shoulder practically all the financial risk, with inadequate security for its capital outlay, and a limited and uncertain net revenue, and (b) the scheme would not cover its costs, unless the existing high prices for groundnuts continued indefinitely and the estimated costs of production could be substantially reduced.[216] The Governor, Sir Gerald H. Creasy, was disappointed and expressed his surprise that

the fact that the project involves a risk, and that there is no guarantee of substantial profits, has been sufficient to decide the Corporation against it, without going further into its merits. If all developments projects in West Africa, or, indeed, throughout the

Colonial Empire, are to be judged solely by this criterion, I doubt whether the Corporation will find much scope for its activities. This is not what I, at any rate, understood by 'adventurous development', as envisaged by Sir Stafford Cripps in his speech to the Governors' Conference last November. Furthermore, this severely materialistic approach to the problem of development is hardly likely to commend itself to Colonial peoples, among whom considerable suspicion already exists that the main purpose of the C.D.C. is 'exploitation' for the benefit of the United Kingdom. Experience such as this is bound to deepen such suspicions.

It continued in the same strain.[217] The Secretary of State felt considerable sympathy with the Governor's point of view, and recognised that issues of principle, of which hitherto the Colonial Office had been mindful, needed clearing up.[218] Discussions continued through the rest of the year, but the intervention of the Colonial Office seemed to exacerbate rather than resolve the conflict.[219] The issue is more appropriately pursued in the context of the CDC's role in Colonial Development than in the present context.

The Nigerian proposals differed radically from those put forward from the Gold Coast in that the settlement of African farmers, rather than employment of paid labour, was envisaged, and in that the Gezira model would be followed. As the scheme was regarded as primarily one of economic development, social aspects were to be financed from Government funds.[220] The estimates for the 12,000-acre pilot scheme in Kontagora showed costs not markedly different from those originally submitted by the Mission, and it was felt that the scheme could evolve 'a sound basis of landlord and tenant, which could continue in spite of the fluctuations in market prices, the continuation or otherwise of mechanisation and of European supervision, modification of cropping rotation, etc.'[221] Even so, it was reported that 'quite a virulent press campaign' had started in Nigeria against the whole project.[222] However, when the project was discussed by the Colonial Advisory Council of Agriculture, Animal Health and Forestry, Mr F. Sykes stated that, in his opinion, the Nigerian Government had not appreciated the agricultural difficulties which might be expected as the result of missing out the first phase of directly-employed labour. He felt that complete control of the labour force was necessary to begin with, particularly in a pioneer scheme.[223] This was reported to the CDC, which was considering the scheme.[224] An experienced agricultural officer, seconded by the Government, was working on the site which had been inspected by the Divisional

Manager of CDC.[225] From this point, the Nigerian scheme also is more suitably discussed in the context of CDC.

The Report was considered by the Colonial Primary Products Committee, which agreed with the main conclusion that further expansion of production was possible only with the introduction of mechanised cultivation. The Committee was anxious to emphasise the reasons why these methods could not be introduced into West Africa as rapidly as in East Africa and did so in this way:

> The East African Scheme has been able to start a technique of cultivation quite foreign to the African and his society without any great dislocation, because the area covered was formerly, for the most part, uninhabitable. In West Africa, this would not be so; and the Committee feels that it is of great importance that no scheme of this kind should be launched until thought has been given to the ways in which the existing structure of society will be affected by, and can be adjusted to, the new conditions. . . . The proposals made by this Mission have been considered by the Colonial Office and the Governments concerned; proposals for pilot schemes of development have been drawn up and are being considered by the C.D.C. The Committee feels that development on these lines must be slow, and that at present it is necessary to concentrate on ways of maintaining production by existing methods at as high a level as possible.[226]

Discussions were strangely innocent of demand and price estimates. By January 1949, the CDC had gone sufficiently far with its consideration of the Report of the Clay Mission to require a firm indication of the Ministry of Food's expected future requirements of groundnuts and expected price level.[227] The Director of Oils and Fats at the Ministry replied:

> We are short of liquid edible oils in relation to other oils to produce margarine and cooking fat from the best possible formula. We are also buying marginal supplies of liquid edible oils from other than Colony or Commonwealth sources, and would prefer not to do so, if possible. We could, therefore, take at least 600,000 tons of groundnuts a year for at least four or five years to come in addition to our present normal supplies. It is difficult to look beyond that period, but I should imagine the demand would continue. In any case, it seems to me that it is not only United Kingdom needs but the shortage of oils and fats generally that must be taken into account in

considering the question of additional production. It is extremely difficult to say what future prices will be. At present, I see no reason for altering the view I took in preparing the Four Year Programme, namely that by 1952 prices will be 20 per cent lower than in 1949. As a buyer, I should hesitate to assume that prices for a long time to come will be lower than I have stated, but as a producer I should take the view that there is likely to be a fall rather than a rise over a long period of years.[228]

SOURCES

1. CM 10(46) item 4.
2. WFS(46) 1.
3. WFS 3(46) item 14, 19 Feb 1946.
4. WFS(46) 22, 15 Feb 1946.
5. WFS 3(46) item 14.
6. WFS(46) 39, 22 Feb 1946.
7. WFS 4(46) item 4, 26 Feb 1946.
8. WFS(46) 60 of 9 Mar 1946 by the Parliamentary Secretary of the Ministry of Food.
9. CP(46) 52.
10. WFS 8(46) item 4, 26 Mar 1946.
11. WFS 9(46) item 7, 9 Apr 1946.
12. SEAF 17(46) item 7, 24 July 1946.
13. SEAF 7(46) item 3.
14. SEAF(46) 31, 12 Mar 1946 by the President of the Board of Trade.
15. SEAF(46) 38, 20 Mar 1946.
16. WFS 8(46) item 8, 9 Apr 1946.
17. SEAF 9(46) item 8, 17 Apr 1946.
18. SEAF(46) 49, 12 Apr 1946.
19. SEAF(46) 50, 15 Apr 1946.
20. WFS 9(46) item 7.
21. SEAF 13(46), 22 May 1946.
22. FO File F 7289/6/61–telegrams of 15 and 26 May 1946.
23. FO File F 7718/6/61–telegram of 23 May 1946.
24. FO File 7562/6/61–telegrams of 22 May, 4/5/12 June, 20/24 July and 14 Aug 1946.
25. Ibid., telegram of 24 July 1946 to Government of India, Food Department.
26. FO File 8839/6/61–telegrams of 15 June, 15/18/24 July 1946.
27. FO File 7562/6/61–telegram of 18 May 1946.
28. SEAF(46) 8, 18 June 1946.

29. File 19606/9/3, Economic 1946 (CO 852/601), item 1, 17 May 1946.

30. SEAF 15(46) item 5, 20 June 1946.

31. SEAF(WA) 1 (46), 26 June 1946.

32. File 19606/9/3, Economic 1946 (CO 852/601), item 90, letter from Mr E. Melville to Mr D. R. Serpell of 21 Feb 1947.

33. Idem.

34. Ibid., minute of 20 May 1946 by Mr G. H. Creasy. Underlining in original.

35. Ibid., item 13, telegram of 5 July 1946 from the Secretary of State to the Governor of Nigeria.

36. Ministry of Food file C 28/4640 (MAF 85/586), letter of 15 Mar 1946 from Mr F. Samuel to Mr Jasper W. Knight.

37. Ibid., letter of 20 Mar 1946 from Sir G. Gater to Sir F. Tribe.

38. Ibid., item 46, Note of meeting of 16 Aug 1946.

39. *Report of the Mission appointed to enquire into the Production and Transport of Vegetable Oils and Oil Seeds produced in the West African Colonies* (Colonial No. 211 of 1947).

40. Files 19606 of 1947 (CO 852/910) and 19606/9/4 of 1947 were Destroyed Under Statute before July 1970.

41. No. 198 to Nigeria, No. 87 to the Gambia, No. 160 to Sierra Leone and No. 151 to the Gold Coast – items 7–11 in Ministry of Food file AG/BF/2 (copies from CO File 19606/9/4 of 1947).

42. Despatch No. 73 of 25 July 1947 – item 14 in ibid. (copied as before).

43. Ministry of Food file AG/BF/2, minute 15 of 2 Sep 1947 by Mr F. Hollins.

44. Ibid., minute 17 of 13 Sep 1947 by Mr F. Hollins following letters of 2 Aug 1947 from Mr J. M. Kisch, Colonial Office, to Mr F. Hollins, and of 12 Sep 1947 from Mr J. F. Cornes, Colonial Office, to Mr S. P. Dobbs.

45. Colonial No 211, para. 133.

46. H. of C. Deb., Vol. 437, cols 407–8, 7 May 1947.

47. *Fifth Report from the Select Committee on Estimates, Session 1947–48, Colonial Development*, 30 June 1948, No. 181–I, pp. xxiii–xxiv.

48. CP(47) 92 Revise, approved by the Cabinet on 18 Mar 1947 – CM 29(47) item 5.

49. Ministry of Food file AG/BF/2, minute of 11 July 1947 by Mr G. H. C. Amos.

50. Ibid., minute of 7 July 1947 by Mr A. E. Feaveryear.

51. Ministry of Food file AG/AL/9, item 16, letter of 14 Aug 1947, from Mr G. H. C. Amos to Brig Grimley, Ancillary Materials Division.

52. File 17025/13, Economic 1947 (CO 852/791), item 43.

53. CM 74(47), item 2, 25 Aug 1947.

54. CP(47) 241.

55. CP(47) 242.

56. File 17025, Economic (Supplies) 1947 (CO 852/790), item 45, letter of 4 Nov 1947 from Mr J. P. E. Henniker, Foreign Office, to Private Secretary to Secretary of State for the Colonies. This was in accordance with the decision of the Fuel Committee in 1946 (see item 50 in ibid).

57. Ibid., item 39, letter of 22 Oct 1947, from Mr J. M. Wilson, Ministry of Supply, to Private Secretary to the Secretary of State for Foreign Affairs.

58. Letters of Mar and Apr 1946 referred to in item 1 in ibid.

59. Ibid., item 1, letter of 13 Aug· 1947.

60. Ibid., minute of 6 Aug 1947 by Mr P. Maynard.

61. Ibid., item 8, letter of 28 Aug 1947. See also letter of 23 Aug 1947 from Mr G. H. Harrison, Ministry of Supply, to Mr F. Hollins, Ministry of Food, on this matter at item 5 in ibid.

62. Ibid., item 26, minutes of the second meeting, on 23 Sep 1947, of the Metals and Minerals Panel of the Colonial Primary Products Committee.

63. File 1/025/12, Economic 1947 (CO 852/791), item 46.

64. File 17025, Economic (Supplies) 1947 (CO 852/790), item 35, letter of 22 Oct 1947.

65. Ibid., item 42, letter of 28 Oct 1947.

66. Ibid., item 51, letter of 21 Nov 1947 from the Minister of Supply, Mr G. Strauss, to the Parliamentary Under-Secretary of State, Mr D. Rees-Williams.

67. File 17025, Economic 1948 (CO 852/790), minute of 19 Feb 1948 by Mr P. Maynard.

68. File 17025/12, Economic 1947 (CO 852/791), item 66, Note of a meeting held in the Chief Secretary's Office on 29 Nov 1947 with Major-General R. G. Fielden.

69. File 17025/12, Economic 1948, Part I (CO 852/792), item 16, letter of 23 Jan 1948 from Mr G. H. C. Amos to General Fielden; also minute of 30 Jan 1948 by Mr P. Maynard.

70. Ibid., minute of 24 Nov 1947 by Mr P. Maynard.

71. Ibid., minute of 2 Feb 1948 by Mr E. Melville.

72. File 17025, Economic 1948 (CO 852/790), item 32, telegram No. 482 of 6 Aug 1948 to the Secretary of State.

73. Ibid., item 33, minute of Meeting of 29 July 1948 of Colonial Development Working Party, Sub-Committee on Railway Requirements.

74. Ibid., item 6, Note of 20 Feb 1948 by Mr W. L. Gorell Barnes.

75. CP(47) 273, 3 Oct 1947.

76. Ministry of Food file AG/AL/9A, item 4, letter of 17 Oct 1947 from Mr W. Strath of CEPS to Mr S. P. Dobbs, Overseas Production Division, Ministry of Food.

77. PC 8(48) item 2, 23 Apr 1948.

78. File 17025/12, Economic, Part I, 1948 (CO 852/792), item 6, letter of 16 Jan 1948 from the Crown Agents to the Colonial Office.

79. Ibid., minute of 4 Feb 1948 by the Adviser on Inland Transport, Mr A. J. F. Bunning.

80. CP(47) 308, agreed by the Cabinet on 18 Nov 1947: CM 89(47) item 1.

81. Ministry of Food File AG/AL/9A, Note of 22 Nov 1947 by Mr G. H. C. Amos.

82. File 17025, Economic 1948 (CO 852/790), item 33, CDWP(SC), 2nd Meeting, 29 July 1948.

83. Ibid., item 30, Circular Telegram of 30 July 1948 from Secretary of State.

84. Ministry of Food file AG/AM/7, item 30, Foreign Office telegram No. 147 of 17 Feb 1947.

85. British Food Mission file 11, Groundnuts East Africa, letter of 3 Nov 1948 from the Chairman of OFC.

86. File 19260/78, Economic 1948 (CO 852/855), item 4, Note of 14 Mar 1948 by Sir S. Caine to Sir T. Lloyd.

87. EPC(48) 35, 27 Apr 1948.

88. Ibid., para. 15.

89. EPC 18(48) item 1, 6 May 1948.

90. File 17025, Economic 1947 (CO 852/790), item 8, letter of 28 Aug 1947.

91. H. of C. Deb., Vol. 444, col. 1127, 19 Nov 1947.

92. Ministry of Food file AG/AC/4, cable of 13 Aug 1947 from Managing Agency and Ministry of Food to Governor of Northern Rhodesia.

93. File 19606/9/4, Economic 1946 (CO 852/601), minute of 26 Nov 1946 by Mr J. M. Kisch.

94. Ministry of Food file AG/AL/11, item 76, letter of 31 May 1947 from Mr G. H. C. Amos, Ministry of Food, to Mr L. Monson, Colonial Office.

95. H. of C. Deb., Vol. 445, col. 72, 3 Dec 1947.

96. H. of C. Deb., Vol. 451, col. 2155, 9 June 1948.

97. Ibid., col. 2158.

98. File 17025, Economic 1948 (CO 852/790), item 53, CDWP(48) 46, 13 Sep 1948.

99. File 17025, Economic 1948, (CO 852/790), item 56, CDWP(SC)(48) 4 of 21 Sep 1948.

100. Idem, para. 15.

101. File 17025/12, Economic 1948, Part I (CO 852/792), minute of 29 Apr 1948 by Mr P. Maynard.

102. Ibid., Appendix B, para. 8, in CDWP(SC)(48) 4. The Crown Agents stated that 'the 150 hopper wagons' should read 'the 100 hopper wagons' – item 56 in ibid.

103. Ibid., item 109, letter of 19 July 1948 from the Chancellor to the Secretary of State.

104. Ibid., item 64, telegram No. 572 of 29 May 1948 from the Secretary of State to the Governor of Nigeria.

105. Ibid., minute of 11 Sep 1948 by Mr K. E. Robinson.

106. Ibid., item 136, letter of 18 Oct 1948 from the Ministry of Supply.

107. Ibid., item 142, telegram No. 1464 of 19 Oct 1948 from the Governor to the Secretary of State.

108. Ibid., item 148, Note of a Meeting at the Colonial Office on 22 Oct 1948.

109. Ibid., item 173, letter of 30 Nov 1948 from Mr E. A. Hitchman of CEPS to Mr W. L. Gorell Barnes.

110. File 17025/12 Part I, Economic 1949 (CO 852/792), item 10, letter of 14 Jan 1949.

111. Ibid., item 13, letter of 25 Jan 1949.

112. Ibid., item 23, letter of 24 Feb 1949 from the Economic Secretary to the Treasury to the Parliamentary Under-Secretary.

113. Ibid., item 28, letter of 2 Mar 1949 from the Parliamentary Under-Secretary.

114. Ibid., item 37A, letter of 22 Mar 1949 from the Minister of Food to the Secretary of State.

115. Ibid., item 38, minute of 25 Mar 1949 by the Parliamentary Under-Secretary.

116. Ibid., minute of 31 Mar 1949.

117. Idem.

118. Ibid., item 57, letter of 14 Apr 1949 (transferred to File 17025/12/10).

119. Ibid., item 62, telegram No. 655 of 22 Apr 1949 from the Governor of Nigeria to the Secretary of State.

120. Ibid., minute of 6 May 1949.

121. Ibid., minute of 19 May 1949.

122. Ibid., minute of 20 May 1949.

123. Ibid., item 96, Secret and Personal telegram of 4 June 1949.

124. Ibid., item 104, Note on Meeting held in the Secretary of State for the Colonies' Room on 2 June 1949.

125. Ibid., item 167A, telegram No. 1694 from the Governor to the Secretary of State.

126. Ibid., item 172, letter of 16 Nov 1949.

127. File 17025/12, Economic 1950, item 14, letter of 20 Mar 1950.

128. Ibid., items 5, 7, 18, 23, 28, 33 and 64.

129. Ibid., minute of 22 Dec 1950.

130. File 17025/12, Economic 1951, item 1, memorandum of 8 Jan 1951.

131. Ibid., item 5, letter of 29 Jan 1951.

132. File 19612/12/8, Economic 1951, item 44, letter of 31 May 1951.

133. Ibid., item 51, Savingram No. 118 of 9 Aug 1951.

134. Ibid., item 63, letter of 21 Sep 1951. A minute of 28 Nov 1951 suggests that the Colonial Office was dubious, although it was thought 300,000 tons of groundnuts could be railed (minute of 29 Nov 1951).

135. File WAF 74/75/02, item 3, letter of 3 Jan 1952 from the Minister of Food, Mr G. Lloyd George, to the Secretary of State, Mr Oliver Lyttelton.

136. Ibid., item 24, letter of 24 Mar 1952.

137. Ibid., item 27, Secret and Personal letter of 18 Apr 1952 to the Governor of Nigeria.

138. Ibid., item 29, Savingram No. 118 of 9 Aug 1951.

139. Ibid., item 40, note of 16 May 1952 to the Secretary of State on Transport Problems in Nigeria.

140. Ibid., item 49, telegram No. 700.

141. Ibid., item 55, letter of 18 June 1952.

142. Ibid., item 65, note of 27 May 1952.

143. Ibid., item 100, note of a meeting at the Ministry of Supply on 19 Sep 1952.

144. Ibid., item 109, Memorandum of 8 Sep 1952.

145. File SUP 70/14/10, 1952–54, item 51, letter of 6 Dec 1952 from the Development Secretary, Lagos, to the General Manager, Nigerian Railways.

146. Ibid., minute of 1 Dec 1952.

147. File SUP 108/14/01, 1954–56, Part B(1), minute of 17 Jan 1957.

148. File WAF 74/75/02, 1952–54, Part B, item 170.

149. Ibid., item 176, letter of 30 June 1953 from the Ministry of Commerce and Industries, Lagos.

150. Ibid., minute of 8 July 1953.

151. File SUP 70/14/01, 1952–54, items 15, 23 and 19.

152. H. of C. Deb., Vol. 511, col. 2074, 23 Feb 1953.

153. File SUP 70/14/01, 1952–54, item 62, letter of 21 Apr 1953.

154. Ibid., item 86, letter of 29 Apr 1953.

155. Ibid., item 87, letter of 1 May 1953.

156. Ibid., item 110, letter of 18 Sep 1953 from Vulcan Foundry to the General Manager, Nigerian Railways.

157. Ibid., item 119, letter of 10 Dec 1953 from Secretary of State to Brigadier A. R. W. Low, MP.

158. File WAF 75/56/01, 1954–56, item 8, statement of Jan 1954 by the Director of Marketing and Exports, Lagos. The £1.5 million figure was given by the Secretary of State to the House of Commons on 24 Feb 1954.

159. File SUP 108/10/01, 1954–56.

160. File WAF 75/56/01, 1957–59, item 40, Savingram No. 2137 of 11 Dec 1957 from the Governor-General, Nigeria, to the Secretary of State.

161. Ibid., item 42, Savingram No. 3122 of 30 Dec 1957 from the Secretary of State to the OAG, Federation of Nigeria.

162. Ibid., item 91, Savingram No. 80 of 14 Jan 1960 from the Secretary of State to the Governor-General, Federation of Nigeria.

163. File 614 of the British Food Mission, letter of 12 June 1942, from Mr Leon Falk Jr, to Mr L. F. Zwarenberg.

164. Minutes of the First Meeting of the CFB, 16 June 1942.

165. Minutes of the Ninth Meeting, 5 Feb 1943.

166. Minutes of the Forty-Second Meeting of the CFB, 13 Sep 1943.

167. Minutes of the Forty-Fourth Meeting of the CFB, 1 Nov 1943.

168. Statement by Mr Jasper Knight to the Committee on Oils and Fats, 24 May 1946.

169. British Food Mission (566F/11) – note of a meeting of 11 Mar 1946.

170. British Food Mission to Ministry of Food, Amaze No. 6849 of 15 Mar 1946.

171. BFM to Ministry of Food, Amaze 6854 of 16 Mar 1946. It had been suggested to the Minister that a personal cable from the Prime Minister to the President might help – Amaze No. X 7032 of 12 Mar 1946.

172. Amaze No. X 7195 of 10 Apr 1946 in reply to Amaze No. 7014 of 5 Apr 1946.

173. BFM 911/0/1, letter of 16 Oct 1946 from Mr Maurice I. Hutton to Mr Jasper M. Knight.

174. BFM to Ministry of Food, Amaze No. 8197 of 19 Dec 1946.

175. Ministry of Food file AG/CD/1, item 1/1, Note of Proceedings, Seventh (1946) Meeting, 20 Dec 1946.

176. Ibid., item 6, Memorandum on Certain Proposals for Expanding Present World Production of Oils and Fats.

177. Ibid., item 48, Note of Meeting held on 2 Apr 1947 at the Ministry of Food (also as item 1 in Ministry of Food file AG/BF/2).

178. File 19612/9/2, Economic 1947 (CO 852/915), item 1, letter quoted in minute of 19 Feb 1947 by Mr W. E. Dawson.

179. Idem.

180. Ibid., item 5, minute of 10 Mar 1947 by Mr W. L. Bloomfield quoted.

181. Ibid., minute of 3 Mar 1947 by Mr W. L. Steemson, Deputy Director of Agriculture in the Gold Coast, quoted in item 5.

182. Ibid., minute of 15 Mar 1947.

183. Ibid., minute of 8 Apr 1947 by Mr J. B. Williams.

184. Ibid., minute of 15 Apr 1947.

185. Ibid., items 6–8, telegrams of 17 Apr 1947, Nos 411, 571 and 161 respectively.

186. Ibid., item 12, telegram No. 397 of 21 Apr 1947.

187. Ibid., item 13, telegram No. 537 of 21 Apr 1947.

188. Ibid., item 14, telegram No. 537 of 21 Apr 1947.

189. Ibid., item 15, letter of 23 Apr 1947.

190. Ibid., item 16, letter of 29 Apr 1947 from Secretary of State to the Minister of Food. The Minister of Food was anxious to extend the investigation to food crops, e.g. rice in The Gambia, and that it should not be confined to groundnuts (item 33 in ibid.).

191. Ibid., minute of 1 May 1947 by Mr K. E. Robinson.

192. Ibid., minute of 2 May 1947 by Mr A. B. Cohen.

193. Ibid., item 48, telegram No. 562 of 22 May 1947 to Governor, Gold Coast.

194. Ibid., item 93, letter of 9 June 1946 from Mr W. B. L. Monson to Mr C. G. Eastwood.

195. Ibid., item 196, telegram No. 582 of 21 June 1947 from the Governor's Deputy, Gold Coast, to the Governor of The Gambia.

196. Ibid., item 93, letter of 9 June 1946 by Mr W. B. L. Monson to Mr C. G. Eastwood.

197. Ibid., item 121, notes on a meeting in the Chief Secretary's Office on 11 July 1947.

198. Report of West African Oilseeds Mission (Colonial No. 224, 2 June 1948).

199. File 19612/9/4, Economic 1947 (CO 852/916), minute of 9 Jan 1948 by Mr C. G. Eastwood.

200. File 19612/9/4, Economic 1948 (CO 852/916), items 8 and 9, letter of 20 Jan 1948 by Mr G. F. Clay.

201. File 19612/9/2, Economic 1947 (CO 852/915), item 148, extract from the minutes of the sixty-ninth meeting on 1 Aug 1947.

202. File 19612/9/4, Economic 1947 (CO 852/916), minute of 26 Nov 1947 by Mr C. G. Eastwood.

203. Ibid., item 20, note of a discussion in Sir Sydney Caine's room on 3 Dec 1947.

204. Ibid., items 21–5: to Nigeria No. 41; to Gold Coast No. 36; to Gambia No. 20; to Sierra Leone No. 49; and to the Office of the West African Council.

205. File 19612/9/4, Economic 1948 (CO 852/916), item 22, letter of 12 Mar 1948 by Mr W. B. L. Monson.

206. Ibid., item 36.

207. Ibid., item 49.

208. Ibid., item 21, Confidential Despatch of 27 Feb 1948.

209. Ibid., item 66.

210. File 19612/12/3, Economic 1948 (CO 852/917), item 1, Confidential Despatch No. 21 and Memorandum of 6 May 1948.

211. Ibid., item 4, Confidential Despatch No. 120 of 26 May 1948 from the Governor's Deputy.

212. Ibid., minute of 11 Feb 1949.

213. File 19612/9/2, Economic 1948 (CO 852/915), item 99.

214. File 19612/10, Economic 1951–52, item 6, report of 30 Sep 1952 by the Colonial Products Advisory Bureau.

215. File 19612/11/1, Economic 1948 (CO 852/916), item 1, covering letter of 25 Apr 1948 from Mr A. Saloway, Secretary for Rural Development, Gold Coast, to Mr Hugh Weeks, Controller of Plans, CDC.

216. Ibid., item 1a, letter of 10 May 1948 to the Governor.

217. Ibid., item 2, Confidential Despatch of 20 May 1948 to the Secretary of State.

218. Ibid., minute of 31 May 1948.

219. Ibid., minute of 1 June.1948 by Mr C. G. Eastwood.

220. Ibid., item 11, note of a meeting held on 16 June 1948 in the Colonial Office.

221. Ibid., item 19 and minute of 23 July 1948 by Mr G. F. Clay.

222. Ibid., item 40, letter of 31 July 1948 from Mr L. Monson, of the West Africa Council, to Mr G. F. Clay.

223. Ibid., item 58, extract from the minutes of the 74th Meeting on 14 Oct 1948.

224. Ibid., item 59, letter of 18 Nov 1948 from Mr C. G. Eastwood to Mr H. Weeks.

225. Ibid., minute of 11 Feb 1949.

226. Ministry of Food file AG/CD/1, item 180, CCP(48) 49 of 12 Nov 1948.

227. Ministry of Food file AG/BF/6, item 20, letter of 21 Jan 1949.

228. Ibid., letter of 1 Feb 1949.

5 The East African Groundnuts Scheme, 1946–1951

1. THE INITIAL PROPOSAL

When Mr Frank Samuel, Managing Director of the United Africa Company (UAC), was visiting Tanganyika early in 1946, the Territory's Director of Agricultural Production, Mr R. W. R. Miller, suggested that UAC should cultivate 100,000 acres of groundnuts in the Colony. At Mr Samuel's request, the Director drew up a scheme. On his return to London, the scheme was expanded by UAC so that the United Kingdom Government might be interested.[1] The general features of the scheme remained substantially unchanged. On 27 March 1946 Mr Samuel discussed his 'Project for the Mass Production of Groundnuts in Tropical Africa' with the Minister of Food, Sir Ben Smith, in order, as he said in a letter to the Parliamentary Under-Secretary of State, Mr Creech Jones, 'to ascertain whether my understanding of the oils and fats position was a correct one'.[2] The paper might be summarised thus:

(1) The project for the mass production of Groundnuts in tropical Africa was based on the assumption that the critical shortage of Oils and Fats was not merely short-term (1946–48) but would continue for many years.

(2) No rapid or substantial increase in world production of vegetable oils could arise, other than by the development of annual crops.

(3) Such an increase in the production could not be expected from the production of peasant cultivators, whose main occupation was, and would remain, subsistence farming.

(4) It could only be achieved by the utilisation of the most modern methods of mechanical agriculture, and would require a negligible labour force.

226

(5) An area of 1,000,000 acres would yield on average about 400,000 tons of Decorticated Groundnuts annually, but to achieve this production and allow for rotational cropping essential to the preservation of soil fertility, a total area of 2,500,000 acres would be required. The development of such an area was the project envisaged. It would be achieved with no more than 350/400 European/Asiatics and about 20,000 Africans.

(6) But the speed of its realisation would depend upon the support and priorities accorded to it, and the sense of urgency with which it was undertaken; but, given these in highest measure, substantial production could be achieved in 1948, and the full programme realised by 1951.

(7) The estimated capital investment for the whole scheme was in the region of £8 million. The production cost of the Decorticated Groundnuts was estimated at £7.13.2 per ton free on rail, without allowing for interest on the capital employed but after allowing for adequate rates of depreciation. Freight to port was not included.

(8) Tanganyika Territory was seen from every aspect to be the most suitable British territory for such a project, and it was believed that land lying between Tabora and Dodoma, adjacent to the Railway, and carrying a negligible population, could be made available.

(9) The project was expected to bring great economic benefits to Tanganyika, and would not disturb the progress or way of life of her peoples.

At the meeting of 27 March 1946, there were present Mr Samuel, Sir Herbert Davis, Sir Roland Wall, Sir Frank Tribe and Mr Jasper W. Knight. Sir Herbert Davis emphasised the long-term nature of the oils and fats shortage.[3] The Minister of Food accepted the general idea of the project and also agreed with the view expressed that such a scheme required the same priority as armaments in wartime and that, for reasons of finance and equipment, it could not be operated as a private venture. He decided to submit the scheme to the Ministerial Committee on World Food Supplies (WFS). In a letter of 28 March 1946 the Permanent Secretary of the Ministry of Food, Sir Frank Tribe, told the Permanent Under-Secretary of State for the Colonies, Sir George Gater, that his Ministry considered that the existing shortage of oils and fats was likely to last for a long time, certainly until new sources of supply were available.[4] From the purely Tanganyika point of view, the project was seen in the Colonial Office as a valuable means of developing the territory by filling the vast empty spaces along the central line of Tanganyika.[5] Within the Ministry of Food at least one official believed that an important aspect of the project was that in addition to producing 'about 160,000 tons of oil for the margarine and cooking fat manufacturers, and about 240,000 tons of cake for farmers, it would also go some way towards relieving the unemployment in the crushing trade which is bound to come' as British crushers were 'in for a very bad time' owing to the shortage of crushing material.[6]

Mr Samuel was anxious to start the project by January 1947. Yet a whole host of questions needed attention. These included (a) whether the soil was suitable, (b) whether there were any insuperable objections from the point of view of native land tenure, (c) how the finance was to be provided, (d) whether the necessary agricultural machinery – assuming the expenditure of £3 million in dollars was authorised – could be quickly procured, (e) whether the medical and social welfare staff for which the scheme provided could be procured. Mr Samuel suggested an aerial survey, but it was felt instead that the Governor should be asked whether a suitable tract of land was available without a formal soil survey, which would take time.[7] The Assistant to the Secretary of State's Agricultural Adviser minuted that, from the agricultural point of view, he did not regard the project with any enthusiasm.[8] His main grounds were seven-fold. First, he stated that about half of the stretch in question, Dodoma to Tabora, was in the Central Province, the most arid in the territory, with a rainfall in the under-30 inches class; over the period 1933–44 inclusive there had been four years of drought and one of badly distributed rainfall. This was denied by Mr Samuel.[9] When risks of this nature were brought to the notice first of the Wakefield Mission (see Section ii below) and later of the Managing Agents of the Groundnuts Scheme (see Section x below) by the Director of the East African Meteorological Service as a result of a detailed study of rainfall distribution in relation to crop requirements, they were rejected on the evidence of 'proved crop yields'. However, in the event the meteorological data proved to be much the more reliable guide to crop hazards.[10] Secondly, it stated that the area was 3000–4000 feet above sea level and undulating, and that the Central Province presented some of the worst examples of soil erosion in the Territory. Thirdly, soil types were said to be variable and less than half of the area was likely to be suitable for groundnuts, while tests on the light soils had suggested they would not be helped by a grass rotation. Fourthly, it was said that, unless groundnuts were planted as soon as there was sufficient moisture Rosette disease would spread, and, even so, continuous cropping with groundnuts tended to lead to the multiplication of the vector of that disease, namely aphides. Fifthly, while, in the initial period, labour could be employed off-season for stumping, clearing and so forth, this could not be continued year after year. Sixthly, while a preliminary selection might be made by aerial survey, the results would need to be correlated with existing knowledge and ground work. Seventhly, difficulty would be found in obtaining the large amount of seed of varieties which were suitable. The Director of Agriculture of Kenya, Mr D. L. Blunt, agreed fully with all this, concluding his memorandum thus: 'In my view, the proper method to produce groundnuts in large quantities in this part of Africa is to ensure the general adoption of rotational cropping by the native.[11]

The Minister of Food mentioned the project to the Prime Minister some time between 27 March and 5 April 1946,[12] when an inter-departmental meeting was held at the Ministry of Food.[13] It was then agreed that a decision in principle had to be obtained but, at the same time, the matter should be explored as quickly as possible so as to be in time for the next crop. Mr Knight was most emphatic about the need for the project despite the Treasury official's doubts. Mr G. M. Roddan, of the Agricultural Adviser's Department, explained his lack of enthusiasm, while Mr A. B. Cohen noted the scheme appeared to have largely ignored both water and fertilisers. It was felt that the Governor should be consulted and a memorandum should be submitted to WFS.[14]

The Governor was sent a copy of the Samuel memorandum and of Mr Roddan's minute, and was asked to state by telegram whether he agreed to the project being explored further and, if so, what kind of expert, or experts, should be sent out.[15] Meanwhile, the proposal was submitted jointly by the Minister of Food and the Secretary of State to the WFS,[16] which invited the Secretary of State to pursue his enquiries further.[17] It was expected at that time that the project would be his responsibility, and the Treasury was asked to agree that it should come under the Colonial Office Vote.[18]

In reply to the telegram of 5 April the Governor of Tanganyika cabled a reply welcoming an investigation and suggesting that an expert in the large-scale growing of groundnuts should be included in any team.[19] In a letter which followed, the Governor confirmed his agreement that the matter should be investigated, emphasised that the Tanganyika Government had no funds to invest in the project, and stated his agreement with his Director of Agricultural Production, Mr R. W. R. Miller, that it was better to avoid the Central Province on account of its uncertain rainfall, and rely on the precipitation of the Western and, possibly, the Lake Province, which would have to be cleared of tsetse.[20] It was not thought safe to count on more than six hundredweights per acre, thus raising costs by some 15 per cent owing to the regular lower yield. For 1949 and subsequent years, some substantial additions to rolling stock would be required to transport the groundnuts to port, where facilities would have to be expanded. A plentiful supply of labour could not be guaranteed.

11. MISSION TO EAST AFRICA

It was decided to send a Mission to Tanganyika to investigate. The Mission consisted of Mr A. J. Wakefield, former Inspector-General of Agriculture in the West Indies, who had also had experience in Tanganyika as a former Director of Agriculture there, as leader of the Mission; Mr D. L. Martin, Head of the Plantations Department and the groundnut expert of the United Africa Company, and Mr J. Rosa of the Economic Division of the Colonial Office, who had been a merchant banker and Treasury representative in Syria. The Permanent Secretary of the Ministry of Food thought that the team combined most of the qualifications needed and did not think that a Ministry of Food representative was required, although he did observe 'that the handling, transport and shipment of groundnuts are almost as important as the growing of them, as was shown by experience in West Africa.[21] Following Mr Samuel's visit to the Colonial Office, Sir Herbert Davis stressed the urgency of an early start and Sir Frank Tribe was urged to press the Colonial Office to accelerate the Mission's departure and also to initiate other schemes.[22] At the suggestion of Mr Samuel, Mr A. L. Gladwell, Managing Director of Messrs Gailey & Roberts Ltd, of Nairobi, the UAC's agents in East Africa, was invited to be associated with the investigation because of his local knowledge of both the area and of mechanised agriculture. The Director of Agricultural Production in Tanganyika Territory, Mr R. W. R. Miller, was similarly to be associated.

The Mission left London on 20 June. Mr Wakefield was able to notify the Colonial Office on 15 August that investigations in Tanganyika and Northern Rhodesia were completed, and it was clear that jointly they could support a project of substantially larger proportions than that originally envisaged.[23] It was agreed that the Mission should not visit West Africa before returning to London.[24] The Mission reported orally at a meeting which took place on 4 September, the day after their return,[25] confirming the optimistic estimates which had been cabled from East Africa. It was stated that Tanganyika alone could provide areas of freely available land, suitable both as to soil and climate, which could, under modern methods of farming, provide crops far in excess of the targets contemplated in London. The three areas demarcated in Tanganyika were virtually abandoned to nature and tsetse, and, to open them would be in the interests of the Colony. In no case, except marginally in the Central province, was there any collision with vested interests, native or otherwise. The Mission had discussed the various technical objections to the scheme and claimed to have convinced many sceptics of the feasibility of the plan. As regard yields, it was thought that once the ground had been 'broken in' and the old cycle of annual impoverishment of the ground by rain and fire interrupted, yields in excess of $7\frac{1}{2}$ cwts per acre would be easily achieved. In fact, it was claimed by the Mission that East Africa would become the lowest cost producer of oil seeds in the world, able to offer them at £8–9s. a ton, free on rail, when the project was fully in its stride. The adoption of modern techniques was stated to be an essential condition. On the financial side, £18 million was thought to be the final figure, as compared with the £8 million originally contemplated, and, allowing for 80 units covering an area of 2,400,000 acres, it would involve a capitalisation cost of under £8 per acre. The £18 million would include £9 million for land clearing, £5 million for permanent installations, including roads, houses and medical centres, and £3 million for agricultural machinery.

In their Report dated 20 September 1946[26] the Mission recommended (i) the setting up by His Majesty's Government of an enterprise to undertake the large-scale production of groundnuts in Tanganyika Territory, Northern Rhodesia and Kenya, as an early and substantial contribution to the world's, and therefore the United Kingdom's, shortage of oils and fats; and (ii) the opening up, over a period of six years, of a total area of about 3,200,000 acres, half of which would, from the fourth year onwards, be under groundnuts. On the assumption that clearing operations would start early in 1947, the following production targets were envisaged:

TABLE 5.1 Production Targets for Groundnuts from 1948 (tons shelled)

1948	56,900
1949	227,700
1950	466,700
1951	609,000

It was estimated that an average yield of 850 lbs of shelled nuts per acre could reasonably be anticipated over the earlier years of the project and, at this level, the average cost of production would be £14.2.7d per ton f.o.b. Better average yields, and therefore lower costs of production, were expected as experience was gained and the fertility of the soil built up. Of the areas recommended for the project, 75 per cent were in Tanganyika, 16 per cent in Northern Rhodesia and 9 per cent in Kenya; all this land was virtually uninhabited and completely undeveloped and was, in fact, not amenable to development by native methods of agriculture nor, indeed, was there a chance that it could be developed fully by any other methods than those of full mechanisation recommended in the Report. It was further recommended that (iii) the clearing operations, and all subsequent agricultural operations, should be undertaken by mechanised means to the maximum extent possible, because only by such means could the vast areas required to achieve the production targets envisaged be brought into production quickly, operated economically, and with a labour force sufficiently small to avoid disrupting other important production in East and Central Africa; (iv) the operation of the project should be entrusted to a Corporation, constituted and operated as far as possible on strictly commercial lines, but sponsored and entirely financed by His Majesty's Government. It was, however, envisaged that the project, which from its earliest years and throughout its existence should make a valuable contribution to the economic life of these Colonial territories and which fitted in well with the development plans of those territories, should, in due course and on terms to be agreed, be transferred to the Governments of the territories concerned and, in the more distant future, to the peasant farmers themselves, perhaps on some co-operative basis.

III. DISCUSSION ON THE MISSION'S REPORT

When the Report of the Mission was submitted to the Secretary of State, Mr Wakefield stated that, although speed had been the keynote from the beginning, the Mission had been meticulous in checking with leading authorities the technical basis and the agronomic principles involved in its recommendations.[27] At a meeting of Colonial office officials, doubts were expressed about the assumptions in the Report regarding water supplies, availability of African staff, research measures, close planting, weeding and the question of off-season employment of labour. The Development Adviser, Sir Frank Stockdale, agreed that the estimated yield was too high. He thought it unwise to accept the scheme on a basis of more than 750 lbs, in which case costs per ton should be estimated at £16–17s., which excluded expenditure on road and railway communications.[28] The Agricultural Adviser, Mr G. F. Clay, thought 600 lb per acre more likely than 850 lb. The need for a preliminary chemical analysis of the soil was stressed. It was felt that the unsuitable distribution of rainfall, the danger of Rosette disease, and the risk from the red and desert locusts had not been adequately taken into account in the Report. Some officials favoured operating the project through a Corporation centred on London, while others favoured more local control. The problem of supplying tractors and fertilisers was stated to be difficult, but this aspect was left to the Ministry of Food.[29]

The Report was discussed by Treasury, Colonial Office and Ministry of Food officials on 3 October 1946.[30] The need for the scheme was generally agreed, both to meet the famine conditions of the next four or five years and, in the long term, to meet the continuing, though less acute, shortage. The Treasury representative questioned the need after ten years. It was accepted that the cost of production estimated in the Report at £14–3s. per ton f.o.b. would be economic even under normal conditions of demand and supply, and so the scheme would be self-supporting in the long run. It was, however, considered that the estimated yield of 850 lbs of shelled nuts per acre was too high, and that various technical points needed to be discussed further between the Secretary of State's Agricultural Advisers and the technical members of the Mission. It was agreed that the scheme should be (i) applied in its entirety, but provision should be made to restrict operations at any time during the development stage; (ii) operated by a Corporation, which should be entirely owned by the United Kingdom Government; (iii) implemented immediately it received Cabinet approval, otherwise part, or the whole, of the first year's crop would be lost. Doubts were expressed whether HMG could afford dollar expenditure of around £7 million on clearing and agricultural equipment, and further consideration was to be given to the use of British equipment. However, a measure of inter-departmental agreement was reached at the official level.

A further meeting of officials with the members of the Mission was arranged in order to take up the technical points, to consider further the financial soundness of the scheme in the light of the upshot of the technical discussion, to estimate the extent to which total capital requirements could be reduced by ploughing back profits, and to discuss whether the project should be organised through a Corporation or on an agency basis, e.g. through UAC. However, some Colonial

Office officials were unhappy with the emphasis in the Note on the discussions on agreement rather than on unresolved issues.[31] Opinion among officials in the Ministry of Food was very favourable towards the project. Thus, Mr, later Sir Eric, Roll wrote an urgent note on 2 October 1946, which stated:

> I have studied the report very carefully and I have come to the view that this is a most important project, which has been very thoroughly thought out and which should be given the utmost possible support and active interest as far as this Ministry is concerned. We are, in some respects, the most interested party or, at least, the most directly interested party, and I think our function should be to help overcome any inertia, or scepticism, there may be in other Departments.[32]

But it is clear from a Note of 24 October by Mr J. Rosa that many of the technical doubts remained after a further meeting.[33] Consequently, it was agreed to use the lower yield basis of 750 lbs for costing purposes, thus raising the cost of production from £14–2–7d. to £15–18–6d. This sum included amortisation of clearing equipment and operations, permanent installations, cost of railway and harbour works, and agricultural machinery, but excluded any provision for interest on capital. Mr Jasper Knight advocated that the UAC should be invited to become Managing Agents because of the Companies' (a) acquaintance with the business of plantations, (b) experience in recruiting and looking after European and native staff, (c) acquaintance with all questions concerning overhaul, upkeep and repair of mechanical equipment, and (d) the excellence of its methods of accounting.[34]

As the project was to supply oil for the United Kingdom food ration rather than being a scheme for Colonial Development, the Secretary of State, Mr Creech Jones, suggested that the Minister of Food, Mr J. Strachey, should take responsibility for it, particularly as the Colonial Office would require statutory authority before it might proceed, whereas the Ministry of Food did not.[35] Mr Strachey's predecessor, Sir Ben Smith, had in fact assumed in the early days that his Ministry would submit the project to WFS as one for food production.[36] The Colonial Office had assumed otherwise, however.

The decision to invite the Minister of Food to take responsibility for the scheme followed the discussions at the meeting of 3 October. The Treasury representative was Mr A. J. D., later Sir John, Winnifrith and his intervention took the form of asking whether it was regarded as a scheme of Colonial development, in which case it would have to be financed, if at all, from CD & W funds, or a scheme to relieve the fats shortage. Some of the members of the committee wondered whether the intention was to make it virtually impossible to proceed with the scheme by compelling the Colonial Office to choose between it and existing commitments elsewhere. Sir John told the author on 15 October 1975, that Treasury doctrine laid down as a cardinal principle that the Department responsible for spending the money should be responsible for accounting for the expenditure, i.e. the executive department should be the accounting department. He had no doubt that in practice the Ministry of Food would propose the policy and execute it. The whole object of the scheme was to secure a large supply of fat for the fat-starved population of this country. Any benefit to the people of East Africa would be a by-product of the scheme. The Department that wanted the groundnuts and the Department that had the commercial expertise on the procurement, transport, processing and marketing of groundnuts was the Ministry of Food and, inevitably, they would be the governing force in the development of the scheme. The Colonial Office would be doing no more than applying a feeble brake from time to time in the interests of the people under Colonial rule. This was his construction of the facts and his application of the doctrine to them. Although doctrine should have settled the matter, Sir John said that he had two further arguments of expediency. The first was that very large sums were going to be spent, and so he thought it desirable that these funds should be under competent financial control. He thought the financial machine of the Colonial Office had inadequate experience of controlling a large commercial operation. The Ministry of Food had had great experience in this field, and Dr E. E. Bailey, their Finance Officer, had a great reputation. Although this perhaps should not have affected his judgement, very early on he had become convinced that Mr Rosa was pressing overmuch to get the scheme adopted. At the time, it was not known that Mr Rosa would transfer from the Colonial Office to the Corporation nor that, in the Ministry of Food, Mr Frank Hollins was to out-rosa Rosa. Looking back nearly thirty years, Sir John said that he felt that 'we were doomed to have a precipitate and disastrous scheme, whichever Department was responsible.' He still felt that it was right to put accounting responsibility with the Department which had to execute the scheme. Also, while the Colonial Office had good Advisers, the financial machine there was lamentably amateur.

Mr Strachey considered that an intensive enquiry into the practicability of the project from all aspects should be undertaken in his

Ministry, with the assistance of the Colonial Office, before submitting a concrete proposal to the Cabinet.[37] This is borne out by the terms of the draft letter which Mr Strachey intended to send to Mr Creech Jones, in which he declared that before he could 'accept Departmental responsibility for it, as you propose, I should want to be much more satisfied than I am at present of its general soundness as a short-term source of supply, that is to say, I should wish to make a much closer examination of the plan than has yet been made or, indeed, than there has yet been any opportunity of making.'[38] However, before the letter could be sent, Mr Samuel spoke with Mr Creech Jones who then discussed the matter again with Mr Strachey, with the result that the latter agreed to abandon the idea of an intensive investigation before submitting the project to the Cabinet, as that would remove any possibility of an early start.[39] Mr Strachey accordingly agreed that a paper should be submitted immediately to the Cabinet, asking for approval of immediate action, and for simultaneous intensive examination of the project as a whole, in order to decide how much further to go in subsequent years.

The draft Cabinet paper to be submitted by the two Ministers followed the recommendations of the Mission's Report with the exception of the yield figure.[40] It was stated that 750 lbs was a reasonable estimate and, at that level, the average cost of production would be £15.18.6 per ton f.o.b. including full provision for amortisation of clearing equipment and operations, permanent installations, cost of railway and harbour works and agricultural machinery. However, some other items, which were either not covered or insufficiently covered in the Mission's Report and which required consideration, had in the meantime been pointed out.[41] These included (i) school buildings and equipment, and teachers; (ii) wells, or other forms of water supply, for African settlements; (iii) cost of clearing land for individual, or communal, cultivation by African labour; (iv) roads, light railways, and rolling stock; (v) airstrips; (vi) inducement goods for African labour. It was stated that the areas recommended could only be developed fully by mechanical means, which would require a labour force sufficiently small to avoid disrupting other production in the area. A wholly Government-owned Corporation, operated on commercial lines, was proposed, though eventually the project would come under the control of the local Governments and, at some stage, be transferred to the peasants themselves. It noted that the Development and Agricultural Advisers of the Colonial Office had agreed that the proposals were feasible. Presumably, this followed a discussion of a paper by Mr Wakefield on

'The Agricultural Soundness of the Project', in which the various technical objections were examined.[42] No note of any discussion has been found, though a minute recorded that 'after full discussion with Mr Wakefield some of the Advisers' doubts were removed.'[43] The need for extra supplies in both the short and long term was reiterated. The total cost was estimated at £25.5 million, but the ploughing back of profits reduced the net cost to £17.92 million. The total capital expenditure was to be spread over six years, which would enable revisions of the programme to be introduced as necessary, although as commitments would have to be entered into in advance the saving in capital would not be exactly proportional to the reduction in the scale of operations. The date by which the capital would be written off depended on whether company tax at current rates was paid in Tanganyika. It was not yet possible to estimate the extent to which British equipment could be substituted for American, although it was noted that East African supplies of groundnuts would reduce the need for dollar supplies. The need for priority in machinery supplies was emphasised if the project was to get off to a good start. While legislation was prepared and a Corporation established, the Minister of Food asked for authorisation to invite UAC to act temporarily as managing agents. However the CEDC was opposed to this and the reference to UAC was deleted at the request of the Secretary of State.[44] The Minister of Food proposed to create within his Department a Special Section, which would be charged with the duty of examining the project, with particular reference to the financial aspects, the availability of equipment, staff and labour, communications, the attitude of the Colonial Governments concerned – in fact, to make a full assessment. It would also make preparations for the first year's activity, involving commitments not in excess of £3 million in advance of a decision of the practicability and cost of the longer-term scheme. Officials from the Ministry of Food and the Colonial Office and persons from commerce with experience in the production and handling of groundnuts would participate.

After discussion with the Secretary of State, a shorter memorandum was drafted which added a reference to the support given by the CEDC to the proposal, and deferred any firm recommendations on the ultimate method of handling the project.[45] The Chancellor of the Exchequer, Dr Dalton, told the two Ministers he would not oppose the proposals set out in the paper.[46] [Sir John Winnifrith told the author that Dr Dalton was keen on the scheme and instructed his officials not to obstruct it. However, the officials were annoyed that the reservations and misgivings of Sir Frank Stockdale and Sir Harold

Tempany had been brushed aside.] The Lord President of the Council, Mr Morrison, was, however, asked in a memorandum on the Cabinet Paper by his economic adviser, Mr P. Chantler, whether it was 'really necessary to buy this £3 million pig-in-a-poke?' because a delay of a fortnight, in order to assess the scheme, could hardly be critical when the scheme would not yield substantial results before 1949–50.[47] Also, it suggested that the Ministry of Food should be asked to estimate the oils and fats position in four years' time. At the Cabinet Meeting of 31 October 1946, the Ministers were authorised to initiate a scheme on the lines indicated, up to a total cost of £3 million, on the understanding that this would not involve interference with other schemes already approved, such as the working of open-cast coal, for which the same type of special equipment was required.[48]

In anticipation of this authorisation, the Minister of Food told Mr Samuel over the telephone on 23 October that his Ministry was considering asking the UAC to act as managing agents in launching the project.[49] At a meeting the following day, Mr Samuel was invited to nominate a member of his business to work for at least four weeks on a full-time basis in the Special Section being set up in the Ministry of Food to report on both the short- and long-term prospects of the scheme. Mr Samuel named Mr W. A. Faure, a Board member of UAC, who was also at the meeting.[50] Mr Samuel suggested that Mr F. J. Pedler would be a suitable Colonial Office representative in the Special Section but Mr J. Rosa was nominated. The Special Section was composed of Messrs F. Hollins, C. Huntley, L. Scott and G. H. C. Amos (all of the Ministry of Food), A. J. Wakefield, W. A. Faure and J. Rosa. Apart from arranging for the first stage to be started,[51] it considered the scheme as a whole. Its report was dated 5 December 1946 and stated that 'advice had been sought from all available authorities in the United Kingdom and overseas who have experience of the problems under examination and of analogous problems.'[52] The conclusions were given thus:

1. A critical examination of the scheme proposed by the Mission leads inevitably to the conclusion that it is a practicable plan for alleviating a world shortage of oils and fats, which is likely to last for many years and which may, indeed, increase in severity, unless bold and vigorous action is taken in good time on some such lines as these.
2. Viewed strictly as a commercial proposition, the scheme involves no unjustifiable finance risks.
3. It would be wrong, however, to make the decision to go ahead

with the scheme or not depend solely on its financial soundness considered as a commercial proposition. Both His Majesty's Government and the Colonial Governments will derive from it many benefits, direct and indirect, some of which can, but many of which cannot, be expressed financially. For example, in assessing the value of the scheme to the Governments concerned, the revenue obtained from United Kingdom and Colonial taxes on the under-taking must clearly be taken into account; they are, in fact, assets to the Governments, though in the financial section of this report, in which the scheme is regarded as a self-contained commercial enterprise, they appear as a liability. Thus, even if the scheme were to turn out to be uneconomic from the point of view from which it has been examined in this report, it might well be financially profitable to His Majesty's Government. Finally, apart from all financial considerations, it might still be desirable because of the incidental good which it would do to the territories, but which cannot be expressed in terms of money, e.g. the prevention of soil erosion and loss of fertility.

4. While in this report the scheme has been examined primarily as a method of obtaining new supplies of fats for the United Kingdom, and can be fully justified solely from that standpoint, it has been seen that it should bring many sociological, economic and political benefits to the people of the territories concerned. Indeed, it may well prove that its permanent importance will lie mainly in its demonstration of the new standards of productivity, health and social welfare which the application of scientific principles of agriculture can bring to Africa. Those who are responsible for carrying out the scheme should, therefore, be specifically charged with the duty of developing the whole area under their control, in such a way as to promote the well-being and advancement of the native population. Suitable local industries should be encouraged, and agricultural research should not be directed solely to increasing the yields of groundnuts, important though this must be.

5. It is only by training Africans for positions of responsibility in such enterprises as this, by getting them to participate first in the running of their own welfare services, and later in the management of the agricultural, commercial and industrial operations of the scheme, that the ultimate political problem facing the British (and other European) Governments in Africa can be solved, and the Africans' capacity for eventual self-government be developed.

6. Early this year, the Food and Agriculture Organisation of the United Nations estimated that the population of the world in ten

years' time from now will be 500 million greater than it was ten years ago. Food production cannot possibly keep pace with this rate of increase, unless large new areas are developed on the most scientific lines. But, if HM Government intend to translate into action the resolution to which they committed themselves after the Hot Springs Conference, they will have to increase food production not merely by enough to keep pace with the growth of population, but by enough to start reducing the chronic undernourishment from which a large proportion of the world's population has always suffered. Viewed from this angle, the East African Groundnuts Scheme is only a small beginning. The possibility of extending it in Tanganyika, Northern Rhodesia and Kenya and, indeed, in other British territories, should, therefore, be constantly in mind. It is not improbable that millions of additional acres in East Africa alone could be profitably developed on similar lines. The possibility of using profits of the scheme to provide capital for further schemes of development should be very seriously considered. The political importance of the United Kingdom giving a lead in the economic development and social and political advancement of Mandated Territories needs no emphasis.

7. It is of vital importance to the success of a scheme so unprecedented as this that the Agency directly responsible for carrying it out should be told in the broadest possible terms (yet precisely) what is expected of them, and that they should have as much freedom as possible in the choice of the means whereby they achieve this goal. This applies equally to the Managing Agents and the Corporation. Any attempt to control them with too tight a rein from Whitehall will be likely, in a venture of this sort, to lead to waste and loss of money rather than to the assurance of economy which it is designed to secure.

The agricultural aspects had been commented on by Mr E. M. Crowther, Head of the Chemistry Department, Rothamsted Experimental Station, and Mr Dunstan Skilbeck, Principal, Wye Agricultural College, neither of whom claimed first-hand experience of groundnuts in East Africa. They welcomed the scheme 'wholeheartedly as offering the means for applying modern methods of agricultural development to some of the most difficult and wide-spread conditions in Africa'. At existing prices, they felt that an initial production of 500 lbs of shelled nuts per acre was hardly alarming, so the whole question of yield per acre was not crucial. They pointed out that much administration at various levels would be involved and doubted whether it had been fully realised. Personnel, rather than technical problems, appeared to be the more difficult to cope with, and they wondered whether the necessary personnel could be attracted to the scheme in sufficient numbers to make it work. They ended by quoting David Lilienthal's summary of the lessons of TVA that there must not be a single fixed plan but a rapid succession of development plans and 'the people must be in on the planning'.[53] The Labour Adviser to the Secretary of State, Major Orde Browne, felt that the project was very large in proportion to the labour resources of East Africa and, unless well organised, would be liable to disastrous failure, upsetting other local activities. The provision of the main incentive to work, in the form of imported goods, was essential, as was the full use of local building material.[54] The Director of Costings at the Ministry of Food, Mr J. A. Dyson, considered the venture on a long-term basis, on the information available, to be a fair commercial proposition, though the necessarily estimated nature of the figures was stressed.[55] This last was originally a report to the Under-Secretary, Finance, at the Ministry of Food, Dr E. E. Bailey, to whom the Special Section was answerable.[56]

The Special Section's Report was not signed because, while the members were willing to accept responsibility for the body of the Report, they were not prepared to assume such responsibility for the Conclusions themselves, which were drawn by Mr Hollins alone. It was agreed to submit the Report unsigned.[57] The Under-Secretary, Finance, at the Ministry of Food felt unable fully to associate himself with the Report and addressed a memorandum to the Permanent Secretary on 20 December 1946 setting out his differences. He stated that (i) there was no evidence that the necessary equipment was available for 1947; (ii) personnel would be difficult to recruit and the adaptation of local labour to mechanised cultivation under a shift system was not to be assumed lightly; (iii) the implications of changing the first year's operations from the Southern to the Central Province of Tanganyika had not been allowed for in the timing of the financial outlay on capital installations, particularly the Lindi Railway; (iv) the views of local Executive Councils had not been obtained; (v) the results of failure, rather than success, on East Africa had not been considered; (vi) costs had climbed steadily as investigation had proceeded, as had the total capital outlay, while the date of repayment had been put back from 1953–54 to 1964 so that a short-term development was not a practical proposition. Consequently, he was unable to accept Conclusion 1 of the Report that a critical exam-ination of the scheme led 'inevitably' to the conclusion that it is a practicable plan for alleviating the world shortage of fats as 'There is unfortunately no inevitability about any of the conclusions to be drawn from this Report.'

In the first place the Memorandum was prepared jointly by the Under-Secretary and the Permanent Secretary,[58] who discussed it on the same day, 16 December 1946, with the Minister.[59] Four days later it was addressed by the Under-Secretary to the Permanent Secretary in the latter's capacity as Accounting Officer of his Ministry.[60] As the Accounting Officer, Sir Percivale Liesching wrote as follows to his Minister on 20 December 1946:

1. As Permanent Secretary of the Ministry of Food I recognise in this scheme a project which, if successful, will make a valuable contribution to our supplies of oils and fats and alleviate a situation of shortage and high prices. In that capacity I support the scheme also as a large-scale experiment of great potential benefit to the economic and social advancement of the natives in the East African dependencies, and I regard this aspect as being, on any true perspective, the major reason for launching the scheme and for pursuing it with all vigour.

2. I had not thought, until Ministerial decisions to that effect were taken, that financial and administrative responsibility should properly rest with the Ministry of Food for what is in its major aspect a Colonial development scheme, even though that scheme is designed to provide a commodity of which the Ministry of Food is anxious to secure additional supplies. The pronouncement in the House of Commons on November 7th 1945 establishing the Ministry of Food as a permanent Ministry suggests that the functions of the Ministry run through 'procurement, distribution and sale', but do not go beyond procurement to responsibility for production. Be that as it may, the responsibility for this particular scheme now rests with this Ministry.

3. It follows that as Accounting Officer, not as Permanent Secretary, I must 'on the finance side . . . exercise in detail those functions of control before expenditure takes place, which are exercised, necessarily in less detail, by the Treasury (in approving the estimates from time to time submitted to them), and still more generally by the House of Commons (in granting supply). This control involves provision of funds and *criticism of the financial aspects of all proposals for expenditure* ['Notes for the use of Accounts Branches of Government Departments', 4th ed., para. 95. The emphasis is mine.]

4. It has been my duty, therefore, with the assistance of my Under Secretary (Finance) personally to scrutinise the report of the Special Section which has now been submitted to you. The Under-Secretary's views are annexed. I agree with his comments which call attention to a number of points at which the uncertainties necessarily existing at the time of launching this enterprise involve a number of risks which cannot lightly be dismissed. These, if the outcome is unfavourable, will inevitably be reflected in the financial liabilities for which, as Accounting Officer, I shall be personally responsible not only to yourself as Minister but also directly to the House of Commons through the Public Accounts Committee.

5. Without neglecting other points to which the Under-Secretary (Finance) draws attention, I am myself chiefly perturbed by the fact that, whereas the success or failure and therefore the financial results of the project depend above all things on the African labour force, it is on this very point that the greatest doubts exist in the mind of the most expert opinion that has been brought to bear. I need not repeat the points made by the Under-Secretary in para. 2 of his Memorandum, but I trust that his criticisms and the relevant section of the Special Section's Report to which he refers (Appendix D pp. 58–69) will be read *in extenso*. In my opinion the financial outcome depends predominantly on whether the hopes and expectations (it would be unfair to describe them as assumptions) with regard to African native labour are or are not realised.

6. As Accounting Officer I cannot be expected to do otherwise than place on record that I have no means of ensuring success at this vital point in the whole scheme, and that if, with this uncertainty and its possible financial effects clearly recognised, Ministers decide that we should proceed with the enterprise, they will do so with the knowledge that I have been unable to advise, on the evidence available, that there is any assurance that the scheme will not falter or fail on this account, with financial results which, from the nature of the case, cannot be estimated with any degree of accuracy.

Mr Strachey replied on 13 January 1947 as follows:

I have spoken in detail to the Chancellor on this point and he is fully assured, as I am, that your position will be fully covered at the P. A. C. by the decision which the Cabinet took today. Now what we have to do in order to discharge our duties is to see that the most efficient possible public corporation is set up to operate the Government's decision.[61]

The Under-Secretary came later to regret that less than justice had been done not only to his own Minute of 20 December 1946, but also to that of Sir Percivale Liesching's of the same date. In his Minute of 6 October 1949, previously referred to, Dr E. E. Bailey added in reference to the Special Section, which he thought had meantime been badly maligned, that 'while I, in effect, rejected their Report, I cannot associate myself with any wholesale depreciation of it or of the work which in many quarters of the Ministry was subsequently devoted to this subject. They and others were the objects of Ministerial pressure of the severest kind, a factor which should never be left out of account in any judgment founded only on the documentary record.'

It is somewhat surprising, too, that at the time there was apparently no decisive discussion of two aspects which were crucial. The first concerns the evidence on yields given in the Mission's Report. The second concerns the appropriateness of mechanised agriculture. It was stated that

In arriving at the figure of 850 lbs of shelled groundnuts per acre, as the acreage output to be expected over the whole project, we have taken into consideration data of the production of groundnuts in the regions concerned. Figures of output and yields per acre were obtained from the publication *Agriculture in Tanganyika* issued by the local Department of Agriculture, and test weighings were made by ourselves whenever crops were found on the ground. The main producing areas are in the Western Province where the figures given by the Department show an average yield of 615 lbs per acre for the years 1943 and 1944.[62]

The pamphlet referred to[63] showed (p. 28), for the Western Province, estimated production in tons by Districts. In 1943 the total for the Province was 4250 tons and for 1944 only 2500 tons. Over the two years, the average acreage per grower was 0.65, the average number of growers was 124,200 and the average return per grower was 400 lbs. It was from these latter averages that the Mission calculated its figure of 615 lbs per acre. Groundnuts were said to be the main cash crop in the Nyamwezi Administrative Area, which consisted of the Tabora District and the Kahama District taken together, accounting for a total of 3200 tons and 2000 tons in 1943 and 1944 respectively. Efforts to extend production in other Districts had not been very successful. Production was said to fluctuate with seasonal variations and the incidence of Rosette disease.

Tanganyika Territory: Proposed Areas for Groundnuts
Production Scheme

Map planned by A. E. Kelleway,
Historical Section, Cabinet Office.

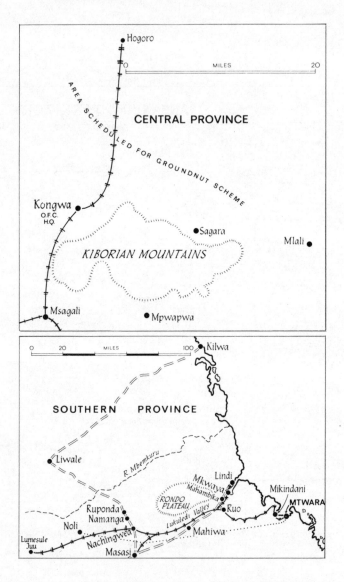

Tanganyika Territory: Sketch Maps of Central Province and
Southern Province

Map planned by A. E. Kelleway,
Historical Section, Cabinent Office.

However, the Western Province was intended to have only ten units of 30,000 acres each while the Southern Province was to have fifty-five units and the Central Province fifteen units. In the Southern Province, according to the pamphlet (p. 42), production for sale in tons had fluctuated over the years 1939 to 1944 between 2428 tons in 1939 and 1104 tons in 1944. In the seven Districts comprising the Province, average acreage per grower varied from 0.5 in five to 0.1 in one. The crop was said to be capable of expansion, especially in the Masasi District, though the extension of the bunch type was necessary in the drier areas. In the Central Province, according to the pamphlet (p. 15), groundnuts were again the most important cash crop and in years of average rainfall good yields of excellent quality were harvested. Over the years 1940 to 1944, production varied between 3511 tons in 1942 and 871 tons the following year, the average production being 1982 tons and the average acreage per grower 0.28. According to the account in *The Groundnut Affair* by Mr Alan Wood, who was Head of the Information Division of the Overseas Food Corporation from April 1948 until September 1949, it was after the Mission had returned to Dar-es-Salaam, having chosen a region in the Southern Province about 100 miles inland from Mikindani, and a region in the Western Province near Tabora, that its attention was directed to the Central Province by a Rhodesian farmer, Mr Tom Bain. The latter, according to Mr Wood's account,

organised Africans to cut tracks through the bush so that the Mission could get in to inspect the soil. Groundnuts had been grown by Africans for many years in the Kongwa area; and the Wakefield Mission, coming on a wayside field, made a check of the yields. They marked off one-tenth of an acre, Tom Bain got Africans with hoes to dig up all the groundnuts in it, and the weighings showed yields of between 1200 and 2000 lbs per acre. These results were confirmed by some twenty checks taken over a wide area by Government Agricultural officers. Wakefield decided that the only reasons why such fertile ground had not been used before were the impossibility of clearing the tangled bush by primitive methods and the absence of domestic water supplies.[64]

The author continued thus: 'There was, however, perhaps another reason. An official rainfall map, published in 1942, showed Mpwapwa lying just outside, and the projected groundnut areas well inside, a yellow band which marks the lowest rainfall in Tanganyika – under 25 inches'; and he quoted an account of a missionary's attempts of 1878 to develop agriculture in the area, which failed because of the shortness and uncertainty of the rainy season. However, Mr Wakefield was apparently unaware of this at the time because in his 'Note on Agricultural Soundness of Scheme' he merely repeated from his Report the evidence from the Western Province and stated that 'the random tests of one-fortieth of an acre taken within fields of native-grown groundnuts on the red loams gave from 1,200 to 2,000 lbs of shelled nuts per acre in a season of extremely poor rainfall.'[65] It was not apparently realised that these yield figures were not based on adequate statistical sampling procedure. Nor was it recognised that land cannot be safely regarded as a homogenous factor of production over large areas and that, even if it were, the rain which it received would vary from place to place and from time to time. Consequently, it is not surprising that the yield figures calculated so simply should turn out to be so erroneous.

An outside observer might reasonably presume that it was the expected economies of mechanised agriculture which explained the Mission's perfunctory investigation of likely yields. Indeed, in paragraph 11 of its Report, the Wakefield Mission had declared: 'Areas of sparse population unencumbered by native or other rights are necessary if operations are to be started quickly. Uninhabited, tsetse-infested and waterless areas therefore offer special attraction to the project, provided the soil is suitable and rainfall adequate; this type of country is almost limitless in Tanganyika and Northern Rhodesia.' Yet the economies of mechanisation were also seriously doubted at the time. When the Clay Mission was on its way to West Africa, Mr F. Sykes read the Report of the Wakefield Mission and believed it was ill-advised in its reliance on mechanisation. As the result, the following paragraphs were included in the Report of the Clay Mission specifically to cover the point:[66]

Limitations on use of mechanisation

2. The information set out in the preceding chapter is admittedly incomplete for the purposes of full development and requires to be supplemented and confirmed before such development could be started. This confirmation and such additional information as may be required should, however, be provided by the detailed surveys of topography, soil conditions, vegetative cover and water resources of each of the areas which are at present being undertaken by the Governments in West Africa. We are in any event satisfied on two points at this stage; first, that there would be little or no opportunity to select very large blocks of land of such uniform topography and

soil that they would be ideally suitable for development by mechanisation; and secondly, that the work of the machine would have to be supplemented to an appreciable extent by hand labour.

The latter point requires some further explanation. It arises primarily from the fact that to produce as economically as possible, the labour and machinery load must be evenly spread. With the introduction of the tractor, the peak labour load would come not at the breaking of the land, as it does with hand hoe cultivation, but at harvest time. Where groundnuts are concerned, there is a particular limitation which would apply at that time. For the crop must not be lifted before it is nearly ripe, or there will be loss from under-development of the nut in the shell. It cannot at the same time be left too long in the ground, since a short time after the nuts are fully ripe the stalk on which they grow becomes brittle and would not stand the strain exerted on it during the lifting operations. There is also a limit on the time the crop can be left in windrow after lifting. This arises from the tendency of the nut to fall off the haulm after exposure to a desiccating sun. The time for this to happen varies. Early in the season when the nut is slightly under-ripe, it may be left for about a week before stooking and without loss from shedding. Later, when the nuts have ripened in the soil, it is only three to four days before they fall off the haulm and are lost unless subsequently gleaned from the soil. In these circumstances, the time for safe harvesting is limited to about 20 days from the time lifting commences to the time when the crop is all in stock, and the maximum area which can be economically put under groundnuts is that acreage which can be lifted and stooked without loss within 20 days or so. Harvesting in this period is not difficult for the farmer and his family working on a small farm, but it could only be done under mechanised farming if the work of the tractor were sup-plemented by a considerable amount of hand labour. On our present estimation, we would not put the maximum area for groundnuts higher than 200 acres per tractor, and consider that to achieve harvesting over the acreage a gang of fifteen men would need to work in conjunction with the tractor, the latter lifting the crop and the men stooking it. In fact, under the conditions for groundnut production we saw, machinery could be used to greater advantage as an adjunct to hand labour rather than as a replace-ment for it.

The reaction of one Colonial Office official had been unfavourable as early as 2 April 1946 to the Samuel scheme on this score. Mr Clauson

had argued that 'The project seems to be in essence one for doing in
Africa what had been done with disastrous results in America, that is
an attack on the land with heavy instruments. Our experience on the
whole is that the use of heavy instruments on the land in African
conditions produces one or two good crops and then devastating soil
erosion.'[67] The official surmised also that 'if the soil is good, one is
disposed to wonder whether the tsetse fly would ever have been
allowed to get in.' Sir Harold Tempany, the Secretary of State's
Agricultural Adviser, on first seeing the scheme after three months'
absence from the Colonial Office, expressed doubts on several aspects
and general surprise that 'the proposal should have received such very
cursory scrutiny from the agricultural point of view in the initial
stages', and did not think a comparable engineering scheme would
have got as far without full preliminary examination of the technical
aspects by a committee of experts. He doubted in particular whether
entire reliance could be placed on mechanical means to carry out the
weeding in the early stages of growth, as experience with cotton in the
Sudan showed that it could not be.[68] The Ministry of Food was aware
in October 1946 of 'a cleavage of opinion in the Colonial Office about
the agricultural feasibility of the scheme'.[69] It might reasonably be
asked why the agricultural advisers of the Colonial Office did not press
their initial doubts further. Sir Leslie Monson told the author that he
suspected that, having expressed doubts and secured the appointment
of a Colonial agricultural expert of their own choosing to lead the
Mission, namely Mr Wakefield, they found the ground cut from under
their feet by his wholesale advocacy of the Samuel scheme, particularly when the tide of Ministerial opinion was running so strongly in
favour of the idea.

IV. WHY THE PROJECT WAS LAUNCHED

Doubts were thus expressed in several quarters. Why, then, it must be
asked, did the matter proceed despite all the doubts? A large part of the
answer is certainly to be found in the atmosphere created by the
desperateness of the oils and fats situation, coupled with pressure from
Washington to help ourselves more vigorously. The feeling of the time
was expressed by the Lord President, Mr Morrison, in June 1947 in a
Cabinet paper entitled 'Planning for Expansion',[70] in which the
shortages of new materials, fuel and food were seen to underlie many of
the economic troubles of the time. 'All our planning', he feared, would
'be brought to naught and economic crisis will recur unless we can

recreate the ample flow of supplies of commodities which is the life-blood of our economy.' So vital a matter should not, he stated, be left 'too much to the self-interest of producers who have little incentive in present conditions and are up against heavy odds'. He went on to state that 'The Minister of Food has been developing, in such examples as the Canadian Wheat Contract and in the Tanganyika groundnut scheme, the type of planned attack which might well be more widely adopted.' Expansion of world production of foodstuffs and raw materials was basic to all else – productivity increases, freer trading, improved incentives and the easing of world political stresses. The Cabinet accepted the argument expressed, and approved the proposals made to expand supplies of scarce commodities.[71]

Recent experience of war also strongly influenced thinking, and the scheme became widely regarded as a campaign between machines and nature. Thus, the Minister of Food, when seeking the secondment of two RAMC officers, prefaced his request with the view that:

In many respects, the planning and carrying out of this scheme resemble a military operation. We are working against time and we have to move very large quantities of constructional machinery and equipment, mobile workshops, heavy tractors, etc., over difficult country, while maintaining all the personnel and equipment ourselves, in much the same way that a military formation has to supply all its own maintenance services. We shall be employing hundreds of Europeans and many thousands of Africans in these at present uninhabited areas, and the proper planning of our medical and hygiene services will obviously be of the highest importance.[72]

In his address of 29 September 1947 to the First Conference of the British Society of Soil Science, Mr Wakefield stated that his Mission had 'considered that the Samuel scheme was practicable and, if it was dealt with as a Mulberry operation of war, that it could be implemented.'[73] The analogy of a military operation was misleading. It is true, if fanciful, to say that in this case tracts of uninhabited land were 'the enemy'. But the other ingredients of a military operation were absent; in a nutshell, the careful mustering of men and materials to carry out a well-considered plan based on sound strategy and well-tried tactics. It was perhaps more analogous to a haphazard assault on nature than to the opening of a campaign. Thus, in the first paragraph of the Memorandum on Progress to 31 January 1947 by the Managing Agents, it was stated that 'The urgent need for progress, dictated by the desire to have a crop in the Spring of 1948, has rendered it impossible to enter the scheme on a fully planned basis. The planning of future development will, therefore, largely have to be done concurrently with the execution of the earlier programme.'[74] The Memorandum concluded with the following:

> Although adequate transport to and from the Southern Province for large crops cannot be available until the 1949 harvest, it has been decided at a very early date to commence operations on a smaller scale in that area, so as to plant at least several thousand acres, in order to gain experience. Apart from that, operations will be concentrated in the Central Province, where it is hoped to complete four or five units each of 30,000 acres.

The military operations analogy was wholly misleading, for the logistics of the operation had been largely overlooked. With a high proportion of tractors in disrepair by the end of 1947 and with the problems of providing for the needs of a new community starting from nothing in the desert, in the words of Mr Alan Wood, 'The Groundnut Army was in fact, in very much the same position as an army which had gone into action in a fit of absentmindedness, and forgotten to take the RASC with it.'[75]

v. VIEWS OF THE GOVERNOR OF TANGANYIKA

But this is to anticipate. On 29 October 1946 the Governor of Tanganyika, Sir William Battershill, considered the Wakefield Report with his officials. It was felt that further information was wanted with regard to labour before the estimates in the Report could be fully accepted. On the agricultural side, it was said that local officials would not have chosen the Mpwapwa District without further investigation, the practicability and cost of using phosphate fertilisers required exploration and, while breaking down the land for cultivation would reduce tsetse, much additional clearing would be necessary to eliminate it, which would not be economic. The Tanganyika Government was in no position to finance roads, railways and ports as required for the scheme apart from what was in hand already.[76] The reaping of a harvest in 1947 from the Southern Province was stated to be dependent on railway materials and personnel being available by the end of 1947.[77] The Governor missed no opportunity of disclaiming any local financial contribution – thus, in answer to a proposal that, when the scheme was announced, it should be stated that it would

eventually be transferred to the Government of the Colonies concerned,[78] he declared that, while he agreed with the principle and had
no objection to its announcement, at the same time 'it would mislead
to give the impression that the people of the area concerned, nearly all
of whom are among the less advanced tribes of the Territory, would,
within the next generation, be able themselves to accept financial
responsibility for, and to manage, mechanised and scientific production on the scale visualised for the scheme.'[79]

vi. MISSION TO THE USA

Meanwhile, the Special Section decided to send a mission of two to the
United States, both to discuss American experience in the cultivation
of groundnuts on mechanical lines in Virginia and to purchase as
much of the agricultural machinery required for Tanganyika as was
available, after investigating the supply position of the types of
machinery needed.[80] The Mission consisted of Messrs D. L. Martin of
UAC and K. W. Wilson, a specialist in agricultural machinery in the
Ministry of Agriculture. As the contents of the Wakefield Report and
the Cabinet decision to preceed were as yet unannounced and, even
when announced, the Ministry of Food wished 'to avoid making a
splash in America', the purchases were to be made through com-
mericial rather than governmental channels.[81] The Mission left
London on 14 November and returned on 25 December 1946. After
visiting the growing areas of South Georgia and finding how little
mechanisation was used, mules being preferred to tractors, it was
decided that similar investigations in Virginia and Carolina were not
justified.[82] In their visit to the groundnut areas of Texas, the growing
side was seen to be not everywhere mechanised nor generally efficient,
because farms were rarely over 100 acres.[83] Spanish Bunch seed was
advised as being more tolerant of drought and lime-deficient soils than
Virginia bunch seed. The approved rate of seeding was 65 lbs per acre,
not 40–45 lbs as recommended in the Wakefield Report. Early seeding
was stated by experts to be essential, and only experience could show
whether in East African conditions this increased the spread of Rosette
disease. Implements for carrying out the digging and combine-
threshing operations were not as advanced as those for other
operations, and needed trying out in the first year to decide which were
the more suitable. They found that American manufacturers were able
to supply only some 60 agricultural tractors with attendant implements, out of the 180 to 200 needed in the first year, with deliveries

commencing by mid-1947. However, Messrs Massey-Harris of Toronto, Canada, was prepared to supply 150 tractors and their attendant equipment before July 1947, provided the total requirements for the second and third years were also ordered from them. The report stated that 'Based both on what we saw and discussed, we are convinced that harvesting in East Africa can be fully mechanised.'[84] As the result of this visit, a contract was placed, through Messrs Balfour Guthrie of New York, with the Massey-Harris Company for machinery to the value of over $5 million. Nearly four-fifths of this was to come from the Company's factories in the USA, and when it was thought that those supplies would be subject to export licensing restrictions the BFM was asked to take the matter up with the United States authorities.[85] The Secretary of Agriculture, Mr Clinton P. Anderson, was asked to support the application for extra licences, which he did.[86] However, while the Special Section were under the impression that the Massey-Harris contract covered the whole of the requirements for 1948/49 and half of the requirements for 1949/50, it appeared that the percentages for tractors in the two years were 62.5 per cent and 36 per cent.[87] It was explained that, until a firm programme was received from East Africa, 'it must be anybody's guess with regard to the agricultural equipment required', although in six months' time it would be easier to assess requirements of heavy tractors for clearing operations.[88] Much depended, it was said on the performance of tractors in 1947.[89]

VII. CABINET DECISIONS

Apart from statements by the new Secretary of State, Mr Creech Jones, at his Lobby Conference on 16 October 1946,[90] the first Ministerial pronouncement on the scheme was made in the House of Commons by the Minister of Food, Mr Strachey, on 25 November 1946. He mentioned the further investigation in hand, but believed that 'the need for additional supplies of oils and fats in this country is, however, so pressing that this further investigation, necessary as it is, cannot be allowed to delay the start of the project. For work must start early next year, if a crop is to be reaped in the 1947–48 season.'[91] The interim arrangement with UAC and the intention to establish a Public Corporation, if the scheme was to continue, were reported. The publication of a White Paper was promised.[92] The statement was well received by members generally.

The Minister proceeded to prepare two memoranda for Cabinet

decision. In the first of these,[93] he reported that the prospects for clearing 150,000 acres of bush in Tanganyika in time for planting in 1947 were not favourable, although, even if the whole area cleared could not be planted in time, 'the development in that year will provide, as well as some crop, invaluable experience for subsequent operations.'[94] He stated that he had accepted the conclusions of the Report by the Special Section and asked for authority to develop approximately 3 million acres in Tanganyika, Northern Rhodesia and Kenya over the next six years. Maximum cash requirements were not likely to exceed £23 million, apart from special provision for railway, road and harbour construction. After the crop year 1949/50, estimated receipts were expected to exceed annual expenditure on capital equipment plus running costs, so that repayment to the Treasury could then begin, being completed by 1964. In addition, £2 million was required to finance railway, road and harbour works. An average yield of 750 lbs per acre was assumed, along with a market price of not less than £30 per ton f.o.b. East African port during the first four crop years and, thereafter, not less than £20 per ton, while the total average cost per ton of shelled groundnuts f.o.b. East African port at the time of the maximum indebtedness to the Treasury would be £17.18.0. He recommended that HMG should not be committed firmly either to localities or to a development programme, so that any adjustments suggested by experience in the initial operations could be made. He proposed legislation to establish a public Corporation which would be able to take over from UAC by August 1948, when UAC wished to relinquish control.[95] August was the end of the financial year chosen for the project to permit of the planting and harvesting of the crop falling within the same financial year. UAC offered to act as managing agents for the first year without charging a fee, but if asked to continue after that they expected to receive a full commercial fee.[96] Until then, he recommended that UAC should act as Managing Agents under an agency agreement. Finally, he proposed that a White Paper on the scheme be published after agreement with the Chancellor of the Exchequer and the Secretary of State.

In his covering memorandum[97] the Minister asked his colleagues, rather than consider the risks inherent in the project, to consider the risks of not undertaking it – first, the possibility in 1950 of having the same, or a lower, margarine ration than that available currently; and, secondly, too few dollars to buy other indispensable imports if large purchases of fats from dollar sources were needed. He also claimed that 'a large enterprise of this type is the only way in which our Central African possessions can be rapidly developed so that they may become

256 DEVELOPING BRITISH COLONIAL RESOURCES

an economic and strategic asset instead of a liability.'[98] In a minute on the draft Memorandum, Mr F. Hollins of the Special Section revealed another strongly-held argument of the time for proceeding with the project. He believed that HMG would

> be driven into schemes of this kind sooner rather than later in any event by the pressure of inescapable economic facts – principally the rapidly increasing population of the world, which will not even be able to maintain its present inadequate levels of consumption unless we get down to the business of applying modern science to food production. We shall probably be attacked in the United Nations by both the Americans and the Russians, and driven into schemes of this kind, quite possibly at a time when they will not be financially profitable. . . .

He suggested the addition of:

> Finally (though this is really a point for the Colonial Secretary) I do not believe that we, as a Socialist Government, can justify our Colonial Empire at all before the world unless we take bold action to develop its resources by schemes like this for the benefit of its people and the rest of the world.[99]

This last suggestion was not taken up, but the sentence appeared in the concluding paragraph of CP(48) 18 of 18 January 1948, which accompanied the draft of a White Paper reviewing progress in East Africa to the end of November 1947. In a comment on the draft of CP(47) 10, Mr Rosa felt that it was both hazardous to estimate the profits over 25 years, and rather pointless, as a more general argument for the project would carry more weight. He proposed the following:

> Sooner or later, if not for the relief of our food situation then for the purpose of Colonial development, we may well see ourselves forced to embark on a project of this nature and scale, and at a far less financially propitious moment. If it is only a matter of time before we have to face up to this problem, let us face up to it now when market conditions, during the next few years at least, offer the optimum conditions for success.[100]

Outside the Special Section and, to a much more limited extent, the Colonial Office, comments were critical and doubtful. The Lord President of the Council, Mr Morrison, was presented, for example, with a highly critical brief on the two draft memoranda by Mr Max Nicholson.[101] He was reminded of wartime failures of ambitious schemes in East Africa. He was warned that it was most unlikely that a commercial undertaking would ever seriously contemplate sinking a really large sum in an untried plantation crop in a part of the world where there was no adequate previous experience of success in growing it, and where there was a long history of expensive failures of other crops. Given the risks of delay and failure, a long-term contract with the French West African Colonies for the expanded supply of groundnuts was thought to be a better proposition. But these points were not mentioned when the two memoranda were considered by the Cabinet on 13 January 1947. After receiving reassurances on various points that were raised, including the continuing need for the additional production, the Cabinet approved the proposals outlined, authorised the Minister of Food to make an early announcement of the scheme in a White Paper and invited the Minister to arrange for the necessary legislation to be prepared in time for its introduction at the outset of the 1947-48 Session of Parliament.[102] The Wakefield Report was published in February 1947, though not in full as an appendix to a statement of the intention to press ahead with the scheme was modified following further re-examination by the Special Section.[103] The statement was an expanded version of the Cabinet paper submitted by the Minister in January 1947.[104] It concluded with this sentence: 'If this large-scale experiment succeeds, it may well prove to be an important step towards the Food and Agriculture Organisation's goal of a world freed from want.' (Cmd 7030, para. 26.)

VIII. THE LOCAL CONTRIBUTION TO THE SCHEME

In order to assess the East African groundnuts project in the context of Colonial development, it is necessary to consider both its contribution – intended, as well as actual – to local development, and also the calls which the project made on local resources, material and financial. While the first of these involves some general account of the progress, plans and revisions of the scheme, the latter is more closely defined and, for that reason, is more conveniently taken first.

Owing to the decision to make an early start, the Secretary of State cabled in November 1946 a series of questions to the Governor of Tanganyika, asking for replies to be sent by telegraph as soon as possible. The questions and answers were as follows:[105]

(i) Whether the Government of Tanganyika was in general agreement with the project proposed in the Report. *Answer*: Yes.

(ii) Were there comments on the Report of a fundamental nature which the Secretary of State should know before the project was launched? *Answer*: The Government of Tanganyika was unable to finance extensive railway, port and road undertakings as suggested by the Mission.

(iii) Whether the Government would lease to HMG at a nominal rent the land recommended in the Report. *Answer*: Yes.

(iv) What was considered a reasonable term of years for the lease, and when might it be terminated to enable the transfer of the project to the Government of Tanganyika. *Answer*: 33 years with the option of two renewals of the same period. [Sir Edward Twining, the new Governor, advised the Secretary of State that it would be possible to revert to 99-year leases.[106] The Secretary of State thereupon withdrew his objections.[107] However, it was not possible to forecast a firm transfer date and only the possibility of the transfer could be noted.]

(v) Would there be political, or other, objections to employing UAC as agents in the initial period. *Answer*: None, providing UAC was employed only until a Public Corporation was established and it had no capital investment in the project.

Later in the month, the Secretary of State extended his catechism. The questions and answers were as follows:[108]

(i) In order to express the intention to transfer of the ownership of the project, the Governor was asked if he would agree to the statement that: 'It is the intention of HMG and of the Governments of the Colonial Territories concerned that the ownership of the project will in due course be transferred from HMG to those Governments, at a time and on terms to be agreed.' *Answer*: Agreed.

(ii) Whether it would be agreed that no export duty or cess be imposed for the first ten years of the project. *Answer*: Agreed.

(iii) Whether imports, other than consumer goods, required for the scheme would be exempt from import duty. *Answer*: Agreed in principle, details to be worked out in order to avoid anomalies.

(iv) Whether political, and other, objections would make it impossible to exempt the undertaking from income and profits taxes for ten years and, if so, whether the local Government would invest the amount collected in income and profits taxes in the scheme. *Answer*: There would be strong objections to exempting the project but a substantial proportion of the tax raised could be invested in the scheme, subject to an annual vote of the Legislature.

On account of the secrecy and urgency of the exchange of teleerams, the Governor had been able to consult his officials but not the unofficial members of his Executive Council. It was considered to be politically impossible to use the official majority in the Legislative Council to force through a measure opposed by unofficial opinion and so the caveat under point (iv) was significant.[109]

The possibility of some local contribution towards the capital cost of the scheme was discussed on 24 February 1947 by officials of the Colonial Office, Ministry of Food and the Treasury. It was proposed by the Colonial Office that monies voted by the Legislative Council should be placed in a fund and used to buy the railway and port installations constructed for the groundnuts scheme, although this did not exclude the use of other monies in addition to finance the transfer of these installations. After they had been transferred, tax receipts would continue to be paid into the fund and invested in the scheme, although it was premature to discuss details. The Colonial Office felt, however, unable to ask the Tanganyika Government to invest in the scheme part of other revenue increases due to the scheme.[110] The Chancellor of the Exchequer, Dr Hugh Dalton, was advised, following this meeting, that the scheme would 'confer great benefits on Tanganyika', that something like £250,000 would be spent 'on the erection of hospitals, welfare centres, schools, etc.', and that the territory would 'obtain approximately £500,000 a year in taxation from the project'.[111] However, he was warned that it was 'not so clear what contribution the Colony will be willing and able to make'. The Chancellor underlined 'willing', putting an exclamation mark in the margin. He minuted: 'Thank you. These Colonial Governments must be made to pay a reasonable share of the costs. H.D.'[112] The official, therefore, felt justified in pressing for a contribution, feeling that, while HMG charged interest on the funds provided, it was 'carrying all the risks – Tanganyika most certainly isn't carrying any real risk.'[113] It was minuted in agreement with this view that 'If Tanganyika forgoes interest, it will be her first real bit of sacrifice in connection with the scheme.'[114] The Ministry of Food was told that in the Treasury view 'the main thing to be settled here and now is that Tanganyika should agree in principle to let us have all the money she can, as fast as she can, without charge.'[115]

The Treasury was not altogether happy about the Colonial Office proposal that the money voted by Tanganyika for purchasing the railway and port installations should be allowed to accumulate in a fund. It was argued that: 'If it is to be of maximum assistance to HM Government, this money should be made available (free of interest) to the Corporation (or the Exchequer) in one way or another as soon as possible each year.'[116] While accepting the view that the Tanganyika Government could not be pressed to invest in the scheme income tax receipts indirectly derived, the Colonial Office was asked to urge the Tanganyika Government 'to increase their annual investment in the scheme by the use of other revenue, in particular customs revenue arising from supplies imported in connection with the scheme'. The Colonial Office reaction was one of disappointment – neither could Tanganyika be denied interest when the Treasury itself was to receive its $2\frac{1}{2}$ per cent, which was the intention as stated in Cmd 7030, nor could the official majority in the Legislative Council be used to allocate income tax receipts. As one official minuted, such action would be 'quite indefensible before the Trusteeship Council, and would savour of nothing less than the old-fashioned Colonial exploitation. The scheme was undertaken to supply the United Kingdom with fats. We really cannot countenance what the Treasury now suggest.'[117] Consequently, the Colonial Office felt unable to put the proposal to the Governor.[118] The Ministry of Food supported this view, adding that the agreement to pay interest 'might be a protection against damaging claims, which the Tanganyika Government could make if they consider that they are being badly treated, and might avert political pressure for ultimate disposal at a knock-down price'.[119] The Colonial Office insisted that, as the Finance Committee of the Legislative Council was predominantly unofficial in character, though there was an official majority in the Legislative Council, it was politically impossible to use that majority to force through financial measures opposed by unofficial opinion. The Treasury regarded this as 'a rescission of the Colonial Office views at the meeting of February 24 when Mr Cohen was confident that, if necessary, the Secretary of State could exact full compliance from the Tanganyika Legislative Council'.[120] The official added: 'I can't see that, in fact, Tanganyika can very well resist the proposal, however.' But in view of the reaction to their proposals from the Colonial Office and the Ministry of Food, the Treasury agreed that the Territory should be treated on a par with HMG, i.e. with a return on its investments and without a special lien on particular assets.[121]

After further discussion between the three Government departments, a Despatch was sent on 26 September 1947 to the Governor of Tanganyika Territory, proposing that 'the full revenue accruing to the

Tanganyika Government from income tax payments by the proposed Overseas Food Corporation should be re-invested in the scheme by means of an annual vote of the sum involved by the Legislative Council.'[122] Such monies would, in time, enable the Government to acquire the railway and harbour works in the Southern Province. Equally, it was suggested, the proceeds of customs and excise duties arising from the scheme should be invested in the scheme. The Governor was asked to consider these proposals and, if he agreed, to discuss them with the members of the Legislative Council. At the same time, a semi-official letter was sent to the Governor, giving the background and hoping that something would be accepted along the lines of the Despatch.[123] But, before putting it to the members of the Legislative Council, the Governor came to doubt the wisdom of submitting the proposals when there was a distinct chance of non-acceptance of them. He felt the proposals (a) could be criticised on political grounds, as the insistence on local investment in a project some were opposed to could be alleged to be exploitation of the African under the cloak of development; (b) the sum at stake over the initial ten years would be small, and it would be unfortunate to hold over the benefits of that sum for ten, or even, twenty years; and (c) when, in a year or two, there was an unofficial majority in the Legislative Council, the Governor might be compelled to certify the vote against its wishes, and this done regularly would make 'a complete nonsense of the Constitution'.[124]

It was decided not to press the Governor further but instead to go back to the Treasury on the whole issue,[125] in the belief that 'our main hope must be that the new Chancellor, Sir Stafford Cripps, will not now be so intransigent as his predecessor, who was determined "to make those Colonies pay up".'[126] The Ministry of Food officials accepted the Governor's views also.[127] In the Colonial Office four arguments were put forward. It was argued, first, that it was difficult to apply the principle generally, i.e. wherever there was a similar project in any Colony. Secondly, there was 'a good deal of Colonial suspicion that our whole new policy in Colonial development is only a disguised form of exploitation', and many, including the Prime Minister, had become concerned about the belief that our intention was one of exploitation for United Kingdom benefit. Thirdly, as so little revenue would be derived for some years, the political odium was out of proportion to the financial benefit; and, finally, transfer should not be tied to earmarked revenue receipts, but determined by the progress of the scheme and the state of the territory's finances.[128] These were regarded in the Treasury as objections 'to the means we suggested for

Tanganyika to find an immediate contribution – i.e. the setting aside of taxes on the scheme – and not objections to seeking a contribution from Tanganyika'.[129] However, at a meeting at the Treasury on 6 October 1948, it was agreed that the question of a direct contribution from Tanganyika, either from the proceeds of taxation or otherwise, should be left over for three years, and then reviewed in the light of the progress made by the Corporation and of the Tanganyika Government's financial position.[130] The good sense of a distinguished Governor had, with the support of the Colonial Office and a more liberal attitude in the Treasury, prevailed.

ix. PORT AND RAILWAY FACILITIES IN THE SOUTHERN PROVINCE

The second financial involvement of Tanganyika concerned the port and railway in the Southern Province. When the East African groundnuts scheme was adopted by HMG in 1946, it was realised that progress was impossible in the promising Southern Province owing to the lack of a railway and an adequate port.[131] It was decided to build both forthwith so as to minimise delay in development of the scheme. The siting of the port presented a problem for, while the Tanganyika Government favoured the enlargement of the small port of Lindi, as proposed by the Wakefield Mission, it was realised that its capacity could not exceed 500,000 tons a year, whereas a tonnage of some 900,000 tons was expected. A technical mission under the Ministry of Transport's Adviser on Shipping in Port was therefore despatched to examine possible sites. It recommended the construction of a port in the hitherto undeveloped natural harbour of Mto Mtwara, some forty miles south of Lindi.[132] This recommendation was accepted by HMG and a contract for a two-berth port was let to Messrs Balfour Beatty and Company. The railway contract was split in two. Part went to the Tanganyika Railways, who were to construct the line from the inland rail terminal to Ruo and thence to Lindi Creek, where Mkwaya was to be prepared as a temporary landing-place while the new port was being built; the rest went to Messrs Paulings and Company, a subsidiary of UAC, who, to save time, were to construct the remaining stretch from Ruo to Mtwara, a distance of some forty miles, by mechanical means.

Although these projects were initiated by HMG it was realised from the outset that it would be anomalous for the Overseas Food Corporation (OFC) to retain ownership of a public utility. The

Government of Tanganyika was unable to provide finance but, when the amalgamated East African Railways and Harbours Administration (EARHA) was created on 1 January 1948, the OFC negotiated an agreement whereby EARHA undertook to buy out the new railway and port as soon as possible, from loan funds, in return for a guarantee of the interest and sinking fund on the loan to the extent that these were not covered by revenue from all traffic handled or carried.[133] That guarantee was revised in January 1950 to cover operating costs also while, in the event of the abandonment of the Corporation's activity in the Southern Province and the consequent withdrawal of port and railway services, the Corporation was to accept responsibility for the redemption of the loan to the extent of the shortfall in the sinking fund, after allowing for the realisable value of assets and any renewal funds accumulated.

The railway from the inland terminal to Ruo and through to Mkwaya was completed in October 1949. Mkwaya had meanwhile become a temporary landing-point. But, as regards the railway link between Ruo and Mtwara, the contractors reported on 27 June 1950 that losses were being incurred because of the inadequacy in both quality and quantity of the labour available, increases in the cost of rations, unforeseen expenditure in the construction and maintenance of feeder roads and increases in the cost of oil fuel because of sterling depreciation. Subsequently it was agreed that EARHA would complete the work by manual methods, which were the least expensive in the Province.[134] Work on the port was held up by the gradual and uneven subsidence of the quay.

It was, however, not because of these technical difficulties but rather because of a reassessment of the traffic that the Colonial Office, the Ministry of Food and the OFC concluded, in August 1950, that there was no need to proceed further with either project. As this conclusion was one of prime importance to the Tanganyika Government from the political and development points of view, the issue was referred to the Governor. He was told that, unless he could see the need in the near future of facilities greater than those available at Mkwaya and Lindi, there would be no reasonable alternative to recommending a suspension of work on both the railway and the port.[135] The General Manager of EARHA was asked to provide information on the financial and technical implications of such a suspension and whether, if suspended, it could be resumed without undue expense at a later date.[136] The Governor viewed 'with dismay' the suggestion that work on the railway and port should be suspended. He felt it was not just a matter of money, for, as a result of the extensive publicity given to the projects, their abandonment would both damage British Colonial prestige and undermine confidence in the future of Tanganyika. Also, the Government and private enterprise had spent money on facilities of various kinds on the basis that the two projects would be completed. So he asked for a survey to assess the likely volume of traffic, and for an examination of means of economising on the work of completing the projects.[137]

The Governor attended a conference on the subject at the Colonial Office on 28 and 31 August 1950, at which all concerned, including the Chairman of the East Africa High Commission, were present. The conference set up a working party to examine and set out the position. It dealt only with the short-term economic aspects, leaving aside both longer-term and political considerations.[138] Until two uncertain factors were clarified it was felt to be impossible to recommend a final solution. The factors were (i) the outcome of the OFC's review of plans, which might affect the estimates of their traffic; and (ii) the outcome of the technical investigations into the subsidence of the quay wall at Mtwara, which might involve further expenditure. A decision was, therefore, postponed and, meanwhile, work was to proceed on both projects.[139] The OFC later agreed that a decision on the future of Mtwara should await a decision on the future of the groundnut scheme as a whole.[140] At a meeting of the East Africa High Commission in November 1950, an understanding was reached between the High Commission and the Government of Tanganyika in the following terms:[141]

1(a) The Government of Tanganyika would accelerate as much as possible the development of the Southern Province, with the aim of increasing the potential exports and imports of the region which would move, via the Mtwara route, to an aggregate of 190,000 tons by 1960, including Overseas Food Corporation traffic. To implement this intention, the Government signified its willingness to undertake substantial capital expenditure on basic services such as roads, water supplies, etc., and on the provision of additional administrative and agricultural staff, marketing schemes and other incentives such as would promote higher production throughout the area. It also intended to transfer the Administrative Headquarters of the Province from Lindi to Mtwara.

(b) The Tanganyika Government and the East Africa High Commission would ensure, so far as each was responsible, that the railway was throughout used to the greatest extent practicable. This would be achieved by the construction of suitable feeder roads, the enactment of appropriate legislation for the licensing of road services, the encouragement of well-organised road transport facilities, and the adoption of an appropriate railway tariff.

(*c*) The East Africa High Commission and the Tanganyika Government, so far as each was responsible, would proceed with

(i) the extension of the railway from KM 126 to Lumesule Juu, and

(ii) the connecting road between the new inland railhead and the Masasi-Tunduru road, so that both would be ready for use by the time the Ruo-Mtwara route was first opened for traffic. The extension of the railway to Lumesule was regarded by the High Commission and the Tanganyika Governmen as the first stage of a rail route through the Songea District to Lake Nyasa.

(*d*) East Africa High Commission would do all they reasonably could to secure the recognition by the Conference Lines of Mtwara as a berth port, as soon as the facilities were ready for use.

2(*a*) In consideration of the foregoing, the representatives of the Overseas Food Corporation stated that the Corporation agreed to the completion of the port of Mtwara and the Mtwara-Ruo section of the railway line, and they welcomed the decision to extend the railway to Lumesule. The Corporation accordingly was prepared to guarantee the annual deficits in respect of interest, sinking fund, depreciation and operating costs on the port of Mtwara and the railway system, including the extension to Lumesule, to the extent of four-fifths of these deficits. The Tanganyika Government, for their part, was prepared, subject to the agreement of the Legislative Council, to meet one-fifth of these deficits.

(*b*) The representatives of the Tanganyika Government, the East Africa High Commission and the Overseas Food Corporation furthermore agreed that any annual surpluses in respect of the port and railway system, including the extension to Lumesule, should be credited to the Tanganyika Government and the Overseas Food Corporation in the same proportions as the guarantee of deficits; but such payments in the aggregate should not exceed the total payments made by them in respect of deficits.

(*c*) These arrangements were to take effect from the date of the first opening to traffic on the Mtwara route, until which time the deficits should be on capital account. These arrangements were also to be subject to review after ten years. If an extension of the railway was made beyond Lumesule, the proportion of the deficits guaranteed by each party should be subject to renegotiation.

(d) The Overseas Food Corporation also agreed that any expenditure on port equipment provided by the East Africa High Commission to secure the recognition of Mtwara as a berth port should be an addition to the capital account in respect of the port, and accordingly subject to the above arrangements for guarantee of deficits, etc.

(e) Notwithstanding the terms of their guarantees to the East African Railways and Harbours Administration, the Overseas Food Corporation would accept such tariffs, common to other users, not necessarily standard with the main East African system, as that Administration might deem necessary to obtain the maximum revenue from the port and railway facilities in the Southern Province.

(f) The East Africa High Commission agreed that, subsequent to the opening of the port of Mtwara and the Mtwara-Ruo railway, consideration should be given to the abandonment of the line from Mkwaya to Ruo, but this should be subject to the economy of that section, with particular reference to the possibility of traffic arising along it for export via Mtwara.

The Governor of Tanganyika was satisfied with the outcome of the negotiations as outlined in this statement of intentions.[142] Local considerations, had, once again, strongly influenced the outcome of somewhat involved discussions.

x. THE UNITED AFRICA COMPANY BECOMES MANAGING AGENT

On 7 November 1946 two officials of the Ministry of Food, Messrs Huntley and Hollins, had a preliminary discussion with Messrs Samuel and Faure on the nature of a possible agency agreement.[143] Mr Samuel reported that UAC would be prepared to act as Managing Agents, if requested to do so by the Ministry of Food. He assumed that the Agents would have a free hand to incur expenditure within certain global figures established for broad headings without reference to the Ministry, though any expected overrunning of the broad headings would be reported to the Ministry. Full progress reports would be made but it would not be possible to operate as a commercial organisation unless expenditure within the global figure could be made without prior agreement. It was agreed to seek Treasury approval for this general principle. It was agreed also that the agreement should continue until the statutory public Corporation that was to be established was ready to take over, after an agreed period of notice. It was agreed that the Agents would have to have a free hand in the engagement of staff generally without reference to the Ministry, though in respect of senior staff there would be prior consultation. Salaries would be paid at commercial rates. Staff would be told on engagement that there was a reasonable presumption that their services would be retained when the Agency arrangement was terminated. It was agreed that some basis should be found to allocate to the costs of the Agency a share of the total administrative expenditure of the firm undertaking it, so as to cover office space and facilities, part-time services of the staff not wholly concerned with the scheme, etc. In addition to these costs the Agents would receive a fee for their services which would be revised from time to time. At the next meeting, Mr Samuel proposed a formula according to which UAC would receive a fee made up of three parts – the first 1 per cent of the estimated all-in costs of the scheme, the second a payment per acre for the first agricultural operations on newly-cleared land, and the third a payment of $2\frac{1}{2}$ per cent of the estimated costs of all subsequent agricultural operations. But he further suggested that, if the Government wished and if after the initial period of organisation the management could be handed over to some other body, UAC would agree to charge no fee at all in the calendar year 1947. If, however, UAC was required to continue the work after 1947, the fee charged would be based on the threefold formula.[144] According to the UAC, this formula would mean a fee of £80,000 if applied to 1947 and £180,000 in 1948. This was thought to be excessive and the Treasury agreed to a counter-offer of £100,000 for all the work to 31 August 1948. However, Mr Samuel argued that such a fee bore no relation to their estimate of the value of their services while it deprived them of the credit of taking no fee for 1947. So he preferred to accept no fee to 31 August 1948, or possibly up to 31 December 1948. It was said, in reply, that HMG might not wish to accept that offer and, while it was not easy to evaluate the disadvantages to UAC in operating the scheme, it was no easier to evaluate certain advantages of the scheme to the parent organisation. These included (a) the experience gained in carrying through a pioneer scheme without risking any of their own capital, (b) the early supply of oilseeds for the firm's crushing mills and cake mills in the United Kingdom, many of which were idle for lack of raw materials, and so would be of direct financial benefit to them, and (c) the increased prosperity of East Africa was a matter of interest to the Company in many ways. After it was agreed that the Company was deeply interested in the prosperity and expansion of trade and development of Africa, the Ministry of Food officials recommended that the financial basis of the Agency should be payment in full by the Ministry of all direct and allocable indirect expenses incurred by UAC, but with no fee to represent an element of direct profit on the Agency.[145] The Minister agreed with the Chancellor of the Exchequer on this basis of remuneration.[146] It was agreed that UAC might properly use its subsidiaries, The Construction Co. Ltd (Paulings) and Messrs Gailey & Roberts Ltd, along with other unconnected companies, as sub-contractors.[147]

The Agreement between the Minister of Food and UAC was signed on 17 June 1947.[148] It provided for the efficient carrying out of the scheme in East Africa by the UAC as Agents, until a Statutory Corporation was established to take over its functions. The Agreement followed the lines discussed earlier, specifically providing for certain arrangements, including (i) the keeping of such books, records and accounts as might reasonably be required by the Minister, (ii) supplying such information and making such reports as might from time to time reasonably be required by the Minister, particularly a quarterly report 'on the progress of the actual work done in East Africa, and of the planning and preparations for subsequent development', (iii) obtaining the Minister's agreement before entering into any agreement (a) for the execution of works involving expenditure of over £25,000 in any period of twelve consecutive months, (b) under which payment was made on a 'cost-plus' basis, and (c) with Lever Brothers and Unilever Limited, Lever Brothers and Unilever NV or any companies or firms in which those companies were financially interested. The Agreement was deemed to have come into operation on 6 November 1946 and was to continue in force until 31 August 1948 unless terminated by six months' notice by either party.

XI. OVERSEAS RESOURCES DEVELOPMENT ACT, 1948: THE OVERSEAS FOOD CORPORATION AND THE COLONIAL DEVELOPMENT CORPORATION

Meanwhile, the Minister of Food invited Mr L. A. Plummer to become Chairman-designate of the Overseas Food Corporation, which was to be responsible for the project, and discussed with him and the Secretary of State, Mr Creech Jones, the structure of the Board and possible members. The Minister's first aim was, he told the Chancellor of the Exchequer, efficiency and enterprise – hence his choice of Chairman, and his acceptance of the Chairman's view that there should be six full-time working members, who would share the executive responsibility for the whole undertaking, and a number of part-time members, who would share responsibility for general policy but would normally attend only the regular Board Meetings.[149] The Chancellor felt it would be consistent with the policy adopted in similar cases, such as the New Towns Development Corporations, if the members of the Corporation, other than the Chairman, Vice-Chairman and General Manager, were salaried officers of the concern.[150] But the Minister was already committed to offer seats on the Board and so it was accepted. The Minister of Food announced the membership of the proposed OFC on 16 May 1947[151] as follows: Chairman – Mr, later Sir, Leslie A. Plummer; Vice-Chairman – Mr James McFadyen, JP; General Manager in Africa – Major-General Desmond Harrison, CB, DSO, MICE; members of the Corporation – Sir Charles Lockhart, KBE, Mr J. Rosa, OBE, Mr A. J. Wakefield, CMG; and, on a part-time basis, Mr Frank Samuel and Lord Rothschild, GM. These members, while still holding appointments in a designate capacity pending the passage of the Bill through Parliament, began selecting a nucleus organisation during the early autumn of 1947. From that time onwards, the designate members devoted an increasing proportion of their time to the affairs of the scheme. The Chairman-designate became full-time as from 1 September 1947 and others followed in quick succession.[152] In September–October 1947 the Chairman-designate and the General Manager-designate visited Tanganyika to study operations in the field. From the date of their return to London, it became increasingly the practice for the managing Agents to consult with the designated members of the Corporation, two of whom, Messrs Wakefield and Rosa, had transferred from the Managing Agency, on policy matters as they arose. The Ministry of Food encouraged this consultation, as it provided a means of ensuring continuity of policy when the Corporation was established and was able to assume control.

The previous experience of the member was as follows. Plummer was Assistant General Manager and a director of Express Newspapers Ltd. Before that he had been business manager of the *New Leader*, the *Miner* and the *Socialist Review*, and Assistant Manager of the *Daily Herald*. McFadyen was a director of the Co-operative Wholesale Society Ltd and a member of the Colonial Economic Development Council. General Harrison, a civil engineer, had been Director of Works at the War Office and before that Engineer-in-Chief, South

East Asia Command. Lockhart was Economic Adviser to the East African Governors' Conference, and had been Chairman of the East African Production and Supply Council and Chief Secretary to the East African Governors' Conference. Rosa, one of the signatories of the original report recommending the groundnuts project, was a member of the banking form of Helbert, Wagg & Co. During the war he had been Treasury representative in Syria and the Lebanon, and later a member of the Economic Division of the Colonial Office. Wakefield, another original signatory, had been Director of Agriculture in Tanganyika Territory and Inspector-General of Agriculture in the West Indies. Samuel, managing director of UAC, had been the first to propose the project. Rothschild was a biologist and a former Fellow of Trinity College, Cambridge.

By the autumn of 1947 it had become clear that the progress of the clearing work at Kongwa in Tanganyika, the site of the main operations in 1947, was far slower than had been expected and it was not proving possible to maintain an adequate force of clearing tractors in operation. By the end of October 1947, although 12,700 acres of bush had been flattened and 9750 acres windrowed, the first rooting operation had been effected on only 1086 acres, and there was considerable uncertainty about the speed with which the rooting of the remainder of the cleared area could be achieved. The proportion of unserviceable machinery was large. From the beginning of July to mid-October the average number of tractors at Kongwa was 246, of which the average number operative was only 105. Thereafter the position deteriorated sharply.[153] Moreover, evidence was accumulating of difficulties in the control of stores and the accounting arrangements. There was, therefore, at that time difficult questions of administration and policy for settlement in regard to the strengthening of the organisation at Kongwa, the recruitment of additional technical staff, and the acquisition of special types of equipment. As the situation developed, it became increasingly clear that the transfer to the Corporation should take place as soon as possible. By the beginning of 1948, when the desirability of expediting the transfer of control was generally recognised in the Ministry of Food, the Overseas Resources Development Bill had passed its Committee Stage in the House of Commons, and there was a reasonable expectation that the Bill would secure the approval of Parliament rapidly, and with little amendment. There existed a nucleus staff, recruited by the members-designate of the Corporation, as the basis from which an organisation capable of assuming full control of operations in East Africa could be rapidly established. As provided in the Agreement between the Minister and the UAC, the services of staff appointed specifically for the scheme were to become available to the Corporation when the transfer took place.

Consequently, the Minister discussed informally with the Managing Agents and the Corporation-designate the possibility of an early transfer. He requested the latter to submit a recommendation as to the earliest date, assuming the ORD Bill would be passed, that the Corporation could accept responsibility for the control of operations in East Africa, and asking that their recommendation should be made after full discussion, and preferably in agreement, with the Managing Agents.

The Corporation-designate reviewed the whole position and on 30 January 1948, with the full agreement of the Managing Agents, they recommended to the Minister that the Corporation should become generally responsible for the development of the scheme with effect from 1 March 1948, and that, with effect from 1 April 1948, they should also assume full responsibility for the management of the operations in Tanganyika. At the same time, it was reported that the Corporation-designate would continue for the time being to use the merchandising services of Unilevers as the buying agents of the Corporation's own Supply Department.[154]

On 11 February 1948 the ORD Bill received the Royal Assent.[155] The Minister on 12 February accepted the recommendation of the Corporation, made in its delegate capacity, and on 1 March 1948 the assets of the scheme were transferred from the Ministry of Food to the OFC, and on 1 April 1948 the Managing Agents relinquished to the OFC full responsibility for the management of the scheme. Sir Frank Stockdale, the Development Adviser to the Secretary of State, became full-time Deputy-Chairman of the CDC. He was appointed an unpaid part-time member of the OFC as a link between the two Corporations.[156]

The foregoing indicates the urgency felt within the Ministry of Food for setting up the OFC. However, Colonial Office officials regarded legislation for the powers the Secretary of State wanted as even more urgent than the legislation for the East African groundnuts scheme, because the scheme was in being, whereas the Colonial Office lacked power to initiate any scheme.[157] An inter-departmental meeting had been held on 30 May 1947 to consider the draft of a Bill, prepared by the Ministry, for giving joint powers to the Minister of Food and the Secretary of State to promote schemes for producing agricultural products in the Colonial Empire, and also the draft of a Bill prepared by the Colonial Office for setting up a Colonial Development

Corporation.[158] The former was designed to give the two Ministers powers to prepare schemes for developing agricultural production in the Colonies, the schemes to be made effective by Order, after approval of both Houses. The latter was intended to give the CDC extensive powers to promote production of all types of product in the Colonies without further sanction by Parliament. The proposal for a CDC was first mentioned to the Minister of Food by the Colonial Secretary in a letter of 11 April 1947. It had already been approved in general terms by the Prime Minister, but not discussed with the Chancellor of the Exchequer.[159] Each draft contained provisions under which the East African Corporation would be established. Officials of the Colonial Office argued that, if the Minister of Food proceeded to take his more limited powers, even jointly with the Secretary of State, the wider project, which provided the means of embarking upon real Colonial development in every form, would be postponed for two years, if not indefinitely. However, the officials of the Ministry of Food felt that this would transform a non-controversial into a controversial measure, possibly postponing the establishment of the OFC until after 1948. It would be better in their opinion to get the new Colonial policy accepted before introducing legislation to establish a Development Corporation, which would do the same things, and a great deal more, and do them with less Parliamentary supervision than the Ministry of Food proposed for schemes promoted under its own Bill. Finally, it was agreed that only Ministers could determine whether there was a reasonable hope of getting the wider project through Parliament in the following session. The two Ministers and their officials had in fact already discussed this without coming to a decision on 15 May 1947.[160]

Following a meeting with the Lord President, who felt both bodies would help to implement the policy he had just advocated in his paper 'Planning for Expansion',[161] the Minister of Food requested his officials to discuss further with the Colonial Office and the Treasury. As a result, two memoranda were submitted to the Cabinet. Two Corporations were proposed. The CDC was to have wider powers to develop mineral resources, improve communications, develop water power, etc., as well as to produce food and other agricultural products, such as rubber, cotton, fibres and so forth; in so far as it produced food in the Colonies, it would normally do so as a part of its plans for the general development of the Colonial Empire, whereas the OFC would be concerned primarily with production of food for export to the United Kingdom as part of the Ministry of Food's overseas procurement programme. The Minister of Food proposed that the capital ceiling of the OFC should be £50 million.[162] The Secretary of State proposed that CDC's capital should be obtained mainly by the raising of money by public issues under Treasury guarantee, with a total borrowing power of £100 million and with provision for some initial contribution direct from the Exchequer. Despite risks of loss on individual projects, CDC was to be expected to 'break even' on its whole operations over a number of years.[163] The Cabinet, subject to further discussion between the Ministers concerned and the Chancellor of the Exchequer on finance and between them and the Lord President on the socialisation aspects, approved the proposals and agreed that the necessary powers should be obtained in an ORD Bill to be introduced early in the 1947–48 Session.[164]

Inter-departmental meetings were held at the Treasury to discuss the financial aspects.[165] The Colonial Office representatives argued that £100 million was a suitable figure for the CDC because (a) it would free them from any sense of financial constriction, and would give them a target to work up to; (b) they foresaw that commitments in general over a period of five years would mop up the whole sum; and (c) they wished to avoid giving the impression that the project was being starved of money. While it was hoped that CDC would 'break even', there was no intention of it repaying its capital. In any case, the total capital turnover would be comparatively slow, say twenty years. The OFC was expected to make a profit, and to repay its capital by a combination of selling its physical assets piecemeal to Colonial Governments and of making profits on the sale of its products to the Ministry of Food. The capital turnover was expected to be much quicker than in the case of the CDC. It was agreed that (i) the figures of £100 million and £50 million for the CDC and OFC respectively should be accepted as realistic estimates, and (ii) it should be stated in the draft that the OFC would be expected to break even. The Treasury proposal that, on grounds of simplicity and flexibility, the capitalisation of the two Corporations should be by Exchequer advances was agreed. The capital was to be advanced through the responsible Minister, who would be accountable to the Public Accounts Committee. As a consequence, it was recognised that there would be need for temporary borrowing powers, the limits of which required further consideration.

The Cabinet had directed that there should be discussion also with the Lord President on the socialisation aspects of the ORD Bill. The Lord President thought it was desirable to ensure that the legislation should conform to the principles with the Socialisation Committee of the Cabinet had laid down for Public Corporations. The main questions of public policy concerned (*a*) the control of policy by Ministers and the degree of responsibility of Ministers to Parliament for the action of statutory bodies; (*b*) the appointment, tenure and salaries of members of public Boards and Corporations; (*c*) the staffing, salaries, pensions and recognition of trade unions by public bodies; (*d*) the financial controls to be exercised over public bodies by Ministers and by Parliament; (*e*) the provision of information and annual reports by public bodies to the Ministers responsible for them and to Parliament; and (*f*) the principles of compensation when existing commercial undertakings were socialised. The last did not apply in the present case and the Lord President felt that the ORD Bill conformed to the policy of the Socialisation Committee.[166]

The OFC, according to the Cabinet Paper, 'would be concerned primarily with production of food for export to the United Kingdom as part of the Ministry of Food's overseas procurement programme'.[167] However, after a discussion between Lord Trefgarne, the Chairman-designate of the CDC, and Mr Plummer, the Chairman-designate of the OFC, the Minister of Food wrote to the Secretary of State to suggest that the only area in which there was overlapping of functions was in agricultural products within the Colonial Empire, but the OFC dealt 'exclusively with schemes for the large-scale mechanised culti-vation of agricultural products on land hitherto mainly uncultivated' and so was differentiated from the CDC which would 'handle all schemes for assisting the population to develop the production of new agricultural products'.[168] However, this was not the basis on which officials had co-operated. Nor did it provide a workable definition, as there could be various degrees of mechanisation as there could of 'large-scale'. At a meeting under chairmanship of the Minister of Food and attended by the Parliamentary Under-Secretary of State for the Colonies, Mr Ivor Thomas, Lord Trefgarne asked again for a redefinition of the respective spheres of action of the two Corpo-rations.[169] Further discussion did not bring about agreement, with the result that the Prime Minister asked the Parliamentary Under-Secretary on 30 September 1947 to let him have particulars of the difficulty which had arisen over the overlapping functions between the two Corporations. He did so next day in a memorandum[170] in which both he and the Secretary of State expressed their wish, as far as the Colonial Empire was concerned, to limit the OFC to the groundnut scheme in East and Central Africa, and to operations ancillary to it. The Minister of Food criticised the argument in a further memoran-dum, which he addressed to the Prime Minister, as he wished to leave open the possibility of further schemes in the Colonial Empire.[171] The

Prime Minister circulated the two memoranda to senior Cabinet colleagues with whom he intended to discuss them. The Secretary of State for Foreign Affairs, Mr Ernest Bevin, circulated a comment, supporting the Colonial Office argument. He declared that:

> We must be careful that our plans for the development of our Colonial Dependencies cannot in any way be represented as springing solely from our own selfish interests. It is, above all, important that in their presentation there is no possible suggestion of exploitation of the Colonial populations. In either case, we may find ourselves exposed to bitter criticism in the United Nations, and be obliged to defend ourselves against quite baseless charges. We know from experience that the possibilities of misrepresentation in this field are almost endless.[172]

Meantime, the Minister and the Parliamentary Under-Secretary, now Mr D. Rees-Williams, had managed to resolve their differences. The Colonial Office recognised the objections to placing narrow limitations on the OFC by statute, while the Minister of Food recognised the political difficulties which might arise if the OFC began to operate in any Colonial territory where its activities were viewed with unjustified, though real, suspicion. Consequently, it was agreed that the Bill should provide that OFC should not engage in any activities in a Colonial territory, except at the express invitation of the Secretary of State.[173] Subsequently, at the Legislation Committee, the Minister of Food said there was a complete answer to the question whether there was need for OFC as well as CDC, because it was clear that OFC would promote one or more schemes outside the Colonial Empire which could not be carried out by CDC, coming as it did under the Secretary of State for the Colonies. The Parliamentary Under-Secretary of State agreed.[174]

The Second Reading of the Bill was opened by the Minister of Food and wound up by the Parliamentary Under-Secretary of State for the Colonies on 6 November 1947.[175] The Third Reading took place in the House of Commons on 20 January 1948.[176] As stated earlier, the Bill received the Royal Assent on 11 February 1948.

xii. PROGRESS IN EAST AFRICA, 1946–1948

Following the Minister of Food's Statement in the House of Commons on 25 November 1946, Mr Frank Samuel wrote to thank the Minister for the references to the UAC and, at the same time, to warn the Minister that it already seemed unlikely that the figure of 50,000 tons envisaged for 1948 in the Wakefield Mission's Report could be achieved, 'having regard to the time factor and the unlikelihood that the whole of the required plant will be available on time and that everything else will work exactly to schedule'.[177] There was, unfortunately, good grounds for the warning. Some still doubted both methods and the choice of crop. Thus Mr Sykes was becoming unpopular with the Managing Agents because of his view that 'suitable crops for mechanisation must be grown, rather than the application of machinery to any old crop which happens to be most needed.'[178] In addition, he warned that maximum usage of machines was being assumed, which was unlikely under African conditions with relatively unskilled labour and, for technical reasons, he advocated sunflowers instead of groundnuts.[179] However, the Managing Agents decided that 'the Combine Harvester would be a satisfactory machine with which to harvest the groundnut crop, and were satisfied that the number of combines required were being provided'.[180] But it was 'agreed not to give any more figures on the question until actual experience had been gained in East Africa'.[181] In a comment, Mr Sykes quoted two agriculturalists from East Africa, who insisted that even twenty days was too long for harvesting as the rains did not end as suddenly as in Northern Nigeria, whereas the Managing Agents were planning on a harvesting period of eighty-two days.[182] As an official minuted, it was a disturbing difference.[183]

No less disturbing was the upshot of the Managing Agents' Progress Reports Nos 8 and 9 for September and October 1947.[184] Earlier reports had included estimates of the acreage which might be planted by the end of 1947, but the September report did not, nor did it comment on the causes of the continued slow progress. The figures of acres cleared spoke for themselves. Up to the week ending 25 September 1947, the figures were, in acres: bush flattening, 12,608; windrowing, 3797; rooting, 152.[185] To the end of October 1947 the figures were in acres: bush flattening, 12,740; windrowing, 9774; rooting, 158.[186] These figures represented the total work done in preparing the land for the plough from the time clearing operations started on a substantial scale at the beginning of July, very little clearing having been done before that date. At the beginning of July, the total number of heavy tractors at Kongwa was 119, of which only 14 were operative, and all were engaged on bush flattening. At the end of October, the total number of heavy tractors at Kongwa was 303, of which 115 were operative and, of these, 81 were engaged on preparing the land for the ploughing and 31 on the training of drivers and miscellaneous operations. These totals for heavy tractors compare well with that of the Wakefield Report of 150 to clear 150,000 acres in the first year and the Special Section's estimate of 200. So the slow rate of progress was not due to the shortage of equipment, but rather to (a) the low proportion of the total tractors on the site which were operative at any one time; (b) the much slower rate per operative tractor-hour at which the land could be prepared for ploughing compared with early estimates; and (c) the operative tractors were being employed for only four or five hours per day compared with the ten-hour day postulated in the Wakefield Report. The improvement of maintenance and servicing was expected to raise the average proportion of operative tractors to tractors on the site from 43 per cent to a possible 80 per cent. The slow rate of progress per tractor-hour was more disturbing. Earlier, it was thought that each heavy tractor should clear and prepare for ploughing half an acre of heavy bush and two-thirds of an acre of light bush per hour. Windrowing was assumed to be unnecessary as there was assumed to be sufficient labour to stack and burn the debris. Also bulldozers were expected to rip out the roots of the bush at the second, if not at the first, attempt. But the considerable difficulty encountered in extracting the roots of the rhino-bush severely limited the acreage ready for ploughing.[107] The low performance in hours per day was due to the same cause as those which were holding tractors completely idle, i.e. supplies were not moving smoothly and adequate servicing facilities were not yet available.[188]

The Minister of Food held a meeting of officials and members of OFC on 11 November 1947, to review progress to October 1947. The General Manager considered that there was no valid conclusion as to future progress to be drawn from the experience of operations at Kongwa at that time, because the state of affairs obtaining there was 'the negation of organisation'. The Chairman of OFC mentioned various causes of the slow progress which were currently being rectified. These included maintenance of tractors, port congestion, road and rail links with Kongwa, unexpected rooting problems and unreliable contractors. He said that the Managing Agents expected to clear 250,000 acres by the end of 1948. The Minister thought a revision of the financial estimates was, in the circumstances, premature.[189] As a result of the meeting, the Minister directed that officials and members of the OFC should jointly consider whether there were valid grounds for revising the estimates in the original Wakefield Report, and asked his officials to prepare a progress report for submission to Parliament, with a covering note for the Cabinet. He instructed that 'the Report to

Parliament, and also the covering note to the Cabinet, must demonstrate clearly why there is at present insufficient evidence to revise in either direction the financial and other quantitative estimates contained in the original White Paper.'[190] It was a month before the Director of Costings completed his review. He concluded that:

> While there are many original estimates not yet capable of final revision, two major ones being the yield per acre and the future selling price of groundnuts, both of vital importance and at present, as far as can be seen, conservatively estimated, it is clear that, on present information, the costs of the scheme will be much greater than originally contemplated.[191]

But, after consideration by officials, it was decided that there were still too many uncertain factors to warrant the publication of revised estimates.[192] The Minister minuted that the review confirmed his opinion that 'any attempt to reassess the finance of the scheme at this moment must be worthless'[193] and proceeded to complete the draft of a paper for the Cabinet which was to accompany the draft White Paper.

The Minister reported that the progress of large-scale clearing operations in Tanganyika had been delayed by difficulties of obtaining tractors and other equipment, by problems of maintenance, and by the intractable character of the bush. The area cleared and planted for the 1948 crop would therefore be no more than 10,000 acres, as compared with the original estimate of 100,000 acres, and it would not be until 1949 that the scheme would make an appreciable contribution to the supply of oils and fats. (The 10,000 acres were further reduced to 'some 8,000–10,000 acres' in para. 7 of the White Paper at the suggestion of the Chairman of OFC – see note of 17 January 1948 by Mr F. Hollins in Ministry of Food file AG/AA/9.) As the result of the rise in world prices, the original estimates of the capital cost and annual operating cost of the scheme were likely to be exceeded by £5.7 million and £1.6 million respectively. The revenues of the scheme were also likely to be substantially above the original estimates as a result of increases in the prices of its products. The Minister restated his belief in the scheme, declaring: 'It is along the lines of this and other public schemes undertaken both by the OFC and the larger CDC that the urgent problems of the people of our Colonial and dependent territories can be solved, and at the same time our need for ample and reasonably priced primary products be met.'[194]

The Cabinet approved the draft White Paper submitted,[195] invited the Ministry of Food to consider, in consultation with the Treasury, the adequacy of the arrangements for local financial control, and directed that the operation of the scheme should be integrated with the general plan of Colonial development.[196] On the latter point, the Colonial Office did not consider that special action was required. The scheme would clearly have to be integrated in any general plan or allocation of materials for Colonial development while it was intended to link OFC with a reconstituted CEDC.[197]

When the Cabinet approved the launching of the scheme, it did so 'on the understanding that this would not involve interference with other schemes already approved'. However, in practice, Government Departments and commercial firms were helpful, although the scheme enjoyed no formal priority.[198] Indeed, there was some complaint, made in the House of Commons Standing Committee on the ORD Bill, that the scheme was obtaining more than its fair share of available supplies and facilities, for which there would inevitably be competition with existing private enterprise in the Colonies. The Secretary of State, Mr Creech Jones, admitted that in order to get the project under way 'it probably did happen that other producers were obliged to withhold their claims and that their claims were pushed a little into the background'.[199] The arrangements for the allocation of iron and steel, and for the granting of priorities for special requirements, became of increasing importance when the groundnuts scheme entered the stage of getting constructional work started in the port, railways, housing, storage and other buildings needed in connection with the scheme. On 31 March 1948, an inter-departmental meeting was held at the Treasury to consider, on the instruction of the Chancellor of the Exchequer, the steel requirements of the scheme. The Chairman, Mr F. W. Smith of the Treasury, thought that it had to be accepted that the screened requirement of the Corporation should be met. Ministers had strongly supported the scheme, public funds had been granted, and an Act of Parliament passed with the object of developing Colonial resources. Therefore, he stated, it was unthinkable that the whole project should be jeopardised by the lack of a comparatively small quantity of steel.[200] As a result, the OFC was assured of essential steel requirements for which the Ministry of Supply would negotiate direct with the suppliers.[201] East Africa thus received a preference which was never extended to West Africa, except from time to time on a purely *ad hoc* basis.

Progress had thus been slow and targets nowhere nearly reached by the end of 1947. In the Progress Reports Nos 10–11 for November–December 1947,[202] emphasis was placed on the regrouping which followed the visit of Messrs Plummer, Harrison and Faure to the area.

The Report not only confirmed the technical difficulties and their effect on the first year's progress, but it also recorded the need to switch the bulk of effort from development work to the creation of better living conditions for personnel, both European and African. The OFC decided that administrative, technical and welfare arrangements should in future be made before agricultural operations were attempted in any new development area.

The Reports of the Managing Agents were naturally not concerned to show the general effects of the scheme on the territory. The Paymaster-General, Mr H. A. Marquand, reported on his return from Africa in March 1948 that 'The initiation of the Groundnuts Scheme is already placing a considerable strain on the economy of Tanganyika, and it is an open question whether other large-scale agricultural development should be attempted for the time being.'[203] It might well be no coincidence that officials of the Colonial Office began by the end of April 1948 to wonder what were the advantages, in terms of employment and new sources of wealth, of the scheme to the local community.[204] It was thought that such a general appreciation should be obtained at the earliest possible moment.[205] The Governor, Sir William Battershill, was asked whether he could provide periodically such a general appreciation of the impact of the scheme on the economic position of the territory, and a forecast of any impending benefits, or the reverse, which the scheme was likely to bring in its train.[206] The Governor promised to report quarterly, except for any special reports that might be necessary between such reports.[207] In passing this on to the Secretariat in Dar-es-Salaam, the official mentioned an article in *The Times* of 17 June 1948, and the letter in reply by the OFC two days later, stating: 'Although the letter answers most of the points, . . . the answers have an air of unreality about them and are given from the book rather than from actual practice.' It was hoped to get the latter kind of information from the quarterly reports.[208]

Early in January 1949 the Parliamentary Under-Secretary of State, Mr Rees-Williams, spoke to the Acting Governor, Mr E. R. E. Surridge, about the matter, with the result that a report was sent on 2 March 1949.[209] It explained that the Government's information about the groundnuts scheme was mainly derived in the normal course of business when the activities of the scheme, or its repercussions, impinged on Government. Monthly meetings had recently been started with representatives of the OFC when matters of mutual interest were discussed. The Agricultural Department had little first-hand knowledge of the scheme, but visits by members of the department were being arranged at the invitation of OFC. The main source of information on matters of policy had been the OFC's monthly publication *Our World*. No other information on land utilisation and the general agricultural policy of the OFC was available.

The long-term benefits to the Government of Tanganyika derived from the Corporation's activities were regarded as:

(1) The new port and railway in the Southern Province would be a great asset to the Province and to the Territory as a whole, particularly if the mineral deposits to the south and west of Songea justified an extension of the railway to the west.

(2) The Corporation's activities would result in the opening up and development of large areas which would otherwise remain undeveloped for a long time to come, thus increasing the general prosperity of the Territory.

(3) Other industries might be established in connection with the Corporation's activities – e.g. timber and fertilisers.

(4) It was hoped that this scheme would eventually result in a new African agricultural economy on co-operative lines.

In the short term, the scheme had resulted in increased revenue in the following ways:

(1)(*a*) Customs duties on equipment, etc., directly imported by the Corporation had amounted to £160,000 to date. The figure was comparatively small because much of the material directly imported consisted of articles on the 'free' list – e.g. agricultural machinery.

(*b*) Customs duties on equipment imported by associated contractors. No figures were available.

(*c*) Licences on Corporation vehicles, amounting to about £25,000 per annum.

(*d*) Customs and Excise duties and taxes paid by employees of the Corporation and associated contractors. Again no figures were available, but the total was considerable.

(2) The activities of the Corporation had stimulated trade and had led to a greater interest in Tanganyika.

(3) The Corporation had assisted Government in various minor ways – e.g. by providing messing facilities at Mgulani Transit Camp for Government officials temporarily accommodated there.

But problems had also arisen, requiring action by the Government. These could be described under the following headings:

(1) General administration. The closer administration which the development of the groundnut areas had necessitated had entailed the opening of two new administrative stations, at Kongwa in the Central Province and at Ruponda in the Southern Province, involving the construction of offices and housing, and the diversion of staff from other duties. Mushroom villages of an insanitary type, which were the haunts of prostitutes and other undesirables, had sprung up in the vicinity of the groundnut camps and presented a problem, both to the Administration and to the native authorities in whose areas they were situated. The growth of these settlements had been stimulated by the absence of married quarters for all but a small proportion of the African employees of the scheme. Such action as was possible under the Native Authority Ordinance to control the settlements had been taken and a Development Areas (Control) Bill, designed to provide for the enforcement of public health and similar measures in specified areas, was before the Legislative Council. An Administrative Officer had been sent to Northern Rhodesia in 1948 to study the methods which had been evolved there to deal with similar problems on the Copper Belt.

(2) Maintenance of law and order. The concentration in remote areas of large numbers of European and African workers, and of large quantities of valuable stores and equipment, had attracted thieves and other miscreants from all parts of the Territory and from neighbouring territories. A police station had been opened at Kongwa and, from the records, it already appeared to be one of the busiest in the Territory. The posting of police to Urambo, Ruponda and Mtwara was proposed. The Resident Magistrate at Dodoma visited Kongwa from time to time to assist with the growing volume of judicial work, and a *Liwali* had been appointed to preside over a native court in the Kongwa minor settlement. An Auxillary Police Ordinance had been passed under which the Corporation was establishing their own police force. Government had seconded a Police Officer to assist with the training of this force.

(3) Labour. The Labour Commissioner and other officers of the Labour Department had been obliged to devote such time to the labour problems of the Corporation and their contractors. So far it had been possible for the scheme to meet its requirements of labour without undue interference with existing industries, but the position

in the Southern Province, where labour for railway construction had been scarce, gave cause for anxiety. A conference with the Corporation's representatives had recently been held for the purpose of examining the labour requirements for the future.

(4) Education. The manner in which schools established for the Corporation's African employees were to be assisted by Government would require further considerations. Preliminary discussions had taken place but no schools had been opened. As regards European education, the sudden and rapid influx of European employees with their families had meant a demand for places at Government and assisted schools, which were already full to capacity. Primary day schools had been opened by the Corporation at Urambo and Kongwa with Government assistance to the extent of the full recurrent cost. In order to ensure that the maximum number of children received a school (as opposed to a correspondence course) education, priority in the allotment of places in the Government primary boarding schools was being given to children who were not within reasonable reach of a day school. The position would be eased when the proposed new Government primary boarding school was built. The demand from Corporation employees for secondary education for their children would aggravate the problem raised by the not unreasonable decision of the Kenya Government that Tanganyika must pay the full cost of secondary education for Tanganyika children in Kenya; fees paid by parents amounted to less than half this cost. While Corporation employees would be liable for the Non-native Education tax, which had been imposed simultaneously with the establishment of the European Education Authority, the contributions of the growing number who arrived in the Territory with children already of secondary school age would be insignificant in comparison with the cost to the Authority, which would have to bear the difference between the fees and the charge made by the Kenya Government.

(5) Food supplies. As far as African labour was concerned, the diversion to the project and ancillary works meant that in 1948 for the first time African staple foodstuffs had had to be sent to the Southern Province, which had hitherto been an exporting area. The OFC had undertaken to grow sufficient grain in future for its own labour force, although this would not provide for those engaged on ancillary works or make up for the food which that labour force would otherwise have grown for sale. The growth of the European population, especially in Dar-es-Salaam and Lindi, which was

partly the result of the scheme, had resulted in shortages of milk, meat, fish and vegetables and schemes were in hand to deal with the problem.

(6) Port congestion. Efforts were being made to improve the situation, which was particularly acute at Dar-es-Salaam.

(7) Curtailment of Territorial development schemes. The super-imposition of a scheme of the size of the Groundnut Scheme on top of a programme of development already planned by the Government inevitably resulted in some dislocation of the original plan in a Territory with bad communications and a population of only seven million. For instance, limitation on the amount of cement shipped to Dar-es-Salaam meant a considerable curtailment of the Government's own building programme.

(8) Inflation. The large amount of money being spent locally by the Corporation, in a country where there was considerable expenditure on development and an inadequate supply of consumer goods, had naturally led to a certain amount of inflation, and there had been considerable rises in local prices in the areas where the Corporation was operating. Building costs, in particular, had risen enormously throughout the Territory. Yet supplies of many classes of consumer goods were increasing and price control had been suspended over a large range of imported goods because they were being sold below the maximum controlled price.

(9) Roads. A great strain was placed on many roads, which were carrying a volume of traffic for which they had never been built to stand. Both the OFC and the Public Works Department were attending to the problem.

(10) Unsuitable European employees. A number of the European employees of the Corporation and its contractors had been attracted to the Territory because of high pay offered, and had no interest in Africa or the Africans. This was bound to be the case in a venture of this type, but the fact remained that some of them were quite unsuited to living amongst a backward people, and their behaviour was likely to do considerable harm. The Corporation was, however, fully alive to the problem.

The only two really unsatisfactory repercussions of the scheme were the dislocation being caused to the Territory's own development programme, and the introduction of unsuitable types of Europeans into the territory. To some greater or lesser extent the adverse effect on the local development plans were compensated by the effects of the groundnut project itself. For the second adverse repercussion, there could be no easy or quick solution. However, the Parliamentary Under-Secretary was shocked by the revelation that the local Agricultural Department relied for their information on OFC's *Our World* and, to a lesser extent, on 'informal talk' with OFC's officers. He instructed that the Administration be brought to realise its duties in respect of land utilisation.[210] The Acting Governor was written to accordingly[211] and he explained that until recently UAC, and then OFC, had 'no real desire for proper discussions with our Agricultural Department.[212] By September 1949 it was possible to tell the Governor that the Chairman and General Manager (Agriculture) of OFC were very pleased with the arrangement established for liaison between the OFC and the Tanganyika Government, including the Agricultural Department.[213] It was at last possible for the Colonial Office officials to feel able to substantiate the argument that some thought had been used rather glibly in connection with the groundnuts scheme, namely that it was designed to be of mutual advantage to the Territory and to the United Kingdom and not simply a scheme to exploit local resources in such a way that the main benefit accrued to people outside the Colony itself.[214] Other Departments, it was added, could be left to worry over the equally important question 'whether the exploitation, in terms of capital and manpower employed in it, is really worth while'.[215] To that question much anxious thought was destined to be given soon after the OFC took over responsibility for the project.

XIII. REVIEW AND REASSESSMENT, 1948–1951

When the OFC took over executive control of the scheme on 1 April 1948, decisions had been taken, including the location of the three main production centres and the new port and railway, and action was in hand, including the purchase of equipment and the engagement of personnel, which had already settled the pattern of future development in accordance with the original plan.[216] The OFC accepted the view, expressed by the Managing Agency in their report of the first year's performance, that it should be possible to develop the original plan and thus achieve the expected results by the end of the six-year period. But reasons to doubt this view arose when, by the beginning of 1949, it became apparent that the estimates of the cost of clearing the African bush, both in Mr Samuel's original proposal and in the Wakefield Mission Report, were so faulty that there was no prospect of attaining the White Paper estimates of cleared areas within the limits of the financial resources available under the ORD Act. In the initial years, the cost of clearance per acre before experience had been gained was about ten times the original figure and, even with experience, the Board of OFC could not reduce the cost below four times the original figures in the Wakefield Mission Report. The estimate of clearing costs was even further out in Mr Samuel's proposal. While there were other miscalculations, none was of the same order of importance as this one. The Board of OFC calculated that, to carry out the original plan, would require borrowings of £67 million. The Chancellor of the Exchequer rejected this, and the Board was asked to produce a plan which limited the deficit on the East African scheme to £40–45 million.[217] The rate of expenditure was reduced for the year March 1949 to March 1950, and action was taken to end the cost-plus contracts for bush clearing. Thus, capital expenditure for the financial year beginning March 1951 was to be little more than one-third of the rate for the first quarter of 1949–50. Such drastic economies necessitated a reduction in the acreage to be cleared. The Board proposed that, by the end of 1954, twenty units, i.e. a total of 600,000 acres, should be the total cleared. This was the amount to be both cleared and under groundnuts given for 1948 in the original programme. To do so involved an extra expenditure of £13 million by 31 March 1954 over and above the expenditure of £32 million to 31 March 1950.[218] The Board argued that the alternative was to close down at once, losing the committed expenditure of around £30 million, which was committed by the date of the Board's proposal and could not then be reclaimed. The Minister of Food, Mr J. Strachey, felt that, in addition to the financial loss, the abandonment of the scheme would be a national setback for a Colonial Power and he quoted Field-Marshal Smuts and the Governors of Kenya, Sir Philip Mitchell, and Tanganyika, Sir Edward Twining, in support of this view.[219] In addition, he argued that, if the revised plan were adopted, 'the Commonwealth would have acquired a large-scale pilot project which would show whether or not, and if so, how, the large-scale mechanised developments of agriculture in undeveloped parts of the work could be undertaken.'[220] Finally, he asked: 'If we are to abandon a scheme simply because it turns out not to be a commercial proposition, in the sense that it does not pay interest in full on the capital invested, are we not denying the very reason which prompted us to undertake such large-scale investment in the first place?'

The Chancellor awaited his officials' reactions before seeing the Minister.[221] Meanwhile, the Permanent Secretary of the Ministry of Food, Sir Frank Lee, discussed with Sir Edwin Plowden and Mr E. A. Hitchman of the Central Economic Planning Staff. He stated that the

Ministry of Food had decided that there would be a loss on the profit-and-loss account, instead of the profit shown in the OFC's estimates, that the scheme could not operate successfully at a lower scale than that proposed, because it would lose its good men, and that, if the scheme continued, it should become the responsibility of the Colonial Office.[222] The Treasury favoured the writing-off of lost capital and the making of a fresh start under new management, if the scheme could not be closed down because of Imperial repercussions. In that event, it was felt that Ministerial responsibility should go over to the Colonial Office.[223] The proposal was that £19 million should be written off, the existing assets written down to £13 million, £15 million should be invested, and the scheme should then earn 3 per cent, amortising its capital over 50 years. It was thought wiser to go to only 300,000 acres, i.e. ten units, by 1951 and review the matter then. Also, it was felt that the Treasury could not justify the issue of money from the Consolidated Fund under a statute which required the Corporation to conduct its operations so as to provide interest and sinking fund, when it was obvious that that requirement could not be met. It was held that finance ought to be provided from Votes of Parliament, so that Parliament could effectively control the continuance of the operations. Colonial Office management was not favoured as economic considerations were then thought likely to become subordinated to those of welfare.[224] In reply, it was said that the Ministry was willing to accept a private review after two years, and mentioned that a Committee to bring the OFC's performance under constant and critical review was being established.[225] The reply added that 'Our experience with the Managing Agents was that we inevitably lacked the technical experience which they possessed and were forced to accept their assurances without further enquiry.'

However, the Chancellor, Sir Stafford Cripps, felt unable to agree with either the proposal to limit production to ten units of 30,000 acres each, because he felt that he lacked the material on which to make a reasoned judgement, or with the proposal concerning Vote procedure, because it was not practicable in the current Session.[226] At an inter-departmental meeting, neither the Ministry of Food nor the Colonial Office was prepared to accept the official Treasury proposals. At the same time, the Secretary of State's Agricultural Adviser, Mr G. F. Clay, and other Colonial Office experts expressed their continued misgivings over the proposals made by the Minister of Food. They still doubted whether the assumed yield of 750 lbs per acre could be achieved, and also whether it was right to concentrate on oilseeds. While they favoured a further four-year programme, it was felt that it should be on a smaller scale than proposed, with cotton, coarse grains and cattle in addition to groundnuts.[227]

The Minister of Food submitted to the Cabinet OFC's proposal for clearing 600,000 acres in the period to November 1953, at a total cost of £47 million.[228] He regarded the plan as technically feasible as the result of departmental advice. Thus the Permanent Secretary, Sir Frank Lee, had stated in his 17-page submission to the Minister; 'The broad conclusion is that, on the evidence presented to us, the Corporation's clearing programme in the period up to 1954 is not unrealistic, despite the inevitable risks involved and the high rate of clearing assumed in the later years.'[229] The Minister relied on the advice of the General Manager (Agriculture) to support the assumption of an average yield of 750 lbs per acre of both groundnuts and sunflower, but concluded that price forecasts were so uncertain that the scheme could make a surplus, or a loss, 'mainly according to the prices reached for the product'. Consequently, the scheme could not be recommended on purely financial grounds, and its future had to be determined 'by reference to wider considerations'. The Permanent Secretary had advised strongly against the Treasury proposal.[230] The Minister said that he regarded the choice as between abandonment or acceptance of the OFC proposal, as he rejected the Treasury proposal of an interim 300,000-acre scheme on the grounds of its uneconomic size and its effect on morale. In his paper to the Minister Sir Frank Lee stated:

> Clearly, however, it is impossible to consider the future of a scheme of this nature without weighing the issues, other than financial, which are involved. Our standing as an Imperial power in Africa is to a substantial extent bound up with the future of this scheme. To abandon it would be a humiliating blow to our prestige everywhere – at home, in the Colonies, in the international field. It has been acclaimed as a vast pioneering enterprise directed to the opening up of under-developed areas. As such, it forms part – indeed it may be regarded as the British contribution to – the wider plans put forward by President Truman as constituting the duty of the civilised world towards less-developed areas. It forms part of our own plans for developing the food production potential of the sterling area.

In the Cabinet paper, the Minister argued strenuously against closing down as premature, as inconsistent with the need to expand the world's food supply, and as a blow to British prestige in both Africa and the

United States. It was, therefore, on the basis of these wider considerations that he recommended the revised programme.

The Secretary of State strongly supported the recommendation, and welcomed the suggestion made by the Minister that there should be consultations between the Corporation and his agricultural advisers, hoping that that this would cover not only crop rotation and selection 'but also the general organisation of production, so that the experience which my agricultural advisers have gained of methods of mechanical cultivation can be drawn upon'.[231] He stated that liaison was satisfactory in technical agricultural matters, and in other fields, between the Government of Tanganyika and the OFC.

The Cabinet agreed that, for the reasons stated in the two Papers, there could be no question of abandoning the project and, after further discussion, accepted the proposal to clear 600,000 acres by November 1953.[232] It was expected that the Opposition would argue in the Debate of 21 November 1949 that the scheme had been initiated with undue haste, and on too grandiose a scale and that the Government had relied on unsuitable persons for the planning and administration of the scheme. In answer to the first criticism, it was held that the world food shortage made it necessary to accept abnormal risks. In reply to the second, it would be admitted that grave mistakes had, in fact, been made. The main responsibility for this lay partly with those who had prepared the original estimates and partly with the Managing Agents. Yet neither the OFC nor the Government was blameless.[233] As far as the revised plan was concerned, its merits were not, it was stated, to be judged solely by reference to its ultimate capacity to earn a profit. The possible transfer of the scheme to the Colonial Office, and the adoption of Vote procedure for financing the revised programme were not raised. The rate of interest on Exchequer advances to Public Boards, including OFC, was increased, without public notice, to $3\frac{1}{2}$ per cent as from 1 January 1950.[234] On 24 November 1949 the ORD Act, 1949 (12 and 13 Geo. 6, Ch. 65), was passed empowering the Treasury to guarantee other charges as well as interest, which was permitted under ORD Act, 1948, in respect of loans made to the OFC and CDC.

The Board of the OFC was reconstituted in December, 1949. Sir Donald Perrott (Deputy Secretary of the Ministry of Food since the beginning of 1947) was appointed Deputy Chairman in place of Mr J. McFadyen, who remained a full-time member of the Board responsible for supplies and transport. Sir Eric Coates was appointed a full-time member, with special responsibility for financial matters. (He had been Financial Adviser, War and Supply Finance, to the

Governor of India; subsequently Finance Member on the Governor-General's Council and lately Financial Adviser to the United Kingdom High Commission in Germany.) Messrs J. Rosa and A. J. Wakefield ceased to be members of the Board on the termination of their appointments by the Minister of Food. In May 1950 the new Minister of Food, Mr Maurice Webb, announced that Sir Leslie Plummer was relinquishing the Chairmanship. Sir Eric Coates became Chairman as from 1 July 1950.

It soon transpired that still all was not well with the scheme. On 11 December 1949 Mr Strachey left for Africa with the Prime Minister's instructions to deal with the situation which had been created by the action of certain executives of the OFC who had protested about a statement made by the Minister in Parliament, and who, it was reported, were threatening to resign.[235] He saw the joint General Managers in Nairobi on the night of his arrival, and at once informed them of the Government's determination to sustain its declarations of confidence in the Chairman and the reconstituted Board, and to support the Board in accepting the resignations of any member of the staff, including their own, who wished to resign. One General Manager welcomed this decision and promised to ensure that the executives concerned realised its full implications to themselves. The other was more non-committal but made no threat of resignation. Mr Strachey then turned to the narrower issue of his admittedly badly expressed statement in the House, told them what he did and did not mean, and informed them that this explanation would be made publicly in the House of Lords. They accepted his statement. During the Debate of 14 December 1949, the First Lord of the Admiralty, Viscount Hall, stated that:

> On November 21 the Minister of Food said in another place that on his visit to Africa last June he had been careful to interview privately and alone the senior members of the Executive, and to ask them their opinion and attitude, and that their replies had not borne out the allegations made by the Opposition speakers that there was a general lack of confidence in the Chairman and in the leadership of the Corporation. The Minister realises that people outside Parliament and in East Africa might have read this statement as an assertion that he had solicited a positive expression of confidence in the Board and the Chairman of the staff in East Africa. This was certainly not what the Minister wished to convey. He would not, of course, have put a direct question to the staff in the form 'Have you confidence in the Board and Chairman of the Corporation?' It

would have been quite wrong for him to do that, and I do not suppose there was any misconception in another place on this point. If there has been a misunderstanding, the Minister regrets it and will certainly be prepared to make his statement more precise. His object was to ascertain the general condition of the morale of the organisation, and he took a full note of a meeting with the executives and the Chairman collectively in which Professor Phillips expressed himself along the following lines. Although there had been a period of strain, things were settling down considerably. The men were realising that the management were not rushing ahead regardless. They were trying to think and plan. Previously people were sceptical about statements which had been made by the management. In the Southern Province people felt that the sound planning was going ahead. At Urambo the spirit was excellent – it had always been good there. There had been a general improvement at Kongwa. As the management settled down to plan with a clear consistency of purpose, morale would continue to improve. The management were agreed that it was 'works and works alone' which made morale. He thought that if the Minister could make a definite statement about continuity of employment, the improvement in morale over recent months would continue steadily. Mr Raby expressed views which are similar to those which were expressed by Professor Phillips.[236]

On reaching Kongwa two days later, the Minister met the disaffected executives together with the joint General Managers and Sir Charles Lockhart, a member of the Board of OFC. He repeated the statement he had made in Nairobi and was assured that there would be no resignations, though, by a curious coincidence, three of the four signatories of the original telegram of protest concerning his statement of 21 November were due over the next few months to leave the scheme in order to take up other appointments. In his report to the Prime Minister, Mr Strachey said that the opportunity for bringing on the crisis was provided not only by his error in the House, but also by the fact that, when the Chairman took over in January 1949 active day-to-day direction of affairs, the scheme was almost in ruins and expense had to be cut, staff reduced and those who had failed to measure up to their responsibilities had to be dismissed.[237] It was his considered view that, if Sir Leslie Plummer had not taken a grip of the situation and done all the highly unpopular things which had to be done, the scheme would have broken down during the first half of 1949.

Even so, it was difficult to understand why the hostility, which the

Chairman inevitably aroused in the spring, should have increased steadily among the group at Kongwa since he returned to the United Kingdom in June, when one would normally have expected that with his departure the feeling against him would have begun to die down. In fact, that happened in all staffs at Urambo in the Southern Province and at Kongwa itself among those who were running the scheme in the field. Mr Strachey was surprised also by the timing of the attack on Sir Leslie. It came when the whole project was under heavy political pressure, and despite the fact that the Government had decided to provide a further £18 million over the next four years and that the decision had been supported by Parliament. Mr Strachey concluded that the relatively minor grievances of some executives had been sedulously fanned up at Kongwa in order to discredit Sir Leslie Plummer to the point at which his resignation could be forced, with consequential discredit of himself, the Secretary of State, the First Lord of the Admiralty and the Lord Privy Seal, and indirectly of the Government on behalf of which they had expressed their confidence in Sir Leslie. In other words, the Minister concluded that the local disquiet was politically motivated. It was settled by his firmness, without resignations or other untoward consequences, and must be placed greatly to his credit in any appraisal of his handling of the scheme. Mr Strachey was succeeded by Mr Maurice Webb on 28 February 1950. On 24 May the new Minister announced that, in view of the change in the scope of the Corporation's activities from that assumed by all parties concerned at the time of Sir Leslie Plummer's appointment, it had been agreed that he should relinquish the Chairmanship as from 30 June 1950.[238]

By the end of March 1950 the Ministry of Food's 'Domestic Committee', which had recently been set up to keep the scheme under review, concluded 'that, in their view, the Corporation should be informed that the Ministry had noted that the long-term plan submitted in September, 1949, had already proved to be incapable of achievement and was being modified. The Ministry would consider the Corporation's revised development plan which should be submitted with the minimum of delay.'[239] The cost of clearing had again been underestimated and the average yield overestimated, the latter being reduced to the more realistic figure of 525 lbs an acre. The Board of OFC was asked 'to hasten the date by which the revised long-term plan is submitted'.[240]

The Minister held an informal meeting on 16 June 1950 with his officials, Sir Eric Coates and Sir Donald Perrott of the OFC.[241] The reconstituted Board of OFC considered that there were two tasks to tackle: (i) to get the scheme under control, and (ii) to recast the long-term plan for the scheme so that the Board could see clearly where it was going. The first task involved instilling respect for the Board following the commotion of December 1949, streamlining all the Corporation's activities, undertaking a reorganisation of the administration and a financial reorganisation. The second task facing the Board was the recasting of the long-term plan. The first problem involved was the future of Kongwa, about which a Working Party was about to begin its survey. The Chairman felt that it was premature to set up an independent Commission to enquire into the whole scheme. Such an enquiry could only be of real use if, when the long-term plan was clear, the Corporation and the Ministry were in real doubt about whether to go forward. The Board undertook to consider whether statistical data could be regularly published so that the public was better informed. Finally, the Minister favoured a visit by an all-Party delegation of Members of Parliament to visit East Africa, possibly in January 1951.

In September 1950 the Parliamentary Secretary to the Ministry of Food, Mr F. T. Willey, visited East Africa.[242] He found morale was good, partly because the unsuitable employees had left, but also because of the underlying assumption that, whatever happened, the Government would always support the scheme, although he admitted that new recruits were more realistic on this score. He was, in general, surprised how recently only that past experience had been turned to good account. Even at the time of his visit, he felt that there was still marked lack of consultation with men on the job, which suggested the need for the institution of consultative machinery. His impression of the administrative organisation was unfavourable, as it appeared too unwieldy for the kind of production – agricultural – involved. The high turnover of African labour was thought to be due to both lack of experience and lack of sympathy on the part of expatriate staff. As a result, there was insufficient drive to obtain a better utilisation of African labour. The need for a firm assessment of the scheme was thought, therefore, to be a matter of urgency and appropriate reorganisation necessary before the project could be handed over to the Colonial Office. This transfer, he maintained, was inevitable once the original objectives were seen to be unattainable and the Colonial development aspect became predominant. He concluded that:

> However rhetorically the Scheme may be spoken of, it remains today a scheme organised by the British for the British, which happens to operate in East Africa. Only by its transformation will

the Scheme have the chance of gaining public support and goodwill in Tanganyika and be recognised as an indigenous development bringing benefit not only to ourselves but also to the people of East Africa.[243]

After visiting East Africa but before writing his report, the Parliamentary Secretary read the Report of the Kongwa Working Party and stated his conviction that, while the Report was somewhat cautious, there was no alternative but to accept the recommendations made.[244] Land clearing was finished in Kongwa at the end of 1949, by which time just over 100,000 acres had been cleared, of which 70,500 acres were planted for the 1950 harvest and the remainder was either unsuitable for cultivation or used for housing, roads, soil conservation measures and the like. Yields at Kongwa were poor, partly because of the bad distribution of rainfall and, in the case of sunflower, the thick growth of convolvulus at a late stage. The OFC appointed in March 1950 a Working Party 'to recommend the long-term and short-term agricultural policies to be pursued by the Corporation in the Kongwa Region in the light of the results achieved to date and other evidence'. The Party was a well-balanced group drawn from the OFC itself, the Colonial Office, the Tanganyika Government and independent bodies, with four officials of the Tanganyika Government service as observers. Sir Charles Lockhart of the OFC was Chairman. The members were Professor J. F. V. Phillips (Chief Agricultural Adviser to the Corporation and General Manager, Agriculture), Mr G. F. Clay (Agricultural Adviser to the Secretary of State for the Colonies), Mr A. M. B. Hutt (Member for Development, Tanganyika Government), Mr J. C. Muir (Member for Agriculture, Tanganyika Government), Mr H. H. Storey, FRS (Deputy Director, East African Agricultural and Forestry Research Organisation) and Professor S. H. Frankel (Professor of Colonial Economic Affairs, Nuffield College, Oxford).

The Working Party submitted its recommendations to the Board of the Corporation on 18 August 1950. Briefly, their view was that, while the attempt to establish a viable pattern of arable agriculture for Kongwa should not be abandoned, the Corporation would be ill-advised to continue large-scale agriculture on the lines hitherto practised. It was recommended that, for the next three years, 24,000 acres should be set aside for four farms of varying sizes and cropping should be restricted to the cultivation of groundnuts and sorghum on approximately 12,000 acres each year. The balance of the cleared land, some 70,000 acres, should, it was suggested, be used for grazing store cattle. It was not felt that the long-term agricultural future of the region could be determined until the results of the three years' experience on this limited acreage were known.

The Working Party based their recommendations on a detailed study of the experience and information available about conditions at Kongwa. These, in fact, differed significantly from those described earlier by the Chief Scientific Officer, Dr A. H. Bunting, who had concluded his report of 22 February – 22 March 1947 thus:

> On grounds of accessibility, rainfall and temperature, topography and soil fertility the Mpwapwa area, i.e. the Kongwa region, stands out as being by far the best of those so far surveyed. It is evident from the vegetation and the soils that the rainfall is higher than has been supposed. It is therefore recommended that production be developed to the fullest possible extent there, possibly to 15 units.[245]

In his report, dated 31 March 1947, the Chief Scientific Officer had set out the main characteristics of the areas in a table. The rainfall and temperature complex was the main governing factor and, on that basis, he advised that 'Mpwapwa and Tabora should be developed to the fullest extent made possible by transport, with a higher priority for Mpwapwa than for Tabora because of the higher fertility levels at Mpwapwa.'[246] [It is interesting to note that, in his talk to the Parliamentary and Scientific Committee of the House of Commons on 21 March 1950, on 'The Scientific Aspects of the Groundnut Scheme', Dr Bunting stated (p. 6): 'At Kongwa where the rainfall is probably on the average rather over 20 inches annually, we have always known that conditions are marginal. The agricultural system there must therefore be based on dryland methods, involving the accumulation of moisture in soils and subsoils.' – item in Brief for OFC Debate, 18 July 1950, File 375A (F 3/2), Ministry of Food.] The problem of weeds suggests there was no adequate soil survey, while the assertion that 'the rainfall is higher than has been supposed' indicates that the evidence to the contrary had been dismissed. That such evidence had been provided both to the Wakefield Mission and the Managing Agents was stated by the former Head of the East African Meteorological Service, Mr A. Walter, who, as consultant in climatology to the Managing Agents, had pointed out in July 1947 the danger of undertaking large-scale operations in a marginal area, and the likelihood of wasting vast sums of public money if this was persisted in. He asserted that, for technical reasons, 'the vegetation could not in consequence be a guide in replacing a rainfall chart in judging the suitability of the area for groundnuts or any other economic crop.' The statement was made by Mr Walter in *The Times* on 6 October 1950, in a comment on an article in the same paper two days earlier written by Professor S. H. Frankel, a member of the Kongwa Working Party, who had alleged, *inter alia*, the lack of adequate meteorological information. Apparently, Mr Walter was dismissed from his post after nine months for reasons which were not stated.[247] According to an independent statistical examination of the available data for the Kongwa region, it was concluded by Mr H. L. Manning that 'Even from the records of no more than eleven years, it may be predicted with confidence that the Kibaya [i.e. Kongwa] area will be subject to serious risk of a crop failure from drought on the one hand and torrential rains on the other.'[248]

According to the Report of the Kongwa Working Party, other causes of failure were 'broadly summarised as being an attempt to deal with too large an acreage for the number of staff and quality of equipment available, farm units of unmanageable size, European staff lacking adequate experience, equipment deficient in quantity and not in all cases yet well adapted to its task, operation by African staff of insufficient training and with insufficient supervision'.[249]

Despite the crucial importance of economic evaluation, OFC had but one Agricultural Economist, who was assisted by a temporary colleague and a clerk. The Agricultural Economist, Mr J. F. Cameron, calculated the costs per acre, including depreciation, for the year April 1949–March 1950 on three units at Kongwa with a total acreage of 65,000. The figures were as shown in Table 5.2.[250]

The first striking point brought out in this table is the relatively minor contribution made by the mechanised operations in the total cost of production. They accounted for only 20 per cent of the total cost as compared with from 35 to 45 per cent for materials (seeds, fertilisers and bags) and for the indirect cost of European and African labour, transport and haulage, and other miscellaneous expenditure. Over-mechanisation has been generally blamed for the failure of the scheme, but this analysis of production costs casts doubt on the sufficiency of that criticism. Certainly, serious losses were caused by the maltreatment of machinery, but these were associated principally with clearing rather than with agricultural operations. The second point brought out is the extremely high cost of fertilisers and, with groundnuts, of seeds and bags. The third point is the relatively small proportional contribution to the total cost by the employment of European personnel. It came to be accepted by the Board of OFC that more effective supervision, made possible by a larger European cadre, would result in improvements in farming technique and, therefore, in crop

TABLE 5.2 Groundnuts and Sunflower: Costs of Production on three units at Kongwa, April 1949–March 1950

	Cost per acre						
Operation or item	Groundnuts				Sunflower		
	£ s. d.		£ s. d.	£ s. d.			£ s. d.
Discing, harrowing and planting	16 11				16 2		
Cultivating	8 2				4 1		
Lifting and combining	13 11				9 6		
Total mechanised operations			1 19 0 (19.7%)				1 9 9 (19.6%)
Seed	1 1 6				1 6		
Fertiliser	1 13 —			1 13 —			
Bags	1 10 —				15 —		
Miscellaneous[a]	4 3				3 —		
Total materials			4 8 9 (44.9%)				2 12 6 (34.3%)
European personnel	1 3 1			1 3 1			
African labour[b]	16 8				16 8		
Transport and haulage	1 — 4			1 — 4			
Building maintenance, etc	10 8				10 8		
Indirect expenditure			3 10 9 (35.4%)				3 10 9 (46.1%)
Total cost per acre			£9 18 6 (100%)				£7 13 — (100%)

[a] including hand labour.
[b] excludes casual labour and that part of the tractor driver's pay included with the tractor.

yields. Finally, the table brings out the fact that there were slight differences in the costs of cultivation and harvesting, and in the costs of seeds and bags, but the basic costs remained the same. This again shows that the attainment of higher crop yields was the main factor in securing more profitable production.

Differences between yields obtained on small experimental plots and yields obtained from large commercially-cultivated areas are, in fact, quite usual. Whereas the actual yield of groundnut kernels per acre harvested in 1949–50 was 184 lbs, experiments giving over three years' yields of between 900 and 1000 lb were reported by the Chief Scientific Officer. The problem was to generalise the experimental results, and this led back to the factors affecting the variation, especially climate, organisation and technique. Meanwhile, the Working Party did not feel able to recommend that the attempt to establish a pattern of agriculture suitable to the cleared area should be abandoned without further experiments on a field scale.

The Board of the OFC accepted the view that it was unwise to press on with large-scale agriculture for another season and was authorised by the Minister of Food, Mr Maurice Webb, to act on the recommendations of the Working Party in the season 1950–51. However, when the Minister reported to the Cabinet this decision to act on the recommendations, Ministers felt that to introduce cattle-rearing on a large scale at Kongwa needed further consideration.[251] Accordingly, the Working Party's Report was circulated, together with a further memorandum by the Minister of Food which stressed (i) the urgency, owing to the closeness of the planting season, and (ii) there was no intention to embark hurriedly on large-scale cattle-rearing.[252] The Minister told the Cabinet that, if no use at all was made of the land that was not to be used for arable cultivation, it would speedily revert to bush and be lost. The proposal that this acreage should be used for the fattening of store cattle was founded on experience in the rearing of African cattle in the area and would not, unlike the breeding of cattle, involve heavy capital outlay. It was regretted that the Report of the Working Party did not set out all the facts so that the public could fully appreciate the points at issue. However, as OFC's general review was due in November, the Cabinet agreed that effect should be given to the recommendations of the Working Party and that the Report be published.[253]

The Revised Long-term Plan was signed by the Chairman, Sir Eric Coates, on 15 November 1950. It had been found that the plan of November 1949 to bring a total of 600,000 acres into production by 1954, with a total capital provision of £48 million, could not be fulfilled in the time or within the capital provision. The Corporation now proposed (i) a seven-year programme of agriculture and development, with detailed agricultural plans for the years to 1954 and a review of the development side of their activities at that time; (ii) no more clearing at Kongwa or Urambo, and the further clearing proposed for the Southern Province would be effected by a slower and less costly method, partly mechanical and partly by hand labour; (iii) the total cleared in the Southern Province would be increased to about 105,000 acres by 1957, with a further 45,000 acres felled and in various stages of preparation for agriculture; and (iv) a net expenditure to 1957 of £45 million. The Corporation stated that the scheme could not be regarded as a commercial enterprise for the large-scale production of oilseeds and, therefore, could not fulfil the financial provisions of the ORD Act. A new basis was required for both operating and financing the scheme, if, indeed, the scheme was to continue. The arguments of 1949 for continuing – the Colonial development argument, the world long-term need argument and the deplorable political repercussions of abandonment argument – still held. So the Minister of Food, Mr Maurice Webb, and the Secretary of State, Mr James Griffiths, recommended to the Cabinet 'that work in East Africa should go on and that its continuance should be based on the need for a development project designed to establish the economics of bush-clearing and agriculture which, in particular will: (i) make the best use of the agricultural assets of the old scheme; (ii) make some contribution to the further development of Tanganyika; (iii) provide experience in clearing and cultivating land which may be of value to the whole Colonial Empire.'[254] As a corollary, the two Ministers recommended a transfer of responsibility for the scheme to the Colonial Office, having decided against a transfer to either the Tanganyika Government or the CDC. In the new circumstances, the Ministers agreed that the scheme should be financed by Votes of Parliament.

The Plan implied a fundamental change in outlook. The original scheme of the Wakefield Mission envisaged by 1953 an output from 3,200,000 acres of 600,000 tons of oilseeds, rising, as methods improved, to 800,000 tons. It was essentially a scheme for the large-scale production of vegetable oils for Britain, at a time when an acute shortage of fats existed and a prolonged shortage was anticipated. The revised plan would yield about 9000 tons of oil, or less than 1 per cent of Britain's annual supplies as compared with between 20 and 25 per cent in the original proposals. Clearly, the further expenditure involved in the revised scheme could not be justified on the grounds that it would provide essential supplies of fats for the United Kingdom. Nor would the simultaneous grain production from the scheme make a substantial contribution to the needs of Tanganyika, which then produced over 500,000 tons of grain annually and imported only some 12,000 tons at an annual cost of £150,000. While the existing fat supplies of the United Kingdom were reasonably satisfactory, although too low to be de-rationed, and while the Oils and Fats Division of the Ministry of Food did not expect any deterioration of supplies over the following five years, the long-term forecast was less assuring. Supplies were likely to be consumed increasingly in producing countries and the Oils and Fats Division could see no alternative new sources of supply, other than possibly 100,000 tons from South-East Asia. It was felt that, that, if the revised scheme could, over the following five years, surmount the technical and organisational difficulties on which the original scheme had foundered, it would go far to justify the heavy costs already incurred and still envisaged. Unless it could either assure that information or show that, even with the best techniques and management, the difficulties were insurmountable, both past and recommended expenditure would have been largely wasted. Consequently, given this view, the future size and nature of the operations should be based on the minimum essential for securing the essential 'know-how', rather than on the acreages which happened to be available for clearing, or on the extent which the balance of the original financial allocation could cover. Yet the size of the scheme had to be sufficient to enable large-scale operations to be conducted, as the problems of farm management and organisation and the determination of the profitability of the various farming methods were as important as the detailed study of the land-clearing and agricultural techniques. The Chief Scientific Adviser of the Ministry of Food, Dr N. C. Wright, noted:

> One omission from the revised plan is the allocation of any average to native cultivation. If, as a result of the work on the four proposed farms, it should still prove uneconomic to grow crops by mechanised methods and if, in addition, large-scale ranching should also prove uneconomic or the meat fail to find a market, the only alternative would be either to abandon the region completely (and lose the whole of the benefit of the expensive clearing) or allocate it for native settlement. An experiment based on the application of native methods of cultivation – either independently or under a scheme comparable with the Sudan Plantation Syndicate – with, of course, advice and guidance from the Corporation or the local Department of Agriculture – might weigh the balance in favour of ultimate native settlement, and would – if successful – provide encouragement to potential native settlers.[255]

The Cabinet, after discussing the memorandum on the future of the scheme, invited the Chancellor of the Exchequer, Mr Hugh Gaitskell, to confer with the two Ministers, the Chairman of the OFC and the Governor of Tanganyika on the financial implications of the proposals.[256] As the result, the Chancellor circulated a memorandum in which, in addition to complete abandonment, three alternative courses were considered. In each of these, farming would continue as planned on the land already felled at Kongwa and Urambo, and they differed only in the extent of development in the Southern Province. The latter might be (i) 105,000 acres, (ii) 60,000 acres, or (iii) as it existed, i.e. 20,000 acres. There seemed no need to go as far as (i) immediately, while (iii) would never be viable. So the choice was between (ii) and abandonment. The latter involved further expenditure, estimated to exceed the further expenditure if alternative (ii) were chosen, or £4,500,000 as against £4,380,000. The non-economic arguments for continuance on a reasonable scale turned the decision firmly towards proceeding, despite the hazardousness of the estimates. The Chancellor, with the concurrence of the Secretary of State and the Minister of Food, therefore recommended alternative (ii).[257] The Cabinet agreed. The Lord President, Mr H. Morrison, who was unable to attend the Cabinet meeting, wrote to the Prime Minister that 'On the picture we are given of the scheme and our known international economic prospects, I think on balance we would gain more credit and suffer less embarrassment from closing down the scheme as soon as we conveniently can than from refusing to face the inescapable realities.' He therefore favoured discontinuance of the scheme.[258] It was also agreed that the Minister of Food should issue a White Paper in the terms of the Chancellor's Cabinet Paper and should arrange for the drafting of the necessary legislation to amend the ORD Act.[259] It was to be the last occasion when the East African Groundnuts Scheme was a matter for Cabinet decision.

In the White Paper, *The Future of the Overseas Food Corporation*, issued later that month, the history of the scheme was reviewed, the OFC's proposals summarised and the Government's decision explained.[260] It was stated that the scheme had to be regarded henceforth solely as 'a scheme of large-scale experimental development to establish the economics of clearing and mechanised, or partly mechanised, agriculture under tropical conditions'.[261] Funds were to be available for a minimum period of seven years so that the experiment should be adequately tested.

The necessary legislation followed and on 21 March 1951 the ORD Act, 1951, received the Royal Assent.[262] The Act came into force on 1 April 1951. It transferred to the Secretary of State responsibility for the OFC, charged the OFC with the duty of investigating, formulating and carrying out of projects 'for production or processing in Colonial territories in East Africa of foodstuffs or agricultural products other than foodstuffs, and for the marketing of foodstuffs or such products'; and required the OFC so to conduct its operations that 'as soon as practicable' revenues would cover outgoings 'taking one year with another'. Additionally, the Act transferred to the Minister of Food all rights concerning the Queensland Food Corporation. Sir Eric Coates asked to be released from his appointment as Chairman of OFC. At the same time, it was announced that Sir Donald Perrott and Mr McFadyen would be leaving the Board of OFC and, with the transfer of the Corporation to East Africa, the London office would be reduced from a staff of 115 to about a dozen by mid-1951.[263] The changed circumstances of the scheme suggested that someone of practical experience of East African agricultural problems and techniques, i.e. a technical administrator, would be most appropriate and also ensure close collaboration with the local agricultural and veterinary departments.[264]

Mr, later Sir Stuart, Gillett was appointed Chairman-designate, becoming Chairman when Sir Eric Coates retired. (He had been born in 1903 and joined the Colonial Agricultural Service in Kenya in 1928, becoming Director of Agriculture in 1948. In 1955 he became Chairman of the Tanganyika Agricultural Corporation, the successor organisation to the OFC, staying until 1958 when he became London representative of the Kenya coffee industry. He retired in 1966 and died in April 1971.) With the new plan of work to be undertaken over the following six years in mind, which amounted to a large-scale version of work which had been developed for some years in Kenya for the effective application of capital and scientific research to backward areas and peasant agriculture, the Governor, Sir Philip Mitchell, unreservedly recommended Mr Gillett for the post, despite the serious loss to Kenya.[265] He had experience of large-scale financial administration as Chairman of the European Settlement Board and then in connection with the African Agricultural Betterment Fund, which was involved in projects in African areas which included clearing and settlement.

xiv. A COMMENT

The author is indebted to Professor S. H. Frankel for discussing the Kongwa Working Party Report with him on 2 July 1970; to Sir Bernard Keen, FRS, for discussing various technical aspects on 21 July 1970, and to Sir Walter Coutts for a general discussion of East African developments on 15 June 1972. The author alone is, of course, responsible for what is written below.

The Groundnut Project was the product of an unique set of circumstances. In the first place, there was the desperate nature of the oils and fats situation facing both the United Kingdom and the dependent territories in South-East Asia. The Ministry of Food was, as a result, prepared to clutch at any straw which promised a speedy contribution to supplies. In the second place, other Departments were anxious because of the considerable pressure which the United States Administration was exerting on the United Kingdom for us to help ourselves through a development of our Colonial resources. Both those who were concerned to maintain the current fats ration, and those who were required to show in Washington what we were doing to help ourselves, were wholly absorbed in the immediate short-term problem, which they conceived as immediate in the sense that even two years was too long.

Separate from, but superimposed on, this immediate issue was the longer-term problem that many others were concerned about at the same time. This arose, in part, from such legacies of war as the decimation in Europe of store cattle, and in part from concern with the general problem of world population outpacing world food supplies. This latter was an intermittently recurring fear, which at this time was compounded of world shortages, forecasts of greatly increased world populations, and the increased expectation of the less well-fed areas that diets would be improved. This longer-term need for developing supplies was often mentioned by those absorbed in the short-term situation though few, if any, seemed able to appreciate both problems, with the result that there was no common ground for policy and planning. This was the third of the set of circumstances.

In the fourth place, with the absorption in the immediate situation, there was the conviction that the scale and urgency of the problem demanded new methods of food production. The wholly misleading analogy of warfare was used by those who saw the solution in terms of a massive mechanical onslaught on virgin land. With the wars in Europe and Asia only recently ended, the appeal of this analogy, both to those using it and to those hearing it, is understandable, even though it misconceived the nature of a successful military campaign. It also, unfortunately, helped to brush aside the cautions and warnings of traditionalists in tropical agriculture, just as the cautions of those reared on horsedrawn transport might have been ignored at the time of the industrial revolution by the enthusiastic devotees of steam power.

Above all else, it was the pressure for immediate action and quick results which explains why so many ill-fated shortcuts were taken. It largely explains the failure to consider the project carefully before action was taken. Mr Strachey's decision to await a technical appraisal before any action was taken was set aside after Mr Samuel had convinced Mr Creech Jones that the next harvest would be lost if the project awaited appraisal. Mr Strachey might well have hesitated to put the project forward if he had persisted with his first decision and received the Special Section's report. But it was not to be: when that report was available, Mr Strachey dealt only with his Permanent Secretary's concern over his accountability for the project. The compromise with Mr Creech Jones meant that the project was launched and the urgency and scale meant that it passed quickly beyond recall. The scheme had come when there was no other proposal, it had come from a reliable source, it was supported by men who knew the product and by men who knew the territory in which it was to be grown. Once launched, it had to be steadily supported while it showed any likelihood of success. Mr Strachey gave it that support. By the end of 1949, evidence was overwhelming that the persistent opposition at Kongwa to the Chairman of the OFC, and through him to Ministers, was politically motivated. Mr Strachey dealt firmly and successfully with the matter, though he could not wholly repair the damage done to the scheme in the meantime.

Owing to the immediacy of the problem as it was conceived, no soil survey was undertaken before operations began. When the land was eventually cleared – and the problem and cost of clearing remained the biggest error in the scheme and the estimates – the dormant weeds germinated. Binder weed had a veritable field-day, the stems becoming as thick as one's index finger. The soil was so dry that the blades of the plough were worn and bent. It was assumed that once the bush was cleared and the new plants were rooted, they would draw up the water from the subsoil. It was a plausible hypothesis but turned out to be untrue, for water will not rise more than three feet. Experiments based on the assumption of appropriate soil and sufficiency of water therefore found no application. In the course of a debate in the House of Lords in June 1966 on Bechuanaland's food shortage and water supply, Lord Ogmore gave this account of the position:[266]

When people fly over Africa (this, unfortunately, was one of the causes of the trouble with the groundnuts scheme) they see this enormous expanse of apparent grassland; they think how wonderful this is, and how many thousands of head of cattle it would sustain. But not a bit of it. This is scrub, and it is there because it has a very long root which can get down to the calcrete layer. When that scrub is pulled off and grass is sown, the grass tends to die, because it cannot get down through the calcrete layer to the water, with the result that, having taken away the scrub (and this is what happened with the groundnuts scheme), you produce a desert. The sun beats down, there is no shade, and the result is something like a concrete runway. I visited the groundnuts scheme at the time, and this is what happened.

There was, in part, a lack of basic knowledge and, in part, lack of application – or acceptance – of what was known. While the first might be placed at the door of immediacy and possibly some of the second, not all of the second can be excused. Warnings by the Colonial Office's agricultural staff and by officials of the Government of Tanganyika were ignored. For example, the decision to go to Kongwa was taken against strong advice. While it might well have been right to place the project under the Minister of Food, his Ministry lacked the ability for technical appraisal which the Colonial Office possessed. The Managing Agents had perhaps, a freer hand, as the result, than otherwise they might have had, but Mr Sykes' repeated warnings might have been heeded if the Colonial Office had been in control. A minute written on 1 November 1949, following an inter-departmental discussion of the Minister of Food's proposals with respect to the future operations of the Overseas Food Corporation, described the views of the Colonial Office thus:[267]

The Colonial Office brought along several of their agricultural experts, including Mr Clay, their Chief Agricultural Adviser. These experts had grave misgivings about the present proposals of the Corporation. They doubted, as they have in the past, whether the assumed yield of 750 lbs per acre can be achieved. They criticised the way in which, in the past, the Corporation have failed to consult agricultural experts either in the Colonial Office or in Tanganyika. They also doubted whether it was right to go on basing plans mainly on the production of oilseeds. They thought that the Corporation should be allowed to go ahead for another four years, but thought that development during the period should be on a smaller scale than the 600,000 acras proposed by the Corporation. At one stage it looked as though they thought 300,000 acres would be enough. Development on this scale for four years would not be markedly different from the sort of thing we have in mind over two years. These experts thought that there ought to be drastic modifications in the agricultural plans, e.g. oilseeds should be given less prominence and at least one-third of the area cultivated should be devoted to cotton and another one-third to coarse grains. Proper arrangements should also be made for rearing cattle during the fallow periods when land is under grass. They thought that a drastic modification of this kind might give a better chance of showing a definite operational profit, but in their view it would take at least four years to try out a new plan of this type. Only then would it really be fair and reasonable to decide the future of the scheme, and whether it could fully pay its way after the appropriate writing down of capital in the light of firm data about clearing costs, etc., etc. Although I did not, of course, commit myself to anything of this kind, I must confess that I was rather attracted.

It was concluded from the evidence that, if heeded, the advisers in the Colonial Office would have proposed a far less ambitious and much more tentative scheme than the one adopted. Sir John Winnifrith told the author that he doubted whether, in the circumstances of the time, they would have been heeded. While the Colonial Office was still the responsible department, their advice was brushed aside by the political heads of the Colonial Office, the Ministry of Food and the Treasury. He feared that the Ministry of Food might well have been still more irresponsible in pressing the scheme if the Colonial Office had remained the responsible department. In his opinion, all Ministers were besotted with the scheme at the time.

In this context, it is well to recall the conclusions of Dr E. E. Bailey as given in his retrospective Note of 6 October 1949.[268] They were as follows:

If anyone is minded to draw lessons from our experience in this field, I feel that the following lessons cannot be ignored.

In the first place, extreme Ministerial pressure on officials who are charged with forming objective judgments is a bad thing and may lead to disastrous results.

In the second place, the Private Office channel of communication should be used with great discretion and should never be allowed to cut across the Civil Service channel or the Civil Service chain of reporting and responsibility.

Finally, objective judgment by officials is difficult, if not impossible, in the face of conflicting Ministerial decision in the same field.

In Volume 4, Chapter 4, the second and final phase, covering the period 1951–64, is discussed. The story is quite different. The scale was reduced to manageable proportions. Immediacy was replaced by an attempt to provide a viable pattern for African agricultural development. There were revisions and setbacks, the latter causing anxiety, in particular in the Treasury, which was, quite understandably, sceptical and exercised. The project was brought to a successful conclusion and taken over gladly by the Government of Tanganyika. Apart from avoiding the impossible target of quick crops, the project differed in phase two from the situation in phase one by having, in the person of Sir Stuart Gillett, one of the best agriculturalists that the Colonial Agricultural Service, which can rightly claim a high standard for its officers, ever produced. He had the vision to see what would be viable, the ability to sort out smoothly matters of administration, profound knowledge of African agriculture and of Africans themselves, together with careful attention to detail in execution. He made a superb contribution, as the Secretary of State's advisory staff came to recognise. Unfortunately, there is reason to doubt whether other territories derived as much benefit from his contribution as they might have.

When, at the end of 1950, the Secretary of State and the Minister of Food jointly proposed in CP(50) 289 that the project be converted into one for the large-scale experimental development to establish the economics of clearing and mechanised, or partly mechanised, agriculture under tropical conditions, some doubted whether such valuable knowledge and experience, over and above the experience already gained, would be obtained as to provide a worthwhile dividend for the benefit of other areas.[269] It was a fair question. Apparently, no action was taken to monitor, evaluate and assess the Tanganyika scheme as it developed under Sir Stuart Gillett's guidance. That was a serious shortcoming of the arrangements. It was not unique, however.

When the Colonial Development Corporation was about to consider in 1953 whether it should withdraw from the Niger Agricultural Project, near Mokwa, Nigeria, the Resident at Niger, Mr M. V. Backhouse, prepared a brief survey of some of the achievements and some of the mistakes that had occurred since the Project was started in 1950.[270] The Project arose from the recommendations of the West African Oilseeds Mission of 1947, which reported that two areas in Nigeria appeared to offer possibilities for large-scale mechanised production of groundnuts, namely an area in Bornu Province, centred on Damaturu, and an area in Niger Province, in the neighbourhood of Kontagora. After a survey of the two areas, the Government chose the latter as the more promising, mainly because of its better water supplies, higher rainfall and easier evacuation problem. The CDC was invited to participate in a scheme of development with the following objects: (i) an increase in cereal and oilseed production for Nigerian markets and for export; (ii) the settlement in an unpopulated area of new village communities in which collective mechanised farming could be combined with local agricultural skill and experience; and (iii) the formulation of a new pattern of farming which, if successful, could be extended to cover the whole of the 2300 square miles of cultivable land in the area, and could be applied to other parts of the country as well. The form of project finally adopted was modelled largely on the successful crop-sharing undertakings which were evolved in the Sudan for cotton growing. According to Mr Backhouse, while much was learnt from the Gezira Cotton Scheme on the administrative side, it had not learnt

> the paramount lesson that success can only come gradually. The Gezira scheme took over fifty years to reach fruition in a million acres and, in its initial stages, moderate targets were often being reduced in scope. From the disastrous operations of the Overseas Food Corporation a great deal was learnt, but not enough; it was still felt that nature might be bustled a bit.[271]

He went on to say that

> some other mistakes have been made by the Management such as those partially responsible for the failure of the groundnut crop in 1952, namely the use of bad seed, which germinated unevenly, and the failure of the tractor maintenance programme at a critical moment, which involved late preparation of the land and, as a fatal result, late planting.[272]

The dividend would have been appreciable if knowledge gained, often at high price, in one territory had been available as a matter of routine elsewhere in the Colonial Empire. It was a matter which, as seen earlier, the advisory staff of the D and W Organisation in Barbados was anxious to handle but they found it difficult to proceed without some *locus standi* in the territories they serviced. In East Africa, Governors were generally unaware of what was taking place in West Africa or in French Africa. To return to groundnuts, it is most unfortunate that phase one became notorious because of its failure, while phase two remained largely unknown because its success was local. For neither phase were the technical aspects evaluated and made known.

SOURCES

1. File 19612/4/1, Part I, Economic 1947 (CO 852/912), item 94A, letter of 27 Mar 1947 from Mr R. W. R. Miller to Sir Frank Engledow.

2. File 19612/11/1, Part I, Economic 1946 (CO 852/603), item 1, letter of 28 Mar 1946, enclosing a copy of the project.

3. Ministry of Food file AG/AA/8A, minute of 29 Mar 1946 by Mr G. R. P. Wall.

4. File 19612/4/1, Economic 1946, Part I (CO 852/603), item 4, letter of 28 Mar 1946 from Sir Frank Tribe, Ministry of Food, to Sir George Gater, Colonial Office.

5. Ibid., minute of 29 Mar 1946 by Mr A. B. Cohen.

6. Ministry of Food file AG/AA/8A, item 5, letter of 28 Mar 1946 from Mr Jasper W. Knight to Sir Frank Tribe.

7. File 19612/4/1, Economic, Part I, 1946 (CO 852/603), minute of 2 Apr 1946 by Mr E. V. Rochfort Rae.

8. Ibid., minute of 4 Apr 1946 by Mr G. M. Roddan.

9. Ibid., item 17, letter of 1 May 1946 from Mr F. Samuel to Mr S. Caine.

10. Ministry of Food file A/445, p. 4, 'Report on the OFC's East African Groundnut Scheme' by Dr (later Sir) Norman C. Wright, dated Nov 1950.

11. File 19612/4/1, Economic 1946, Part I (CO 852/603), item 54.

12. Ministry of Food file AG/AA/8A, minute 10 of 8 Apr 1946 by Sir Frank Tribe.

13. Ministry of Food file AG/AA/1, item 6A, Note of an inter-departmental meeting on 5 Apr 1946.

14. File 19612/4/1, Economic 1946, Part I (CO 852/603), item 15, letter of 25 Apr 1946 from Mr A. B. Cohen to Mr G. H. C. Amos pointed out that the Note did not sufficiently bring out the Colonial Office view that there were a number of knotty technical problems requiring investigation on the spot.

15. Ibid., item 7, letter of 5 Apr 1946 from Mr S. Caine to Sir William Battershill.

16. WFS(46) 01, 10 Apr 1946.

17. WFS 10(46) item 7, 16 Apr 1946.

18. File 19612/4/1, Economic 1946, Part I (CO 852/603), item 32, letter of 27 May 1946 by Mr W. L. Gorell Barnes.

19. Ibid., item 16, telegram No. 379 of 24 Apr 1946.

20. Ibid., item 19, letter of 23 Apr 1946 from the Governor to Mr S. Caine.

21. Ministry of Food file AG/AA/8A, item 20, letter of 13 May 1946 from Sir Frank Tribe to Mr S. Caine.

22. Ibid., minute of 23 May 1946 by Mr G. R. P. Wall.

23. File 19612/4/1, Economic 1946, Part I (CO 852/603), item 69, telegram no. 792 of 15 Aug 1946.

24. Ibid., item 70, telegram no. 571 of 17 Aug 1946.

25. Ibid., item 76, Note of meeting in Mr S. Caine's room on 4 Sep 1946 by Mr W. F. Dawson.

26. *A Plan for the Mechanised Production of Groundnuts in East and Central Africa* (Cmd 7030, Feb 1947).

27. Ibid., item 81, letter of 26 Sep 1946 from Mr A. J. Wakefield to Mr S. Caine.

28. Ibid., item 111, minute of 11 Oct 1946.

29. Ibid., item 94, note of a Meeting held on 1 Oct 1946 for the initial discussion of the Report.

30. Ibid., item 104, note on the Discussions of the Report of the Groundnut Mission of 1 Oct 1946.

31. Ibid., item 105, minute of 7 Oct 1946 by Mr J. B. Williams.

32. Ministry of Food file AG/AA/1, item 10, note of 2 Oct 1946 by Mr E. Roll.

33. Ibid., item 135, note of 24 Oct 1946 by Mr J. Rosa.

34. Ibid., minute of 4 Oct 1946 by Mr J. W. Knight.

35. File 19612/4/1, Economic 1946, Part I (CO 852/603), item 112, letter of 15 Oct 1946 from the Secretary of State to the Minister of Food.

36. Ministry of Food file AG/AA/8A, minute of 29 Mar 1946 by Mr G. R. P. Wall.

37. File 19612/4/1, Economic 1946, Part I (CO 852/603), minute of 25 Oct 1946 by Mr S. Caine.

38. Ministry of Food file AG/AA/7, item 15, draft letter for the Minister to send to the Secretary of State.

39. File 19612/4/1, Economic 1946, Part I (CO 852/603), minute of 26 Oct 1946 by Mr S. Caine.

40. Ministry of Food file AG/AA/1, item 22.

41. Ibid., item 39, note of 13 Nov 1946 by Mr F. Hollins.

42. Ibid., item 28, paper of 17 Oct 1946 by Mr A. J. Wakefield (also item 13 in file AG/AA/7).

43. Ibid., item 29, para. 9.

44. Ministry of Food file A/SO37/4, items 3 and 4 of 25 and 29 Oct 1946 by Dr E. E. Bailey.

45. CP(46) 402, 29 Oct 1946.

46. Ministry of Food file AG/A/8, Part II, item 17, Note of an interview with the Chancellor on 29 Oct 1946.

47. Office of the Minister of Reconstruction file 1731/15, item 2, Memorandum of 30 Oct 1946 to the Lord President by Mr P. Chantler.

48. CM 93(46) item 6, 31 Oct 1946.

49. Ministry of Food file AG/AA/7, item 17, Note of 24 Oct 1946 by Mr A. E. Feavearyear.

50. Idem.

51. Ministry of Food file AG/AB/1, for progress reports for the period 4 Nov 1946 to 16 Jan 1947.

52. Ministry of Food file EAG I, 5 Dec 1946.

53. Idem, Appendix C.

54. Idem, Appendix D.

55. Idem, Appendix H.

56. File 19612/4/1, Economic 1946, Part I (CO 852/603), item 153, letter of 2 Nov 1946 by the Permanent Secretary of the Ministry of Food, Sir P. Liesching to Sir J. G. Lang of the Admiralty and other Permanent Secretaries.

57. MAF 85/589, note of 6 Oct 1949 by Dr E. E. Bailey.

58. Ministry of Food file A/SO37/4, draft joint minute of 16 Dec 1946.

59. Idem, handwritten marginal note by Dr E. E. Bailey.

60. MAF 85/589, minute of 20 Dec 1946.

61. Ibid., minute of 13 Jan 1947 by Mr J. Strachey.

62. Cmd 7030, para. 32.

63. Pamphlet No. 41, Department of Agriculture, Tanganyika Territory, 1945.

64. *The Groundnut Affair* by Alan Wood (The Bodley Head, London, 1950) p. 37.

65. Ministry of Food file AG/AA/1, item 28.

66. Colonial No. 224, p. 21. The author is grateful to Sir Leslie Monson, a member of the Mission, for telling him this on 3 Aug 1970.

67. File 19612/4/1, Economic 1946, Part I (CO 852/603), item 10, letter of 2 Apr 1946 by Mr G. L. M. Clausen to Lt-Col Liddle.

68. Ibid., minute of 30 Apr 1946 by Sir Harold Tempany.

69. Ministry of Food file AG/AA/7, minute of 2 Oct 1946 by Mr G. H. C. Amos.

70. CP(47) 169, 2 June 1947.

71. CM 52(47) item 2, 5 June 1947.

72. Ministry of Food file AG/AA/8, Part II, item 19, letter of 16 Dec 1946 from the Minister of Food to the Secretary of State for War.

73. Ministry of Food file AG/AO/11, item 1.

74. Ministry of Food file AG/AA/8, Part II, item 24.

75. *The Groundnut Affair* by Alan Wood, p. 93.

76. File 19612/4/1, Economic 1946, Part II (CO 852/603), item 166, report of 2 Nov 1946 from the Governor to Mr S. Caine.

77. Ibid., item 151, telegram No. 1065 of 4 Nov 1946 from the Governor to the Secretary of State.

78. Ibid., item 180A, telegram No. 028 of 25 Nov 1946 from the Secretary of State to the Governor, Tanganyika Territory.

79. Ibid., item 188, telegram No. 1167 of 29 Nov 1946 from the Governor, Tanganyika Territory, to the Secretary of State.

80. Ministry of Food file AG/AB/1, item 1, meeting of 4 Nov 1946.

81. Ministry of Food file AG/AK/3, item 8, note of 5 Nov 1946 by Mr John Rosa for Mr E. Melville, Colonial Office.

82. Ibid., item 23, Savingram of 4 Dec 1946 from British Food Mission, Washington, to Special Section.

83. Ibid., item 24, Savingram of 6 Dec 1946 from BFM to Special Section.

84. Ibid., item 33, report of a visit to the USA by Messrs D. L. Martin and J. V. Wilson.

85. Ministry of Food file AG/AL/2, item 1, cable of 13 Feb 1947 from the Ministry of Food to the BFM, Washington.

86. Ibid., item 9/B, letter of 18 Mar 1947 from the Secretary of Agriculture to Major-General Philip B. Fleming, Temporary Controls Administrator, Office of Emergency Management.

87. Ibid., item 4, letter of 19 Feb 1947 from Mr F. Hollins to Mr W. A. Faure, UAC.

88. Ibid., item 6, letter of 27 Feb 1947 from Mr Lionel T. Scott, UAC, to Mr C. F. Huntley.

89. Ibid., item 12, letter of 10 Apr 1947 from Mr J. Goss, UAC, to Mr G. H. C. Amos.

90. Ministry of Food file Ag/AA/8, Part II, item 10, letter of 24 Oct 1946 from Mr Noel Sabine, Head of Information Department, Colonial Office, to Mr R. Wentworth.

91. H. of C. Deb., Vol. 430, col. 1262, 25 Nov 1946.

92. Ibid., col 1264.

93. CP(47) 4, 4 Jan 1947.

94. Idem, para. 2.

95. File 19612/4/1, Economic 1947, Part I (CO 852/912), item 3A, note of 7 Jan 1947 by Mr J. Rosa.

96. Idem.

97. CP(47) 10, 4 Jan 1947.

98. Idem, para. 4.

99. Ministry of Food file AG/AA/4, minute of 20 Dec 1946 by Mr F. Hollins.

100. File 19612/4/1, Economic 1947, Part I (CO 852/912), Item 3, minute by Mr J. Rosa.

101. File of the Office of the Minister for Reconstruction 1731/15, item 9, brief of 11 Jan 1947 by Mr E. M. Nicholson for the Lord President.

102. CM 5(47), item 3, 13 Jan 1947.

103. *A Plan for the Mechanized Production of Groundnuts in East and Central Africa*, Cmd 7030, Feb 1947.

104. CP(47) 4, 4 Jan 1947.

105. Ministry of Food file AG/AC/1, items 6, 7, 8 and 11; questions are in Telegrams Nos 760 and 761 of 2 Nov 1946 and answers in Telegrams Nos 1065 and 1066 of 4 Nov 1946.

106. Ministry of Food file AG/AE/4, item 4, letter of 29 Sep 1949.

107. Ibid., item 47, 10 Feb 1950.

108. Ibid., items 13 and 15, telegram No. 815 of 20 Nov 1946 from the Secretary of State to the Governor, Tanganyika Territory, and telegram No. 1133 of 22 Nov 1946 from the Governor, Tanganyika Territory.

109. File 19612/4/1, Part I Economic 1947 (CO 852/912), item 52, letter of 3 Mar 1947 from Mr B. L. Monson to Mr D. R. Serpell, Treasury.

110. Ibid.

111. Treasury file S 53997/3, Interim Report of 12 Mar 1947 to the Chancellor on the Question of the Contribution by the Tanganyika Government towards the Capital Costs of the Groundnut Project by Mr W. H. Fisher, pp. 20–2.

112. Ibid., minute of 18 Mar 1947.

113. Ibid., minute of 28 Apr 1947 by Mr W. H. Fisher.

114. Ibid., minute of 28 Apr 1947 by Mr D. R. Serpell.

115. Ministry of Food file AG/AC/1, item 23, letter of 30 Apr 1947 from Mr W. H. Fisher to Mr C. F. Huntley.

116. File 19612/4/1, Economic 1947, Part I (CO 852/912), item 91, letter of 2 May 1947 from Mr D. R. Serpell to Mr W. B. L. Monson.

117. Ibid., minute of 9 May 1947 by Mr A. B. Cohen.

118. Ibid., item 93, letter of 28 May 1947 from Mr W. B. L. Monson to Mr D. R. Serpell.

119. Ibid., item 103, letter of 29 May 1947 from Mr C. F. Huntley, Ministry of Food, to Mr D. R. Serpell, Treasury.

120. Treasury file S 53997/3, note of 4 Mar 1947, by Mr D. R. Serpell on the letter of 3 Mar from Mr W. B. L. Monson.

121. File 19612/4/1, Economic 1947, Part I (CO 852/912), item 104, letter of 17 June 1947 from Mr L. M. Helsby to Mr W. B. L. Monson.

122. Ibid., items 129–35, despatch No. 203 of 26 Sep 1947 from the Secretary of State to the Governor, Tanganyika Territory.

123. Ibid., item 128, letter (Personal and Confidential) of 26 Sep 1947 from Mr A. B. Cohen to the Governor.

124. File 19612/4/1, Economic 1948 (CO 852/913), item 7, letter (Confidential No. 16765/39) of 28 Jan 1948 from the Governor to Mr A. B. Cohen.

125. Ibid., minute of 9 Feb 1948 by Sir Sydney Caine.

126. File 19612/4/1, Economic 1947, Part II (CO 852/912), minute of 3 Dec 1947 by Mr W. F. Dawson.

127. Ministry of Food file AG/AC/1, minute of 13 Feb 1948 by Mr G. H. C. Amos.

128. File 19612/4/1, Economic 1948 (CO 852/913), item 8, letter of 9 Feb 1948 from Sir Sydney Caine to Mr J. Crombie, Treasury.

129. Treasury file AF 77/289/05, minute of 4 Aug 1948 by Mr A. Mackay.

130. File 19612/4/1, Economic 1948 (CO 852/913), item 42, letter of 12 Oct 1948 from Mr A. B. Cohen to Mr E. R. E. Surridge, OAG, Tanganyika.

131. Cmd 7030, paras 10 and 107.

132. *Report of a Mission to investigate and make recommendations on the suitability of certain sites for the construction of a deep water port required primarily for the shipment of groundnuts to be grown in the Southern Province of Tanganyika Territory*, by P. E. Millbourn, N. Willcock and O. Hardie (The Government Printer, Dar-es-Salaam, 1947).

133. Ministry of Food file AG/AC/1, item 49 of 12 Apr 1948. EARHA reported that expenditure in Southern Province on railways and ports was estimated at £4,650,000, the whole of which would be met by the Transport Administration. Expenditure on Kongwa Branch line was £175,000. Proportion of general expenditure on rolling stock of central line and harbour improvements in Dar-es-Salaam due to estimated requirements of OFC was £1,350,000 out of a total of £2,400,000 – Telegram No. 86 of 3 Dec 1949 from EARHA to Ministry of Food – item 85 in Ag/AC/1.

134. Ibid., item 114A, Confidential Despatch No. 65 of 25 July 1950 from Sir E. F. Twining, Chairman, East African High Commission, to the Secretary of State, Mr J. Griffiths.

135. Ibid., item 122, meeting of 17 Aug 1950 at the Colonial Office, referred to in top Secret Telegram No. 463 of 18 Aug 1950 from the Secretary of State to the Governor, Tanganyika.

136. Ibid., item 123, Top Secret Telegram No. 51 of 18 Aug 1950 from Secretary of State to Governor, Tanganyika Territory.

137. Ministry of Food file AG/AC/1, item 126, Top Secret Telegram No. 474 of 21 Aug 1950 from Governor, Tanganyika Territory, to the Secretary of State.

138. Ibid., item 162.

139. Ibid., item 145.

140. Ibid., items 149, 151, 152 and 154, letter of 18 Sep 1950 to Sir Eric Coates, Chairman of OFC, and letters of 20 and 28 Sep 1950 from Sir Eric Coates.

141. Ibid., item 163A, Secret Telegram No. 649 of 11 Nov 1950 from the Secretary of State to the Governor, Tanganyika Territory.

142. Ibid., item 163, Secret Telegram No. 645 of 13 Nov 1950 from the Governor, Tanganyika Territory, to the Secretary of State.

143. Ministry of Food file AG/AE/1, item 3 and minutes 1 and 2 of 9 and 11 Nov 1946 respectively.

144. Ibid., item 12, Notes on Management Agency Agreement by Mr Samuel. On 11 Dec 1946 UAC was authorised to inaugurate the project so that there would be no delay pending the finalising of the Agreement. A limit of £250,000 was placed on commitments. See letter of 11 Dec 1946 from Mr F. Hollins to the Managing Director of UAC – item 17A in ibid. At first the restriction was regarded as unacceptable by UAC but when it was explained as an interim matter and the Ministry appreciated 'the necessity for the Managing Agents to have the widest possible authority to take action without prior reference in the carrying out of this scheme' it was accepted – see items 19/1, 19 and 20 in ibid.

145. Ibid., minute of 19 Dec 1946 by Mr F. Hollins.

146. Ibid., minute of 13 Jan 1947 by the Minister of Food, Mr J. Strachey.

147. Ibid., item 22, letter of 10 Jan 1947 from Mr W. H. Fisher, Treasury, to Mr C. F. Huntley, Ministry of Food.

148. Ibid., item 85A.

149. Ministry of Food file AG/AQ/3, Part I, item 14, letter of 30 Apr 1947 from the Minister of Food to the Chancellor of the Exchequer.

150. Ibid., item 15, letter of 5 May 1947 from the Chancellor of the Exchequer to the Minister of Food.

151. H. of C. Deb., Vol. 437, cols 1881–4, 16 May 1947.

152. Ministry of Food file AG/AQ/3, Part I, item 15. The Chancellor of the Exchequer had agreed in his letter of 5 May 1947 that members-designate could be paid until the Corporation was set up under sub-head J. 2 of the Ministry of Food Vote. Mr McFadyen joined on a full-time basis on 1 Jan 1948; Sir Charles Lockhart on 1 Dec; Mr Rosa on 1 Oct; Mr Wakefield on 1 Jan. See letter of 13 Jan 1948 from Mr J. Rosa to Mr F. Hollins – item 31 in ibid.

153. Ministry of Food file AG/AQ/14, item 22A, note of 4 May 1948 by the Overseas Production Division, Ministry of Food.

154. Ministry of Food file AG/AQ/3,Part I, item 42A, notes of a Conference between Mr J. McFadyen and Messrs Samuel and Faure at Unilever House on 28 Jan 1948, and letter of 30 Jan 1948 from Mr J. McFadyen to the Minister of Food – item 52A in ibid.

155. 11 and 12 Geo. 6, Ch. 15, Overseas Resources Development Act, 1948.

156. Ibid., item 58.

157. Ministry of Food file AG/AD/1 – minute of a meeting on 9 May 1947 between officials by Mr F. Hollins dated 12 May 1947.

158. Ministry of Food file AG/AB/4, item 6, note of a meeting at the Ministry of Food on 30 May 1947, Sir Percivale Liesching in the chair.

159. Ministry of Food file AG/DA/1, item 11: a note on the proposal to form a CDC was sent by the Colonial Secretary to the Chancellor and the Minister of Food on 28 Apr 1947 – item 15A in ibid.

160. Ibid., item 23.

161. File of the Office of the Minister of Reconstruction 1731/15, item 28, note of 9 June 1947 from Mr E. M. Nicholson to the Lord President.

162. CP(47) 176, 8 June 1947.

163. CP(47) 175, 6 June 1947.

164. CM 53(47) item 5, 10 June 1947.

165. Ministry of Food file AG/DA/1, item 71 and 87, notes of the discussions of 17 and 25 June 1947, Mr Crombie of the Treasury in the chair.

166. Ibid., item 80, brief on 19 June 1947 by Mr F. Hollins for Minister of Food's meeting with the Lord President and minute of 20 June 1947 by Sir Herbert Broadley.

167. CP(47) 176.

168. Ibid., item 125, letter of 23 Sep 1947 from the Minister of Food to the Secretary of State.

169. Ibid., item 144, note of a meeting held on 25 Sep 1947.

170. Cabinet Office file 6/15/24, Part I, item 3, 1 Oct 1947.

171. Ibid., item 3, 6 Oct 1947, ref. PM 47/22.

172. Ibid., item 3, ref. PM 47/139.

173. Ibid., item 4A, minute of 16 Oct 1947 from Mr John Strachey and Mr D. R. Rees-Williams to the Prime Minister.

174. HPC 21(47) item 5, 21 Oct 1947.

175. H. of C. Deb., Vol. 443, cols 2018–124, 6 Nov 1947.

176. H. of C. Deb., Vol. 446, cols 63–156, 20 Jan 1948.

177. Ministry of Food file AG/AD/5, item 15, letter of 26 Nov 1946 from Mr Frank Samuel to the Minister of Food.

178. Ministry of Food file AG/AA/8, Part A, item 9, letter of 26 July 1947 from Mr Frank Sykes to Mr Frank Hollins.

179. Ibid., item 12, letter of 30 July 1947 from Mr Frank Sykes to Mr Frank Hollins.

180. Ibid., item 17A, minutes of a meeting held on 20 Aug 1947 at Unilever House.

181. Idem.

182. Ibid., item 20, letter of 16 Oct 1947 from Mr Frank Sykes to Mr Frank Hollins.

183. Ibid., minute of 21 Oct 1947 by Mr F. Hollins.

184. Ministry of Food file AG/AB/3, items 8 and 9.

185. Ibid., item 8, p. 1.

186. Ibid., item 9, p. 19.

187. Ministry of Food file AG/AA/9, minute of 27 Oct 1947 by Mr F. Hollins.

188. Ministry of Food file AG/AH/21, minute of 4 Nov 1947 by Mr C. F. Huntley.

189. Ministry of Food file AG/AA/9, item 14, note on a meeting held on 11 Nov 1947.

190. Ibid., minute of 17 Nov 1947 by the Minister.

191. Ministry of Food file AG/AH/21, item 11, report by Director of Costings, Mr J. A. Dyson, to Under-Secretary (Finance), Dr E. E. Bailey, 17 Dec 1947, para. 58.

192. Ministry of Food file AG/AA/9, minute of 29 Dec 1947 from Sir Herbert Broadley to Mr E. S. Bishop, the Minister's Private Secretary.

193. Ministry of Food file AG/AH/21, minute 15 (undated) of Dec 1947 from the Minister to the Under-Secretary (Finance).

194. CP(48) 18, 14 Jan 1948.

195. Cmd 7314 of January 1948: *East African Groundnuts Scheme–Review of Progress to the end of November 1947*.

196. CM 5(48) item 4, 19 Jan 1948.

197. File 19612/4/1, Economic 1947–48, Secret Annexe, minutes of 7 and 11 Feb 1948 by Mr A. B. Cohen and Sir S. Caine.

198. Ministry of Food file AG/AL/9A, minutes of 8 and 10 Dec 1947 by Mr G. H. C. Amos and Mr F. Hollins respectively.

199. H. of C. Standing Committee A, Official Report, 25 Nov 1947, col. 15.

200. Ministry of Food file AG/AL/9A, item 36, note of a meeting held on 31 Mar 1948 at the Treasury.

201. Ibid., item 40, letter of 9 Apr 1948 from Mr F. W. Smith, Central Economic Planning Staff, to Mr D. C. V. Perrott, Ministry of Food. The Minister minuted 'Splendid' on seeing the letter – item 46 in ibid.

202. File 19612/4/25, Economic 1947 (CO 852/914), item 10.

203. File of the Office of the Lord President 1731/5, report by the Paymaster-General on his visit to Africa, 16 Jan to 9 Mar 1948 (dated 2 Apr 1948) Section B, para. 7(c).

204. File 19612/4/25, Economic 1948 (CO 852/914), minute of 30 Apr 1948 by Mr E. Melville.

205. Ibid., minute of 12 May 1948 by Sir S. Caine.

206. Ibid., item 5, letter of 21 July 1948 from Mr E. Melville to the Governor, Tanganyika Territory.

207. Ibid., item 6, letter of 25 July 1948 from the Governor to Mr E. Melville.

208. Ibid., item 7, letter of 27 July 1948 from Mr E. Melville to Mr S. A. S. Leslie.

209. File 42553 East Africa: Tanganyika, 1949 (CO 691/204), item 2, Savingram No. 16861/83 of 2 Mar 1949 from the Governor, Sir Edward Twining, to the Secretary of State, Mr Creech Jones. Reports on the labour problems connected with the scheme had been sent on 4 Nov 1948 and 16 Feb 1949 in Savingrams Nos 957 and 164 (File 12259/4/49).

210. Ibid., minute of 10 Mar 1948 by the Parliamentary Under-Secretary of State.

211. Ibid., item 3, letter of 14 Mar 1949.

212. Ibid., item 8, Confidential letter No. 16861/91 of 19 Apr 1949.

213. Ibid., item 20, letter of 3 Sep 1949.

214. File 19612/4/25, Economic 1948 (CO 852/914), minute of 30 Apr 1948 by Mr E. Melville.

215. Idem.

216. Overseas Food Corporation, Report and Accounts for 1948–49 (HMSO No. 252, 27 Sep 1949).

217. Treasury file AF 77/289/01, Part A of 1 June – 2 Nov 1949, item 3.

218. CP(49) 231, 11 Nov 1949, annex dated 28 Sep 1949 – Memorandum on East African Groundnuts Scheme.

219. Treasury File AF 77/289/01, Part A, 1 June to 2 Nov 1949, item 93, letter of 10 Oct 1949 from Minister of Food to Chancellor of the Exchequer.

220. Idem.

221. Ibid., item 94, letter of 12 Oct 1949 from the Chancellor, Sir Stafford Cripps, to the Minister of Food.

222. Ibid., item 107, note of meeting on 21 Oct 1949.

223. Ibid., item 108, minute of 27 Oct 1949 by Mr E. S. Compton.

224. Ibid., item 112, minute of 28 Oct 1949 by Sir Bernard W. Gilbert. The points concerning size and concerning transfer to a Vote of Parliament were made in a letter of 2 Nov 1949 from Sir Bernard Gilbert to Sir Frank Lee, Permanent Secretary of the Ministry of Food – item 167 in ibid.

225. Treasury file AF 77/289/01, Part B, item 38, letter of 8 Nov 1949 from Sir Frank Lee to Sir Bernard Gilbert.

226. Ibid., minute of 8 Nov 1949 by the Chancellor of the Exchequer.

227. Ibid., item 120, minute of 1 Nov 1949. The Note of the meeting of 1 Nov 1949 is item 43A in File 42533, East Africa/Tanganyika, 1949 (CO 691/004).

228. CP(49) 231, 11 Nov 1949.

229. Ministry of Food file A/PO-758, 'The Permanent Secretary's Study of the Groundnut Scheme', 27 Oct 1949, para. 11.

230. Ibid., paras 23–5.

231. CP(49) 232, 11 Nov 1949.

232. CM 66(49) item 3, 14 Nov 1949.

233. File of the Cabinet Office, 6/15/20, item 14. Suggestions that the Government should frankly acknowledge this were made in a brief of 12 Nov 1949 by Sir Norman Brook, Secretary to the Cabinet, to the Prime Minister. It was reproduced, in part, in the Cabinet Conclusions.

234. Ministry of Food file AG/AH/30, item 128, letter of 28 Dec 1949.

235. Secret Ministry of Food file AG/AK/16, Dec 1949–Jan 1950.

236. H. of L. Deb., Vol. 165, cols 1540–1, 14 Dec 1949.

237. File of the Office of the President of the Council 13/2/04, item 15, Top Secret Report of 22 Dec 1949, reference PM 49/12, from the Minister of Food to the Prime Minister on his visit to Africa.

238. H. of C. Deb., Vol. 475, cols 2077–8, 24 May 1950.

239. Treasury file AF 77/289/02, item 14, quoted in a minute of 30 Mar 1950.

240. Ibid., item 16, letter of 4 Apr 1950, from the Permanent Secretary, Ministry of Food.

241. Ministry of Food file A/5037/7, 1950, Note of an informal meeting held on 16 June 1950.

242. Ministry of Food file A/444 – Confidential Report by the Parliamentary Secretary to the Ministry of Food on his visit to Tanganyika, Sep 1950.

243. Idem, para. 84.

244. Idem, para. 16.

245. Ministry of Food file AG/AB/3, item 2, Second Progress Report by the Managing Agents for the period 23 Feb to 31 Mar 1947, p. 9.

246. Ibid., item 3, Sixth Progress Report of the Areas in Tanganyika and Kenya, by the Chief Scientific Officer, p. 11.

247. File 42553 East Africa/Tanganyika, 1950, Part I, item 39.

248. Ministry of Food file A/445 (OFC/23), quoted by Dr Norman C. Wright in his Report on OFC's East African Groundnut Scheme, dated Nov 1950.

249. CP(50) 213, 25 Sep 1950, Annex: Report of the Kongwa Working Party, para. 9(a).

250. Ministry of Food file A/445 (OFC/23), quoted by Dr Norman C. Wright in his Report on OFC's East African Groundnut Scheme, dated Nov 1950.

251. CM 60(50) item 5, 18 Sep 1950.

252. CP(50) 213, 25 Sep 1950.

253. CM 62(50) item 2, 28 Sep 1950.

254. CP(50) 289, 30 Nov 1950, para. 24.

255. Ministry of Food file A/445 (OFC/23), Report on the OFC's East African Groundnut Scheme, Nov 1950, para. 135.

256. CM 83(50) item 4, 7 Dec 1950.

257. CP(50) 324, 29 Dec 1950.

258. File of the Office of the Lord President of the Council 13/2/04, item 28, memo of 31 Dec 1950.

259. CM 1 (51) item 7, 2 Jan 1951.

260. Cmd 8125 of January 9, 1951. The revised long-term plan of OFC was given in an appendix.

261. Idem, para. 14.

262. 14 and 15 Geo. 6, Ch. 20.

263. Ministry of Food file AG/AQ/45, item 54A, text of press announcement for release 21 Mar 1951.

264. Ibid., item 58, confidential letter of 23 Feb 1951 from Dr N. C. Wright, Chief Scientific Adviser to the Permanent Secretary, Sir Frank Lee.

265. File of the Office of the Lord President of the Council 13/2/09, quoted in minute of 23 Feb 1951 (ref.PM51(1)) from the Secretary of State to the Prime Minister.

266. H. of L. Deb., Vol. 275, col. 438, 23 June 1966.

267. Treasury file AF 77/289/01 Part A, 1 June to 2 Nov 1949 item 120, minute of 1 Nov 1949.

268. Ministry of Food file MAF 85/589, Note of 6 Oct 1949.

269. File of the Office of the Lord President of the Council 13/2/04, item 22, memorandum of 6 Dec 1950, on CP (50)289.

270. File WAF 77/253/01 (1951–1953), item 34, Appendix II, Memorandum of 2 Apr 1953 on the Niger Agricultural Project.

271. Idem, para. 2.

272. Idem, para. 3.

6 The Colonial Development Corporation, 1947–1952

1. FORMATION OF THE CDC

At its thirteenth meeting, on 10 March 1947, the Colonial Economic Development Council discussed a Note prepared by the Chairman, Viscount Portal, which recommended the institution by Act of Parliament of a Colonial Development Corporation (CDC) to promote increased Colonial production on an economic and self-supporting basis, with particular reference to the production of foodstuffs and raw materials where supply to the United Kingdom, or sale overseas, would assist the balance of payments.[1] At the same time, by increasing the output of the Colonies, the latter would become more prosperous and so there would be mutual advantage. This latter point was stressed at the meeting of the CEDC, where some members, while accepting the proposals in principle, were anxious that there should be no suspicion of exploitation and that particular care should be taken to avoid large-scale production in the Colonies of commodities in only temporary short supply.[2] It was not felt economic to organise on an *ad hoc* Colony by Colony basis as that would be wasteful of experienced personnel. Instead, a general CDC was proposed which would be able to initiate projects in any Colony and which, once they were launched, would normally transfer the ownership and management to subsidiary companies. The CDC's primary purpose would thus be investigation and promotion, although it would be able also both to operate new industries, wherever that was appropriate, and to provide finance for subsidiary companies by taking up shares or debentures, or otherwise. It was recognised that the Corporation would need to have access to substantial sums of money and it was suggested in the Chairman's Note that the sources from which it might obtain money would include (i) CD & W funds, (ii) Exchequer loans, (iii) borrowing on the London capital market on its own account, but with a Government guarantee, and (iv) loans obtained from the London balances of Colonial Governments. No estimate was made of the sums that were expected to derive from these sources. It was recognised that the Corporation could operate in any Colony only after receiving the full consent of the Government of the Colony concerned, and it was stated that the CDC would collaborate closely with any local Development Corporation that existed or was set up. The CEDC indicated the desirability of encouraging peasant production and industries as well as using plantation methods of production, and warned that care was needed in presenting the plan to the public as 'Any hint of substantial profits being made by the Corporation and taken out of a Colony would be likely to arouse strong adverse reactions locally, whether or not such criticism was reasonable in itself.' After revision in accordance with the views expressed, the Chairman was invited to submit the revised memorandum to the Secretary of State on behalf of the CEDC[3] so that the necessary legislation might be introduced in the next Session, possibly jointly with the legislation establishing an East African Groundnuts Corporation, which the Cabinet had agreed to do at its meeting on 13 January 1947.[4]

The Prime Minister was happy for the Secretary of State to 'Go ahead with the Chancellor',[5] who was, in turn, agreeable to the proposal being examined by officials. The latter, realising that the proposal had come because 'the ostensible purpose of the Corporation would be to increase the supply of Colonial foodstuffs and raw materials', decided, nevertheless, to consider it in terms of Colonial development as a whole.[6] Ten-year Development Plans were at the time in various states of preparation; a few had been completed. Under Section 1 of the CD & W Act, 1940, which still applied, the Secretary of State was empowered to make schemes 'for any purpose likely to promote the development of the resources of any Colony or the welfare of its people'. However, it was found difficult, in practice, for the Secretary of State to ensure that a balance between 'development' and 'welfare' would be secured when local pressures tended to favour social amenities, which were, admittedly, usually badly needed, rather than income-yielding schemes, which would involve postponing the enlargement of welfare services for a time. It was accepted that an improvement in the quality of, say, labour by providing better medical and educational services, or of communications by building better roads, might well be the *sine qua non* for economic development. Despite the vetting procedure of the Colonial Office and the CEDC, the Secretary of State could hardly insist that any Colony should spend CD & W, or other, funds on schemes other than those to which the Colony itself attached most immediate importance. Consequently, some Colonies' development programmes gave considerable emphasis to the welfare side. So, while the use of CD & W funds could not be severely criticised, the need for provision for the development of industries remainded. One official considered that

> the establishment of a Colonial Development Corporation with funds of its own, not subject to Colonial Governments, may well be the best method of achieving this. Certainly, the establishment of the Corporation would enable the Colonial Office to put through schemes of economic development in which Colonies themselves would be reluctant to invest sufficiently large sums from their own resources for fear of prejudicing their development programmes.[7]

It was realised that, while the allocation under the 1945 CD & W Act were not sacrosanct, any diversion of CD & W funds from Colonies to the CDC would be strongly resisted and would, as a result, be likely to be small. Also, as the purpose was in large part to benefit the United Kingdom, any diversion of CD & W funds would virtually amount to a reversion to the principles of the Colonial Development Act, 1929, which had been so frequently condemned.[8]

The impression given by officials of the Colonial Office at a meeting on 14 May 1947 with officials of the Treasury was that the Colonial Office believed that the time was over when private enterprise could be relied on to provide the technical experts and the capital required to investigate the economic potentialities of the Colonies and to promote the schemes necessary to realise these potentialities.[9] The purpose of the new Corporation was seen as 'primarily to operate big *ad hoc* development schemes in the Colonies on a "break-even" basis, the reason being that the Colonial Office feel that on grounds of general policy big industrial developments in the Colonies ought not to be exploited by private enterprise and, in any case, they hold that private enterprise is not likely to show the necessary degree of activity.'[10] This view was readily accepted in the Treasury, where officials were 'convinced that the proposal is on the right lines and that it does represent a necessary stage in Colonial development'.[11]

The exact shape of the Corporation and the provision of finance raised several questions. There was, first of all, the nature of the relationship with CD & W. One suggestion was that there should be a token once-for-all capital contribution of £2 million to £3 million from the CD & W reserve to the CDC.[12] Then there was the relationship with the Colonies themselves, who might contribute substantially from the Joint Colonial Fund, which then stood at over £20 million. More important still was to get a clearer idea of the total capital required, as so far only the CEDC had made a proposal, quoting the sums available to the United Kingdom's Finance Corporation for Industry of £25 million capital, with borrowing power of a further £100 million. It was thought, though without any obvious relationship to Colonial potentialities, that 'about half of the sums mentioned would be enough to make a very handsome start.'[13]

At the informal discussion between Treasury and Colonial Office officials on 14 May 1947, the Chairman enquired whether the Colonial Office would be able satisfactorily to meet any charges that the proposed CDC was being set up to exploit the Colonies (a) in the interests of the United Kingdom or (b) through its use of the funds available to it, for the benefit of private firms.[14] The Colonial Office representatives did not expect any criticism under (a) as there was little prospect of new ventures being undertaken except by the kind of Corporation proposed. As regards (b), it was stated that 'in view of the present trend of HMG's policy, it might not be desirable for large-scale new developments in the Colonies to be undertaken by private enterprise, even if private enterprise was prepared to find the necessary funds.'[15] After further discussion on the question of ministerial responsibility, the relationship with other interested organisations, the constitution and the financing of the Corporation, it was agreed that the Colonial Office should proceed, in the light of the discussion, to draft a memorandum for the Cabinet which would be discussed in draft with the Treasury.

The Colonial Office drafted a Bill, some clauses of which were modelled on the British Overseas Airways Act, 1939. This was sent to the Ministry of Food, which had also drafted a Bill. While the ideas of the two Departments were much the same on the actual provisions required to set up the two Corporations, there was a difference of method. The Colonial Office was proposing that the Act itself should establish the two Corporations, while the Ministry of Food proposed that the Act should be a short enabling Act and that the actual establishment of the Corporation should be made by Order. While not dissenting from the objects of the Colonial Office draft, the Ministry of Food officials felt that there would be parliamentary opposition to the setting up of the two dissimilar Corporations in one Bill and, in any case, a place had only been reserved in the legislative programme for a comparatively short Bill. The Treasury had formed no view on these points, and reserved their position. The matter was referred to Ministers. As a result of a discussion with the Lord President of the Council, Mr Herbert Morrison, the Minister of Food withdrew his objection to the combined Bill and accepted the Colonial Office draft as a basis, subject to certain amendments which he specified when he discussed with the Secretary of State. On the CDC, the Minister of Food said that the Lord President had told him that he thought the inclusion in the terms of reference of special mention of secondary industries might cause difficulty in Parliament. It was, therefore, agreed to omit 'industrial', leaving 'agricultural or other economic development', which was considered quite adequate.

In his submission to the Cabinet, the Secretary of State repeated much of the memorandum from the CEDC in making a case for the establishment of a CDC.[16] He proposed the Corporation should have a broad representation of persons with experience in business, applied science, administration and trade union matters in the Colonies, or elsewhere, and that its capital should be obtained mainly by raising money by public issues under Treasury guarantee, with a total borrowing power of £100 million and provision for an initial contribution direct from the Exchequer. As the purpose was to initiate genuinely new development, the risk of loss on individual projects had to be accepted, though the Corporation was to be expected 'to "break even" on its whole operations over a number of years'. A departmental committee would be set up to keep in general touch with the operations of the Corporation and provide guidance on policy matters. The Cabinet agreed with the proposal, subject to further discussions with the Chancellor of the Exchequer on finance and with the Lord President on the socialisation aspects.[17]

The Colonial Office argued the case for total borrowing powers of £100 million on the basis of both the costliness of large-scale projects, as exemplified by the East African groundnuts project and the Cameroons Corporation, and the desire to avoid the need to seek Parliamentary sanction for further funds for some time. It was recognised that the provision of aggregate borrowing powers of £100 million would not provide the Corporation with *carte blanche* to borrow up to that amount, as each new instalment of borrowing would be subject to Treasury approval.[18] It was, however, hoped that there would not be detailed Treasury control of each project undertaken by the Corporation. After discussion, the limit of £100 million was accepted.[19] The Colonial Office resisted a Treasury proposal that there should be an allocation of CD & W funds to the Corporation, because their purposes would overlap to some extent, arguing that (i) the projects to be financed by the two organisations were not the same, as those of the CDC were to be of a quasi-commercial character; (ii) CD & W funds were largely allocated to particular Colonies; and (iii) the transfer of token sums would merely arouse suspicions that the funds were being whittled away, particularly if such contributions became repayable by the CDC to the Treasury. It was agreed that the question should be left for Ministerial decision.

The Treasury decided that capital for both the OFC and the CDC should be provided by means of Exchequer advances, mainly because this method gave 'some latitude for financial arrangements between the Corporation and the Exchequer under which the Corporation paid low interest, or no interest, on part of their capital in the initial period. Ideally, this would be recovered by payment to the Exchequer of the equivalent of profits, i.e. interest in excess of a gilt-edged rate if earned in a later period when fructification had taken place.'[20] The Colonial Office and the Ministry of Food agreed to accept this on grounds of simplicity and flexibility.[21] As a consequence, the Corporations required only temporary borrowing powers, the limits of which were to be considered by the sponsoring Ministries. It was agreed that a direct accounting relationship between the two Corporations and the Exchequer should be avoided, and that capital would be advanced to them by the responsible Minister, who would be accountable to the Public Accounts Committee.[22]

It had been suggested to the Secretary of State that it would be useful to have a shadow Board in existence before the CDC was established by statute.[23] This was recommended, partly because such a Board could put in much preliminary work and so save several months of time when the Corporation was established, and partly to avoid speculation with regard to the membership of the Board while the Bill was debated. It was suggested that, apart from the Chairman and the chief executive, members, some half-dozen in all, should be part-time. As a consequence of the setting-up of the CDC, it was suggested that the continuance of the Colonial Research Committee should be brought under review and the CEDC reconstituted so as to include the general supervision of research within its scope and a greater concern with the principles of economic policy rather than matters of detail, thus bringing it more closely to resemble the CEAC which preceded it. If there was a change in the chairmanship, the Parliamentary Under-Secretary should, it was suggested, become Chairman, as under the CEAC.[24] However, the Secretary of State was doubtful of the usefulness of part-time members, as he felt that they were usually unable to give sufficient attention to matters arising. But, as it was thought difficult to ensure a sufficiently varied and wide experience on the basis of full-time members only, it was agreed that a Board of, perhaps, four full-time and four part-time members should be considered.[25] It was further agreed that, if possible, the following special varieties of experience, some of which might be combined in one individual, ought to be represented on the Board: finance, agriculture (especially tropical), other branches of natural science with special relation to industry, engineering, business organisation and, possibly, general economics. Mention was made, but no decision reached, of the possibility of appointing someone with experience of co-operatives, and of the possible desirability of including a specific representative of the labour side.

After consulting the Lord President, the Chancellor of the Exchequer, the Ministers of Food and of Transport and others, the Secretary of State decided to seek the Prime Minister's agreement to the appointment of a Chairman and Deputy Chairman and about eight part-time directors selected for their experience and special knowledge.[26] The reasons for the change-over from full to part-time directors, apart from the Chairman and Deputy Chairman, were not, unfortunately, given. It can be surmised that the OFC and the CDC were treated differently in this respect because, whereas the former had a large operational project, the latter was expected to be concerned with small schemes which would, as they became viable, be 'hived off' to local companies. Lord Trefgarne was favoured as Chairman 'because his approach to Colonial development accords with that of the Party, he has a first-hand knowledge of Colonial conditions, has general commercial experience and knowledge of public policy and administration, and has age, health and capacity for movement on his side.'[27] The Prime Minister agreed and, after discussing the possibility with Lord Trefgarne, the Secretary of State made him a formal offer at a salary of £5000 per annum for five years, in the first instance.[28] The Chairman was expected 'to give to the service of the Corporation such time as is needed, and would without necessarily giving up all other interests regard their activities as definitely subordinate to this principal one.' [As Mr Garro-Jones, Lord Trefgarne had been a Labour MP in the war years, and Parliamentary Secretary to the Minister of Production. He withdrew from active participation in politics in 1945 and held various directorships. Some, including those where he was a substantial shareholder, he was allowed to retain while being Chairman of the CDC.] Sir Frank Stockdale, the Secretary of State's Adviser on Development Planning, became Deputy Chairman. The other directors were to be part-time, giving between one-quarter and one-third of their time to the affairs of the Corporation and receiving payments ranging from £500 to £1000. Seven such directors were appointed – Mr Robin E. Brook (Bank of England), Sir Charles Darwin (scientist), Mr H. M. Gibson (CWS – co-operatives and labour), Mr H. Nutcombe Hume (City finance), Mr J. Rosa (representing OFC), Mr E. C. Tansley (Managing Director of the Gold Coast Marketing Company and of the Nigerian Produce Marketing Company Ltd) and Sir Miles Thomas (Deputy Chairman, BOAC). The appointments were for three years, in the first instance. They were made, it was said, not in order to include in the Board men who were expert in the various categories of Colonial economic activity, such as agriculture, manufacturing, mining and so forth, but rather those with 'general business experience and broad vision'.[29]

A rough draft of the ORD Bill was sent to Lord Trefgarne and other members of the Board on 5 September 1947.[30] It was discussed, rather inconclusively, at a meeting presided over by the Parliamentary Under-Secretary and attended by Colonial Office officials, Parliamentary Counsel, Lord Trefgarne, Sir Frank Stockdale and Mr R. Brook on 24 September 1947.[31] Susequently, Lord Trefgarne requested that before the Bill was put in its final form he should have a full explanation of the meaning and effect of the financial clauses in the Bill.[32] Lord Trefgarne met Treasury and Colonial Office officials on 21 October 1947 to discuss these clauses. He asked whether it was agreed that the CDC should set out to be a paying concern and was told that both Departments regarded that as the objective. The Colonial Office thought that if the Corporation were making money it would lower its standard of risk, i.e. be ready to take on schemes having somewhat smaller chance of success. It doubted whether it would ever be politically practicable for the Corporation to earn large profits on any particular scheme, because if a particular scheme proved extremely profitable steps were likely to be taken to acquire the greater part of such profits for the area in question. Lord Trefgarne then raised the question of Clause 9(2), which read: 'In framing programmes involving substantial outlay on capital account, the Corporation shall act on lines settled from time to time with the approval of the Secretary of State.' He realised that there were precedents for such a clause in other Bills – Transport, Electricity and Coal – but he did not think the precedent was exact, as, in those cases, it would not be the main duty of the Board to undertake substantial capital outlay whereas, in this case, it would be its duty. He argued also that it put the Minister under an obligation to exercise discretionary control, which could be embarrassing to the Minister as well as wrong in principle. But the Treasury thought that Parliament would wish the responsible Minister to have continuing control over large sums of money. The matter was left on the understanding that it would be raised at the Legislation Committee later that day. Lord Trefgarne then raised questions relating to

Clauses 12(1) and 15(1), as he was anxious that the provision in Clause 12(1) that working capital might be included on capital account and the provision in Clause 15(1) for 'breaking even' 'taking one year with another' should allow for initial expenses to be charged to capital account, which Lord Trefgarne said was usual, and should provide sufficient cover in case a loss was made for a number of years, as was quite possible. The Treasury promised to consider these points. While officials there wished to adhere to the two clauses, though with the addition of the words 'initial expenses' in Clause 12(1), the Financial Secretary to the Treasury felt that other clauses in the Bill adequately covered the Treasury's interests, and he was not disposed to press Clause 9(2) as drafted. Instead, he proposed that an understanding could be reached with the Corporations by an exchange of letters under which they would undertake to seek the approval of the responsible Minister in framing their capital programmes, and suggested that the Corporation could, if necessary, be induced to give the necessary assurances by the threat to use powers of direction under Clause 9(1) of the Bill.[33] This was agreed.[34] The Treasury then wished to ensure that there was a common understanding of Clause 15(1), which made it a duty of the CDC to balance its revenue account 'taking one year with another'.[35] The Treasury recognised that, during an initial period, expenditure would outrun revenue and that, thereafter, the Corporation would be expected to break even as a whole, and not in the case of each project. Indeed, the Treasury stated it would 'not take exception to a situation in which the richer undertakings of the Corporation "carried", perhaps for an extended period, less immediately profitable schemes because of their value, or potential value, to the Colonies or to this country'.[36] When the Colonial Office questioned whether this latter could have importance because there would, on the one hand, be strong local political objections to subsidising projects in one territory from those in another and, on the other hand, local interests would be likely to wish to participate in, or take over, profitable enterprises, the Treasury thought the argument 'a bit disingenuous' in raising the exploitation bogey after relying previously on the view that the Corporation should be run, generally speaking, on commercial lines. The Treasury recognised that it was unlikely that the Corporation would reach the stage of taking large profits out of any territory as the enterprise would be likely to be taken over by local interests before that came to pass, and so there was little between the two views.[37]

The differences between the Colonial Office and the Ministry of Food were not so easily resolved. The Parliamentary Under-Secretary for the Colonies, Mr Ivor Thomas, mentioned them to the Prime Minister, who asked for details of the difficulty which had arisen over the overlapping of functions between the CDC and the Ministry of Food's OFC. A memorandum was sent to the Prime Minister next day.[38] The issue arose from the Minister of Food's statement in CP(47) 176, para. 4, that

> The Colonial Development Corporation would have power . . . to produce food and other agricultural products such as rubber, cotton, fibres and so forth; in so far as it produces food in the Colonies, it would do so as part of its plans for the general development of the Colonial Empire, whereas the Overseas Food Corporation would be primarily concerned with the production of food for export to the United Kingdom as part of the Ministry of Food's overseas procurement programme.

However, when the Bill was drafted this definition was seen to be inadequate in demarcating the functions of the two Corporations, and unsatisfactory in not acknowledging the primacy of the Secretary of State in matters of Colonial development. Also, while the OFC was primarily to be concerned to procure foodstuffs for the United Kingdom, the CDC was primarily intended to develop the Colonies, and so Parliament would not readily accept that the OFC should have a wide scope in the Colonies. Therefore, it was suggested that the OFC should be restricted to the Groundnut Scheme in East and Central Africa and operations ancillary to it 'but no other schemes in the Colonial Empire'. The Minister of Food reacted sharply to the Memorandum, stating that the solution proposed meant that 'the Government would be imposing limitations on its own chosen instrument of Socialist development which it would not impose on any Capitalist organisation', and the limitations would cause inefficiency as they would result in the waste of its specialist knowledge and experience.[39] However, the Foreign Secretary strongly supported the Colonial Office arguments, adding that care should be taken that our plans for Colonial development should provide 'no possible suggestion of exploitation of the Colonial populations'.[40]

This last point was a matter of some concern, for the first reaction to the announcement by the Secretary of State in the House of Commons on 25 June 1947 of the proposal to establish a CDC[41] was the appearance of articles in certain sections of the British press which gave the impression that the Colonies were to be 'exploited' in order to help Britain out of her difficulties.[42] 'Africa as the larder for Britain' was an example of the headlines which appeared in certain newspapers at that time. In a note on the Second Reading debate of the ORD Bill, *The Economist* (15 November 1947) reflected and reinforced the current attitude with the conclusion that 'Suspicion is engendered in the Colonies as easily by official British policy as by the activities of private British firms, and it has arisen over the proposed new Corporations. That suspicion will be intensified by the appearance of the Ministry of Food, which is mainly interested in obtaining food for the British consumer at the lowest possible price.' The Parliamentary Under-Secretary of State held a Lobby Conference on 4 November 1947 to attempt to dispel the suspicion and confusion. In a Note used at the Conference,[43] he stated:

> We've seen some rather dramatic headlines about these two new Corporations which suggest that the British have suddenly found some neglected estates which they are now going to exploit in a big way in order to solve all their difficulties. Well, these alleged estates are, in fact, a number of countries scattered around the world which, though they may not have full self-government, have minds of their own, and they don't like being spoken of as chattels of Whitehall, or anybody else. These headlines have got repeated back to them, and they're not feeling very happy about it, as you can see from comments in their own newspapers. They are wondering if our motives are not entirely selfish and what they are going to get out of it. And don't let's make any mistake about it. Unless we carry the peoples of these countries with us, we shan't get very far. Their interests have got to be considered just as fully as our own. We are responsible ultimately for their well-being and good government, and we've got to discharge those responsibilities.

It proved difficult to correct the misunderstanding of the position because (i) Britain did stand to benefit from the economic development of the Colonies, (ii) Government Departments, other than the Colonial Office, thought in terms of the British public in connection with the development of the Colonies, and (iii) the fact that the Ministry of Food was responsible for the OFC provided a convenient peg for those, like political extremists in some Colonies, who were looking for pretexts to accuse HMG of exploitation. Further attempts were, therefore, recommended to convince the United Kingdom press that a primary purpose of increased Colonial production was that it should benefit the Colonies themselves, and to get all Government Departments with an interest in Colonial development to think of

Colonial development as a matter of mutual benefit between the United Kingdom and the Colonies.[44] It was thought of no less importance that the leaders of opinion in the Colonies should understand this mutual interest.[45] It was recognised that deeds would achieve more than words, so it was stated firmly that 'Decisions on government policy affecting the Colonies should ensure that Colonial interests are not subordinated to British interests.'[46] It was thought well to recognise that the foundations for development had been laid in most Colonies, éven though further progress would be hard going. As an incidental advantage to the adoption of a policy of stressing benefits to the Colonies and pressing developments as fast as póssible, it was realised that the vulnerability of HMG to attacks of foreign powers would be reduced.[47]

When the Foreign Office received a copy of the draft Cabinet paper on the CDC for comment, it asked for clarification on one point 'since it may affect the way in which our proposal is accepted abroad, particularly in the United States'. The point was whether the Corporation would have 'a monopoly of, or first refusal on, all development schemes in the Colonies, or will it be possible for private companies to invest money in new enterprises subject only to approval of their plans by either the Corporation or the Colonial Development Council to prevent over-lapping?' If the latter was the case, it was suggested that it should be made known. It was recalled that HMG was 'under obligation in the United Nations Charter to allow equal treatment to all cases' and HMG would not wish to depart from it.[48] 'A quite categorical' assurance was given that there was no intention of monopoly or first refusal implied: the Corporation was intended to complement, rather than displace, private enterprise, undertaking projects which private enterprise was unwilling or unable to put in hand or which 'for particular reasons may be unsuitable for private operation'.[49]

II. THE ROLE ENVISAGED FOR THE CDC

By the beginning of August 1947 Lord Trefgarne felt there were enough Board members to make a start.[50] By the end of October, although the Corporation had not found suitable premises or an adequate staff, the Board had agreed upon the general lines on which the Corporation would begin to operate.[51] Lord Trefgarne submitted the draft of a paper, 'The CDC: Method of Operation', which had two purposes, namely (i) to convey to Colonial Governments some information of the lines on which the Corporation would work and the nature of its powers, and (ii) to invite Colonial Governments to submit projects to the Corporation. Although the first purpose was strictly for the Secretary of State, Lord Trefgarne explained that he was 'making an effort to bring the Corporation into being as a working machine within two or three months' of the Act being passed. The paper was accepted as the basis for a Despatch.[52] Governors had been told, by secret telegram[53] on 15 June 1947, of the Cabinet's consideration of plans for establishing an OFC and a CDC in order to fill 'a gap in the machinery for Colonial evelopment'. The telegram emphasised that the purpose was 'not to supplant private enterprise, but to supplement it, so long as it is in harmony with the plans of the Government for social and economic development'. The Secretary of State expressed his anxiety lest the impression should be given that HMG intended to use the Colonial Empire 'merely as a field of production to be exploited for their own interests'. A circular telegram followed on 24 June and that was followed, in turn, by a Circular Despatch on 10 July 1947.[54] In the latter, the Secretary of State assured Governors that (i) the Corporation would operate in individual Colonies only with the consent of the Colonial Government concerned, (ii) it was not intended to give the Corporation any monopoly powers, and (iii) it was intended that the Corporation should supplement, not supplant, existing enterprise. It was hoped that the Corporation would be given power to assist any development project which was both in the interests of the Colonies concerned and had a prospect of being sufficiently remunerative to cover the costs incurred. The latter criterion distinguished the CDC from CD & W. It was stated to be permissible for a Colonial Government to provide assistance from its CD & W allocation in order to make an 'uneconomic' project sufficiently economic for the CDC to be able to accept it. Colonial Governments were invited to submit projects that suggested themselves, but not to work them out in detail at that stage.

The matter was discussed at the Conference of African Governors in November 1947.[55] The Secretary of State, who presided, said that the idea of the Development Corporation had been simmering in the minds of the Government for a long period, and its emergence as a proposal at a time of shortage was coincidental, not deriving from any thought of Colonial exploitation. Lord Trefgarne saw it as the development of work which had been going on in the Colonies for many years. Governors were to be invited to put forward projects for the Corporation's consideration. Sir Frank Stockdale emphasised that the Corporation was not to be merely a financing house, but an organisation to enter into partnership with business concerns and to encourage local enterprise. The Governor of Nigeria, Lord Milverton, while welcoming the ORD Bill as 'an act of wisdom wrung out of our needs', thought its Achilles heel was the requirement to act as a commercial concern and pay its way. The Economic Adviser to the East African Governors' Conference, Sir Charles Lockhart, agreed that it was going to be difficult to reconcile Colonial development and the making of commercial profits. The Governor of Kenya, Sir Philip Mitchell, observed that, if the obligation of profitability meant that dividends were to be withdrawn from the Colonial territory, then that was a very vulnerable criticism from the point of view of the private businessman as well as from that of the people of a Colony. The Chief Secretary of the East African Governors' Conference, Sir George Sandford, said that a solution of the agrarian problem was by far the most important subject for action in East Africa, but, viewed as a purely commercial proposition, development of these vast areas of unoccupied waste land might not pay. He thought that if the Corporation was to help in a solution of the problem the financial limitations placed upon it would have to be very liberally interpreted. Lord Trefgarne replied that, although the principal criterion which the Development Corporation would apply in determining whether or not to undertake any particular project would inevitably be the probable financial profitability of that project, rather than the more general criteria of social and economic advantage to the territory concerned, yet those wider criteria would certainly be applied to a greater extent in the Corporation's activities than would ever be the case with developments undertaken by purely private, profit-making enterprise. The Governor of Nigeria held that this involved the profit-and-loss criterion, which was inappropriate for what was a Government undertaking. Sir Sydney Caine concluded that some Governors appeared to think that the £100 million should have been added to the £120 million already available under the CD & W Act for financing development of the type envisaged in the ten-year plans. However, schemes of a generally commercial, but non-profit-making nature, could be financed under the CD & W Act, while, once the commercial criterion was abandoned for the CDC, there would be no limit to the kind of development that might be included. Yet, in view of the immediate need, first, to increase resources of equipment, staff and finance; and, secondly, to invest these resources in schemes which would give quick results beneficial to the Colonies and the United Kingdom, experience of CD & W-type expenditure was less important than provision for CDC-type, which, inevitably, competed for resources and funds which could be elsewhere employed. He added that the generosity of HMG in launching the CDC consisted in offering these resources to the Colonies without laying down that the schemes on which they would be employed should do more than pay their way. The Secretary of State, in winding up the discussion, stressed that the Corporation had its origin not in the immediate needs of the United Kingdom but as an extension of Colonial development policy. It was an instrument which could be adapted in the light of experience, in much the same way as the machinery of the Colonial Development Act had been adapted and elaborated over the years 1929–45. Meantime, HMG was still in the early stages of planning the operations of the Corporation.

This discussion was taken into account[56] in drafting the Despatch and enclosed memorandum, which was sent to Governors on 17 December 1947.[57] The primary task of the CDC was said to be 'to assist the development of Colonial resources and thus to help to strengthen the resources of the Sterling Group as a whole, and so prove of considerable benefit to all the members of that Group and not only to the Colonies themselves'.[58] Governors were asked to co-operate in achieving these objectives. It was said that the 'shadow' Board had done much preliminary work, and expected to be ready by 31 March 1948 to examine projects and draw up a programme of initial projects. The memorandum enclosed stated the information the Corporation would require before it could consider any scheme submitted. The CDC could receive schemes also from the Colonial Office or private individuals, and was free to make its own plans.[59] The policy considerations which would govern the acceptability of any given project were stated to be (i) the economic need of the Colony for the proposed scheme and its practicability without adverse repercussions in the territory, it being assumed that Colonial Governments would be mindful of the social implications of any projects proposed; (ii) the potentialities of the project for the reduction of dollar imports, the promotion of dollar exports or of the supply of commodities in short supply in the United Kingdom and the Commonwealth; (iii) a measure of equitable geographical distribution of projects over Colonial territories as a whole; (iv) the capacity of the early organisation to handle projects in each of the six broad categories mentioned, namely (a) animal products, (b) agricultural or forestry products, (c) fisheries, (d) mineral, mining or fertiliser production, (e) civil engineering and public works projects, and (f) manufacturing and processing projects; (v) in the intial stages, projects would be preferred which required a minimum of capital goods, either from sterling or still more from dollar sources, in relation to their expected yield; (vi) initially, short-term projects would be preferred to long-term; (vii) schemes of a preparatory or ancillary character, such as the production of fertilisers, packing materials and possibly building projects, would be considered; (viii) the commercial soundness of the scheme would in most cases be 'vital' after the previous criteria were studied. At the suggestion of the Treasury, the Despatch stated that with the advent of the CDC it was 'not intended that CD & W money should in future be used for schemes of a commercial nature which could properly be undertaken by the Corporation'.[60]

This last statement puzzled the Administrators of the Windward Islands. Accordingly, the Acting Comptroller of the D & W Organisation asked the Colonial Office whether all such projects should be removed from their sketch-plans of development, and the funds so released applied elsewhere.[61] Much agricultural development was of a commercial nature, and, once withdrawn from the sketch-plans, finance would be difficult, if not impossible, to find should the CDC then not agree to undertake the projects. The Acting Comptroller had advised that only those projects likely to yield a sufficient return should be withdrawn, but sought confirmation of this view. The Colonial Office agreed but, in turn, consulted the Treasury,[62] which asked how the Colonial Office would interpret the distinction involved between 'schemes of a commercial nature' and 'projects of a character which makes them appropriate for financing by the CDC or OFC'.[63] It was noted that the promise made in the joint memorandum by the Minister of Food and the Parliamentary Under-Secretary of State to make a statement 'in the course of the debate on the Bill that recourse will not be had to the CD & W Vote for funds for projects of a character which make them appropriate for financing by either Corporation'[64] had not been made, and the Colonial Office was asked to explain the omission. Apparently, Ministers were unwilling to make a statement, and the question remained. It was argued by the Colonial Office that the CDC could not have 'the power of financial decision as to what projects of a commercial character should be assisted from United Kingdom funds, because it would not be possible to give the Corporation direction to undertake individual schemes.'[65] The Treasury accepted the argument, seeing the demarcation between the CDC and the CD & W Act as 'very much a matter of good sense and individual instances'. The CDC was not expected, though operating under section 15 of the ORD Act, 1948, to 'pay the same regard to pure motives of commercial profit as would a private enterprise', and so it would normally accept all commercial projects. Where this was, for any reason, inappropriate, the Treasury was willing to 'consider the possibility of arranging for the proposition to be carried on by some other means, with perhaps assistance from CD & W funds'.[66] The Colonial Office was authorised to write to the Acting Comptroller accordingly. He was assured that 'the last thing that the Secretary of State wants is that the setting up of the Corporation should make any aspect of Colonial development more difficult. That would of course by plumb contrary to the underlying intention of the Act.'[67] It was noted that 'the Treasury have gone so far as to agree that a commercial project might be financed from a Colony's allocation by means of a CD & W loan. This was virtually no concession at all, since no Colony, if it could find the money elsewhere, would accept a loan chargeable to its allocation, since that would mean forfeiting free grants of an equal amount.'[68]

It is noteworthy that Mr Frank Samuel, Managing Director of the United Africa Company, who regarded the East African Groundnuts project as a non-commercial venture to provide a new source of oils, took quite a contrary view regarding the CDC. After Sir Sydney Caine had explained the nature of CDC during an address at Unilever House on 10 September 1947, Mr Samuel said that, in the course of his remarks, Sir Sydney

referred to these enterprises being expected to make a reasonable rate on the capital invested. It may well be that in his present state of mind Mr Dalton would regard $2\frac{1}{2}$ per cent as a reasonable rate but I think that we all agree that on these terms obviously the City of London even a month ago would scarcely have been willing to compete for anything in the way of enterprise which had not got assured success ahead of it. I would say, speaking in this room in front of a lot of businessmen, that allowing for good years and bad years and for building up reasonable capital reserves in industrial enterprise in new markets where there are so many hazards and difficulties to be overcome, a rate in the neighbourhood of 8 per cent would not be regarded as being an exaggeration of the term 'a reasonable return', over an average. Some years less; some years you will make more. But I am just wondering whether, as a Government Corporation, they have got some standards of what is a reasonable rate which it would be very difficult to match in ordinary private enterprise and which, if that were the case, would make a Corporation of this kind in industrial and commercial activities a very difficult competitor to private enterprise. I don't believe from what I know of it that this is the intention. But this question of the definition of a reasonable rate of interest I think does go very much to the root of the future management and purpose of the Corporation.

In reply, Sir Sydney said he expected a margin over the minimum gilt-edged rate, but considered that over a long period, assuming that the general level of interest rates remained more or less steady, net earnings, after providing for specific but not for general reserves, averaging 4–5 per cent would be quite satisfactory.

Mr Samuel also showed a different attitude towards the operations of the CDC than he had to the Groundnuts Project. The latter he was anxious to launch virtually regardless of further investigation once the Wakefield Mission had reported. But, in the case of CDC, he said:

We all hope that the availability of so vast a sum of money will not tempt the Board of this Corporation to embark too rapidly on schemes which have not been fully considered: it is a danger, and I think Sir Sydney will probably share this view, that with the immense publicity that has been accorded to this in the Press, and with the natural eagerness of men given the responsibility for a development of this nature, that there might well be a sense of urgency which might lead to developments which, with greater consideration and greater study might not then appear to be so desirable. And I have no reason to doubt myself that one of the first acts of this great Corporation will be to establish a section which will do work which our French friends I believe always refer to as Société d'Etude. There is an enormous amount of investigation to be done, and I am sure that the lasting and great success of this Corporation will arise from the fact that it is not going to attempt to proceed at anything like breakneck speed.

III. **THE RELATIONSHIP OF THE CDC WITH GOVERNMENT DEPARTMENTS, 1948**

Clearly, whether the developmental efforts of Colonial Governments were eased, or further complicated, depended on the willingness of the CDC to accept projects and, no less, the speed with which decisions were taken. Early in 1948 the Chairman of the CDC indicated that he was not happy about the machinery for obtaining quickly the concurrence of the Colonial Office and the Treasury for his proposals, and a meeting to discuss the matter was suggested by the Colonial

Office.[69] In preparation for this, a meeting was held at the Treasury on 19 April 1948 to discuss the machinery for the examination by HMG of the programme of the CDC.[70] The Treasury felt itself to be in a strong position, because when the old clause 9(2), which read, 'In framing programmes involving substantial outlay on capital account, the Corporation shall act on lines settled from time to time with the approval of the responsible Minister', was dropped, it had insisted that a letter be sent to Lord Trefgarne on which the broad principles of HMG's control of the Corporation's expenditure would be based.[71] It was on the strength of that letter that their case for requiring the submission of satisfactory programme was held to rest. In the words of the draft letter, 'the general idea would be that HMG should have the same facilities to ask questions, or influence broad policy, as the shareholders in an ordinary company which is seeking to raise fresh capital for a new venture.' The Treasury went further than this sentence implied in wishing 'to control the Corporation in three ways – forward control, i.e. knowledge of what the money *will* be spent on, current control, i.e. what it *is* being spent on, and review powers, i.e. what it *has* been spent on', adding: 'Obviously, however, we must have a pretty loose rein on all three, as is the intention of the Act.' Later still, more detail was felt to be necessary, including the annual rate of expenditure and, in order to gauge the inflationary effects on the Colony, an estimate of local expenditure.[72]

The Parliamentary Under-Secretary, Mr Rees-Williams, and Sir Sydney Caine meantime suggested that there might be regular monthly meetings between the CDC and the Colonial Office where outstanding questions could be discussed.[73] The Chairman agreed in principle, but was thought to wish to formalise the meetings over much.[74] The first meeting was arranged for 21 June 1948, and thereafter there was to be a meeting on the second Monday of each month.

Beforehand, the Parliamentary Under-Secretary conferred with the Chairman,[75] and later a meeting was held in the Colonial Office by the Secretary of State with the Parliamentary Under-Secretary and five officials.[76] In the first of these, the Chairman asked for information on such matters as the surveys and missions in hand and in prospect in the Colonies, and the position with regard to State Broadcasting Corporations in the Colonies. He also complained that the OFC had become involved in both Fiji and the High Commission Territories without receiving the Secretary of State's invitation to do so. In the second of the meetings, the Secretary of State referred to complaints by the Chairman about access to Ministers, the number of checks to which the Corporation was exposed, and the delays in dealing with its business. For the latter, the Chairman particularly blamed the Treasury, although he felt that the Colonial Office conducted unnecessary consultations with other Departments. Thus, he instanced consultation with the Ministry of Food on the proposed poultry farming project in The Gambia, and considered that checks and consultations on that scale would make the work of the Corporation impossible. In the discussion, it was thought by Sir Sydney Caine that the Chairman had some cause for complaint, because originally it had been intended that the CDC should have a free hand. Subsequently to the decision to establish it, there had been a development of central planning, so that neither the Colonial Office nor the CDC could any longer have a completely free hand.

At the meeting of the Economic Policy Committee on 6 May 1948[77] the Chancellor of the Exchequer, Sir Stafford Cripps, pointed out that the report by the Paymaster-General on his visit to Africa and the interim report by the Colonial Development Working Party were complementary. They first drew attention to the urgent problem of raising native standards of farming, to the shortage of trained staffs, and to the need for substantial new capital investment in transport, particularly railways, as a condition precedent to the expansion of production in Africa. The Working Party had also concluded that the pace of Colonial development was limited by the shortages, not of sterling finance, but of material resources, especially iron and steel. Consequently, the first priority was to improve the productivity of existing facilities, in particular transport and communications, as these would yield the quickest returns for a given outlay of resources. This was accepted by the Committee, as were the specific proposals made by the Chairman of the Colonial Development Working Party, Sir Edwin Plowden, head of the Economic Planning Board, in his covering Note to the report. The intentions were stated to include making estimates for the following three years of likely Colonial exports, examining likely Colonial needs for imports from dollar sources and, on that basis, proposing dollar-saving measures whose practicability would, in turn, be assessed. It was claimed that 'This process will also assist in setting up some standards by which investment policy in the industrial and commercial field can be regulated, thus forging a link between this line of enquiry and that which the Working Party has been pursuing hitherto.'

The Parliamentary Under-Secretary had supported the Working Party's recommendations that the immediate need was to concentrate on the repair and improvement of existing facilities, especially transport and communications. No mention had been made of the role of the CDC, whose operations necessarily involved new capital formation rather than improving existing facilities. As the Chairman of the CDC had several times insisted, his Corporation was unlike the other statutory corporations, such as the National Coal Board, in not taking over physical assets. But the desperateness of the economic situation caused the exceptional nature of the CDC to be overlooked. At the Colonial Office meeting of 18 June it was agreed that, in the national interest, the CDC's schemes had to be judged against other schemes demanding scarce materials, and that they should be asked at the meeting of 21 June to provide sufficient information to enable this to be done.

At that meeting,[78] the Chairman stated his concern with the amount of information the Colonial Office seemed to require in regard to a comparatively small scheme for producing eggs, poultry and pigs in The Gambia. He took it amiss that the Colonial Office had referred to the Ministry of Food on this. He regarded it as contrary to the agreement contained in Sir Sydney Caine's letter of 16 December 1947 that the CDC should be required to enter into detail regarding the Corporation's proposals. The letter of 16 December arose out of the Treasury's desire, in view of the loss of the original Clause 9(2) from the ORD Bill, to get a clear understanding with Lord Trefgarne as to the arrangements for keeping HMG informed of CDC's general programmes. In the agreed draft, which was sent to Lord Trefgarne on 16 December, it was stated that 'although neither the Treasury nor the Colonial Office would wish to examine the details of any proposition, they might well find it necessary to examine with you the main headings of expenditure and revenue on which the Corporation bases its plans for any major undertaking. Similarly, they would like to see aggregated figures for the bulk of the smaller schemes under the same headings.'[79] The Gambia scheme was said to be a special case, because it was proposed to borrow $300,000 from the International Bank. On the general side, it was stated that control over capital investment had become much closer in order to ensure that the United Kingdom's dollar resources and commodities in short supply, such as steel, fertilisers, and cement, were used to what was considered to be the best advantage. The Chairman viewed this as a change of the procedure envisaged in the letter of 16 December. He felt there would be inordinate delay if, after the Corporation had completed its investigation on the 25 or 30 schemes being considered, they were considered in detail by the Colonial Office and inter-departmentally. The Ministers and Sir Sydney Caine explained they were the prisoners of circumstance and, while shortages continued, detailed planning was unavoidable. It was not the commercial soundness of a scheme, but whether it fitted in with the national programme that the Colonial Office wished to determine and it wanted sufficient data for that purpose. The Parliamentary Under-Secretary emphasised that the Corporation would not be more severely tested in this regard than any private concern.

While the change of general economic policy was held responsible for the new requirements this was not, in fact, the only impetus. For on 28 May 1948 the Chairman of the CDC had written to the Secretary of State to request that £1 million 'be drawn from the Treasury pursuant to Section 12(1) of the Overseas Resources Development Act, 1948, and held available for immediate advances at the future request of the Colonial Development Corporation'.[80] The Secretary of State was surprised by the request and minuted: 'I assume that, in all the Corporation schemes, this Office is given some opportunity of agreeing, or criticising or opposing, that the Colonial Government is also required to be a willing and co-operating party, and that safeguards will operate so far as welfare, native rights and interests, etc., are concerned.'[81] The Parliamentary Under-Secretary thought that, in addition, it would be necessary to determine 'a list of priority targets and notify them to the CDC, otherwise the CDC will be approving projects for which no steel and technicians will be available'.[82] The Colonial Office was disturbed, as it had been understood that the Corporation would submit an initial programme a few months after the Act had been passed and a detailed procedure would be followed in vetting schemes. But 'unfortunately, owing to delays in the Treasury, we have not yet written to Lord Trefgarne describing the details of the procedure',[83] although this hardly excused the failure to submit any programme at all. It was felt necessary to insist on such a programme, if the Office was to keep any control, even though the Chairman was likely to regard such a request as obstruction. The Secretary of State decided to discuss the matter at the meeting of 21 June.

There is no evidence to explain the Chairman's somewhat cavalier approach of 28 May. Whether he hoped to avoid control or, instead, to bring the matter to a head, cannot be determined. What he in fact did was to shock both Ministers and officials and lead, in all probability, to a tighter control than otherwise might have been pressed. This view received support from time to time in Treasury files, most notably in 1955. The Chairman's point of view was then given its due measure of appreciation by a Treasury official concerned with what had become the perennial problem of capital sanction procedure for the CDC.[84] The minute of 1955 was written to review Treasury thinking over this matter, as discussions in the Colonial Office–CDC Working Party had revealed that one of the main differences still between the CDC and the Government was over that procedure. The Treasury had argued over the years that detailed examination of the schemes was necessary to enable Ministers to discharge their responsibility to Parliament for the use of public funds. The CDC had argued that this was not required by the Act, and they were willing to give all the information desired after the event, but the decision should be left to the Board and the funds issued without further enquiry when demanded, subject only to such prior Ministerial directions as may have been given under Section 9 of the Act. Ministers in this way, it was argued, would show their confidence in the Board, otherwise it should be replaced, rather than its work redone by reinvestigating proposed schemes. The CDC argued against detailed re-examination of schemes before advances were made on five grounds: (i) the examination took time when the CDC often needed to make a quick decision; (ii) negotiations sometimes involved commitments, e.g. to prospective partners, and it was embarrassing to go back on these later; (iii) the Board of the CDC was an expert body, while civil servants were less expert; (iv) re-examination involved wasteful duplication; and (v) Ministers should not be closely identified with the decisions of the CDC if they were not to be held responsible for any failures concerning the Corporation. However, the Treasury maintained that detailed examination was necessary before advances were made from public funds on these grounds: (a) although the capital sanction procedure was not explicitly laid down in the Act, under Sections 11 and 12 of the Act Ministers had responsibility for the proper use of the Corporation's borrowing powers; (b) as Ministers were responsible for the use of public money, they could not accept without question the CDC's demands for advances; (c) schemes might well conflict with general Government policy, and it was impracticable to issue prior directions to cover every possible such conflict; (d) the record of the CDC did not justify any departure from strict control as losses to 31 December 1953, were £9.6 million; and (e) Parliament expected such control to be exercised, as shown by the interest of the Public Accounts Committee. However, the Treasury minute of 1955 went on to state that, while there was some analogy between the CDC and nationalised industries, there were also important differences. These included:

(a) With the Nationalised Industries, the Minister has the responsibility of protecting the consumers' interests. It was for this purpose, primarily, that the power to give general directions was taken. With the CDC, there is no consumer interest in this sense. This is an argument for less close Ministerial control of the CDC than of nationalised industries. (b) CDC schemes are by intention more speculative than those of Nationalised Industries. The purpose of the CDC is to finance ventures which normal sources of finance would not undertake alone. This is an argument for closer Ministerial control of the CDC since greater risks are being undertaken with public money.

In a comment of 18 April 1955 on the minute, it was suggested there was 'an even more fundamental difference: Coal, transport, etc. were nationalised because they were thought to be basic services which should not be run for private profit, but the CDC was set up to stimulate development in the Colonies by supplementary private enterprise.'[85] The minute concluded that

> there is force in the CDC's arguments. There might be a case for relaxing the capital sanction procedure, not examining schemes in detail before advances are made, but relying on the Corporation's judgment, if we were starting from scratch. But we are not. As things are, I think the dismal record of the Corporation and the resulting Parliamentary interest outweigh the arguments for relaxation. . . . [Accordingly] we must hold to the present line and insist on full information and examination of details of schemes, and that the Government must take an independent decision (and accept the responsibility) before each advance of money is made.

Later in the year, there was a discussion of whether the Treasury should consider some relaxation of capital sanction control in the light of an opinion put forward by the CDC's lawyer on a case concerning housing. The official then minuted:[86]

> I would myself adhere to the views expressed in my minute of April 18. Now that I have a little more personal experience of the working of capital sanction procedure, I should be a bit more sceptical of its efficiency. We are not, in practice, able to form much of an independent judgment about the merits of these schemes. And very likely we could form as good a judgment as we do with less detail than is supplied in the agreed form of CDC application. . . . [Yet he

continued:] But having just, laboriously, agreed on a form of application, I should not like to upset it now. Nor am I in favour of any modification of the procedure in substance. What has happened in the housing case merely demonstrates the need for close control. Admittedly, we have tumbled on the legal point almost accidentally. But we *have*, in the end, got on to it, and that we did not do so more directly is rather an argument for strengthening the control, or working it more carefully, than for relaxation.

The last point was accepted – 'We must stick to fully detailed control.'[87]

So much then for the alleged exigencies of the situation, whether in 1948 or succeeding years. The upshot of the meeting of 21 June 1948 was that a letter modifying the procedure set out in that of 16 December 1947, was to be sent to the Chairman. In private discussion later with the Parliamentary Under-Secretary, the Chairman said his main objection to the proposals put forward was the possibility of delay as the result of inter-departmental consultation, and he suggested that a high-placed Treasury official should attend the monthly meetings. The Secretary of State agreed.[88] However, a further meeting with officials was indecisive. It seemed, at least to some, that in effect Lord Trefgarne was asking that the Corporation be treated 'as an authority with greater independence of Government control and supervision than any private concern in the country', and this seemed impossible at the time.[89] The Chairman felt unable to continue under the strict regimen which was being proposed.[90] The Parliamentary Under-Secretary thereupon made proposals that the Chairman found acceptable. The principal one was that all projects needing Colonial Office help in the way of capital goods or finance should be notified to the Colonial Office by the CDC at an early stage, and the Colonial Office would be free to consult other Departments as it thought fit. If the Colonial Office did not agree, it would so inform the Chairman. They were then put to the Secretary of State, who was, at the same time, asked officially not to agree to any restriction on the freedom of the Colonial Office to consult with other Departments. The argument was that 'HMG is an indivisible entity and it is not possible to carry on the work of any one Department if there is any bar on consultation with other Departments which may be interested.' The Chairman had expressed his fear to Sir Sydney Caine and Mr C. G. Eastwood that he did not wish information supplied to the Colonial Office to be sent round Departments on a quest for observations and objections.[91] The Secretary of State reacted somewhat emotionally to the minutes.[92] He expressed the 'hope that Mr Rees-Williams' agreement, with the important proviso in Sir Sydney Caine's Minute regarding Colonial Office freedom of consultation, will settle these differences, which I must say seem to arise from Lord Trefgarne's unreasonable demands and suspicions. We have not given the Colonies and British capital over to the Corporation for them to proceed as they determine. Ministers have a responsibility to Parliament. British policy must be worked *as a whole* . . .'; and so forth, ending more reasonably thus: 'He must be made to appreciate that we do not want to invade his territory, but we have responsibilities too.' The Parliamentary Under-Secretary suggested a further meeting with the Chairman, who submitted a fourteen-page memorandum on the CDC's relationship with Departments.[93] This was taken into account in drafting a nine-page letter from the Secretary of State to the Chairman, in which it was proposed that 'at regular intervals, the Corporation should let the Office have reports on all schemes of any significance which are under way, and a note of all new projects under active investigation.' The regular monthly meeting would consider all schemes in hand and under active consideration. Advances would be made at, say, six-monthly intervals on the basis of details of funds in hand and to be received, on the one side, and funds likely to be disbursed, on the other, with an allowance for contingencies. It was agreed that the Corporation was to remain sole judge of the commercial soundness of schemes. Yet this view of the matter was also questioned in the minute of 1955 referred to earlier,[94] in which it was recalled that:

The CDC have said that, in principle, they accept the need for something like the capital sanction procedure. But, in fact, they do not accept that this should mean detailed examination of the schemes proposed before funds are issued. In particular, Lord Reith, while not averse to giving *Ministers* details of schemes for information, objects to their examination by comparatively junior officials in the Treasury and Colonial Office before any decision is taken. Secondly, the Government has said that it does not seek to interfere with the 'commercial judgment' of the Corporation. But it is doubtful if commercial judgment can really be distinguished from other elements involved in the decision on a scheme.

But, be that as it may seven years later, the Treasury approved the letter to the Chairman in July 1948 'on the clear understanding between us that HMG would get, by these various means, the information needed to form a proper judgment' as set out in their draft.[95] For in the Treasury, it was believed that 'If the battle is not joined now, the Colonial Office will find that their Secretary of State (and HMG) will have allowed the final control of the most important aspect of Colonial development to pass into the hands of a Chairman of a public corporation.[96]

The Chairman was, however, unwilling to accept what he regarded as 'the continuous review of projects', but wished instead to have notice of acceptance or refusal of a project at an early stage and, once sanction was given, be free to cope with the project as circumstances required.[97] After discussion with the Chairman, the Secretary of State replied[98] that (i) the procedure outlined in his letter of 15 July was agreed, (ii) the Corporation would give a measure of priority to the consideration of schemes suggested by the Office, (iii) 'every project, on being submitted as a synopsis at an early stage, shall receive approval or otherwise with the minimum of delay', and such approval would authorise the Corporation to commit capital up to the amount agreed, providing no major change in the scheme was made without prior consultation. Grounds for refusal would be stated. An uneasy peace was thus restored, committing the Colonial Office, once a project had been approved, to support any requests the CDC might make for scarce materials and hard currency. On the morrow of the agreement, this latter undertaking was seen to be a clear source of future difficulty.[99] It was decided to see what actually happened.

iv. THE OPERATIONS OF THE CDC TO
    31 DECEMBER 1948

The second monthly meeting between the CDC and the Colonial Office took place on 12 July 1948, with Mr Rees-Williams in the chair and Mr D. P. Pitblado representing the Treasury.[100] Lord Trefgarne handed in requests for an advance to cover (a) British Guiana Consolidated Goldfields Ltd (£200,000), (b) Gambia Poultry Project (£500,000), and (c) Administrative Capital (£100,000, of which one-half was required immediately). The Colonial Office promised a decision as soon as possible. It was stated that Lord Milverton's appointment to the Board was to be published next day. Lord Trefgarne explained that five regional corporations (in Malaya, West Africa, East Africa, Central Africa and the West Indies) were to be set up and for three of them regional directors had been appointed. Local residents would be appointed to the Boards. The Colonial Office raised no objection to the Corporation's intention to form a Hotels Division, with a view to the construction of hotels in the West Indies and elsewhere in the Colonies. It was noted that this proposal had both a dollar-earning aspect and a development aspect. It was agreed that the Corporation was free to undertake investigations in the High Commission Territories, and the Corporation was asked to keep both the Secretary of State for the Colonies and the Secretary of State for Commonwealth Relations informed of any major developments there. These were the main items discussed. The Colonial Office sent a Note on the meeting to the CDC and was surprised to hear that the Chairman felt strongly that, in the case of an informal meeting of this kind, the 'minutes should be confined to decisions and matters on which agreement had been reached'.[101] This insistence on informality was quite contrary to what was feared when the monthly meetings were proposed, namely that the Chairman would wish to formalise the meetings. As a result, the Colonial Office produced an abbreviated version called the 'Minutes', which was agreed with the CDC, and a longer 'Supplementary Record', which has been used for present purposes.[102]

The Secretary of State took the chair at the third monthly meeting, on 20 September 1948.[103] He expressed the hope that the Corporation would be able to undertake the salt scheme in the Turks and Caicos Islands on mutually acceptable terms, as it appeared to provide the only means of livelihood for the islanders. The Corporation was asked to consider the recommendations of the Evans Commission on Settlement in British Guiana. The Chairman was rather perturbed by the impression that the CDC could be expected to carry out any undertaking, however all-embracing and whether remunerative or not, which was beyond the competence of the ordinary administration. He felt that the primary function of the CDC was to undertake self-contained propositions which showed a prospect of commercial return, a view with which the Secretary of State expressed sympathy. The Chairman reported that he was going to Nyasaland to investigate further a promising scheme, estimated to involve capital expenditure of £1.4 million on tung trees and wattle. Aden fisheries and cattle in Fiji were among the schemes to be investigated further. Several Colonies had suggested that the CDC's profits should be invested in the Colony in which they had been made. However, the Chairman thought it would be premature to reach an agreement on this, as the Corporation had not made excessive profits so far and needed to balance profits against losses, any residual profit being at the disposal of the Secretary of State. It was decided to leave the matter for the time being.

The first Quarterly Report on schemes in operation was dated 5 November 1948,[104] and included three items. The Gambia project was reported to be well under way. Mr Phillips, the Project Manager, and about 80 members of the staff, including the sawmill and tractor teams and some 30 Bahamians, had arrived in the Colony. Negotiations were proceeding on the final terms of the lease to the CDC of the first 10,000 acres of land. Most of the equipment had been ordered and a building contract signed. Two comparable crawler tractor teams were being built up, one of American and the other of Italian machines, so that it could be established whether the Italian were a reliable dollar-substitute for American machines. The equipment was later to be used elsewhere in East Africa. A supplementary submission for capital sanction was to be made. Preliminary clearing work for the building sites was about to begin; land clearing would begin when the heavy tractors and American saws reached the Colony, possibly in December. Secondly, the Loan Agreement between the CDC and British Guiana Consolidated Goldfields Ltd had been executed, but no money had been advanced. A dredge was to be purchased in the USA. Thirdly, no final decision had been taken concerning the timber concession in British Guiana.

At the fifth meeting, on 8 November 1948, the question of revealing estimated costs of projects in answer to Parliamentary Questions was discussed in connection with a question tabled by Mr Turton for oral reply on The Gambia poultry project.[105] It was agreed that the Secretary of State should not be put into the position of having to explain and justify subsequent alterations to estimates announced in Parliament. Detailed questions would be referred to the Corporation, which would not be bound to answer them. At the seventh meeting,[106] the Chairman said that in order to devote sufficient time to the study of important projects already received, it had been decided to examine no new projects for the next four months.

The first Annual Report was issued on 21 June 1949, covering the period beginning in July 1947, when the Chairman-designate was requested by the Secretary of State to prepare the first plans for the establishment of the new Corporation, until 31 December 1948.[107] The initial organisation was described, being along functional lines in London and regional lines in the Colonies. The need to train and provide guidance for the regional units was stated, and the tentative nature of the initial arrangements for what was said to be a Corporation unique with its widespread and diverse functions was noted. It was asserted that 'in the short and in the long run, the objective of reducing the dollar deficit is closely linked with the objective of raising the standard of living in the Colonies.' The production of both local foodstuffs and simpler manufactures was relevant to that objective. Africa was believed to be the most promising field for large-scale development, and the need for greater supplies of manufactured goods by local production and imports was stressed. The Far East illustrated an aspect of the Corporation's task: those areas, notably Hong Kong and Singapore, which had resources of capital and skill, would be left to private enterprise. Other areas, not so well endowed, which would not attract sufficient private capital, would be where the Corporation's main efforts would be made. In a section of its Report on the Corporation's internal relationships with the Colonial Office, the Treasury and Colonial Governments, the Board felt compelled 'to state their conviction that if real achievement is to be attained against all the physical difficulties of Colonial development, a certain measure of freedom to venture and to act in circumstances of doubt should be accorded to the Board and executives and local managers of the Corporation'. In the choice of projects the Board felt it necessary 'to avoid all-embracing and grandiose economic development plans in favour of the selection of more concrete proposals', even if they were less ambitious in their size and scope. Consequently, development schemes could 'not be expected to conform rigidly or exactly to an elaborate list of priorities', and the Board expressed the hope that their applications for capital sanction would continue to be examined 'in the light of certain simple and paramount criteria, of which the benefit in the local economy' was the first. The difficulty of assessing schemes for which varying estimates of yields and prices were made was stated, as was the expense of providing housing and communications and the minimum necessary services, which together amounted 'in typical cases to a doubling of the normal capital cost of an undertaking'. Thus in order to develop a large area of Nyasaland, beginning with the cultivation of tung on an estate of 20,000 acres, it was necessary to spend £557,000 on residential buildings, welfare and recreational buildings, water supply, electrical installations, a jetty, feeder roads and nearly half the cost of 70 miles of main road. This represented 34 per cent of the estimated total capital expenditure on the project by the CDC, which felt that this kind of expenditure should be separated from the rest if its commercial programme was to be expanded. The Secretary of State was invited to pay special attention to this problem. As agreed with the Secretary of State, the Corporation did not regard public utilities as an important part of its concern, which would instead be with ordinary share risks. Given the kind of risks to be undertaken, large profits were not to be expected. In the development of various projects, particularly tropical agricultural projects, where land clearance and subsequent plantings of tree crops were concerned, there was likely to be a prolonged fructification period during which large expenditures would be incurred and no revenue earned. By the end of 1948 the number of undertakings in operation was nine and the number of projects under serious consideration was 57, spread over 24 territories. The undertakings in operation were (i) gold dredging in British Guiana, (ii) timber concession in British Guiana, (iii) salt production in the Turks and Caicos Islands, (iv) managing agents and consulting engineers to the Government of St Lucia for the rebuilding of Castries, (v) sealing in the Falkland Islands, (vi) poultry and general farming in The Gambia, (vii) tung growing in Nyasaland, (viii) fisheries of Lake Nyasa in Nyasaland, and (ix) manila hemp in North Borneo. The total capital commitment was just over £3 million, excluding the cost of rebuilding Castries. The estimate capital commitment of the projects under investigation, if all were accepted in their existing form, was estimated at £32–33 million. The Board, in expressing its appreciation of the manner that its work had generally been received, noted that 'scarcely any of the undertakings which have been announced have been immune from criticism (some of it misinformed) of various kinds', although it was regarded as understandable that interests who expected to be adversely affected by a scheme would so inform political and commercial circles. The Board, therefore, expressed its hope that 'the spirit of constructive criticism and suggestion' hitherto experienced would continue to prevail.

The first Report thus provided, on the one hand, details of its organisation and methods and, on the other hand, muted expression of its somewhat uneasy relationship with Government Departments, Colonial Governments and other interests. It is not necessary to rehearse here the material fully reported annually in the Reports. The files provide material for two matters that in the nature of the case would not be fully reported. These matters are, first, the perennial problems of control by the Colonial Office and Treasury and, secondly, a full account of several schemes. These, then, are the matters to be examined. The first will bring out the strengths and weaknesses of the Corporation method of commercial development, while the second will show how a few selected schemes were developed.

v. THE CONCORDAT OF 1949 BETWEEN THE CDC, THE COLONIAL OFFICE AND THE TREASURY

The agreement of 30 July 1948 restored an uneasy peace over the control of capital issues. It is true that the Chairman complained in September of that year to the Chancellor of the Exchequer about the delays in getting his projects through the Colonial Office, and the Chancellor undertook to have the matter investigated.[108] But when the Economic Secretary to the Treasury saw the Chairman in January 1949, the latter was reasonably happy with the existing position, while the Economic Secretary found himself wondering whether there was too little Government say in the selection of major schemes rather than too much.[109] In fact, officials assured him that 'the procedures laid down were adequate to ensure that the Corporation would not be able to launch out on projects which the Government thought unsuitable on any particular grounds',[110] and he was content that the existing arrangement should be allowed to run for a while.

However, matters were brought to a head over the project for tung oil. The Treasury sought justification for the project in terms of the criteria laid down by the Colonial Development Working Party, particularly as the initial yield was not expected to be available until the year 1960. The criteria, as given in the Report of the CDWP, were (a) the resulting product should satisfy an effective and continuing demand, (b) the period between starting work on the project and reaping results should be short, unless the long-term need was particularly important, (c) the proposed development should be a paying proposition over a reasonable period of time, and (d) the scarce resources required for the project should have no better alternative use. The Treasury expected the Colonial Office to obtain the necessary information from the CDC and pass it on, the project being regarded as intrinsically worth while and also for its contribution to the future development of the Vipya Highlands area of Nyasaland.[111] But the request brought to a head the broader relationships of the Colonial Office with the CDC as it was realised that the need to estimate scarce currency requirements involved a departure from the agreement of 30 July. It was suggested that, as the Chairman was likely to resent having to provide information of the kind set forth in the CDWP report, the Secretary of State should first discuss with the Chancellor,[112] which was agreed. Meanwhile, in the absence of the Chairman in the West Indies, the CDC provided the necessary information and the Secretary of State was recommended to give capital sanction for the project.[113]

The basic issue remained and was the subject of a discussion between the Chancellor, the Parliamentary Under-Secretary and the Chairman on 1 April 1949, when the Chairman reluctantly agreed to accept the need to fulfil the CDWP criteria. He requested that a memorandum should be prepared to define the future machinery for liaison between the CDC, on the one side, and the Colonial Office and Treasury on the other.[114] A memorandum was drafted by the Colonial Office and the Treasury[115] but rejected by the Chairman, who produced his own,[116] which the Parliamentary Under-Secretary was anxious to accept, if that was at all possible without surrendering the Colonial Office's basic requirements.[117] While the memorandum was under discussion, the Chancellor of the Exchequer sent a most tactful explanation of the Treasury's need to examine with the CDC the whole picture in relation to our foreign exchange position and so to receive a programme of operations. Such estimates as were provided would, he stated, be expected to include provision for unforeseen contingencies. The Chancellor mentioned a sum of around £100,000 a year for that item.[118] The Chancellor's persuasive prose did not, however, meet the point at issue over the memorandum which was, according to the Chairman, that 'the CDWP report would draw the Corporation into a new procedure' which, in the view of the Board of the CDC, was unworkable.[119] Therefore, the Board felt the need to press for some definition of the limits of its obligations concerning Departmental consultations. The negotiations appear to have an admixture of the unreal about them when it is found that the Treasury official involved felt 'strongly that, as a matter of policy, we should be unwise to yield on all Lord Trefgarne's points – even if, in fact, to yield on most of them should not make any immediate practical difference'.[120] The exchange continued until the end of September 1949, when agreement was reached.[121]

There was mild rejoicing in the Colonial Office, as there were thought to be 'one or two passages' in the Despatch making the new agreement available to Colonial Governors at which the Chairman 'might have jibbed, but has not'.[122] The prolonged negotiations, resulting in what became known in the Colonial Office as the 'Concordat', led to the Circular Despatch of 20 January 1950 entitled 'Colonial Development Corporation: Procedure and Relationships of Government Departments'.[123] The Secretary of State defined the main object of the procedure outlined as providing the CDC with the maximum freedom for its operations that was compatible with both the Secretary of State's statutory obligations and with 'the need for ensuring that its projects comply with the general policy decisions of

HMG regarding, for example, hard currencies, or materials in short supply, or other factors affecting the national economy generally'. Governors were told that the CDC was not entitled to any privilege, or priority, that was not available to their competitors in the same sphere of activity. He endorsed the Corporation's policy of avoiding undue publicity, and asked Governors to co-operate with the Corporation in this as exaggerated hopes would beget subsequent criticism. Colonial Governments were asked to co-operate fully with the Corporation in its task of developing the resources of Colonial territories.

The contentious paragraph 7 of the Concordat read, in its final form, as follows:

It is recognised that there must be some differences between the relationships between Government Departments themselves and the relationship between Government Departments and the Corporation. The former relationship cannot exclude from consideration, as between Departments, any question which such Departments consider to be relevant. But, as between the Treasury and the Colonial Office, on the one hand, and the Corporation, on the other, a different relationship exists, and these Departments felt it necessary, in that field, to define the main principles. The first is that the requirements of official administration should not nullify that measure of independent executive responsibility that has been laid upon the Corporation by Parliament: the second is that the Corporation should be in some degree insulated from the complex and many-sided internal procedures upon which Government policy is founded. The Secretary of State has always recognised that these procedures, involving, as they must, a considerable degree of inter-Departmental interrogation and discussion, might come to impose, if applied equally to the Corporation, an undue administrative burden on the Corporation's executives.

The Concordat continued, with six sub-headings. First, there was the application for capital sanction. The requirements laid down in the CDWP report were stated. When once approved, the Corporation was free to handle a project, providing it abided by Government decisions concerning scarce currencies, or materials, or other national economic factors. Secondly, there would be guidance, as necessary, from the Secretary of State on general Government policy, while the Corporation would provide a quarterly list of projects being planned and of undertakings in operation. Thirdly, the Board would determine administrative expenditure, except where scarce currencies were involved or any specific directions or representations made by the Secretary of State arising from the annual report of the auditors. Fourthly, the commercial soundness of a project was the exclusive concern of the Board of the CDC. Fifthly, the Corporation would, from time to time, provide estimates in broad categories of its expected foreign currency expenditure, making, in addition, provision for 'unforeseen dollar expenditure of an urgent character', which could not be particularised under the headings of the programme. Sixthly, should the Corporation borrow from IBRD, the Treasury would exercise any necessary control at the time when the Corporation asked permission to seek the loan.

The Board was glad to report in the Annual Report for 1949 the conclusion of the agreement, which included the acceptance of the principle that it was the sole judge of the commercial soundness of any project submitted to it for it was 'a principle which the Board regard as indispensable to the discharge of their task'.[124] This was the concession which an official of the Treasury was most unhappy about, suggesting to an official of the Ministry of Food that neither of them 'would be prepared to allow it in the case of the Overseas Food Corporation, at least in connection with the East African Groundnuts Scheme'.[125] His uneasiness had to be contained until May 1951 when the Chancellor, Mr Hugh Gaitskell, proposed that 'the Colonial Office and the Treasury should have the power to question the commercial soundness of a project, if it seemed right to them to do so'.[126] The private view of the Colonial Office is suggested in but one minute, where the main defect of the Concordat was said to be that it reflected the Chairman's 'anxiety not to be caught in imaginary meshes of Government bureaucracy and to be given as free a hand as possible in carrying out Corporation's functions', which, by overstressing the fear, had handicapped 'that type of free, frank and informal collaboration with the Corporation' that was desirable.[127] To the outsider with the benefit of knowing the later views of the Treasury, the Chairman's anxieties do not appear as exaggerated or his requirements as questionable as the officials apparently believed at the time. There was a conflict of method and purpose, which was seen overmuch as one of personality. Officials rarely seem to have thought through the issues sufficiently before taking up a position which they tended to consider as not negotiable. This was perhaps largely due to the lack of guidelines. The implications of having a Corporation of the kind had never been thoroughly studied. Much was left to be worked out *solvitur ambulando*, which is necessarily a piecemeal approach and liable to maximise conflicts once things begin to go wrong. The agreement on the Concordat was an important step forward, but it should have come much earlier. Given the lack of preliminary study and the changing economic environment, the Corporation owed much in its first three years to the understanding Parliamentary Under-Secretary, Mr Rees-Williams.

On 23 August 1950 the Chairman wrote to the Secretary of State to confirm his request that he might relinquish his appointment at the end of his third year, an option he was granted by the then Secretary of State on accepting the chairmanship.[128] The Corporation was then running 49 projects. The Chairman said he had come to the conclusion that it needed 'an objective appraisal from within of the methods and future plans', and this would be 'best carried out by a fresh mind'. The Secretary of State was loath to think, in view of the way the Corporation had been developed by the Chairman, that the time had come 'for a new man at the helm', and he would have preferred the Chairman to have continued, but reluctantly agreed to the request to be released.[129]

Lord Reith was appointed Chairman at a salary of £5000 per annum for a term of five years as from 7 November 1950.[130] In one of several attempts to get the salary raised, the new Secretary of State, Mr Oliver Lyttelton, stressed that the duties of the Chairman of the CDC were different from the management, as in the case of some nationalised industries, of 'a going concern controlling assets which have already been successfully erected by someone else'. He went on to state that the tremendous variety in the schemes involved, the need to create new undertakings in all types of conditions and the numerous pitfalls and snags would, by themselves, justify a higher salary, but in addition he was anxious that the taxpayers' money had to be safeguarded and 'the cause of Colonial Development should not have a setback from repeated failures'.[131]

VI. THE GAMBIA POULTRY SCHEME

'Failures' was a new word to enter the vocabulary of the CDC. It had not existed when Lord Trefgarne wrote in his letter of 23 August 1950: 'It is my belief that the organisation so created is running satisfactorily, and even efficiently, though that may be thought rather a bold claim for such a young concern.' It entered, suddenly and unexpectedly, on 15 February 1951 when the new Chairman wrote to tell the Secretary of State that The Gambia Poultry Scheme could not be carried out in the form originally conceived, and that about half the capital of £900,000 might have to be written off.[132] The CDC has, perhaps, never fully recovered from that traumatic shock, certainly it cast a shadow over the Corporation for some considerable time. The story cannot be traced in detail before January 1950 as the appropriate file (File 19889/62/10 of 1949) has been Destroyed Under Statute. However, the early essentials were established in the course of an independent enquiry conducted by Mr Gerald R. Upjohn, KC, over the period 2 June 1951 to 23 April 1952 and published in a White Paper.[133] The salient points were: (1) The Chairman had been asked by the Governor of The Gambia to help the Colony (p.7 of Cmd 8560); (2) The Chairman thought it might be a good plan to establish a Poultry Farm under the management of an American poultry farmer, Mr Millard J. Phillips, whom he had met in Bahamas in January 1948, where he managed a large poultry farm containing some 75,000 birds (p.7); (3) On 18 March 1948 Mr Phillips was appointed and requested to report on the practicability of producing in The Gambia on intensive lines poultry, eggs and, possibly, hogs (p. 8); (4) A scheme was proposed which was expected ultimately to produce 20,000,000 eggs and 1,000,000 lb of poultry per annum (p. 8); (5) The Ministry of Food raised objections to the scheme in June 1948 and, as he felt this raised a point of principle, the Chairman took up the matter with the Chancellor of the Exchequer in September 1948, and the Chairman's views were approved (pp. 9–10); (6) Dr Fowler, who joined the CDC as Head of the Animal Products Division, was critical of the assumption made concerning the amount of food required for the laying flock and the yield per acre of coarse grains to be grown in The Gambia for the flock (p. 11); (7) The assumptions underlying the revised estimates accepted by the Board were: (a) that the timber from the land cleared would realise approximately £237,000; (b) egg production would be 200 eggs per bird per annum; (c) selling prices would be 2s. 6d. per dozen c.i.f. for eggs and 2s. od. per lb c.i.f. for poultry; (d) feeding grain would be produced at 900 lbs per acre (p. 16); (8) Assumption (a) was 'hopelessly wrong and, in 1949, a further sum of £110,000 had to be appropriated to the scheme' (p. 17, para. 56); (9) Assumption (b) could not be assessed because the data were not recorded (p. 17, para. 57);[134] (10) Assumption (c) was a substantial underestimate (p. 17, para. 58); (11) Assumption (d) was an over-estimate, but the failure of the scheme was not due to that. Indeed, as late as October, 1950 [i.e. at the end of Lord Trefgarne's period as Chairman], Dr Fowler himself had great faith in the future of the scheme, in spite of the extremely disappointing crop reports about 207 lbs to the acre, in the meantime.' (p. 18, para. 3). As will be seen, the White Paper was not correct on this question of the necessity, or otherwise, of local production of feedingstuffs.

The rest of the White Paper is not directly relevant here. In the 1950 file, there is a letter dated 19 June 1950 from the Chairman to the Secretary of State asking for the latter's intervention with the Minister of Agriculture as his Ministry intended to refuse entry of all dressed poultry from The Gambia, because Newcastle disease had been discovered among native-kept poultry some seven miles from the CDC's Farm. This was contrary to an earlier assurance that this would take place only if fowl pest broke out among the poultry on the CDC's own Farm.[135] However, the Ministry decided not to proceed and the Secretary of State did not need to intervene.[136] But he did ask the Governor for a full report,[137] which was sent on 7 July 1950.[138] The main points were:

(1) The Manager of the CDC's Farm knew that The Gambia Veterinary Department had diagnosed Newcastle disease in native-kept poultry in September 1949, but had disputed the correctness of the diagnosis.

(2) It had never been suggested that there had been any notifiable disease on the CDC's Farm, and before the first shipment of 10,000 birds left The Gambia on 2 July the disease-free condition had been certified.

(3) Little was known of the incidence of disease in native-kept chickens and, until the establishment of the CDC's Farm, the question was of little importance. It was probable that fowl pest was epidemic, if not endemic.

(4) The Veterinary Department in The Gambia consisted of the Director of Veterinary Services, who was also Director of the Sierra Leone Department, and one Veterinary Officer, and was mainly concerned with cattle disease.

(5) Unless imports of dressed poultry were allowed into the United Kingdom, the CDC's Farm was likely to fail as there was no alternative large-scale market available.

(6) A copy of a circular letter which the National Utility Poultry Society sent round the Colonial Empire was enclosed. It referred to the Ministry and to tropical disease, saying: 'It is not difficult to appreciate that in the event of failure, this Society will not hesitate to gloat and trumpet that as far back as August, 1949, it had protested and had specifically – in their circular letter at any rate – mentioned the possibility of disease. . . . The failure of the

undertaking . . . will be hailed with vociferous delight by the poultry keepers of Great Britain and must have repercussions of some magnitude, particularly following on the report of the Public Accounts Committee on the East African Groundnuts Scheme.'[139] (7) As, at certain times, there was only one Verterinary Officer in The Gambia, it was suggested that the CDC should provide funds for another officer.

The Ministry of Agriculture and Fisheries was perturbed, having first heard 'a few months' previously of the intention to send poultry from The Gambia, because there would be 'unpleasant public comment' if either a serious outbreak of disease followed importation or public money was lost because entry had to be refused. It was suggested that the CDC should consult at any early stage where the possibility of meat imports was involved.[140] While the Colonial Office was agreeable, the CDC was not.[141] When, at the end of September, the veterinary officer certified that the premises and the poultry on the CDC farm were free from Newcastle disease, he added that the flock had Fowl Typhoid and the Governor asked that the certificate be passed on to the Ministry of Agriculture.[142] The CDC objected to the certificate, as only the absence, or presence, of Newcastle disease had to be notified.[143] However, the Colonial Office insisted it should be presented to the Ministry of Agriculture and asked the CDC to forward it.[144] On 26 October there was an outbreak of an unidentified disease on the CDC's Farm, and the veterinary officer was unable to provide the necessary certificate for shipment to take place. A breakdown in the refrigeration plant meantime led to the loss of 100,000 lbs of frozen carcasses valued at some £20,000. (This was given as 70,000 lbs in the Annual Report for 1950, p. 17.) The Manager of the CDC's Farm criticised the veterinary officer, and refused to co-operate further.[145] He went on leave and then resigned, being replaced in January 1951 by Mr H. A. Graves, who was transferred from the Niger Agricultural Project of the CDC.[146]

It was not until the end of October 1950 that misgivings about the scheme came to a head, and an investigating mission visited the Farm early in February 1951.[147] It found that the fertility of the 10,000 acres was poor and difficult to maintain, and that maximum production, after five years' development, was likely to be no more than half the original estimate of 5000 tons.[148] So the scheme, as originally conceived, could not be carried out despite the proof that the original poultry stock, together with their progeny, could be reared successfully in The Gambia and were intrinsically healthy.[149] There had been no fowl pest on the Farm, but outbreaks of typhoid caused the loss of 30,000 birds. The position was brought under control by inoculation and the remaining stock of 50,000 birds was in fairly good condition. The laying stock took the brunt of the typhoid disease, and so most of the remaining poultry was breeding, not laying, stock. Already 38,620 eggs and 51,617 lbs of dressed poultry had been exported to the United Kingdom and a further consignment was on the way when, on 28 February 1951, the Secretary of State explained the position in the House of Commons. The export of eggs had been discontinued. The announcement came at a particularly unfortunate time as the Government had to seek Parliamentary authority for writing off losses in the East African groundnut scheme.[150] In reply to Lord Trefgarne's question whether it was necessary to spotlight in this way the CDC's first failed undertaking, which involved less than 2 per cent of the CDC's committed capital, the Secretary of State explained that the initiative had been that of the CDC itself. With the latter's communication of 15 February and in the light of articles in the press, notably the *Daily Telegraph*, emanating from The Gambia, which probably prompted a series of Parliamentary Questions, he could not avoid making a statement.[151] In the debate which took place on 13 March 1951[152] the Opposition's case was, in part, a suggestion that much of the responsibility for the scheme rested squarely on Lord Trefgarne.[153] The Minister of State urged that other members of the Board at the time were also responsible[154] and this led in time to the independent enquiry by Mr Gerald R. Upjohn to which reference has been made above.[155] Lord Trefgarne made a personal statement in the House of Lords on 11 April 1951.

In a report, dated 26 April 1951, it was stated that it was essential for the CDC to grow its own feeding stuffs in The Gambia if the supply was to be forthcoming and uneconomic imports were to be avoided, and that a 10,000-acre farm could not provide more than one-third of the total requirements, which had in fact been underestimated. A farm of 30,000 acres would be too costly, and so the project should be modified, or abandoned.[156] The Board of the CDC decided, on 3 May 1951, to set up a Working Party representing the Colonial Office, The Gambia Government and the CDC to consider a modified agricultural scheme for the Farm as further efforts to rear poultry were abandoned when Newcastle disease reached the Farm in April 1951. The main recommendations in its report were that (i) an investigational farm of about 400 acres be established on the land already stumped and cleared, (ii) groundnuts, cotton and flue-cured tobacco offered the best prospects, (iii) livestock should form an integral part of the farm,

(iv) trials should be carried out over a five-year period, 1952–56 inclusive, (v) the Colonial Office and The Gambia Government should contribute equally to the annual cost of £10,000, any unused balance from one year being available within the five-year period, (vi) the CDC would contribute £1250 towards the Manager's salary, and (vii) the Director of Agriculture in the Colony would be administratively in charge.[157] Both The Gambia Government[158] and the CDC[159] accepted the recommendations, which were rather unsympathetically described by Lord Reith in the Annual Report for 1951 as 'a sort of salvage operation, to retrieve something from the Poultry Farm Scheme',[160] a style of writing deprecated in the Colonial Office.[161] However, no practical possibilities for commercial development emerged, according to the CDC's Annual Report for 1954,[162] and the Corporation withdrew by agreement at the end of 1954, transferring its assets to The Gambia Government in composition for contributing to the operating expenses over the following two years.

In March 1951, the Lord President wrote to the Chancellor of the Exchequer[163] to say that 'The heavy financial loss on the Gambia poultry farm seems, according to Lord Reith's information, to be another case where a small pilot ecological survey of the ground would have brought to light its fundamental lack of fertility, and its probable response to cultivation in the given climate circumstances.' Financial loss and public discredit resulting through failure to take 'this elementary precaution' appalled him, and he enquired whether the Treasury would insist on such surveys in appropriate cases before sanctioning development expenditure. He felt that 'if it were known that the Treasury were specially watching this aspect, expensive short-cuts would not be attempted in future.' The Chancellor minuted 'Not a bad idea' and told the Secretary of State[164] that Treasury officials would, in future, be required to satisfy themselves, as far as was possible, 'that the known facts, as ascertained by experiment or from experts, justify the undertaking involved'. The Secretary of State was no less anxious to avoid further failures through lack of investigation and, to show the awareness of this by the CDC, he mentioned that in the case of the North Borneo rice scheme, despite pressure from the local Government for early progress, the Corporation had insisted upon a pilot scheme, very wisely as it had turned out.[165] But he pointed out also that the Corporation was charged under the ORD Act 'with the duty of securing the *investigation*, formulation and carrying out of projects for developing resources of Colonial territories',[166] and felt uneasy about any suggestion that Government Departments should attempt to assess the technical evidence on the basis of which the CDC submitted schemes. He thought the CDC might be asked for information on such matters. The Chancellor agreed but thought that judgement on commercial soundness could no longer be left entirely to the CDC as was appropriate earlier, and this matter might be considered by officials.[167] However, some of his officials, quite rightly, doubted the Treasury's ability to go far in that direction because, even if the Treasury had complete powers of objecting to any scheme, they could only do so, as a normal rule, on advice from these same sources, i.e. the Colonial Office and the Colonial Government. For, if the few schemes which the new Chairman felt might have been better conceived and executed were considered, 'the Treasury could have objected to the majority only if the Colonial Office or the Colonial Government had advised it – there was not and could not be any particular act of divination in the Treasury about the commercial soundness or otherwise of these schemes.'[168] Nor did the Concordat prevent, in the last resort, the Treasury refusing capital sanction for a project which was considered to be harebrained.

However, before leaving the Gambia scheme, the observations of the Governor, Sir Wyn Harris, deserve notice. In his view, the overriding cause of the failure of the schemes in his territory was due to the lack of 'basic experimentation and proper investigation'.[169] He believed that as most of the known, sound commercial propositions in Africa had already been taken up by private enterprise, it meant that the Corporation could only take up schemes which, however promising, were necessarily speculative, particularly so if the basic investigational work had not been undertaken. He continued:

> I do not think that the present policy of Her Majesty's Government with regard to the financial structure of the Corporation will lead the Corporation to take a short-sighted view or to go in for schemes yielding quick return, but I do think that any prudent Board is going to think twice before it sinks possibly some tens of thousands of pounds in the necessary investigation and experimentation of what appears possibly even a most helpful scheme.

Commercial firms normally did not take up projects which looked hopeful, if there was a fair risk that they might prove fruitless on investigation; and this was likely to be both expensive and prolonged. The Governor suggested a possible solution to the problem, which, he believed, had to be solved if the Corporation was to function satisfactorily. It was that the substantial sum of the CD & W Vote should be earmarked for investigations into projects which might be suitable for participation by the CDC and Colonial Governments, the CDC being given the first option if the project seemed to be a commercial proposition. He instanced an area of some hundred square miles of saline swamp, the fringes of which were planted to rice, which might possibly be turned into an area suitable for rice if investigations confirmed that the salt of the river could be sealed off. Yet, if the investigation was successful and the area became suitable for peasant agriculture, which would require relatively little capital, it would 'be quite impossible for this Government to make a surcharge for peasant grown rice on the grounds that £45,000 had been spent, £25,000 of which had been spent on investigation work'. Consequently, he felt that, unless there were funds under the control of the Secretary of State for investigation and experimentation, the CDC would never undertake anything 'really worth-while'.

The Governor was told that the Secretary of State and the CDC were agreed that the basic investigation which did not lead directly and in a fairly short period to a profit-making project should be the responsibility of the Government rather than that of the Corporation.[170] In the poorer Colonies, at least, it meant the use of CD & W funds. In fact, the Governor's Upper River Rice Development project was being examined at that time on the lines the Governor outlined.

However, pressures are never all in the same direction. Investigation was time-consuming as well as expensive, and Ministers, while anxious to see that necessary studies were made, were no less anxious that the Corporation should maintain a lively pace, as is explained in the next section.

vii. THE PACE OF DEVELOPMENT, 1950–1951

At the regular meeting of the Colonial Office and the CDC that was held on 18 July 1950, the Chairman, Lord Trefgarne, announced that the Corporation had been seriously considering its rate of growth.[171] One member of the Board had suggested that there should be a period of twelve months' consolidation before any new schemes were undertaken. Although the Chairman did not think that was necessary, he favoured a lull of some six months during which the Corporation would not be 'pushing' schemes very vigorously. Meanwhile, the Corporation was in process of reorganising; it was splitting up the Directorate of Operations and the agricultural section. The Chairman asked the Minister of State at what rate HMG thought that the CDC's resources should be used. The Minister hoped that the Corporation would utilise its resources as speedily as was compatible with sound progress. Schemes under active consideration represented potential commitments of £14 million, and a total of £60 million might be committed over the next two years. The Colonial Office fully appreciated the enormous amount of organisation which the Corporation's scheme entailed, and was glad that schemes had been undertaken in those Colonies which needed them most, although it was hoped that more might be done in the smaller West Indian Islands. In September 1950 the Chairman said he was proposing to submit a paper to his Board on the subject of the further activities of the Corporation. A great deal of the original capital had been committed and there was the danger of overloading the administrative capacity of the Corporation. He suggested a nine months' selective moratorium on further schemes. The Secretary of State, while appreciating the difficulties, indicated HMG's desire to proceed with economic development *pari passu* with political development in the Colonies and felt that there was grave danger of the moratorium being misinterpreted if made public. The Board accepted temporarily the policy of a selective moratorium on the admission of new projects over the period to 30 June 1951.[172] After strengthening the executive side, the Chairman felt that the Corporation could handle the full £100 million provided in the ORD Act.

However, after the meeting of 18 July the Minister of State wondered whether it could effectively handle more than £60 million of investments or whether another Corporation should be set up to take over either a geographical district, such as the West Indies, or a function, such as the industrial section, of the CDC.[173] The immediate bottleneck was not finance but, as the Chairman stated, pressure on staff and the specially difficult problem of getting suitable managerial staff for overseas. A new Corporation would solve neither of these, whereas devolution of functions by the CDC would be of assistance; regional boards were put forward as at least part of the answer.[174] Three additional full-time members of the Board were also advised at salaries appropriate to the level required.[175] It was realised that the new Chairman would have to be in general sympathy with the plan for devolution.

After he had accepted these recommendations, the Minister of State was still doubtful whether any one concern could develop 'on the scale and in the time that we expect the CDC to develop'.[176] He did not feel it was reasonable to expect 'any single organisation in any region to be able to deal with such a variety of enterprises as a gold mine, a hotel and a wattle industry'. When this view was discussed in the Colonial Office, officials were critical, though it was not felt that the problem could be solved either by laying down certain general criteria to govern the selection of projects by the Corporation. As one official minuted:[177] 'We had some experience in trying to lay down criteria of this kind for Colonial development projects generally in the CDWP, and I doubt whether any of us feel very proud of the result.' It was not thought that the time had come for a second Corporation, unless the purpose was changed from that of encouraging and supplementing private enterprise. The main positive recommendations, apart from the appointment of further full-time members of the Board, were effected by the new Chairman and described briefly in the Annual Report for 1950. They were: (i) strengthening the organisation at headquarters, (ii) intention to appoint regional controllers abroad, (iii) transference of self-supporting schemes to local ownership, (iv) improved financial control within the organisation, and (v) a Committee of the Board to assess projects.

The Colonial Office offered, at the monthly meeting held on 15 December 1950, to prepare for the guidance of the Corporation a statement of priorities by region and by commodity.[178] The memorandum was sent on 9 April 1951[179] and neatly summarised by the CDC[180] thus:

COLONIAL OFFICE SUGGESTED PRIORITIES FOR DEVELOPMENT

A. By Colonies	B. By Commodities

A.
I. Assuming principal contribution of CDC to be skill and finance Colonial Office categorises Colonies thus:

(1) Lacking   both   skill   and finance:

British Guiana	Sarawak
British Honduras	Seychelles
Falkland Islands	Sierra Leone
Gambia	Somaliland
Leeward Islands	S African HC
Nigeria	Territories
North Borneo	Windward Islands
Nyasaland	Zanzibar
Pacific HC Territories	

(2) With skill but lacking finance:

Barbados	Malta
Jamaica	Mauritius

Kenya
(3) With finance but lacking skill:
Fiji   Tanganyika
Gold Coast   Uganda
(4) With access to both skill and
finance:
Cyprus   Singapore
Malaya   Trinidad
Northern Rhodesia

II. On the basis of A.I. the Colonial Office suggested priorities thus:
Priority 1: Colonies with no CDC projects at December 31, 1950:
  Leeward Islands   Sierra Leone
  Malta   Somaliland
  Pacific HC Territories   Zanzibar
  Sarawak
Priority 2: Colonies in which Colonial Office consider more should
           be done:
  Jamaica   Uganda
  Nigeria   Windward Islands
  Tanganyika   (apart from Dominica)
Priority 3: Colonies in which Colonial Office consider project should
           be undertaken if possible:
  Cyprus   Gold Coast
  Fiji   Trinidad

B.

I. Primary Products
Priority 1: cotton, coal, basic chemicals, fish, jute and jute sub-
           stitutes, livestock, rice.
Priority 2: Other simple foods for local consumption, cocoa, base
           metals such as copper, zinc, lead and manganese but
           excluding tin, hides and skins, timber especially softwoods,
           coffee, oils and fats.
Priority 3: Gold and diamonds, tobacco, tanning extracts, hard
           fibres, essential oils.

II. Fabricated Products
Priority 1: Steel if economic production possible.
Priority 2: Aluminium – if production proceeds in Gold Coast or in
           North Borneo; doubtful if a further project is practicable.

III. Manufacturing Industries
           Industries where product concerned, e.g. building mat-
           erials, is required to meet important local development
           requirements or to enhance local production through
           more economic utilisation, e.g. sawmills.

IV. Basic Services
Priority 1: Hydro-electric plant, transport, water, etc.
Priority 2: Hotels.

It was recognised that the undertaking of projects should not depend
entirely on priorities. 'Thus, a scheme for production of a low priority
commodity in a low priority territory may well have great potentialities for the advancement of Colonial development as a whole, if
one of its main functions is to demonstrate how productivity of peasant
agriculture can be increased by better methods of cultivation and
provision of mechanical appliances, fertilisers, etc., from central
pools.'[181]

The summary was neat, though it had not managed to be inclusive
for it had not mentioned Malaya and Singapore, which were not put
into any of the three categories by the Colonial Office as their need for
external assistance depended on the level of prices of their exports of
rubber and tin.[182] The memorandum was shelved, largely because the
Board of the CDC was reluctant to adopt any new schemes, however
strong the arguments in favour of them might be. It was felt in the
Colonial Office that what was needed was some form of stimulus to cut
through this lack of confidence and get the Corporation working
again. It was realised that the priority memorandum by itself would
not achieve that result.[183] It was a matter of opinion whether the
considerable falling off in the rate of submission of new schemes was
due to the working of the late Chairman's 'selective moratorium' or to
the 'new broom' activities of the new Chairman.[184] Be that as it may, it
was decided to use the memorandum in the Colonial Office as a broad
guide to policy and the background against which to view individual
applications, unless, and until, the CDC rejected any of it.[185]

VIII. AN APPRAISAL OF CDC, 1951–1952

The Colonial Office memorandum of April 1951 was prepared on the
basis that 'The assessment of the commercial soundness of projects is a
matter primarily for the Corporation and the Secretary of State is not
in a position to judge the commercial soundness of individual projects
or the relative attraction from the commercial point of view of the
different Colonial territories.'[186] In reply to the Chancellor, it was
agreed that officials should examine the question of judging commercial soundness.[187] Although officials agreed on the list of points to
be covered in applications for capital sanction by the CDC,[188] the
Chancellor still wished it to be made clear to the Corporation that, if

the Treasury was not satisfied on any points arising from the information supplied, they might refuse sanction.[189] In practice, the Treasury did not expect to go further than seek information on enquiries concerning commercial soundness or the results of any pilot schemes already undertaken,[190] but the Colonial Office feared that the Treasury's new policy would amount to the certification of the commercial soundness of schemes and, possibly, lead to the resignation of the Chairman of the Corporation, who might well take some of the members of the Board with him.[191] Some officials at the Treasury felt straddled uneasily between the probable demands of the Public Accounts Committee for tighter control[192] and the need to recognise that 'the idea of having a Corporation with a Board of high standing implies that they must be able to carry a certain amount of responsibility and exercise a reasonable measure of commercial judgement'.[193] Others thought differently because they saw the problem differently. For it was held that, unlike the other Nationalised Industries, pressures on the CDC by Colonial Governments, the Colonial Office and the Chairman and Board itself were all one way, namely in the direction of development almost for the sake of development. Consequently, it was argued, at each stage difficulties would tend to be minimised and, therefore, the Treasury should provide a second opinion by studying the evidence assembled and asking questions.[194] The Permanent Secretary and the Chancellor agreed that the Treasury must be entitled to fulfil this role and, if not satisfied, be entitled to refuse sanction.[195] The Chancellor wrote accordingly to the Secretary of State[196] who, despite the reservations of his officials, felt unable to resist.[197] Consequential changes in the Concordat were discussed with the Chairman of the CDC[198] and then with Treasury officials.[199] However, the Chairman of the CDC never answered the letter of 14 August and the whole question had to be reviewed by the new Secretary of State, Mr Oliver Lyttelton, after he took office on 28 October 1951.

Accordingly, a memorandum was prepared in the Colonial Office[200] on the CDC. Its conclusions were that:

(i) the position of the Corporation gave cause for anxiety;

(ii) it was too early to judge how far the Corporation's comparative failure was due to inherent difficulties of its conception and how far to early mistakes of policy and administration;

(iii) there might later on be need for a full review of all the Corporation's implications, economic and political, for the future of Colonial development;

(iv) the Chairman should be pressed to agree to the provision of information requested in the late Secretary of State's letter of 14 August;

(v) the Corporation should not be permitted or encouraged to devote more than a modest proportion of its capital to 'finance house' business;

(vi) no proposal for the writing-off of Treasury advances to the extent of the Corporation's capital losses should be entertained for the time being.

The point concerning 'finance house' business arose from the earlier view of the Colonial Office and Treasury that the London market was the appropriate source for providing loan funds to finance public works in the Colonies. With the possibility that the London market would be unable to supply all the funds required, it was thought better to supply funds direct from the Exchequer at gilt-edged rates rather than via the CDC, which had to charge approximately 1 per cent more to cover overheads, although no service was provided that the Colonial Office could not perform at virtually no cost. In respect of writing-off lost capital, the Colonial Office felt that acceptance at that time would provide an unfortunate precedent for repeated write-offs and, if once-for-all, a write-off should be preceded by careful investigation of causes so that these were also eliminated. Also, it was thought to be just as well that the Corporation should retain its extra incentive for caution. After considering Office views, the Secretary of State minuted as follows:[201]

I have read this penetrating analysis with great interest. I cannot offhand recall any exploitation Company of this kind that has won through in this century. We must, therefore, recognise that the Corporation is unlikely to succeed. Moreover, certain fundamental principles, in my opinion, have been violated by its consitution, aims, organisation. These are (a) that the object of organisation is to face the management at all levels with problems that they are specially trained to solve and that, therefore, businesses should deal as far as possible with homogeneous affairs, commodities or services. To run an hotel not only requires a different management but an entirely different mentality from running a hydro-electric scheme. A Board that tries to do both is either in the hands of an hotelier or an electrical engineer (possibly of both). I blush to state anything so obvious but my excuse is that it is so obvious that it was not seen. (b) The control should be delegated, not centralised. The difficulties of (a) are magnified by the necessary dispersal all over the world.

(c) It has not been quite clear whether the Corporation is designed to be an investment, finance, or operating company.

I am quite prepared to press for more information under (iv). I must, however, point out that the pressing does not require to be carried far before we shall become *de facto* responsible, i.e., 'what is not vetoed must be approved, etc.'. 'The Colonial Office should have stopped this at once.' The argument about 'finance house' business in the sense this term is used seems sound, but the description would, I think, mislead many, especially experts, who differentiate banking, issuing and lending, issuing and underwriting, from financial 'nursing'.

To sum up:

(a) I endorse all the conclusions except (ii).
(b) The trend of the Corporation policy should in my opinion be towards local companies, with Memoranda and Articles reasonably limited to one kind of job and ancillary services.
(c) These local companies should invariably seek local investment, especially corporate, in equity (geared *where appropriate* by the Corporation taking some loan or preference capital).
(d) Even if (c) is unsuccessful, as it frequently will be until confidence is built up, local directors should invariably, or almost invariably, be appointed with adequate fees at the outset and some vista of an occasional K and some CBEs opened out to them.
(e) This policy should go some way, if not to ease, at least to mitigate the heterogeneous nature and huge, though inevitable, geographical sprawl: it should avoid at least the grosser errors springing from ignorance of local conditions and labour.
(f) On this system, the Corporation will emerge more as a finance, or investment, house with wide powers to help the local management rather than an operating company in the first instance. It requires to finance, supervise, advise, admonish, expand or wind up it subsidiaries, not in my view to operate itself.

I add that I have confidence in Lord Reith's approach to his thankless task and I would hope that his assent to the above might be forthcoming.

The minute was discussed by the Secretary of State and the Minister of State, Mr Alan Lennox-Boyd, with officials. One official reflected that a rigid adherence to the principle of participation proposed by the

Secretary of State would not only have eliminated bad and doubtful projects, such as the Gambia Poultry, Atlantic Fisheries, Gambia Rice, British Honduras Hotel, Vipya Tung, Bahamas Agriculture and Tanganyika Roadways, but also it might have prevented the adoption of some projects that were not then, at any rate, in the doubtful category. These included the schemes in the South African High Commission territories, British Honduras livestock, Tanganyika Coalfields and Nigerian fisheries. The CDC was, in fact, trying to get partners and it was felt that further pressure would be useful, although exceptions would have to be made where participation was impracticable though the project was otherwise sound.[202] This was allowed for in the robust letter which the Secretary of State drafted himself, stating that it was 'if not indispensable, at least highly desirable' to entrust each project to a local company with local participation or participation of a United Kingdom company carrying on similar business.[203] The exceptional nature of the Corporation's task was recognised, and the delegation of function that it was making, coupled with the general principles suggested, which included the provision of full information on each project, were thought to give it 'the best chance of success'. The Chairman, in turn, raised issues both with the Minister of State, in the absence of the Secretary of State, and with officials. The Secretary of State proposed a meeting with the Chairman to determine the several outstanding issues. The discussion took place on 31 January 1952 and covered the following issues:

(i) Overspending by the CDC. The third stage of the Bahamas Agricultural Project was put into operation without capital sanction and the Colonial Office reacted to the casual attitude of the CDC on financial control with shocked indignation.[204] Borneo Abaca was also in excess of sanction, and several others either certain or likely to be in excess in the near future.[205] The matter was taken up with the Treasury. As the result, the Secretary of State decided that, in arriving at the amount of capital to be sanctioned for productive schemes, as distinct from loans such as had been made to the Malayan Electricity Corporation, the CDC should include a provision for contingencies which should be clearly shown in the Synopsis. Normally, the provision would be 10 per cent but in appropriate cases, where there was unusual risk, it could be as high as 20 per cent. The 'capital sanction' thus provided was not to be exceeded without prior sanction.[206]

(ii) Investigation expenditure. The Chairman proposed that part, possibly £250,000 per annum, of the Corporation's authorised capital might be made available to the Corporation as a direct grant, instead of a loan, in order to meet unfruitful expenditure on preliminary investigations and pilot schemes. The Secretary of State felt this proposal ran counter to the whole conception of the Corporation as a body which took the rough with the smooth and broke even in the long run. Also, it was thought to confuse the function of the CDC with that CD & W.[207] Indeed, the question of allocating some of CD &W resources had just been the subject of a Despatch, the terms of which the Chairman had agreed.[208] It permitted Colonies to finance investigational schemes which held a prospect of substantial long-term benefit from their CD & W allocation or, exceptionally, from additional funds contributed for the purpose. It was as far as the Colonial Office felt it could go.[209] In fact, there had been much heart-searching in the Colonial Office about this and the Chairman's point of view was, in general, regarded as reasonable. Indeed, had CD & W and the CDC not been instituted at different times, their functions would certainly have been co-ordinated from the outset and, as one official minuted: 'Over a considerable field the two can, and should, be regarded as complementary. In this connection, the old ruling that CDC moneys and CD & W moneys cannot be used on the same scheme has always seemed to me verge on the ludicrous.'[210] But the inadequacy of the existing CD & W reserves made it impossible to make a substantial allocation to CDC, and so the provisions of the Despatch were as far as these sympathies could be effected.

(iii) Writing-off lost capital. The Chairman had proposed that lost capital on abandoned schemes should be written off. The Secretary of State agreed to consult the Chancellor of the Exchequer on the procedure appropriate. The Chairman sought permission for some form of standing authority from Parliament by which bad debts could be written off without further reference at intervals of, say, five years. While the Secretary of State neither liked the idea nor thought it would be acceptable, he agreed to have the matter looked into. However, he asked the Chancellor of the Exchequer, Mr Butler, to agree, in principle, to a once-for-all specific write-off, then roughly estimated to involve £2 million.[211] In his reply, the Chancellor seized on the amount mentioned, saying it could not be held to constitute a very formidable millstone. Nor could he regard the write-off as in the end costless to HMG as it was at least doubtful whether in ordinary circumstances the CDC was required under Section 15(ii) of the ORD Act to pay over its profits to the Exchequer. Finally, he felt that the timing was unwise and suggested, without committing himself, that the new management should have time to show itself first.[212] Instead, the Colonial Office proposed that the Corporation be exempted from the liability to pay interest in respect of advances made for schemes where the capital had clearly been lost.[213] The Treasury agreed, in principle, and was prepared to make it a general agreement, not confined to schemes already abandoned. In return, the Corporation would be expected to obtain prior agreement for the winding-up of schemes.[214] This was the form eventually adopted, though it was not firmly agreed by the Board of the CDC until after the Home Affairs Committee of the Cabinet had agreed to write off capital advanced to December 1953, in the sum of about £5 million.[215] In confirming the agreement of the Secretary of State to the eleventh-hour conversion to a waiver of interest, the Minister of State, Mr H. Hopkinson, said that the proposal for a capital write-off was to be regarded as permanently withdrawn.

(iv) The provision of information. The Chairman maintained that the request that, when an application for capital sanction was made, information and the sources of such information as the Corporation had collected on technical and commercial aspects should be included damaged the constitutional independence of the Corporation and would be opposed by the Board. The Secretary of State insisted on receiving adequate information in order to be in a position to judge whether a *prima facie* case had been made out. Instead of the earlier questionnaire, the Secretary of State proposed an arrangement whereby sanction would be withheld until he had enough information to decide.[216] He informed the Chancellor accordingly; the Chancellor expressed his disappointment that he had 'gone so far to meet Reith in the matter of supply of information without giving [him] a further opportunity to express a view',[217] and he reserved his right to press the Secretary of State to insist on sufficient information being made available. Meanwhile, the Board had agreed to the conclusions arising from the discussion of 31 January 1952.[218] At the same time, the Chairman indicated the difficulties that had been experienced in securing partners, because local investors were rarely willing to lock up money in shareholdings, Colonial Governments were rarely able to invest long-term, while agricultural schemes did not usually attract United Kingdom companies.

By delaying an answer to the letter of 14 August 1951, the CDC had secured an easier arrangement over the information to be provided –

THE COLONIAL DEVELOPMENT CORPORATION, 1947-1952   373

easier, as has been recorded, than the Chancellor wished. The Secretary of State had accepted a great deal of the Chairman's point of view, had acknowledged the unenviable nature of the task and, when he was told that some of the staff had interpreted Ministerial statements since the change of Government to mean that the continued existence of the Corporation was in question, had replied unequivocally. He wrote thus: 'The problems of Colonial development are a challenge to our generation. One of the chosen instruments is the CDC. We have confidence in what you are doing. We shall support you and feel sure that with your efforts the Corporation will prosper and provide a stable and continuing career for all those who are working for it.'[219] The Secretary of State had previously confirmed the continuance of the policy of his predecessor that the CDC should not be deterred from investment in any territory on grounds of political uncertainties.[220] The international situation in the Far East in particular had been in the mind of the Chairman when he requested confirmation.[221]

SOURCES

1. File 19286/4, Economic, Part I, 1947 (CO 852/867), item 8.
1. File 19286/3, Economic 1947 (CO 852/866), item 13, CEDC 13th Minutes, 10 Mar 1947.
3. File 18706/9/68, Economic General 1947-48, items 5 and 6, letter and enclosure of 11 Mar 1947 from Viscount Portal to the Secretary of State.
4. CM 5(47) item 3, 13 Jan 1947.
5. File 18706/9/68, Economic General 1947-48, item 8, minute of 26 Mar 1947 by the Prime Minister.
6. Treasury file IF 239/638/01, Part A, p. 7, minute of 1 May 1947 by Sir Herbert Brittain.
7. Ibid., pp. 9-10, Comment of 8 May 1947 by Mr D. R. Serpell on the Secretary of State's letter of 28 Apr 1947 to the Chancellor.
8. Idem.
9. Ibid., p. 26, note of 14 May 1947 by Mr N. E. Young.
10. Ibid., p. 29, minute by Mr E. A. Shillito.
11. Ibid., pp. 11-12, note of 9 May 1947 by Mr L. M. Helsby.
12. Ibid.
13. Idem.
14. Ibid., p. 34, Note of an informal discussion at the Treasury on 14 May 1947 with Mr. J. I. C. Crombie in the Chair.
15. Idem.
16. CP(47) 175, 6 June 1947.

17. CM 53(47) item 5, 10 June 1947.

18. File 18706/9/69, Economic General, Part I, 1947, item 19, Note of a Meeting in the Treasury on 17 June 1947.

19. Treasury file IF 239/638/01, Part A, p. 95. When the recommendation of his officials was passed to the Chancellor the latter minuted 'I agree. This is a Big Idea and we must back it. H.D. 21/6.'

20. Ibid., pp. 35–9, note of 19 May 1947 by Mr E. S. Compton to Mr L. N. Helsby and letter of 20 May 1947 from Mr L. N. Helsby to Mr S. Caine.

21. File 18706/9/69, Economic General, Part I, 1947, item 27, note of a discussion held at the Treasury on 25 June 1947.

22. Idem.

23. File 18706/9/71, Economic General 1947–48, minute of 19 June 1947 by Mr S. Caine.

24. Idem.

25. Ibid., minute of 25 June 1947 by Mr S. Caine on a meeting of even date between the Secretary of State, the Parliamentary Under-Secretary, the Permanent Under-Secretary and Mr S. Caine.

26. Ibid., item 31, Memorandum of 22 July 1947 from the Secretary of State to the Prime Minister.

27. Idem.

28. Ibid., item 36, letter of 16 Aug 1947 from the Secretary of State to Lord Trefgarne.

29. Ibid., minute of 11 Feb 1948 by Sir Sidney Caine to the Parliamentary Under-Secretary. It arose over a suggestion from the British Overseas Mining Association that a mining expert should be appointed to the Board – item 136 in ibid. Lord Milverton, a former Colonial Governor, and Mr A. J. Mitchell, Colonial Service (PWD, Tanganyika) 1930–49, were appointed part-time Directors on 1 July 1948 and 4 November 1949 respectively. Sir Frank Stockdale died on 3 Aug 1949 and on 1 Nov 1949, Mr R. E. Brook was appointed Deputy Chairman in his place.

30. File 18706/9/69, Economic General, Part I, 1947, items 45–7.

31. Ibid., item 62.

32. Ibid., item 69A, note of 7 Oct 1947 by Lord Trefgarne to the Parliamentary Under-Secretary.

33. Treasury file 239/638/01, Part B, p. 67, minute of 22 Oct 1947 by Mr J. I. C. Crombie.

34. Ibid., p. 82, letter of 24 Oct 1947 from Sir Sydney Caine to Mr J. I. C. Crombie.

35. File 18706/9/69, Economic General 1947, Part II, item 95, letter of 27 Oct 1947 from Mr J. I. C. Crombie to Sir Sydney Caine.

36. Idem.

37. Treasury file IF 239/638/01, Part B, minute of 31 Oct 1947, by Mr I. S. Bancroft and File 18706/9/69, Economic General 1947, Part II, item 100, letter of 5 Nov 1947 from Mr J. I. C. Crombie to Sir Sydney Caine.

38. Cabinet Office file 6/15/24, Part I, item 3, Cabinet Committee Paper GEN 196/1 of 10 Oct 1946 – Memorandum of 1 Oct 1947 by the Under-Secretary of State.

39. Ibid., memorandum of 6 Oct 1947 by the Minister of Food (FM 47/22).

40. Ibid., memorandum PM/47/139 of 4 Oct 1947 by the Foreign Secretary, Mr Ernest Bevin. The issue did not come before the Committee of Ministers called by the Prime Minister for 17 Oct 1947 because meantime a satisfactory compromise was arrived at.

41. H. of C. Deb., Vol. 439, cols 441–6, 25 June 1947.

42. File of the Office of the Lord President 1731/2, item 10, memorandum by the Parliamentary Under-Secretary of State, 'Publicity on Colonial Development', to the Ministerial Committee on Overseas Information Services (OI(48) 3 of 26 Feb 1948).

43. Ibid., item 2.

44. Ibid., item 10.

45. Ibid., item 14, memorandum by the Parliamentary Under-Secretary of State for the Colonies, in conjunction with the Parliamentary Under-Secretary of State for Foreign Affairs and the Parliamentary Under-Secretary of State for Commonwealth Relations, 'Publicity Policy for Colonial Development', to the Information Services Committee (IS(48) 11 of 6 May 1948).

46. Idem.

47. Idem. The Committee discussed the Memorandum at its meeting on 11 May 1948 and invited the Colonial Office to pursue the proposal to provide a central club and additional hostels in London for Colonial students and, if necessary, submit a memorandum to the Lord President's Committee – see item 15 in ibid.

48. File 18706/9/68, Economic General 1947–48, item 40, letter of 19 June 1947 from Sir Edmond Hall-Patch to Mr S. Caine.

49. Ibid., item 41, letter of 21 June 1947 from Sir Sydney Caine to Sir Edmond Hall-Patch.

50. File 18706/9/71, Economic General 1947–48, item 32a, letter of 3 Aug 1947 from Lord Trefgarne to the Secretary of State.

51. File 18706/9/68, Economic General 1947–48, item 54, note of 28 Oct 1947 from Lord Trefgarne to Sir Sydney Caine.

52. Ibid., minute of 4 Nov 1947 by Sir Sydney Caine.

53. Ibid., item 37.

54. Ibid., item 58.

55. Ibid., item 57, minutes of the 10th Session on 14 Nov 1947.

56. Ibid., Instruction of Sir Sydney Caine in his minute of 14 Nov 1947.

57. Ibid., items 64 and 65.

58. Ibid., item 63. The sentence down to 'whole' was suggested by the Treasury – letter of 9 Dec 1947 by Mr D. R. Serpell to Mr C. G. Eastwood.

59. Ibid., item 88, letter of 15 Apr 1948, from the Minister of State, the Earl of Listowel, to the Governor of Singapore, Sir Franklin Gimson.

60. Ibid., item 63, letter of 9 Dec 1947 by Mr D. R. Serpell to Mr C. G. Eastwood.

61. File 18706/9/95, Economic 1948, item 1, letter of 10 Feb 1948 from Mr S. A. Hammond to Mr G. F. Seel.

62. Ibid., item 11, letter of 10 Mar 1948 from Mr R. Newton to Mr D. R. Serpell.

63. Ibid., item 13, letter of 20 Mar 1948 from Mr D. R. Serpell to Mr R. Newton.

64. HPC(47) 75, 17 Oct 1947, para. 9 – item 77 in file 18706/9/69, Economic General 1947, Part II.

65. File 18706/9/95, Economic 1948, item 17, letter of 19 Apr 1948 from Mr C. G. Eastwood to Mr D. B. Pitblado.

66. Ibid., item 42, letter of 20 July 1948 from Mr D. B. Pitblado to Mr C. G. Eastwood. Also see pp. 188–92 in Treasury file IF 580/01, Part C.

67. File 18706/9/95, Economic 1948, item 43, letter of 24 July 1948 from Mr C. G. Eastwood to Mr S. A. Hammond.

68. Ibid., minute of 6 Aug 1948 by Mr H. A. Harding.

69. Ibid., item 15a, letter of 7 Apr 1948 from Sir Sydney Caine to Mr J. I. C. Crombie.

70. Treasury file IF 580/01, Part C, pp. 56–7, note on the meeting between Messrs Crombie and Pitblado and Sir Sydney Caine.

71. Treasury file IF 239/638/01, Part C, pp. 122–3, draft letter of 8 Dec 1947 from Sir Sydney Caine to Mr J. I. C. Crombie.

72. Ibid., minute of 30 Apr 1948 by Mr J. P. Bancroft. See also the minutes of 14 May, by Mr W. H. Fisher and of 6 May by Mr A. J. Phelps.

73. File 18706/9/95, Economic 1948, item 25, letter of 4 May 1948 from Sir Sydney Caine to Lord Trefgarne.

74. Ibid., item 24, discussion of 30 Apr 1948 between Sir Sydney Caine and Lord Trefgarne.

75. Ibid., item 28, Note of discussion of 10 May 1948 between the Parliamentary Under-Secretary and Lord Trefgarne.

76. Ibid., item 29, Note of a meeting on 18 June 1948.

77. EPC(48) 18th meeting. The Committee considered a memorandum by the Chancellor of the Exchequer – EPC(48) 35 – covering the two reports.

78. File 18706/9/95, Economic 1948, item 31, Note of a meeting in Mr Rees-Williams' room at 11.30 on 21 June 1948.

79. File 18706/9/86, Economic 1947–48 (CO 852/839), item 10a, letter of 16 Dec 1947 from Sir Sydney Caine to Lord Trefgarne. Lord Trefgarne entirely concurred (letter of 18 Dec 1947 – item 13 in ibid) and the Members-designate of the Board concurred (letter of 7 Jan 1948 – item 14 in ibid).

80. File 18706/9/86, Economic 1947–48, (CO 852/839), item 19, letter of 28 May 1948 from the Chairman to the Secretary of State.

81. Ibid., minute of 31 May 1948 by the Secretary of State.

82. Ibid., minute of 31 May 1948 by the Parliamentary Under-Secretary.

83. Ibid., minute of 5 May 1948, by Mr R. Newton. A draft letter had been sent to the Treasury on 20 Apr but several sections of the Treasury (Capital issues, Balance of Payments, Overseas Finance) had to be consulted and it took some time.

84. Treasury File IF 580/231/01, pp. 65–8, minute of 18 Apr 1955.

85. Ibid., p. 75, minute of 18 Apr 1955.

86. Ibid., pp. 76–7, minute of 19 Oct 1955.

87. Ibid., minute of 21 Oct 1955.

88. File 18706/9/95, Economic 1948, item 31a, minute of 21 June 1948 by the Parliamentary Under-Secretary.

89. Ibid., minute of 26 June 1948 by Sir Sydney Caine to the Parliamentary Under-Secretary.

90. Ibid., minute of 29 June 1948 by the Parliamentary Under-Secretary.

91. Ibid., item 33, minute of 30 June 1948 by Sir Sydney Caine to the Secretary of State.

92. Ibid., minute of 5 July 1948 by the Secretary of State.

93. Ibid., item 38, letter of 6 July 1948 and enclosure from the Chairman to the Secretary of State.

94. Treasury file 580/231/01, pp. 65–6, minute of 18 Apr 1955.

95. File 18706/9/95, Economic 1948, item 42, letter of 20 July 1948 from Mr D. B. Pitblado to Mr C. G. Eastwood. This followed a minute to him of 14 July from Mr J. P. Bancroft.

96. Ibid., pp. 176–7, minute of 14 July 1948 by Mr J. P. Bancroft.

97. Ibid., item 45, urgent letter of 20 July 1948 from the Chairman to the Secretary of State.

98. Ibid., item 48, letter of 30 July 1948 from the Secretary of State to the Chairman.

99. Ibid., minute of 31 July 1948 by Mr W. L. Gorell Barnes.

100. File 18706/9/102, Economic 1948 (CO 852/840), item 2 for the Minutes of the meeting of 12 July 1948.

101. Ibid., item 6, letter of 12 Aug 1948 from Mr J. P. Cunningham, Colonial Liaison Officer of CDC, to Mr R. Newton.

102. Ibid., minutes of 3 Sep 1948 by Mr C. G. Eastwood and of 23 Sep 1948 by Mr A. H. Poynton.

103. Ibid., item 16, Supplementary record of the third monthly meeting held on 20 Sep 1948.

104. Ibid., item 30.

105. Ibid., item 31, Supplementary record of the fifth monthly meeting held on 20 Nov 1948.

106. Ibid., item 46, Supplementary record of the seventh meeting held on 3 Jan 1949.

107. *CDC: Annual Report and Statement of Accounts for the year ended 31 December 1948* (HC No. 188, 21 June 1949).

108. Treasury file IF 580/01, Part D, p. 29, minute of 27 Oct 1948 by Sir Edward Bridges.

109. Ibid., p. 30, minute of 5 Jan 1949 by the Economic Secretary to Sir Edward Bridges.

110. Treasury file IF 580/01, Part C, p. 229, minute of 12 Oct 1948 by Mr J. I. C. Crombie, following a meeting between the Economic Secretary, Sir Sydney Caine, Mr E. A. Hitchman and himself.

111. Treasury File IF 580/01, Part D, pp. 35–9, minute of 4 Feb 1949.

112. File 18706/9/95, Economic 1949, minute of 31 Jan 1949.

113. File 18706/9/102, Economic Production 1949 (CO 852/840), item 12, Supplementary record of the eighth meeting with the CDC on 14 Feb 1949.

114. File 18706/9/95, Economic 1949, minute of 11 Apr 1949.

115. Ibid., item 15, note on Agreement between the Parliamentary Under-Secretary of State, Colonial Office, and the Chairman, CDC.

116. Ibid., item 16, letter and memorandum of 5 Apr 1949 from the Chairman to the Parliamentary Under-Secretary.

117. Ibid., minute of 11 Apr 1949.

118. Ibid., item 23, letter of 9 Apr 1949 from the Chancellor of the Exchequer to the Chairman.

119. Ibid., item 37, letter of 8 July 1949 from the Chairman to the Parliamentary Under-Secretary.

120. Ibid., minute of 30 July 1949.

121. Ibid., item 49, letter of 11 Oct 1949 from the Chairman to the Secretary of State informing him that the Board of CDC had accepted the agreement without reserve.

122. Ibid., a minute of 28 Nov 1949 added: 'and the sooner we can all think of the Concordat as one of the . . . old, unhappy, far-off things, and battles long ago the better'.

123. Ibid., item 89.

124. *CDC: Annual Report and Statement of Accounts for the year ended 31 December 1949* (HC No. 105, 10 July 1950) p. 46.

125. Treasury File IF 580/01, Part F, pp. 118–19, letter of 29 Nov. 1949.

126. File 97357, Economic General, Part I, 1950–1–2, item 18, letter of 9 May 1951 from the Chancellor of the Exchequer to the Secretary of State.

127. File 97357/75, 1950–1, minute of 3 Oct 1950.

128. File 97357/70/1, Economic General 1950, item 1, letter of 23 Aug 1950 from the Chairman to the Secretary of State.

129. Ibid., item 5, letter of 25 Sep 1950 from the Secretary of State to the Chairman.

130. File 97357/70/13, Economic General, 1950–1–2, item 9, letter of 6 Nov 1950 from Sir T. Lloyd to Lord Reith.

131. Ibid., item 44, letter of 25 Mar 1952 by the Secretary of State, Mr O. Lyttelton, to the Chancellor of the Exchequer, Mr R. A. Butler. The Chancellor accepted neither the arguments nor the proposal in his reply of 13 May 1952 – item 49 in Ibid.

132. File 33326/1, West Africa–Gambia, Part I, 1951, item 8A, letter of 15 Feb 1951 from the Chairman to the Secretary of State.

133. *CDC: Report on the Gambia Egg Scheme* (Cmd 8560, May 1952). References are to pages and paragraphs of the White Paper. The events leading up to the Enquiry are stated on pp. 3–4 of the Report. It might be added that in its Report for 1950 the Chairman and the Board of CDC stated 'the Chairman assumed direct charge in July 1948' (p. 16, para. 32(2)(iv)).

134. File 33326/1, West Africa–Gambia 1950 item 40. According to the CDC Quarterly Report (No. 7) on Schemes in Progress Feb–Apr 1950, 109, 740 eggs were laid during the quarter ending 30 Apr 1950, an average of 16 eggs per bird per month.

135. Ibid., item 35, letter of 19 June 1950 from the Chairman to the Secretary of State.

136. Ibid., item 40, letter of 6 July 1950 from the Chairman to the Secretary of State.

137. Ibid., item 41, Priority Telegram No. 122 of 4 July 1950 from the Secretary of State to the Governor, The Gambia, Mr P. Wyn Harris.

138. Ibid., item 42, Priority Savingram No. 205 of 7 July 1950 from the Governor, The Gambia, to the Secretary of State.

139. Ibid., item 48, in a letter of 31 July 1950 the Governor drew attention to an article appearing in *The Times* of 24 July that showed that pressure to ban imported poultry was not entirely disinterested.

140. Ibid., item 49, letter of 8 July 1950.

141. Ibid., item 69, letter of 14 Sep 1950.

142. Ibid., item 74, Savingram No. 325 of 29 Sep 1950 from the Governor, The Gambia, to the Secretary of State.

143. Ibid., item 75, letter of 10 Oct 1950. This was confirmed by the Ministry of Agriculture on 1 Nov 1950 – item 86 in ibid.

144. Ibid., item 76, letter of 23 Oct 1950 from the Minister of State for Colonial Affairs to the Chairman.

145. File 33326/1, West Africa–Gambia 1950, item 92, letter and enclosures of 10 Nov 1950 from the Governor, The Gambia.

146. File 33326/1, West Africa–Gambia, Part I, 1951, item 8A, letter of 15 Feb 1951 from the Chairman to the Secretary of State.

147. *CDC: Annual Report for 1950*, p. 18. In a letter of 5 Mar 1951 to the Secretary of State, Lord Trefgarne stated that: 'In the December quarterly report (prepared after my departure) it was stated that, with certain changes, the scheme could still, despite those setbacks, be pushed to success' – item 34 in file 33326/1, West Africa–Gambia, Part I, 1951.

148. File 33326/1, West Africa–Gambia, Part I, 1951, item 8A, letter of 15 Feb 1951 from the Chairman to the Secretary of State.

149. *CDC: Annual Report for 1950* para. 7(v) p. 17

150. File 33326/1, West Africa–Gambia, Part I, 1951, item 8E, draft minute of 23 Feb 1951 from the Secretary of State to the Prime Minister.

151. Ibid., item 35, letter of 19 Mar 1951 from the Secretary of State to Lord Trefgarne.

152. H. of C. Deb., Vol. 485, cols 1327–80, 13 Mar 1951.

153. Idem, Mr Nugent at col 1371 and Mr Ellis Smith at cols 1364–5.

154. Idem, cols 1375–6.

155. H. of L. Deb., Vol. 171, cols 229–37, 11 Apr 1951.

156. File 33326/1, West Africa–Gambia, Part I, 1951, item 65, Report of the Gambia Poultry Farm Mission by Sir Ernest Wood and Messrs Fowler and Telford.

157. Ibid., item 86.

158. File 33326/1, West Africa–Gambia, Part II, 1951, item 105, Savingram No. 221 of 4 July 1951 from the OAG, The Gambia, to the Secretary of State.

159. Ibid., item 115, letter of 27 July 1951 from Mr A. M. Telford, CDC, to Sir Geoffrey Clay, Colonial Office.

160. *CDC: Annual Report and Accounts, 1951*, para. 63(1)(b), p. 64.

161. File 33326/1, West Africa–Gambia, Part II, 1951, minute of 22 July 1952 by Messrs Osborne and Rowland.

162. *CDC: Annual Report and Accounts, 1954*, para. 69(2), p. 47.

163. Treasury file IF 580/01 Part F, letter of 2 Mar 1951 from the Lord President of the Council to the Chancellor of the Exchequer, at p. 249.

164. File 97357, Economic General, Part I, 1950–1–2, item 11, letter of 21 Mar 1951 from the Chancellor of the Exchequer to the Secretary of State.

165. Treasury file IF 580/01, Part G, pp. 39–41, letter of 10 Apr 1951 from the Secretary of State to the Chancellor of the Exchequer.

166. Underlined in letter. The Secretary of State had argued thus in the House of Commons on 13 Mar 1951 (H. of C. Deb., Vol. 485, cols 1356–7).

167. File 97357, Economic General, Part I, 1950–1–2, item 18, letter of 9 May 1951 from the Chancellor of the Exchequer to the Secretary of State.

168. Treasury file IF 580/01, Part G, pp. 63–4, minute of 24 Apr 1951.

169. File 97357, Economic General, Part II, 1952, item 57, letter of 23 July 1952 from the Governor of The Gambia, Sir Wyn Harris.

170. Ibid., item 58, letter of 12 Aug 1952 to the Governor of The Gambia, Sir Wyn Harris.

171. File 97357/85, Economic General, 1950–1, item 1, extract from the Supplementary Record of the 23rd Meeting with the CDC held on 18 July 1950.

172. Ibid., item 6, letter of 3 Oct 1950 from the Chairman to the Secretary of State.

173. File 97357/88, Economic General, 1950, minute of 19 July 1950 by the Minister of State.

174. Ibid., minute of 3 Aug 1950.

175. Ibid., memorandum of 26 Sep 1950 and minute of 26 Sep 1950.

176. Ibid., minute of 28 Sep 1950 by the Minister of State to the Secretary of State.

177. Ibid., minute of 10 Oct 1950.

178. File 97357/85, Economic General, 1950–51, item 16, extract from Supplementary Record of 27th Meeting with CDC held on 15 Dec 1950.

179. Ibid., item 32, letter and enclosure of 9 Apr 1951 from the Minister of State to the Chairman of CDC.

180. Ibid., item 33, letter and enclosure of 11 Apr 1951 from the Chairman to the Minister of State.

181. Idem.

182. Ibid., item 32, memorandum, para. 8.

183. Ibid., minute of 30 July 1951.

184. Ibid., minute of 31 July 1951.

185. Ibid., minutes of 31 July 1951 and of 1 Aug 1951.

186. Ibid., item 32, memorandum, para. 2.

187. File 97357, Economic General, Part I, 1950–1–2, item 19, and in Treasury file IF 580/01, Part G, p. 104, letter of 26 May 1951 from the Minister of State to the Chancellor of the Exchequer.

188. File 97357/75, Economic General, 1950–1, item 19.

189. Ibid., item 21, letter of 11 June 1951 and minute of 12 June 1951. Sir Edward Bridges informed Sir Hilton Poynton that the Treasury could not, meantime, wholly accept the view put by Poynton and the Chairman of CDC to the Public Accounts Committee on 14 June 1951 – ibid., item 22, letter of 15 June 1951.

190. Treasury file IF 580/01, Part G, pp. 80–92, Treasury Control over Capital Expenditure of Public Corporations, para. 19.

191. File 97357/75, Economic General, 1950–1, minute of 9 July 1951.

192. Treasury file IF 580/01, Part G, pp. 97–99, minute of 22 May 1951. The minute concluded: 'I do not think we have yet solved the problem of how to deal with this particular category of public body and I suspect, moreover, that we have set the CDC a directive which comes perilously near to self-contradiction.'

193. Ibid., minute of 5 June 1951 by Sir James Crombie.

194. Ibid., pp. 127–8, minute of 6 June 1951 by Sir Bernard Gilbert.

195. Ibid., minutes of 8 June 1951 by Sir Edward Bridges and the Chancellor of the Exchequer.

196. File 97357/75, Economic General, 1950–1, items 26 and 28, letters of 6 July 1951 and 2 Aug 1951 from the Chancellor of the Exchequer to the Secretary of State.

197. Ibid., item 29, minute of 13 Aug 1951 by the Secretary of State in ibid., and letter of 14 Aug 1951.

198. Ibid., minute of 23 Aug 1951 by Sir Hilton Poynton.

199. Ibid., minute of 30 Aug 1951.

200. File 97357, Economic General, Part I, 1951–2, item 2, memorandum of 1 Nov 1951.

201. Ibid., item 3, 6 Nov 1951.

202. File 97357, Economic General, Part I, 1951–2, minute of 9 Nov 1951.

203. Ibid., item 8, letter of 26 Nov 1951 by the Secretary of State to the Chairman of CDC.

204. File 97357/75/1, Economic General, 1951–2, item 4, letter of 19 Sep 1951. See also the letter of 9 Oct 1951 from Sir Hilton Poynton to the Chairman – item 5 in ibid.

205. Ibid., item 8, letter and enclosure of 29 Oct 1951 from the Chairman to Sir Hilton Poynton.

206. Ibid., item 15. The Secretary of State's decision was stated in a letter of 15 Feb 1952 from Sir Hilton Poynton to the Chairman. The Deputy Chairman was told on 22 Feb 1952 that this decision was final – see minute of 3 Mar 1952.

207. File 97357, Economic General 1951–2, minute of 1 Feb 1952 by Sir Hilton Poynton.

208. File 97357, Economic General, Part I, 1950–1–2, item 39, Circular Despatch 36/52 of 15 Jan 1952.

209. Confidential file 97357, Economic General 1951–52, item 13, Brief for the Secretary of State. As noted in the previous Section (vii), the Governor of The Gambia put forward a similar suggestion in his letter of 23 July 1952 as something he had thought out and the Circular Despatch of January was not mentioned – items 57 and 58 in file 97357, Economic General, Part II, 1952.

210. Ibid., minute of 24 July 1951.

211. Treasury file IF 580/01, Part H, pp. 67–9, letter of 25 Feb 1952 from the Secretary of State to the Chancellor of the Exchequer.

212. Confidential file 97357, Economic General, Part II (Annex), 1952, item 25, letter of 31 Mar 1952 from the Chancellor of the Exchequer to the Secretary of State.

213. Ibid., item 30, letter of 25 Apr 1952.

214. Ibid., item 36, letter of 19 May 1952.

215. Secret file EGD/150/01, Part A, item 6, HA(54) 5th Meeting of 9 Mar 1954.

216. Confidential file 97357, Economic General, Part I, 1951–2, items 14 and 15, letters of 13 Feb 1952 from the Secretary of State to the Chairman.

217. Confidential file 97357, Economic General, Part II, 1952, item 25, letter of 31 Mar 1952 from the Chancellor of the Exchequer to the Secretary of State.

218. Ibid., item 21, letter of 17 Mar 1952 from the Chairman to the Secretary of State.

219. File 97357, Economic General, Part II, 1952, item 59, letter of 14 Aug 1952 from the Secretary of State to the Chairman.

220. Secret file 97357/95, Economic General 1951–2, item 3, letter of 31 Jan 1952 from the Secretary of State to the Chairman.

221. Ibid., item 1, note for record: Implications of the international situation for CDC policy (10 Jan 1951). In a minute by Sir Hilton Poynton advising confirmation, he wrote: 'If the Government's own statutory instrument shies off these territories and can quote Colonial Office policy in support of their doing so, the chances of getting any private capital into such territories would be virtually nil.' The Secretary of State minuted: 'I don't think, having made a slight mess, we should roll in it.'

Appendix
The Colonial Office,
1924–1967

1966, 6 April   Rt Hon. Frederick Lee (later Lord Lee of Newton)

MINISTERS OF STATE FOR COLONIAL AFFAIRS (1948–1963)

1948, 5 January   Rt Hon. The Earl of Listowel, GCMG
1950, 2 March   Rt Hon. John Dugdale
1951, 2 November   Rt Hon. Alan T. Lennox-Boyd, CH (afterwards Viscount Boyd of Merton)
1952, 8 May   Rt Hon. Henry Hopkinson, CMG (afterwards Lord Colyton)
1955, 20 December   The Hon. John H. Hare, OBE (afterwards Viscount Blakenham)
1956, 19 October   Rt Hon. John Maclay, CH, CMG (afterwards Viscount Muirshiel)
1957, 17 January   Rt Hon. The Earl of Perth
1962, 19 April   The Most Hon. The Marquess of Lansdowne, PC

MINISTERS OF STATE FOR COMMONWEALTH RELATIONS AND FOR THE COLONIES (1963–1964)

1963, October   The Most Hon. The Marquess of Lansdowne, PC
                           His Grace the Duke of Devonshire, PC, MC

PARLIAMENTARY UNDER-SECRETARIES OF STATE FOR THE COLONIES

1924, January   Lord Arnold
1924, November   Rt Hon. W. G. A. Ormsby-Gore (later Lord Harlech, KG, GCMG)
1929, June   Mr W. Lunn
1929, December   Sir Drummond Shiels, MC
1931   Sir Robert Hamilton
1932   Rt Hon. The Earl of Plymouth
1936   Rt Hon. Earl De La Warr, GBE
1937   The Marquess of Dufferin and Ava
1940   Rt Hon. G. H. Hall (later Viscount Hall)
1942   Rt Hon. Harold Macmillan
1943   His Grace the Duke of Devonshire, KG, MBE
1945   Rt Hon. A. Creech Jones
1946   Mr Ivor Thomas (later Bulmer-Thomas)

1947, 8 October	Mr D. R. Rees-Williams, TD (afterwards Rt Hon. Lord Ogmore)
1950, 2 March	Mr T. F. Cook
1951, 5 November	Rt Hon. The Earl of Munster, KBE
1954, 18 October	Rt Hon. Lord Lloyd, MBE
1957, 19 January	Mr J. D. Profumo, OBE
1958, 1 December	Rt Hon. Julian Amery
1960, 31 October	Hon. Hugh Fraser, MBE
1962, 17 July– October 1963	Mr (later Sir Nigel) Fisher, MC
1964, 21 October	Mrs Eirene White, later Baroness White
1966, 6 April	Mr John Stonehouse

PARLIAMENTARY UNDER-SECRETARIES OF STATE FOR
COMMONWEALTH RELATIONS AND FOR THE COLONIES FROM 1963

1963, October	Mr (later Sir Nigel) Fisher, MC
	Mr John Tilney, TD
	Mr Richard Hornby
1964, October	Lord Taylor
1965, October	Lord Beswick

PERMANENT UNDER-SECRETARIES OF STATE FOR THE COLONIES

1925	Brig.-Gen. Sir Samuel H. Wilson, GCMG, KCB, KBE
1933	Sir John Maffey (afterwards Lord Rugby of Rugby), GCMG, KCB, KCVO, CSI, CIE
1937, 2 July	Sir Cosmo Parkinson, GCMG, KCB, OBE
1940, 1 February	Sir George Gater, GCMG, KCB, DSO
1940, 28 May	Sir Cosmo Parkinson, GCMG, KCB, OBE
1942, 13 April	Sir George Gater, GCMG, KCB, DSO
1947, 1 February	Sir Thomas Lloyd, GCMG, KCB
1956, 20 August	Sir John Macpherson, GCMG
1959, 20 August	Sir Hilton Poynton, GCMG

DEPUTY PERMANENT UNDER-SECRETARIES OF STATE

1931, 15 August	Sir John E. Shuckburgh, KCMG, CB
1942, 18 March	Sir William Battershill, KCMG
1945, 13 April	Sir Arthur Dawe, KCMG, OBE
1947, 1 February	Sir Sydney Caine, KCMG	} Joint
1947, 6 April	Sir Charles Jeffries, KCMG, OBE	

	Sir Charles Jeffries, KCMG, OBE ⎱ Joint
1948, 5 August	Sir Hilton Poynton, KCMG ⎰
	Sir Hilton Poynton, KCMG ⎱ Joint
1956, 1 July	Sir John Martin, KCMG, CB, CVO ⎰
	Sir John Martin, KCMG, CB, CVO ⎱ Joint
1959, 20 August	Sir William Gorell Barnes, KCMG, CB ⎰
1963, 1 June	Sir John Martin, KCMG, CB, CVO
1965, 26 January	Mr (later Sir Arthur) Galsworthy, KCMG

The Colonial Office was combined with the Department of Commonwealth Affairs on 1 July 1966 and discontinued on 7 January 1967. When the Commonwealth Office was merged with the Foreign Office to form the present Foreign and Commonwealth Office, the Secretary of State for Foreign and Commonwealth Affairs became ultimately responsible for the remaining Colonial territories. A Minister of State was deputed to deal with affairs on a day-to-day basis. At the official level, the Permanent Under-Secretary of State was ultimately responsible but normally a Superintending Deputy Under-Secretary dealt with the matter arising. Sir Arthur Galsworthy held the position until 1969 when he was succeeded by Sir Leslie Monson, who retired in 1972.

Index